Lanver Mak is an academic consultant, guest lecturer and Fellow of the Royal Historical Society. He has been Visiting Fellow at the Institute of Commonwealth Studies, School of Advanced Studies, University of London and received his PhD from the School of Oriental and African Studies, University of London.

'Lanver Mak's book is a comprehensive study of the British expatriate presence in Egypt in its prime, filling an important gap in the literature. The author provides a fascinating picture of the British community's fluctuating social, economic and religious character, including much useful data on a foreign body that was always varied and by no means always respectable.

Above all, Mak conveys the variety of British life in occupied Egypt, and mixes sociology with absorbing human interest.'

—*Robert Holland, Emeritus Professor, Institute of Commonwealth Studies, University of London*

'Using census records, as well as court, diplomatic, and missionary archives, Dr. Mak has done pioneering work in establishing the lineaments of the expatriate British community in Egypt. In particular, he offers an intriguing portrait of the internal workings of this community and its interactions with Egyptian society. Along the way, he inserts many anecdotes that offer fascinating insights into the class snobbery and professional misconduct that marked British society, both at home and abroad. The British community was much more than an enclave of upper-class administrators and military officers since it included domestic servants, craftsmen, railway workers and teachers. The stories Mak tells of these forgotten individuals and their struggles are among the best sections of this book and lend to the work a real sense of vividness and color.'

—*Michael J. Reimer, Associate Professor, History Department, American University in Cairo*

THE BRITISH IN EGYPT

Community, Crime and Crises 1882–1922

Lanver Mak

Paperback edition published in 2018 by
I.B.Tauris & Co. Ltd
London • New York
www.ibtauris.com

Hardback edition first published in 2012 by
I.B.Tauris & Co. Ltd

Copyright © 2012 Lanver Mak

The right of Lanver Mak to be identified as the author of this work has been asserted by the author in accordance with the Copyright, Designs and Patents Act 1988.

All rights reserved. Except for brief quotations in a review, this book, or any part thereof, may not be reproduced, stored in or introduced into a retrieval system, or transmitted, in any form or by any means, electronic, mechanical, photocopying, recording or otherwise, without the prior written permission of the publisher.

Every attempt has been made to gain permission for the use of the images in this book. Any omissions will be rectified in future editions.

References to websites were correct at the time of writing.

ISBN: 978 1 78831 088 8
eISBN: 978 0 85773 099 2
ePDF: 978 0 85772 116 7

A full CIP record for this book is available from the British Library
A full CIP record is available from the Library of Congress

Library of Congress Catalog Card Number: available

For Sarah, and Bethany, Amy and Lily

CONTENTS

List of Illustrations	viii
List of Maps	ix
List of Tables	x
List of Rulers in Egypt	xii
British Consul Generals	xiii
Note on Translation	xiv
Acknowledgments	xv
Introduction	1
1. Demographic Overview	15
2. Boundaries of British Identity	49
3. Symbols and Institutions	83
4. Socio-Occupational Diversity	117
5. Crime and Misconduct	145
6. The First World War	177
7. The Revolutionary Period, 1919–22	214
Conclusion	240
Notes	245
Bibliography	296
Index	311

LIST OF ILLUSTRATIONS

Between pages 144–145

1. Entrance of the Shepheard's Hotel, Cairo
2. Taking tea at the English military tournament in Cairo
3. At the Grand Stand, Cairo
4. The Ezbekiyya Square
5. Playing field for British forces at Qasr el-Nil barracks
6. British soldier at Qasr el-Nil Bridge
7. The Barkers and the Rowlatts at Stanley Bay, Alexandria
8. British military parade, Cairo

LIST OF MAPS

1. Map of Greater Cairo 14
2. Map of Central Cairo: Locations of important areas and buildings for the British community 84

LIST OF TABLES

1.1 Population of the British (from the British Isles) with that of British subjects, non-Egyptians and Egyptians, 1882–1917, and its percentage as compared with the non-Egyptian and Egyptian populations.   17

1.2 Rates and percentage of growth of British subjects, 1882–1917.   19

1.3 Rates and percentage of growth of British subjects from British Isles, 1882–1917.   19

1.4 British subjects by ethnic origin, 1917.   21

1.5 Size of British Army of Occupation compared with British civilian population, number of British from British Isles, and total number of British subjects.

1.6 British population compared with other European populations in Egypt, 1882–1917.   25

1.7 British population compared with other European populations in Cairo, 1882–1917.   29

1.8 Number of British subjects and Britons of British origin in various parts of Egypt, 1882–1917.   30

1.9 Population of British community in Cairo and its percentages compared with total foreign population of Cairo and total population of Cairo, 1882–1917.   33

1.10 Number of British subjects, other foreign nationals, and Egyptians, and where they lived in Cairo, 1897.   35

1.11 Number and locations of residence of children who could make use of the Dean's Building School in 1915.   37

LIST OF TABLES xi

1.12 British subjects in Egypt and their religious affiliations, 1897.	39
1.13 British subjects in Egypt and their religious affiliations, 1917.	40
1.14 Age groupings and percentages of British subjects in Egypt, 1897.	42
1.15 Age groupings of British subjects in Lower Egypt, 1897.	42
1.16 Age groupings of Britons from the British Isles and British subjects, 1917.	43
1.17 Literacy and illiteracy rates for British subjects, foreigners, and Egyptians over 7 years of age, 1897.	45
1.18 Literacy rates and percentages (for those 5 years old and above) according to nationality and gender, 1917.	47
4.1 Number of male British subjects in Egypt according to occupations.	123
4.2 Percentage of male British subjects in Egypt according to occupational categories.	124
4.3 Number of female British subjects in occupations.	124
4.4 Number of male British subjects in Cairo and Alexandria categorised by occupations.	126
4.5 Number of female British subjects in Cairo and Alexandria categorised by occupations.	127
4.6 Number of male and female British subjects in Egypt and their occupations.	129
5.1 Number and ratio of British troops infected with venereal disease in 1916.	172

LIST OF RULERS IN EGYPT

Muhammad Ali's line of rulers in Egypt, their years in power, and their family relationships by generation.

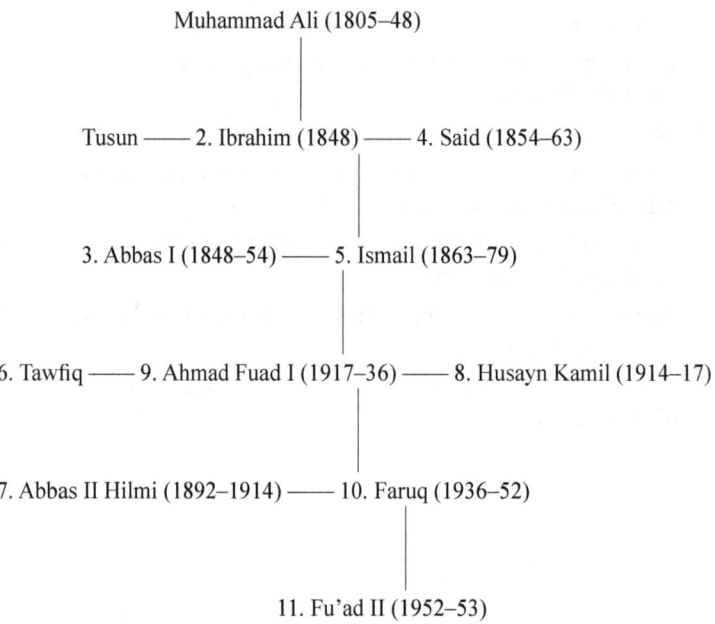

BRITISH CONSUL GENERALS

List of British Consul Generals (1879–1914) and High Commissioners (1914–36) and their years of ascendancy to power.

1879:	Sir Edward Malet
1883:	Evelyn Baring (Lord Cromer)
1907:	Sir Eldon Gorst
1911:	Sir Herbert Kitchener
1914:	Sir Henry MaMahon
1916:	Sir Reginald Wingate
1919:	Sir Edmund Allenby
1925:	Lord George Lloyd
1929:	Sir Percy Loraine
1933–36:	Sir Miles Lampson (Lord Killearn)

Based on Jere L. Bacharach, *The Middle East Studies Handbook* (London: Cambridge University Press, 1984), p.25.

NOTE ON TRANSLATION

The system of transliteration used follows that of the International Journal of Middle East Studies. For most place and personal names, and familiar terms such as Cairo, Alexandria, Zamalek, and Khedive, the most common spellings have been adopted.

ACKNOWLEDGMENTS

Many mentors, friends, family members, editors, and staff of libraries and archives on three continents have assisted, advised, and encouraged me in this project. I will attempt to acknowledge them here with the regretful realisation that there are others who have helped me on this journey that I will inevitably fail or forget to mention.

I want to first acknowledge the Institute of Commonwealth Studies at the University of London's School of Advanced Study and its recent directors Richard Crook, Warwick Gould, and Philip Murphy for giving me the opportunity to complete this task. Alison Stewart, the Institute's administrative manager, was an enormous help. I am deeply indebted to Theodore Balderston for his scholarly mentoring and perceptive observations and to Michael Reimer for his encouragement and many insights that strengthened the manuscript. Much appreciated was Robert Holland's thoughtful reflections and timely support. I thank my project manager Jodie Robson and editors at I.B.Tauris Tomasz Hoskins, Jenna Steventon and Joanna Godfrey for shepherding the publication process. Robin Parry, of Wipf and Stock Publishers, also offered invaluable advice and detailed assistance. However, I take sole responsibility for any shortcomings in this project.

As this book developed from my Ph.D. thesis entitled 'The British Community in Occupied Cairo, 1882–1922,' I want to acknowledge the School of Oriental and African Studies, University of London, for allowing me to engage this research some years ago. Foremost, my supervisor Ulrike Freitag (current Director of Zentrum Moderner Orient) asked important questions and provided crucial direction and many keen insights. Members of my thesis committee Ben Fortna, the late Ralph Smith, and the late R. M. Burrell offered helpful perspectives especially in the earlier stages of the work. I also thank my thesis examiners Paul Starkey and Charles Tripp for their encouragement to publish the study in modified form, particularly the parts based on demographic analyses.

In London, I wish to recognise the help of archivists and librarians at the School of Oriental and African Studies, the London School of Economics, King's College London, the British Library, the Newspaper Library, the Imperial War Museum, the National Army Museum, the Church Missionary Society Library, and the Public Record Office (National Archives). In other parts of Britain, I want to thank the staff at Barclays Group Archives in Wythenshawe, Manchester Central Library, Hove Central Library, Churchill College and King's College at the University of Cambridge, Special Collections at the University of Exeter, the Middle East Centre Archives at St. Antony's College, University of Oxford, and the Universities of Birmingham and Manchester. In Cairo, Father Matthew Rhodes and Rev. David Grafton gave me access to the archives at All Saints' Cathedral and St. Andrew's Church respectively. Ghislaine Alleaume of the Centre d'Étude et de Documentation Économique, Juridique et Sociale (CEDEJ) directed me to helpful demographic data. Prolific writers Max Rodenbeck and Samir Raafat and Egyptian historians Raouf Abbas, Yunan Labib Rizk, and Mursi Saad el Din offered many interesting tips and insights. At the American University in Cairo (AUC), the library staff assisted me with regards to census material and other secondary and Arabic sources while archivists Stephen Urgola and Ola Seif went the extra mile to provide relevant images. During my post-graduate days at AUC, I was grateful to Amira Sonbol and Afaf Lutfi al-Sayyid Marsot for inspiring me to pursue more historical research. In Alexandria, Colin Clement of the Centre d'Étude Alexandrines, Sahar Hammouda and Mohammed Awad, noted historian of the city, gave valuable advice and Ghada Hozayen supported my teaching of some of this material. In Toronto, I am thankful for the staff at the University of Toronto's government publication department and my first tutor James Reilly for fuelling my interest in Middle Eastern history many years ago.

A small portion of this work has appeared in print previously in the form of an article entitled 'More than Officers and Officials: Britons in Occupied Egypt, 1882–1922' in the *Journal of Imperial and Commonwealth History*, Vol. 39, No. 1, March 2011, pp. 21–46. I thank Routledge for permission to reuse the material from that article in this book.

Not least, I thank my wife Sarah and our parents for their indispensable encouragement and support over many years. I'm grateful for my three daughters who tolerated my excessive computer use with understanding and good humour, and numerous friends in Egypt, London, Cambridge, Oxford, Birmingham, and Manchester who provided accommodation at key moments. Above all, I acknowledge God's love for me in Christ.

INTRODUCTION

This is the untold story of ordinary members of the British community in Egypt during the British occupation from 1882 to 1922. It tells the stories of unknown villains like Charles Helfield who committed fraud on three separate occasions by pretending to be a European aristocrat, a British army doctor, and a jewellery salesman; and Michael Ellis who received multiple convictions for stealing from his mother, forging his brother's signature, and assaulting his wife. It recounts the tales of maids, like Elisa Ann Cuff who was raped by her British employer, and working class clerks, like George Osborne Lion who dared to sue his boss, James Francis Waterlow, for wrongful dismissal even though Lion was clearly lazy and incompetent. These characters are only examples of many of the British men and women that this book will introduce as it seeks to answer questions related to the British community, such as: What were the origins, demographics, and residential locations of Britons in Egypt? As the British community was small compared to other foreign communities, how did Britons relate to other expatriates and the indigenous Egyptians? What were the boundaries that defined their British identity and how were they ambiguous? What symbols and institutions strengthened their sense of identity and community? To what extent were they from various class and occupational backgrounds? What were the roles and lifestyles of non-elite Britons? What types of crimes and misconduct did they commit and why? How did the crises of the First World War and the revolutionary period of 1919–22 affect them?

This work brings to light previously underemphasised aspects of the British in Egypt during the occupation because most existing studies deal mainly with their political and economic involvement as well as the lifestyles of the upper middle class British travellers or government administrators.[1] Research engaged with the lives of ordinary Britons and their community during the British occupation seems to be lacking. This book seeks to address this imbalance and tell the important story of the British community in Egypt during the colonial era – a story essential to the understanding of the history of modern Egypt and the British Empire. By using census and court records, certain private papers, and business, newspaper, military and missionary archives, this study highlights discoveries that are made regarding the community's demographic profile, its boundaries and symbols, its socio-occupational diversity, criminal activities, and approaches to the crises of the First World War and the revolutionary period of 1919–22. As the lives and activities of Britons who were not part of the military or civil service elite are examined, one main contention and contribution of this study is to suggest that the British in Egypt were not, as the existing literature tends to imply, a monolithic group. Their diversity, explored in the following chapters, is expressed in differences of income, vocational roles, attitudes towards the law, and responses to challenges of the First World War and the revolutionary era of 1919–22.

Sources

The sources used for this book are primarily concerned with the demographic and social profile of Egypt's British community and its non-elites. Some of these sources have been used recently by other scholars while other sources have been largely overlooked. Though a number of academics have utilised the British Consular Court records, the Church Missionary Society archives, and the Egyptian government census records for a variety of research purposes,[2] this study seeks to unearth from these sources data and stories specific to the British community in Egypt. For example, it appears that British Consular Court cases have not been previously consulted to tell the stories of crimes committed by Britons in Egypt. It is also likely that court probate records have never been gleaned for income levels and other financial details of Egypt's Britons. Though rich with information, the British Consular Courts are limited since it seems that a fair number of crimes went unreported or were never brought to court and many long-term British residents in Egypt did not have probate records in the Consular Courts due to their eventual return to Britain.

The Church Missionary Society archives host a significant collection of British missionary reports in Egypt. Since most of the accounts seem to have been written to mission supervisors in Britain, they may have emphasised the missionaries' progress and commitment more than their failures since few wanted to be called back to Britain for their incompetence or inability to cope. Consequently, they should be interpreted with some care.

As for the Egyptian census records, they are an important resource for demographic data but a clearer distinction between Britons from Britain and other British subjects would have helped the purposes of this study even more. This limitation and other information that the censuses lacked are assessed in the next chapter on the demographic overview of the community.

Many of the private papers of Egypt's British officials – kept at St. Antony's College, Oxford – were observed by Hopwood for his *Tales of Empire*. Other archives of British officials, which appear to have gone largely unnoticed, are found at King's and Churchill colleges at the University of Cambridge. They provide important insight related to boundaries, symbols, and misconduct within the British community, but are limited since their authors are strictly educated upper class civil servants.

Other archives that appear to be largely overlooked in the writing of the history of the British in Egypt are those at All Saints' Church and St. Andrew's Church in Cairo; the Imperial War Museum and the National Army Museum in London; the Manchester Chamber of Commerce minutes and the Anglo-Egyptian Bank correspondences from Barclays' Group Archives near Manchester, plus 'the only English daily'[3] newspaper of the British community throughout most of this forty-year period – *The Egyptian Gazette*. As for assessing the above, the church records, based on the minutes of church meetings, are helpful but generally limited to the activities of the church. The museum accounts, based on diaries, letters, and correspondences of men and women involved in the First World War are very useful for the understanding the Egypt's British community during that time, but are primarily limited to the stories of soldiers and army nurses and reveal little about the wider British population. The bank correspondences and minutes of the Chamber of Commerce crucially reveal the challenges that Egypt's Britons, who were not part of the military or civil service, encountered during the war and the revolutionary period. Although requiring painstaking patience to plough through, the *Egyptian Gazette* provides key insight into the daily lives and struggles of Britons in Egypt during the occupation through its reports, articles, and advertisements. It is hoped that this book can bring to light many of the stories of Britons in Egypt based especially on material that are used sparingly. Where appropriate, Arabic sources are used but since this volume is essentially concerned with the activities, composition, and diversity within the British community in Egypt, the bulk of the sources consulted tended to originate from Britons.

Definitions and Constraints

This work defines the 'British in Egypt' to mean primarily those who originated from the British Isles, of English, Welsh, or Scottish descent,[4] and had become residents in Egypt, as opposed to short-term travellers. It appears that the term 'Britons' was rarely used as they were more likely to call themselves 'English', 'Welch', or 'Scottish' at the time of the occupation. Other Europeans seemed to employ the term 'English' while Egyptians tended to use the word 'Ingiliz'. It seems that the term 'British' was used to denote people when used with the word 'subject' but was used often as an adjective for things such as 'culture', 'hospital', or 'rule'. British subjects from Malta, India, or elsewhere outside the British Isles are excluded in this definition of the 'British in Egypt' since they were, for the most part, not accepted as part of the British community by Britons themselves.[5] On the whole, children born to British parents in Egypt are included in this definition.[6]

Another key term in this book is 'community'. Much has been written by anthropologists and social scientists on the nature of what a community is. Simply stated, 'community' in this book refers to a group defined by common culture and descent.[7] Thus the British community in Egypt refer to those who had British parents, shared a common culture and heritage, and were residents in Egypt. Subsequent chapters will examine in more detail the demographic contours of the community and the complexities of determining its boundaries.

Two important constraints related to time and geography need to be mentioned. This book is concerned with the British community during the forty-year span of the British occupation in Egypt from 1882–1922. This timeframe is chosen because more Britons moved to Egypt during this period than in any previous era while, at the end of the forty years, there was a critical drop in the number of Britons in Egypt. These forty years also represented the British occupation of Egypt[8] and the height of power for upper and middle class Britons in the civil and military services. This provides the background for the contrast laid out in this book with regards to Britons from the lower, working class. Also this study is confined mainly to the British community in Cairo. The vast majority of Britons in Egypt lived in either Cairo or Alexandria while a small percentage resided in Port Said, Suez, and other parts of Egypt. The census records seem to indicate that there were more Britons in Cairo than in Alexandria, yet recent research on foreigners in Egypt during the colonial period has tended to centre on Alexandria.[9] This book attempts to redress that disparity. In spite of the focus on Cairo, this work includes data on the British in Alexandria when appropriate to the central themes of the study and as a source for comparison. Studies of the British community in Egypt before 1882 or after 1922 or of the British in other parts of Egypt will have to be the subjects of other investigations as they are beyond the scope of this one.

Significance

This work seeks to contribute to the study of British imperial history, 'history from below', the history of expatriate communities, and the social history of crime. To a lesser extent, it hopes to add to the urban, missionary, and imperial business histories of Egypt.

In recent years, there has been a resurgence of interest in British imperial history.[10] This study of the British in Egypt during the forty years of the occupation aspires to play a part in the burgeoning academic interest in the British Empire. According to Mrinalini Sinha, 'the most salutary contribution of the new imperial histories…has been a certain integration of empire into the…narratives of Britain'[11] and the overseas territories. This integration between – or 'transnational intermediate zone bridging'[12] – metropole and colonial society is expressed in the distinct experiences of the British in Egypt. In light of this, the book touches on the fluidity of British identity due to diverse perspectives and shifting historical conditions in the colonial context. It compares income levels of Britons in Egypt with those in Britain and ponders economic incentives which may have encouraged British migration to Egypt. It considers factors which may have contributed to British crime and misconduct and the threat that this seemed to have created for the British government's continued dominance over Egypt. It also explores conflicts that ordinary Britons had with the British authorities and the interface between certain British businessmen in Egypt with their managers in Britain during the testing years of the First World War and the revolutionary period from 1919 to 1922. The examples above contribute to this 'blurring of boundaries between Britain's domestic and imperial histories that academics now chart with increasing regularity.'[13]

As for the theoretical debates related to the roots of imperial expansion, it is beyond the scope of this work to contribute at length to this discussion between 'gentlemanly capitalism'[14] and 'informal empire'.[15] Suffice to say that Cain and Hopkins argue for 'gentlemanly capitalism', meaning that economic and political ambition emanating from the City of London fuelled imperial advance. Whereas, Robinson and Gallagher contend that the empire grew informally since conditions at its edges 'were more important than developments in the metropole in both driving imperial domination forward and determining the form it took.'[16] This study is, however, much more concerned with the demography, composition, and challenges facing a particular expatriate community of Britons in Egypt, and not directly with the causes and development of imperial rule.

Perhaps no work has provoked more discussion on imperialism in the Middle East than Edward Said's path-breaking *Orientalism,* first published in 1978. Said's 'Orientalism' refers to the tendency that Western scholars of colonial studies have in portraying the Orient or the East as the exotic, exploitable, and inferior 'Other'. This huge gulf between the Western colonizer and the colonized East renders the West as the powerful 'knower' and the East as the weak objects that are 'known'.[17] The term also refers to the way in which art, history, anthropology, archaeology, and other pursuits glorified the classical civilizations of the East but denigrated the East's post-classical potential.[18] It seems to me that Said, for the most part, tended not explore the diversity among the 'colonizers'. In the case of the Britons in Egypt, there were stark differences with regards to their income levels, occupations, tendencies to crime, and responses to crises. *The British in Egypt* exposes these variations. It suggests some Britons in Egypt were powerful while others were weak and poor. Although it appears that in general, they were still better off then many poor Egyptians, the diversity among Britons in Egypt seems to diverge from Said's binary categorization of the powerful Westerner and the inferior Easterner.

A key contribution that this work aspires to make is to the study of 'history from below', which is a form of historical narrative that focuses on the non-elites or ordinary individuals in society. The term was first popularized in the 1960s by the influential historian E. P. Thompson[19] who sought to 'confer voice and agency upon the inarticulate and anonymous masses...[and] to rescue them from the condescension of traditional elitist scholarship.'[20] Eric Hobsbawn was another prominent historian to encourage 'history from below'.[21] Through the use of tax records, coroner's inquest, court records, property deeds, petitions to charities, and autobiographies, a 'growing group of historians [since the mid 1990s, are developing] a "meta-narrative" very different from the inherently-elitist script.'[22] However, within Middle Eastern studies,

> Historical scholarship on the Middle East and North Africa has conventionally focused on elites, political, religious, military, or other...The mentalities, agendas, and ideological underpinnings of these elites have been relatively accessible to the historian, as they were historically both literate, generating voluminous documentary sources, and also powerful, able to generate a dominant discourse, framing and reinforcing their own versions of themselves ready-made for the scholar. In contrast, comparatively little attention has been paid to the experience of non-elite, 'subaltern' groups in the region.[23]

By drawing attention to British 'subalterns'[24] or lower and working class Britons in Egypt, this book aims to contribute to an often-overlooked area of 'history from below' in Middle Eastern studies.

This monograph also seeks to add to the limited number of studies of expatriate communities in Egypt and of British communities in various parts of the world.[25] Examples of research focused on expatriate groups in Egypt include those by Alexander Kitroeff, P. M. Glavanis, and Sotirios Roussos on the Greek community,[26] and by Thomas Philipp on the Syrian community.[27] As for works centred on British expatriates in the colonial era, there are a number of examples concerning Britons in India by S. C. Ghosh, Veena Talwar Oldenburg, Raymond Renford, and Damayanti Datta,[28] in China by Robert Bickers,[29] in Malaya by John Butcher,[30] in Persia by Valerie Johnson,[31] and in the Arabian Gulf by James Onley.[32] Beyond the colonial context are studies by John Paul Bailey on the British in Argentina[33] and Margaret Harvey on the English in Rome in the late fourteenth and early fifteenth centuries.[34] Since it may be that the study of expatriate communities is still a relatively neglected field of research,[35] this work hopes to be a helpful addition to this genre of historical investigation.

Another growing area of historical enquiry is criminal justice history. A major under-researched area is the management of crime and justice within the British imperial context.[36] Historians are also discovering that the history of crime uncovers a host of useful insights of a given context gleaned from how societies understood crime, how they dealt with it, and how they defined it.[37] In some instances, quantitative analyses, such as links between indictment rates for theft or fraud compared with higher prices or rising unemployment, are considered.[38] Since a significant part of this study uncovers the criminal activities of Britons in Egypt, it is hoped that the work can contribute to the under-researched area of crime history in the British imperial context.

Finally, students of urban history, Christian missionary history, and imperial business history in Egypt may find aspects of this book helpful. Since the book deals with Britons in an urban context, primarily in Cairo and to a lesser extent in Alexandria, some aspects of the book may add to the study of Egypt's urban history already considered in notable works by James Aldridge, Janet Abu-Lughod, Samir Rafaat, Michael Reimer, Robert Ilbert, and Max Rodenbeck.[39] Certain aspects of the British missionary experience are also highlighted in this work and may be of interest to Christian missionary history in Egypt and to this growing area of enquiry within Middle Eastern studies.[40] Since some portions of the book are based on rarely-used business archives and chronicle the experiences and challenges of certain British businessmen in Egypt, it may also contribute to the study of British business history in the imperial context[41] – an area that will benefit from more scholarly research.[42]

Content

To achieve the above objectives, the first chapter aims to document the demographic dimensions of the British community in occupied Egypt. Using census records, it seeks to present quantitative data on Egypt's British community in relation to other foreign communities and the general Egyptian population, as well as their location in the city, religious leanings, age, and literacy rate. Chapter 2 attempts to identify the boundaries of the community and discusses aspects of ambiguity in this task. The third chapter introduces the symbols and institutions that served as rallying points for the community, which also aimed to signify its position of power to both Britons and non-Britons in Egypt. Chapter 4 argues that though many of Egypt's Britons were upper middle class government officials, military officers, businessmen, and professionals, a significant number were also in a variety of less prestigious occupations and came from lower and working-class backgrounds. The fifth chapter further develops the theme of the community's diversity by examining the involvement in crime and misconduct of some of Egypt's Britons to challenge the perception that they were solely law-abiding upper and middle class residents. Chapters 6 and 7 detail the diversity of roles and reactions of the community in the face of two significant crises – the First World War and the Revolutionary Period of 1919–22.

Origins of the British Community

Before embarking on the study of the British community from 1882 to 1922, it may be useful to ask the question: Why was there a British community in Egypt? The story of the community's emergence reveals that Britons settled in Egypt for academic, artistic, and health reasons as well as for economic, political, and religious factors. Prior to 1882, there was already a small but budding group of Britons in Egypt. They started to visit Egypt, a territory of the Ottoman Empire, in the 1790s for academic and health reasons as explorers, archaeologists, and patients seeking recovery in a warmer climate. By the middle of the nineteenth century, many travellers from Britain and other parts of the world were visiting Egypt[43] but some British painters, writers, and artists began to settle in Egypt for extensive periods.

Significant economic factors also increased British presence in Egypt. From the 1840s, when the overland route to India was established, Britons moved into Egypt in higher numbers. This route was an affordable and convenient way for them to travel from England to India, for business or leisure, via transportation on land in Egypt. The route enlarged the British community in Egypt by spawning new businesses. The papers of Henry Barker, longstanding British merchant in Egypt, noted that 'by 1852 the route to India through Alexandria, Cairo, Suez and the Red Sea was in full swing and remained so until the opening of the Suez Canal in 1869.'[44] The surge of travellers encouraged the arrival of British hotel staff and entrepreneurs, such as Samuel Shepheard – founder of Shepheard's Hotel, railway engineers who built the railroad from Alexandria to Cairo to Suez, and travel agents such as John Mason Cook, son of Thomas Cook. By 1859, construction of the Suez Canal was under way and though essentially a French enterprise, British engineers were involved as well. By the 1860s, Egypt had become increasingly integrated into the European economy as a key cotton producer causing the arrival of a growing number of British financiers, bankers, and businessmen and bolstering the population of the British community. By 1872, the Khedive, Egypt's ruler under official Ottoman suzerainty, had acquired such a massive debt – by trying to make Cairo look like a city in Europe through erecting European-style streets, gardens, and buildings – that he was forced to sell his shares in the Suez Canal to Britain. Thereafter, to regulate the Egyptian economy in order to appease British and French creditors, Britain and France instituted the system of Dual Control over much of Egypt's financial affairs, bringing in considerable numbers of British and French civil servants to manage Egypt economically. The argument for the significance of commercial factors contributing to the influx of Britons in Egypt before the occupation is supported by the arrival of British entrepreneurs who serviced the overland route, British engineers who built the railway system and the Suez Canal and British experts who took over Egypt's financial affairs. Thereafter, during the forty-year span of the occupation[45], many more British businesses arrived in Egypt and continued to draw Britons to Egypt.

> The British were important in banking, shipping, and cotton trading. Because of the predominant British political presence in Egypt, British contractors were often successful in competing for bids for major construction projects. British firms did much of the hydraulic construction on the Nile, and they were the chief suppliers of equipment to the Egyptian State Railways and other government departments.[46]

Political and strategic factors also facilitated the emergence of Britons in Egypt. By 1882, in face of the 'Urabi Revolt – led by Colonel 'Urabi with substantial support from the Egyptian public – aimed at overturning European economic control in Egypt, another wave of British personnel, primarily military, arrived in Egypt. Not only did the British military presence crush the revolt, it quickly established a renewed stability under British authority whereby British commercial interests would not be threatened. This form of British rule in Egypt became known as the 'Veiled Protectorate' whereby the Egyptian Khedive and his ministers were officially in control of government departments but in reality, the British Consul-General and his advisers were in charge. Lord Granville, the Foreign Secretary, even established the principle known as the Granville Doctrine, whereby Egyptian ministers who were not obedient to British advisers were dismissed from their posts.[47] In effect, though Egypt was not taken over as an official colony administered by the Colonial Office, it was still under the control and influence of the Foreign Office. For all intents and purposes, Egypt was ruled by the British Empire under the 'Veiled Protectorate'.

The Khedive was expected to name his own ministers, but the choice of them was to be privately dictated to him by the British Agent [or Consul-General]. The Government officials were to wear the Ottoman Fez, but the more important of them were to be English men. These were to give advice, not orders, but the advice was always to be obeyed. It was an ingenious plan, adopted from the Government of British India...[and supported by] the presence...of a sufficient armed force to give emphasis to [the Consul-General's] advice and enforce his will, the Army of Occupation.[48]

During the 40 years of the British occupation, this political system guaranteed the influx of British administrators since Egyptians were not allowed to run, nor believed to be capable of running, the government without British involvement.[49] The political, strategic, and legal safeguards in the form of the British military and the Capitulations (discussed in a later chapter) created an environment which encouraged the longer term presence of Britons in Egypt and their economic gain.[50] It is important to note that the influx of Britons in Egypt came largely as a result of the social and racial inequalities inherent in imperialism. In other words, opportunities for success in business and in the civil service were given to Britons, often at the expense of Egyptians. Without this imperial framework far fewer Britons would have made their way to Egypt.

Throughout the empire, missionary motivations 'to improve the lot of disadvantaged peoples, and to bring to them the good news of the Christian Gospel,'[51] played a part in placing Britons in many countries, and Egypt was no exception. British missionaries had arrived in Egypt in early 1800s, but Britain's occupation of Egypt encouraged them to more open evangelism and attempts at converting Egyptian Muslims to Christianity – believing that they and their converts would receive protection from the British authorities.[52] However, due to their reluctance to stir up more animosity against British rule among the mostly Muslim population of Egypt, the British authorities did not protect converts from the hostility of their relatives nor did they prevent Egyptian courts from applying inheritance laws that disinherited converts. Nevertheless, they did offer stronger protection for the missionaries.[53] In spite of the tensions that many missionaries created with the Coptic Orthodox church (as they were converting Copts to Protestantism) and with the Muslim population, missionaries still enjoyed remarkable freedom in their work during the late nineteenth and early twentieth centuries. They visited countless cities, towns, and villages; they opened schools, clinics, and Sunday schools; they organized outdoor meetings and tent shows, and travelled widely distributing Christian tracts and portions of the Arabic Bible.[54] It is with these purposes and activities in mind that a number of British missionaries were moved to serve in Egypt. Though allowing Protestant missionary activities tended to make governing more difficult, perhaps some within the British authorities felt that part of Britain's 'civilising' mission in Egypt included the promotion of greater religious freedom and expression, as well as the introduction of the Protestant faith to Egyptians.

Cosmopolitan and Historical Context

Given the rise in the body of scholarship exploring cosmopolitanism in Mediterranean history and Egyptian history during the colonial period,[55] it is important to discuss Egypt's British community with reference to its socio-cultural context. The term 'cosmopolitanism' largely refers to the coexistence and flourishing[56] of 'Europeans and Europeanized foreign minorities who resided in Egypt from the middle of the nineteenth century to the middle of the twentieth century.'[57] The phrase implies shared economic concerns and commercial interaction among the foreign communities. It is also 'frequently applied to the upper classes who interacted at the exclusive social clubs and the European cafés, and who sent their children to Western-style schools.'[58] However, drawing from Will Hanley's critique of cosmopolitanism,[59] the term may be less useful for the purposes of this book. Hanley argues that the concept, as it is often used, is reserved for elites and implies 'nostalgia for a more tolerant [and glorious] past, along with grief over modern-day Middle Eastern states and societies.'[60] *The British in Egypt* is not primarily about the elites but includes discussion of British non-elites. It is not about a glorious past but rather a difficult one. It reflects on hardships faced by non-elites, crimes committed by Britons, and struggles encountered during the First World War and the revolutionary period. Hence, this book tends not to use 'cosmopolitanism' – with its implied attention on elites and past glories – as a descriptive framework.

During the forty years of the occupation, the British authorities were by and large successful in absolving Egypt's debts and improving its irrigation and transportation facilities. Yet, by developing Egypt primarily as a cotton supplier to benefit the textile industry of Lancashire, the British administration underdeveloped Egypt's economic potential in other areas. Further, British rule in Egypt for the most part restricted Egyptian officials from gaining influence and power while allowing even inexperienced British officials more authority than experienced Egyptian ones. By 1914 Egypt had become a formal protectorate of Britain in order to more effectively safeguard Egypt and the Suez Canal in light of the threat posed by the Great War. By 1922, after a period of intensive nationalist pressure to secure autonomy, Britain at long last granted Egypt limited independence by ending the protectorate, establishing a parliamentary monarchy, and giving responsibility for internal affairs to Egyptians.[61] British authorities would retain authority over the security of the Suez Canal and imperial communications, defence, foreign affairs, and the protection of minorities. Though Egypt would have to wait thirty more years for full independence, 1922 still marks a watershed for the start of some form of self-rule for Egypt.

Fig. 1. Map of Greater Cairo (not to exact scale). Based on Map of Cairo, no. 64480 (4): Edward Stanford, 12, 13, 14, Long Acre W.C., 16 June: 1906, London and General Map of Cairo, no. 64480(6), Survey of Egypt 1920.

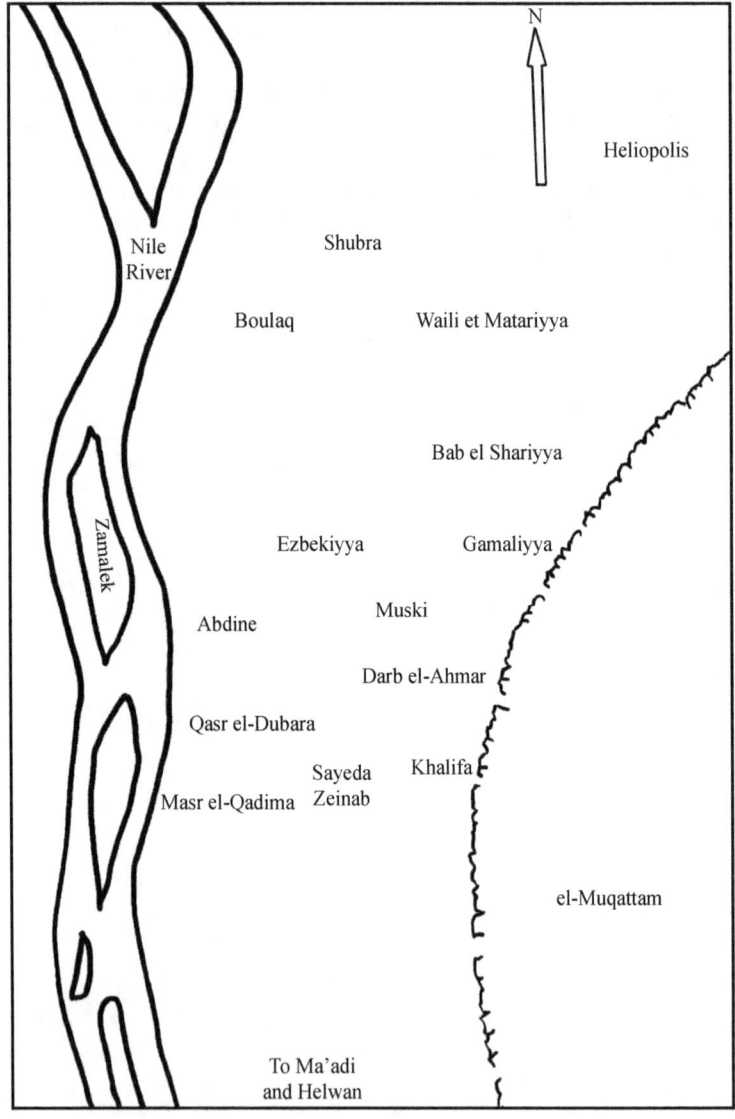

1

DEMOGRAPHIC OVERVIEW

Important demographic information on the British in Egypt is useful in developing a preliminary quantitative understanding of the community in question. Essentially, the Egyptian census records between 1882 and 1922 provide this initial numerical glance with answers to questions such as: How does the population of the British community in Egypt compare with other ethnic groups and the Egyptian populace? Does the population growth rate of the British in Egypt and their locations of residence give further insight into their community? A subsequent chapter will address their work and employment situations.

Using the Egyptian Census Records

Although the statistical information in this discussion is based on a variety of records, the vast majority of the figures come from the limited data collected by the Egyptian censuses of 1882, 1897, 1907, and 1917. Though often called the first 'modern' census, because it made use of European methods – in particular, the enumeration of the population in a single day,[1] the census of May 1882 was most likely flawed. In that census, the Egyptian population may have been undercounted by at least 100,000,[2] since Egyptians were fearful of having their sons conscripted if they gave accurate information of how many children were in their families – especially during a time of military conflict such as the 'Urabi Revolt. Further, rural Egyptians likely gave inaccurate data in the census since they 'mistrusted both the census taker and the tax collector, whom they may well have confused.'[3] Fortunately for the purposes of this book, the figures for the European population in the 1882 census were probably accurate due to the fact that the Europeans would have made 'every effort to be counted...as they were calling for European intervention to protect their privileged status against nascent Egyptian nationalism.'⁴ Notwithstanding these inadequacies, the 1882, 1897, 1907, and 1917 censuses were limited since they present only aggregate data. For example, though the 1917 census claimed to tabulate detailed information of Egyptian families, the actual records were destroyed once the data was aggregated in order to protect the privacy of individual families in the hope of soliciting greater co-operation from them. Therefore, although the existence of four censuses would suggest that there is an abundance of demographic data on the 40-year span of the British occupation, much of the data appears to have been very limited, or destroyed. The censuses lack details such as the size and structure of households, age of marriage for both sexes, information on fertility and family finance, and how these factors may have been altered over time and between regions and classes. Ironically, since data from earlier censuses were never aggregated, there exists in the Egyptian National Archives (Dar al-Watha'iq) more than 5,300 census registers from the middle decades of the nineteenth century (1840s–1870s), making these records far more useful to social historians of today.⁵ Nonetheless, the censuses between 1882 and 1922, though of limited usefulness, are still helpful with regard to data on population according to nationality and location of residents, information on occupations, religious affiliation, age, and literacy.

Population of the British in Egypt

The overall population of the British community in Egypt was notably small compared to the population of other foreigner communities and Egyptians. Table 1.1 illustrates the population of the British in Egypt, over the course of the four censuses, and demonstrates the percentage of Britons as compared with other foreigners and Egyptians. At most, the British community in Egypt (Britons from Britain) represented only 11.07 per cent of the foreign population and only 0.13 per cent of the entire population in Egypt. Remarkably, in spite of its size, the community is significant because it consisted of those who ruled and influenced Egypt politically, fiscally, administratively, commercially and militarily.

From Table 1.1, with the exception of the one in 1882, the censuses make a clear distinction between those who were British subjects from Britain and those who were British subjects from other colonial territories. Since British subjects of Indian, Maltese, and other origins and were generally excluded from the events and relationships of the

Table 1.1: Population of the British (from British Isles) with that of British subjects, non-Egyptians and Egyptians, 1882–1917, and its percentage as compared with the non-Egyptian and Egyptian populations.

Year	British from British Isles	British subjects of Indian origin	British subjects of Maltese origin	Total number of British subjects	Total population of foreigners	Percentage of British from British Isles compared with population of foreigners[6]	Total population of 'native' Egyptians	Total population of Egypt	Percentage of British from British Isles compared with population of Egypt[7]
1882[8]				6,118	90,886	6.73%	6,715,495	6,806,381	0.091%
1897[9]	12,465	617	6,481	19,563	112,574	11.07%	9,621,831	9,734,405	0.13%
1907[10]	14,361[11]	Combined total: 6,292 (includes 'Colonial')[12]		20,653	151,414	9.48%	10,903,992	11,189,978	0.13%
1917[13]	9,042	954	7,761	24,354	203,949	4.43%	12,512,306	12,716,255	0.071%

Britons from Britain, the population of British subjects from the British Isles more accurately reflects the population of the British community. The next chapter will attempt to outline more specifically some of the ambiguities in defining the ethnic boundaries of the British community.

Growth Rates

Second, population growth rates of both the British subjects in Egypt (Table 1.2) and of Britons from the British Isles (Table 1.3) may be derived from Table 1.1. Table 1.2 suggests that there may have been a dramatic increase in the number of British subjects in Egypt during the years 1882 to 1897, whilst for the next 20 years, the growth rate in the population of British subjects increased steadily but far less dramatically.

The growth rate of the British community (Britons from Britain) in Table 1.3 suggests the same pattern of significant growth from 1882 to 1897 and then a slower growth rate from 1897 to 1907. The only variation may be that Table 1.3 points to a decline in the number of British from the British Isles from 1907 to 1917 while Table 1.2 suggests that the population of British subjects in Egypt continued to rise, though moderately, from 1907 to 1917.

What may have caused the similarities between the initial growth rates of the population of British subjects and of the Britons from Britain in Egypt? And what may have caused the diverging developments between the two groups from 1907–17? Perhaps, the initial growth spurt can be attributed to the establishment of the Army of Occupation that, as shall be made clear later, added around 5,000 British men to the already small British community in Egypt. Also, with the consolidation of British administrative power in Egypt under the occupation, Britons came to Egypt to take up new government positions in the judiciary, finance, public works, education, and diplomatic ministries. As a result of the confidence and socio-economic environment established by the new British administration in Egypt, many more British government officials, businessmen, missionaries, professionals, and labourers came to work in Egypt. Further, businessmen, tradesmen and workers from colonial territories such as Malta and India also came to Egypt in search of greater opportunities. However, the rates of growth both for British subjects and for the Britons from Britain decelerated from 1897 to 1907. This may have been due to the fact that the rate of accepting new recruits declined after 1897 since many of the government positions may have already been filled. Further, following the retirement of Lord Cromer,

Table 1.2: Rates and percentage of growth of British subjects, 1882–1917.[14]

Year of Census	Population of British subjects	Absolute increase of British subjects since previous census	Percentage increase of British subjects since previous census
1882	6,118[15]		
1897	19,563	13,445	+219.76%
1907	20,653	1,090	+5.57%
1917	24,354	3,701	+17.92%

Table 1.3: Rates and percentage of growth of British subjects from British Isles, 1882–1917.[16]

Year of Census	Population of British from British Isles	Absolute increase of British from British Isles since previous census	Percentage increase of British from British Isles since previous census
1882	6,118		
1897	12,465	6,347	+103.74%
1907	14,361	1,896	+15.21%
1917	9,042	-5,319	-37.04%

the British Consul-General in Egypt from 1883 to 1907, Sir Eldon Gorst (Consul-General, 1907 to 1911) began to discourage British recruits from entering government service in Egypt in order to bolster the number of Egyptian officials in government.[17] Whatever the reasons, the rate of growth for both categories declined significantly during the last ten years of Cromer's tenure and the initial stages of Gorst's administration.

However, from 1907 to 1917, there appears to be a steady growth in the population of British subjects in Egypt whilst the population of the British community declined significantly. What may have accounted for this divergence? Table 1.4 provides a glimpse into the ethnic composition of those who were British subjects in Egypt in 1917. It appears that not only did the population of British subjects from Maltese and Indian backgrounds increase from 1907 and 1897 (Table 1.1), the population of British subjects from other colonial territories grew dramatically. In 1907, there were only 6,292 British subjects who were from Malta, India, and other colonial lands. But by 1917, there were 15,312 British subjects not originally from the British Isles – an increase of 243.36 per cent. Perhaps one reason for this influx of British subjects from colonial territories may have been the need for military assistance in the case of Australians, Canadians, Maltese, and Indians – although the huge number (up to 400,000)[18] of military personnel from the British Empire during the First World War does not figure into this particular census. The significant growth of British subjects of Greek origin to Egypt provides another reason for this massive influx. Mike Reimer, in *Colonial Bridgehead*, draws from a British consular report that suggests that Greeks in Egypt sought to obtain British nationality in order for them to obtain 'justice', or favourable outcomes, over disputes with local Egyptians and to secure their property from violence and arbitrary acts of the Egyptian authorities.[19] Even though the Greeks had their own Consular Courts and were protected under the Capitulations as Greek nationals, it appears that they felt that being British nationals would afford them even greater protection.

As for the decline of the population of Britons from Britain in Egypt during this time, the reason may be attributed to the personnel needs of the war. The onset of the First World War meant that the British Army of Occupation moved to the European front while a substantial group of able-bodied British men in Egypt, eligible for combat, joined the British war effort in Europe as well. It appears, from the data in Table 1.5, that the size of the British Army of Occupation grew to almost 5,000 in 1897 and continued to grow, albeit marginally, through the ten years leading up to 1907 and beyond. Arnold Wright, in his extensive work, *20th Century Impressions of Egypt,* stated in 1909 that the

> army has varied in strength from time to time…In recent years it has had a total strength of nearly 6,000 men. The British Army Estimates for the financial year 1909–10 show that it will be kept at a strength of 6,015 of all ranks and arms…as compared with 5,719 in the previous financial year [1908–9].[20]

Consisting of 5,000 to 6,000 well-trained and battle-ready men, nearly the entire British Army of Occupation was relocated to the European front at the start of the First World War.[21] Consequently, the population of the British community fell by 5,319, around the same number of British troops that were in Egypt before the war.

DEMOGRAPHIC OVERVIEW   21

Table 1.4: British subjects by ethnic origin, 1917.[22]

British subjects by ethnic origin	British	Maltese	Greeks	Indians	Egyptians	Jews	Australians	Canadians	South Africans	Others	Total British subjects not from British Isles	Total number of British subjects
Number of subjects	9,042	7,761	2,422	954	824	343	103	52	52	2,801	15,312[23]	24,354

Table 1.5: Size of British Army of Occupation compared with British civilian population, number of British from British Isles, and total number of British subjects.

Year	Size of British Army of Occupation	British civilian population	Number of British from British Isles	Number of British subjects from colonial lands	Total number of British subjects
1882					6,118
1897	4,909[24] (or 4,887)[25]	7,556 (or 7,578)	12,465	7,098	19,563
1907	6,835[26]	7,526[27]	14,361	6,292	20,653
1917	–	9,042	9,042	15,312	24,354

As for the mass influx of Britons who came to Egypt during the war, were they not part of the British community? Why were they not counted in the census as British subjects or as British from the British Isles? In the census of 1917, the list of occupations that the British in Egypt were involved in omitted any mention of Britons in the military.[28] This is probably due to the fact that British military personnel who had come to Egypt as a result of the war may have been too numerous (as mentioned, 400,000 under imperial authority) or too transient to be counted in the 1917 census. Also, they may not have been considered part of the British community, unlike the men in the Army of Occupation who had slightly longer-term aspirations in Egypt. British soldiers in Egypt during the First World War were perceived to be visitors in Egypt waiting to fight in Europe or the Middle East, or convalescing until they were strong enough to go home. They did not desire to reside or work in Egypt unlike other members of the British community though they mixed with the British residents in Cairo in churches, hotels, and homes, where many British families provided hospitality for the military.

After the initial influx of Britons into Egypt from 1882 to 1897, their civilian population did not change significantly from 1897 to 1917. In fact, it appears that their civilian population did not change significantly since 1882 if one considers that the 1897 figure (around 7,500) for British civilians in Egypt differed very little from the 6,118 British subjects resident in Egypt in 1882. Compared to the Greek population in Egypt which grew by 65 per cent between 1897 to 1907 (from 38,208 to 62,973) or the Italian population which grew by 43 per cent during those same ten years (from 24,454 to 34,926),[29] the British community was by and large stagnant. Why did the British population stagnate while the Greek and Italian communities multiplied? The difference lies in how the communities perceived Egypt. The Greeks and the Italians generally considered Egypt to be a place where their families would settle. Due to the relative poverty in Greece and Italy, they believed that their descendants would experience more opportunities and a better standard and quality of life than in Egypt. The British, on the other hand, largely viewed Egypt as a temporary location for work, service, or rest. They expected their children to settle in Britain where there was greater opportunity for education, work, and wealth. They also planned to return to Britain for their retirement. In other words,

> the large Greek and Italian populations are colonies of settlers, who, for long periods of years look upon Egypt as their home, whereas

the British...regard Egypt as a foreign country in which, by force of circumstances, they are destined to spend a part of their lives, but do not, as a rule, look forward to the prospect of their children establishing themselves in the country.[30]

Therefore, it was common for British diplomats or businessmen to return to Britain after finishing their terms of service or contracts in Egypt. Even if they decided to stay for a number of years, they continued to send their children to British schools and were likely to encourage their children to settle in Britain. Nearly all sought to retire in Britain. In other words, the population of the British community may have remained stagnant due to the constant influx of new British residents replacing ones that may have left due to completing their terms of service or contracts. Without the settler-mindset characteristic of the Greeks and the Italians, the community did not grow through reproduction because British families encouraged their children to pursue education and work in Britain. For the most part, the British were in Egypt 'only for as long as their work required and their affectionate impulses were all directed towards Home, and the retreats in England to which they hoped ultimately to retire.'[31]

The British Community of Egypt and Near Eastern Communities

Next to population and growth rates, it is important to note the multi-ethnic context that the British community was situated in.[32] Table 1.1 has already indicated that British subjects in Egypt accounted for a minuscule percentage of the entire Egyptian population and were on average between 5 and 11 per cent of the entire foreign population. This foreign population consisted of both Europeans and those from the Eastern Mediterranean and the Near East (or the Levant) such as Syrians, Armenians, and Jews. Since for the most part, Syrians, Armenians, and Jews were Ottoman subjects – and Egypt was still an Ottoman territory at this time – there is a case to be made that they were not strictly 'foreign', especially in the case of some Armenians and Jews whose families had lived in Egypt for centuries. Yet, since Egyptians and other foreigners largely tended to view them as non-Egyptians, Syrians, Armenians, and Jews are classified as 'foreign' in this discussion.

Those from the Levant or Levantines were also called Syrians, a term which refers 'to persons originating from the geographical area containing the modern states of Syria, Lebanon, Israel, and Jordan.'[33] Some had Egyptian citizenship whilst others held European nationalities.[34] There were 35,000 of them in Egypt by the time of the First World War. The initial wave immigrated to Egypt due to civil unrest in mid-nineteenth century Syria. A second group came to Egypt when cheap East Asian imports of silk flooded into the French market at the end of the nineteenth century causing many silk spinners and weavers to find alternative pastures of work and survival. Further the importing 'of cheap and better European industrial products initiated the destruction of a wide variety of traditional manufacturers and crafts. Among the immigrants to Egypt [were] former charcoal burners, gunpowder producers, miners, [and] gunsmiths.'[35] During the 1860s and the early 1870s, Egypt experienced an economic boom based on cotton exports thereby attracting many disaffected Syrian immigrants. However, perhaps the greatest motivator for Syrians to migrate to Egypt was the opportunity of educated graduates to seek employment due to the 'lack of career opportunities commensurate with [their] education and expertise'[36] in Syria. On the contrary, by the later part of the nineteenth century, 'Egypt offered a variety of positions and careers to the educated, professionally trained, and often multilingual Syrian youth.'[37] Many were employed in the Egyptian civil service as accountants, translators, and medical doctors. Due to their education, ability, and Arabic fluency, they were the group that the British civil servants were keen to recommend to administrative posts. Eager to fulfil their desire to improve in material terms, the large majority of Syrians reached a prosperous middle-class status in Egypt by the end of the nineteenth century.[38] Most of them lived in Cairo, Alexandria, or the Suez Canal zone where they worked as professionals or businessmen.[39]

Besides Syrians, Armenians and Jews also represented significant non-European populations in Egypt although, as mentioned, they had been in Egypt for centuries. Armenians worked largely as merchants and artisans,[40] and were particularly adept at the jewellery business.[41] Their migration to Egypt increased considerably during the nineteenth century and prior to and during the First World War when many relocated as refugees in order to escape the severe persecution in Turkey. As for the Jews,[42] they had also been in Egypt for centuries and there was as many as 60,000 in Egypt in 1919.[43] They played an important economic role in Egypt as financiers, merchants, clerks, artisans, and professionals.[44] Wealthy Jewish entrepreneurs ran the big Cairo department stores such as Cicurel's, Sednaoui's, and Orosdi-Back's.[45]

Table 1.6: British population compared with other European populations in Egypt, 1882–1917.

Year	British from British Isles	British subjects	French	Greek	Italians	Germans	Austro-Hungarians	Russians
1882[46]	unknown	6,118	15,716	37,301	18,665	948	8,022	533
1897[47]	12,465	19,563	14,171	38,208	24,454	1,281	7,115	3,192
1907[48]	14,357	20,653	14,591	62,973	34,926	1,847	7,704	2,410
1917[49]	9,042	24,354	8,816	56,731	32,519	157	2,789	4,225

The British and European Communities in Egypt

The most prominent European populations in Egypt during the British occupation (from the 1882 census to the 1917 tabulations) were the Greeks,[50] Italians, French, British, Austro-Hungarians, Germans, and the Russians, as outlined in Table 1.6. By and large, the numbers refer to individuals from Europe or European families and not to colonial subjects of European powers. As for Greek emigration to Egypt, there were a variety of factors behind the phenomenon. The Egyptian cotton boom in the 1860s attracted Greek workers just as it attracted Syrians. Not a few Greek merchants from the Aegean islands followed the trade routes south to Egypt and settled largely in Alexandria. Others, from the mountainous Pelion area, moved to Egypt after the local artisan economy collapsed in the mid-nineteenth century. Greeks from the Peloponnese region migrated to Egypt as a result of overpopulation and lack of opportunities at home.[51] A significant proportion of Greeks in Egypt became grocers and money merchants.[52] Whatever the reason, the Greek migrants formed the single largest non-Egyptian community in Egypt and a significant number acquired Egyptian nationality.[53]

The second largest foreign community in Egypt consisted of the Italians. Many Italians had migrated to Egypt during the time of Muhammad Ali's regime in the first half of the nineteenth century. They served as army officers, professionals, builders, architects, technicians, and staff in manufacturing projects. Muhammad Ali was even attended to by Italian physicians. By the second half of the nineteenth century,

> merchants and workers, both skilled and unskilled, moved to Egypt to enlarge the Italian community there. By this time, many members of the original community had become closely associated with the royal family and held many senior administrative posts. They played an important part in the postal service, the health service and in the public works sector...Outside the civil service... the Italian presence remained strong, especially in the building industry which was noted for the large number of Italians employed in it at all levels, from bricklayers to civil engineers.'[54]

After the Greeks and the Italians, the British and the French formed the next largest European communities in Egypt (Table 1.6). We have discussed earlier the academic, medical, economic, political, and religious factors behind the emergence of Britons in Egypt though a subsequent chapter will discuss the arrival of the British working class. The French relocated to Egypt largely for professional or business opportunities. The majority of Germans, Austrians, and Russians came to Egypt to engage in trade although the number of Germans and Austrians declined dramatically (Table 1.6) at the outset the First World War when their properties were confiscated and assets frozen by the British military authorities. Whatever the case, European entrepreneurs 'were attracted by expanding opportunities [in Egypt] which, thanks to the immunities granted them under the Capitulations, they were privileged to exploit.'[55] Without a doubt, the Capitulations which exempted Europeans from local legal jurisdiction (discussed further in a subsequent chapter) served as a central factor facilitating their ongoing migration to Egypt during this time.

The British and European Communities of Cairo

The European population in Cairo experienced significant growth during the years leading up to and during the British occupation. The gradual integration of Egypt into the world market during the mid-nineteenth century was accompanied by a large inflow of foreigners and foreign capital especially into the capital city of Cairo – the financial, administrative, and political heart of the country. Europeans came to Cairo to staff various public works projects which Khedive Said and Ismail endorsed. Certain Europeans in Cairo established banks to finance the increased trade with Europe, to provide Egypt's rulers with loans, and to lend money to various cultivation and irrigation schemes. Along with the cotton boom in the 1860s, 'the flotation of government loans, allocation of bond issues, [and the] provision of short-term credit provided lucrative work for [an] increasing number of foreign banks.'[56] During the period of 1882 to 1918, there was a virtual foreign monopoly over financial, banking, and trade sectors and various joint-stock companies in Egypt. Further,

> Cairo acted as a magnet for foreigners [since] by the 1890s, it became clear that [British] withdrawal was not near and Europeans could feel secure living in the capital because of the large British garrison. The great majority of the net influx of foreigners was absorbed by Cairo...[and to a lesser degree,] Alexandria. [By] 1897, less than thirteen percent of the foreign community lived

outside these two cities...[because] Europeans...were engaged almost exclusively in commerce (not agriculture).[57]

Though the British military presence in Egypt and the Suez Canal zone provided the stability with which European businessmen prospered during the high tide of imperial competition, British economic policies and aspirations also encouraged European commerce. Primarily, the British authorities did not favour commercial Cairo falling into the hands of Egyptians. They preferred that the accumulation of capital should profit themselves and other Europeans that were helping them. Egypt, with its cheap labour at the time, was to be maintained as a cotton monoculture.[58] In other words,

> it was vital for the sort of commercial investment [the British] were making in Egypt that Cairo at least should be thoroughly organized in a modern way by dependable non-Egyptians. Britain therefore encouraged into Cairo not only her own administrators but commercially inclined foreigners from all over Europe who flocked into the city and took over the Europeanized part of it... This was...a steady process rather than a sudden one.[59]

By 1907, 87 per cent of the annual net increase of the European population took place in Cairo alone and the foreign population outside the governorates was minimal, accounting for only 0.3 per cent of the entire population of Lower Egypt.[60] Table 1.7 below demonstrates the growth of the European communities in Cairo from 1882 to 1907 within a context where Egypt's general population (and undoubtedly Cairo's) nearly doubled between 1882 and 1907 (Table 1.1). It appears that from 1882 to 1907, the British, Greek, Italian, German, and Russian populations in Cairo more than tripled while Austro-Hungarian community grew by 30 per cent and the French community seemed to have been stagnant. However, between 1907 and 1917, most of the communities diminished in size due to the participation of Britons and Frenchmen in the European war effort and the departure of Germans and Austrians when they realised they were in enemy territory and threatened with the requisition of their properties and prohibition from using their assets in Egypt. Greek and Italian populations in Egypt dwindled too due to increased risks in travel, movement, and emigration during the war.

Table 1.7: British population compared with other European populations in Cairo, 1882–1917.

Year	British from British Isles	British subjects	French	Greek	Italians	Germans	Austro-Hungarians	Russians
1882[61]	unknown	1,247	5,193	6,880	4,969	234	2,105	111
1897[62]	unknown	6,727	5,124	9,869	8,670	487	2,262	561
1907[63]	7,207	8,577	5,215	19,419	13,296	923	3,128	1,223
1917[64]	3,202	9,254	3,275	15,250	12,114	31	1,004	1,242

Table 1.8: Number of British subjects and Britons of British origin in various parts of Egypt, 1882–1917.

Location	British subjects 1882[65]	British subjects 1897[66]	British subjects 1907	English, Welsh, Scottish, and Irish 1907[67]	British subjects 1917	British subjects of British origin,[68] 1917
Cairo Governorate	1,247	6,727	8,577	7,207	7,254	3,202
Alexandria Governorate	3,552	8,301	8,190	5,006	10,656	3,115
Port Said and Canal Governorate	791	2,754	1,584	641	2,539	778
Suez Governorate	280	641			933	404
Other Lower Egypt regions			47	35	11	5
Lower Egypt provinces (and Suez Governorate for 1907)	189	662	1,372	924	1,583	802
Upper Egypt provinces	27	445	505	434	983	638
Desert and oases					123	98
Total	6,118	19,563	20,653	14,357	24,352	9,042

Cairo: Home of the Largest Proportion of Britons in Egypt

After observing the origins and extent of the European population in Egypt and in Cairo, attention will now be given specifically to the British population in Cairo. Unfortunately, Egyptian censuses of 1882 and 1897 record only the number of British subjects residing in certain governorates and provinces but do not register the number of Britons from the British Isles. On the other hand, censuses of 1907 and 1917 account for the number of British from the British Isles, the number of British subjects and their locations of residence. This data is presented in Table 1.8.

Though it is unclear as to how many Britons from the British Isles were residing in different parts of Egypt in 1882, it is certain that British subjects (regardless of background) tended to congregate in the governorates of Cairo and Alexandria (Table 1.8). More specifically, about 79 per cent of all British subjects in Egypt resided in Cairo or Alexandria. Overwhelmingly, 96 per cent of all of British residents in Egypt lived in the governorates of Cairo, Alexandria, Port Said, Suez, or the provinces of Lower Egypt. Interestingly, it seems that Alexandria, as a multi-cultural business centre, hosted almost three times as many British subjects as Cairo in 1882.

Similar to the census of 1882, there is no record as to where Britons from Britain actually lived from the census of 1897 – only data on British subjects. However, a glimpse at the religious affiliation of British subjects in Cairo and Alexandria during this time (Table 1.12) suggests that there may have been substantially more Britons from Britain in Cairo than in Alexandria, since there were substantially more Protestants in Cairo than in Alexandria. This projection is based on the assumption that the majority of Britons from the British Isles in Egypt were Protestant. Whether this assumption is made or not, it appears that similar to the distribution of British subjects in 1882, almost 76.8 per cent of British subjects in Egypt lived in the Cairo and Alexandria governorates while 94.3 per cent lived in the governorates and provinces of Lower Egypt (Table 1.8). In 1897, Alexandria still hosted more British subjects than Cairo but by nowhere near the same margin as 1882. Further, the population of British subjects in Cairo quadrupled from 1882 to 1897, unlike that of Alexandria which merely doubled during this same time period. Clearly, Cairo had been established as the focal point for the British administration in Egypt by 1897 and was home to a rapidly increasing number of British subjects and among them were Britons from the British Isles or members of the British community.

Similar to the censuses of 1882 and 1897, the census of 1907 (Table 1.8) suggests that most of the British subjects in Egypt lived in the governorates and provinces of Lower Egypt. A little more than 81 per cent of British subjects resided in the Cairo and Alexandria governorates while 97.55 per cent resided in the governorates and provinces of Lower Egypt. However, unlike the censuses of 1882 and 1897, the census of 1907 also detailed the actual numbers of Britons from Britain and where they lived in Egypt. According to the data, just over 85 per cent of British residents from the British Isles lived in the Cairo and Alexandria governorates while almost 97 per cent resided in the governorates and provinces of Lower Egypt. By 1907, there were clearly more Britons from the British Isles living in Cairo than in Alexandria. The British community of Cairo consisted of approximately 7,200 Britons while around 5,000 Britons made up Alexandria's British community.

The census of 1917 (Table 1.8) details the number of British subjects and those of British origin and their locations of residence as well. It appears that 74.66 per cent of British subjects lived in the Cairo and Alexandria governorates while 95.46 per cent lived in the governorates and provinces of Lower Egypt. Similarly, almost 70 per cent of British subjects of British origin lived in governorates of Cairo and Alexandria while almost 92 per cent resided in Lower Egypt's governorates and provinces. By 1917, Cairo and Alexandria had almost equal numbers of British residents who were from the British Isles. The numbers had diminished since the census of 1907 because British men who were residing in Egypt had left to participate in the war effort in Europe.

Based on the demographic data, it appears that the British community of Cairo comprised of a small group of people in relation to the total population of foreigners in Cairo and the entire population of Cairo (see Table 1.9). The size of Cairo's British community was, at its peak, 19.01 per cent of the entire foreign population of Cairo in 1897 while it was at the most 1.18 per cent of the entire population of Cairo during that same year. Averaging the percentages over the four censuses (and over the four decades of the occupation), the size of Cairo's British community amounted to 11.6 per cent of the foreign population and 0.78 per cent of the entire population – seven times larger than the British population averaged out over all of Egypt during this same time period (0.11 per cent).[69]

Table 1.9: Population of British community in Cairo and its percentages compared with total foreign population of Cairo and total population of Cairo, 1882–1917.

Year	British subjects from British Isles in Cairo	British subjects in Cairo	Total foreign population in Cairo	Percentage of Britons[70] compared with foreign population in Cairo	Percentage of foreigners compared with total population	Total population of Cairo	Percentage of Britons[71] compared with total population of Cairo
1882[72]	unknown	1,247	21,650	5.76%	7.88%	274,838	0.45%
1897[73]	unknown	6,727	35,385	19.01%	6.21%	570,062	1.18%
1907[74]	7,207	8,577	55,987	12.87%	8.55%	654,476	1.10%
1917[75]	3,202	9,042	45,714	7.00%	5.78%	790,939	0.40%

However, though the British community of Cairo was relatively small, it represented the occupying power in Egypt and a good number of its members exuded an aura of authority and influence that deeply affected the development of the city.

It was this sort of super-English presence which began to change the outward appearance of Cairo simply by being there. The English not only took over the court and the politics and the banks, but they introduced the sort of modern city amenities that English colonial society found essential for its comfort and its commerce.[76]

Distribution of Population in Cairo: British Locations of Residence

As far as census records are concerned, the 1897 census offers the most detailed account of the numbers of Britons, foreigners, and Egyptians living in various districts in Cairo.

Table 1.10 only refers to the population of British subjects in certain districts of Cairo and not solely to the population of Cairo's British residents from the British Isles. Nonetheless, it gives an overview of where Cairo's British, foreign, and Egyptian populations may have lived. It appears that the British subjects of Cairo resided primarily in Abdine, Ezbekiyya, Khalifa, and Waili et Matariyya. As discussed later in this chapter, Britons also inhabited locations further from the main commercial and hotel district of Cairo, like Gezira (Zamalek), Helwan, Maadi, and Heliopolis. Although British subjects amounted to a little over 3 per cent of the population in Abdine and Ezbekiyya, these two areas were vital to the British and European communities of Cairo. The district of Abdine housed the British Consul-General at the Residency, the British general commanding the Army of Occupation, and the offices of the ministries of Public Works, Justice, Finance, Interior, and the War Office.[77] The area of Ezbekiyya hosted the European quarter. Among the buildings in Ezbekiyya were the head offices of the Suez Canal Company, the office of Thomas Cook and Son, Shepheard's Hotel, Hotel Continental, Savoy Hotel, Turf Club, British Consulate offices, All Saints' Church, St. Andrew's Church, and offices of the Eastern Telegraph Company. This was the 'quarter of Cairo where most of the well-off foreigners live and move and do their shopping.'[78] In Khalifa and Muski, the percentage of British subjects compared with the rest of the population was only 2.5 to 2.75 per cent while in Waili et Matariyya, the population of British

Table 1.10: Number of British subjects, other foreign nationals, and Egyptians, and where they lived in Cairo, 1897.[79]

	Abdine	Bab el-Chariyya	Boulaq	Shubra	Darb el Ahmar	Ezbekiyya	Gamaliyya	Khalifa	Masr el Qadima	Muski	Sayeda Zeinab	Waili et Matariyyah	Helwan	Total
British men	1164	169	109	99	9	470	66	1049	1	239	21	1535	19	4950
British women	328	153	98	112	6	383	60	112	7	216	27	254	21	1777
British Total	1492	322	207	211	15	853	126	1161	8	455	48	1789	40	6427
Greeks	1103	718	229	447	1290	2221	601	72	112	2500	136	290	150	9869
Italians	1087	905	194	272	242	2132	721	8	5	2360	28	545	171	8670
French	600	217	133	278	458	1419	938	17	11	477	54	470	82	5154
German	108	11	6	50	6	161	6			87	2	32	18	487
Austrian	375	106	59	69	87	646	85	3	8	590	20	133	81	2262
Russian	59	11	11	26	13	78	58	100	5	134	23	32	11	561
Britons	1492	332	207	211	15	853	126	1161	8	445	48	1789	40	6727
Other	103	42	32	49	407	321	336	18	4	161	28	154	30	1685
Total foreign	4927	2332	871	1402	2518	7831	2871	1379	153	6734	339	3445	583	35385
Egyptian	44396	49268	75410	31377	66074	28239	55026	45817	31696	16504	53272	33301	4292	534677
Total	49323	51600	76281	32779	68592	36070	57897	47196	31819	23238	53611	36751	4875	570062

subjects reached over 5 per cent. Since the number of male British subjects in Abdine, Khalifa, and Waili et Matariyya far outweighed that of female British subjects, this disparity suggests that Abdine, Khalifa, and Waili et Matariyya were hosts to the British military (by far the largest male-only occupational domain). Correspondingly, Abdine featured the Qasr el-Nil barracks whilst the Khalifa area hosted the barracks at the Citadel and Waili et Matariyya district featured the barracks at Abbassiyya.[80] It appears that the barracks were strategically located. From the Qasr el-Nil position, the British military watched over the Nile and the centre of Cairo. The troops at the Citadel monitored Cairo from an elevated position east of the city and the forces at Abbassiyya (near Abdine and Ezbekkiya) provided protection for the British Consul-General, other officials and the main European commercial and tourist district.

In addition to census records, there is evidence suggesting that different socio-economic groups among the British from the British Isles may have lived in different districts in Cairo. For example, it appears that a significant number of Britons living in Boulaq, 'an unsavoury part of Cairo'[81] predominantly inhabited by Egyptians, were working in the British railway projects. There were 232 British railway workers by the end of the occupation.[82] In order to meet the education needs of the children of these British railway workers, the Dean's Building School (more on the school in chapter 3), was established to cater for the poorer members of the Cairo's British community. It became a valuable resource for Boulaq's British families. A missionary attached to All Saints' Church, Sister Margaret Clare, did a survey in 1915 'collecting information as to the numbers and district of residence of parents with children likely to make use of the School.'[83] She found that there were a substantial number of poorer British families living in different parts of Cairo who were able to make use of the Dean's School.

Table 1.11 demonstrates that there may have been a reasonable number of British families in Boulaq that may have needed the assistance of the Dean's Building School for their children's education. There seem to have been poorer families in other parts of Cairo, which may have needed the services of the Dean's School as well.

Besides the districts outlined in the census of 1897, four other locations in the Cairo vicinity also hosted British residents during this forty year span – Helwan, Maadi, Zamalek, and Heliopolis. If Boulaq appears to be the place where poorer British workers lived, then Helwan appears to have been the place for sick Britons; 'nearly all the visitors…at Helouan

Table 1.11: Number and locations of residence of children who could make use of the Dean's Building School in 1915.[84]

Location of residence	Boys	Girls	Total
Boulaq	34	32	66
Rod el Farag	8	2	10
Heliopolis	9	12	21
Mataria	6	4	10
Zeitoun	–	2	2
Cairo District	11	6	17
Total	68	58	126

[sic]...[were] invalids, many of them with lung trouble.'[85] Fifteen miles south of Cairo, Helwan featured 'an ancient sulphur spring...developed into a chic spa. Aside from healing baths and luxury accommodation, Helwan...was equipped with a Japanese garden...[and] the fresh air... made it an ideal place for pony rides and picnics.'[86] A small number of Britons from the British Isles lived in Helwan in order to seek the curing powers of the baths and the warmth and the fresh air not found in Britain. The resort town also 'offered swimming, golf, shooting, and racing... in addition to a multitude of treatments to which patients subjected themselves – the electric light bath, the Berthe vapour bath, and the Vichy bath and douches.'[87] By 1904, the number of Britons in Helwan grew to the point where they even established their own church building named St. Paul's.[88]

Maadi, between Helwan and Cairo, also became a place for British and other wealthy European residents to settle during this time. Developed by the Egyptian Delta Light Railways Limited and the Egyptian Delta Land and Investment Company, which were jointly run by Britons and Jews,[89] Maadi featured thirty large villas connected to its power station by 1912.[90] An exclusive suburb, Maadi showcased alpine chalets and Raj-style bungalows close to a sporting club and a yacht club, accompanied by nicely landscaped lawns and streets.[91] Its British occupants 'were former officers of His Britannic Majesty's regiments who had joined the service of the expanding Egyptian government.'[92] They included Sir John Godfrey Rogers (Director of Sanitary Department in the Egyptian Ministry of the Interior), Col. George Gilette Hunter (Director General of Coastguard Administration), Crookshank Pasha (Director General of the

Prisons Administration), and Alexander Adams and Major S. T. Lucey from the Indian service. Other Britons who lived in Maadi, like John Williamson and Percy Wyfold Stout (of Hogg and Stout Stockbrokers), worked in trading houses or, like Robert Devonshire, were lawyers.[93] Unlike Helwan which had acquired a church building for its British residents by the early 1900s, there was not 'even a chapel at a suburb like Maadi [in 1915], where there [were] many English residents.'[94]

Besides Maadi, Zamalek was also home to many British government officials and educated professionals. In F.T. Rowlatt's private papers, there is a residential map of Gezira (or Zamalek), dated 1907, accompanied by a listing of its residents and their public functions.[95] In 1920, the Ministry of Finance published another map of Zamalek with a list detailing similar information.[96] From both of these maps and lists, it appears that the British elite, both in government and business, had very strong representation in Zamalek.[97] Lastly, beginning in 1906, the British government in Cairo authorised a Belgian company, Cairo Electric Railways, to develop a stretch of desert just north-east of Cairo known as Heliopolis.[98] Inspired primarily by the vision of Belgian industrialist Baron Edouard Empain, the ancient town of Heliopolis was converted into a modern residential suburb. Heliopolis featured an abundance of neo-Moorish villas and apartments, high-speed tramlines connecting it to Cairo, and 25,000 inhabitants by 1925, among whom were prominent Britons and other Europeans.[99] It appears that settling in Maadi, Zamalek, and Heliopolis allowed many Britons to limit their exposure to the noise, smell, and dirt of parts of Cairo more densely populated by Egyptians.[100] A subsequent chapter on 'symbols and institutions' will explain further the significance of distinct locations of residence for Britons in Egypt.

Religious Commitment and Affiliations of the British in Egypt

Data on the religious affiliations of Britons in Egypt are only available from the censuses of 1897 and 1917.

Since Britons from the British Isles were most likely Protestants, it appears that more Britons from Britain lived in Cairo than in Alexandria in 1897 (Table 1.12) even though Table 1.8 suggests that a smaller number of British subjects (6,727) lived in the Cairo governorate than in Alexandria (8,301). Also based on the data in Table 1.12, many more British subjects of Catholic backgrounds, like the Maltese, resided in Alexandria than in Cairo. Since censuses at that time did not have categories for secularists or atheists, every British subject in Egypt had

Table 1.12: British subjects in Egypt and their religious affiliations, 1897.[101]

Religion	British subjects in Cairo	British subjects in Alexandria	British subjects in Egypt
Coptic	1		
Orthodox	57	165	275
Catholic	1,966	4,923	8,611
Protestant	4,258	2,718	9,088
Total Christians	6,282	7,806	17,974
Muslim	90	20	578
Jews	305	463	929
Others	50	12	82
Total	6,727	8,301	19,563

to report a religious affiliation and the vast majority (almost 92 per cent) were from Christian backgrounds.

In 1917, a similar pattern can be observed where more British Protestants lived in Cairo rather than in Alexandria (Table 1.13) while more British subjects who were Catholics, like the Maltese, lived in Alexandria. However, Table 1.8 demonstrates that the number of Britons from Britain in Cairo was almost identical to the number of Britons of British origin in Alexandria in 1917. Whatever the case, similar to the data in 1897, a large proportion of British subjects were from Christian backgrounds. As for other non-Christian religious affiliations, mentioned in Tables 1.12 and 1.13, British subjects of Jewish origin may have included someone like Joseph Smouha who dealt with goods from Manchester and had business dealings in Manchester, Mesopotamia, Palestine, and Persia but was based in Egypt.[102] British subjects of the Muslim faith may have referred to a small number of British women who converted to Islam after marrying Egyptian Muslim men. More likely, British subjects of Muslim backgrounds referred to those of Indian or Egyptian origin (Table 1.4) who may have acquired British subject status through being born in a British colony such as India. Moreover, British subjects of Orthodox backgrounds (both in 1897 and in 1917) referred primarily to Greeks, and perhaps some Egyptians, who had also become British subjects.

However, despite the fact that every British subject seemed to be affiliated with a particular religious denomination, there is evidence to

Table 1.13: British subjects in Egypt and their religious affiliations, 1917.[103]

Location	Orthodox	Roman Catholics	Protestants	Other Christian sects	Total Christians	Muslims	Jews	Others	Total
Cairo	1181	2783	2201	21	6186	306	925	107	7524
Alex	1602	5486	1613	236	8935	282	1252	185	10656
Canal	186	1506	398	2	2092	182	178	87	2539
Damietta	4		1		5	6			11
Suez	94	413	259	4	770	108		5	933
Desert	8	29	79		116	2		5	123
L. Egypt	341	171	488	32	1234	231	74	28	1595
U. Egypt	106	283	455	9	853	55	47	18	973
Total	3522	10671	5494	304	20191	1172	2476	435	24354

suggest that a significant number of Britons from the British Isles were not serious or devout about their faith. This is no surprise since Britons of this era considered themselves Christians whether they went to church regularly or not; for almost all had been christened and many had been confirmed. In 1921, in the minutes of St. Andrew's Church of Scotland in Cairo, there is a reference to the many Britons in Egypt who were not religious and labelled 'unchurched'. They included British businessmen, government officials, British military personnel, and some professional women as well.[104] Rev. F. A. Klein of the Church Missionary Society also asserted that most Britons in Egypt were interested in concerts, races, balls, and dances rather than helping with church functions.[105] By 1900, the British residents of Alexandria were lacking in biblical knowledge; as one missionary commented, their 'need...of simple teaching on fundamentals [was] only too apparent.'[106] Due to the perceived spiritual poverty of the British in Egypt, there was even a suggestion that a 'missionary among...the English-speaking residents throughout Egypt...was very much needed...and there was very much work that needed doing.'[107] Obviously, this perspective – that many Britons in Egypt were not devout and were 'unchurched' – seems to have derived from the lenses of a more theologically conservative branch of the church and from missionaries, noted for their zeal. Whatever the case, British subjects in Egypt during the time of the occupation were primarily from Christian backgrounds, though some were Muslims and Jews. Whether devout or not, the British community in Egypt consisted of Britons from the British Isles who may have been mostly Protestants since there appears to be only a few English-speaking congregations in Cairo and Alexandria at that time – namely of Anglican, Wesleyan, or Church of Scotland persuasions.[108]

Age Structure of the British in Egypt

Again, only the censuses of 1897 and 1917 record information on age groupings among the British subjects in Egypt. It appears, from Table 1.14, that 67 per cent of British subjects in Egypt in 1897 were adults (9,890 plus 3,230 out of 19,563) and more than 75 per cent of these adults were men. This outnumbering of male British subjects over female British subjects indicates that perhaps many single men came to Egypt to work in the traditionally male domains of business, banking, engineering, the civil service, and the military.

Table 1.14: Age groupings and percentages of British subjects in Egypt, 1897.[109]

Nationality	Sex	Children		Youths		Adults		Seniors	
		10 yrs +<	%	11–20 yrs	%	21–60 yrs	%	61 & >	%
Egyptian	Male	1,612,698	33.02%	841,898	17.24%	2,239,948	45.87%	189,057	3.87%
British		1,598	11.99%	1,624	12.90%	9,890	74.21%	215	1.61%
Egyptian	Female	1,585,826	33.47%	808,331	17.06%	2,151,958	45.41%	192,115	4.05%
British		1,570	25.18%	1,223	19.62%	3,230	51.79%	213	3.41%

Table 1.15: Age groupings of British subjects in Lower Egypt, 1897.[110]

	0–1	2	3–5	6–10	11–15	16–20	21–30	31–40	41–50	51–60	61–70	71–80	81–90	91–100	100+	Total
Male	275	155	465	672	532	1083	6388	1745	921	508	156	45	8			12,954
Female	259	178	444	669	562	647	1319	1032	553	280	144	48	18	1	1	6,154
Total	534	333	909	1341	1094	1730	7707	2777	1474	788	300	93	26	1	1	19,108

Table 1.16: Age groupings of Britons from the British Isles and British subjects, 1917.[111]

British	<1	1–4	5–9	10–19	20–29	30–39	40–49	50–59	60–69	70–79	80–89	90>	Not stated	Total
Male	91	339	395	485	941	1244	862	418	123	28	3	3	35	4947
Female	89	321	358	539	810	953	569	261	120	45	8	1	21	4095
Total	180	669	733	1024	1751	2197	1431	679	243	73	11	4	56	9042
British subjects	456	1832	2284	3933	4262	4591	3134	1830	812	318	63	10	82	24354

Table 1.15 provides an even clearer picture of the age ranges of British subjects in Egypt in 1897. The data refers to age groupings among British subjects in Lower Egypt where 97.7 per cent of them (19,108 out of 19,563 – the total number of British subjects) lived in Egypt. From Table 1.14, it appears that there were almost five times as many male British subjects between the ages of 21 to 30 as females. This sizeable discrepancy may be due to the young single men from Britain who were recruited for military and diplomatic service in Egypt in the 1890s. Less significantly, there seem to have been nearly twice as many male British subjects as female between the ages of 16–20 and 31–60. Similarly, the presence of a larger number of male British subjects may be attributed to their jobs in the technical, business, educational, governmental, and military sectors.

The census of 1917 clearly refers to the age groupings of not only British subjects in Egypt but more specifically of British residents from Britain (Table 1.16). It is important to remember that the census of 1917 disregarded any data on the huge number of British military personnel in Egypt in 1917. Thus there seems to be no substantial difference between the populations of male Britons and female Britons in any age range, though overall there appear to be more British men than women in 1917. Similar to the data of 1897, the majority of Britons in Egypt were between the ages of 20 and 50. Perhaps, as already mentioned, this can be attributed to the fact that the British from the British Isles viewed Egypt as a temporary place of work. Therefore, many of them sent their children to Britain for secondary and post-secondary schooling while hardly any among them would contemplate retirement in Egypt instead of Britain.

Literacy Rates of British in Egypt

There was a significant rise in literacy in Britain during the last half of the nineteenth century that coincided with the development of publicly provided mass schooling. £6 million were spent on public education by the government and the Church of England compared to almost no funding for education at the beginning of the century. Laws such as the Education Act of 1870 gave local school boards authority to set minimum standards for school attendance making truancy illegal. Other circumstances that increased popular demand for education were 'rapid urbanization, rising working-class living standards, and the development of publications aimed at the working-class market.'[112] As a result, there was a dramatic increase in the percentage of children enrolled in elementary schools and

DEMOGRAPHIC OVERVIEW

Table 1.17: Literacy and illiteracy rates for British subjects, foreigners, and Egyptians over 7 years of age, 1897.[113]

		Male				Female				Both Sexes	
	Total	Literate number	Illiterate %	Literate number	Illiterate %	Literate number	Illiterate %	Literate number	Illiterate %	Literate %	Illiterate %
British in Cairo	6,030	4,403	96.0	193	4.0	1,061	74.0	373	26.0	91.0	9.0
British in Alexandria	7,150	3,890	87.0	577	13.0	1,894	71.0	789	29.0	81.0	19.0
British	17,209	10,509	86.6	1,627	13.4	3,549	70.0	1,524	30.0	82.0	18.0
Foreign	96,684	46,786	83.3	9,385	16.7	24,930	61.6	15,583	38.4	74.0	26.0
Egyptian	7,341,325	389,407	10.5	3,306,401	89.5	10,269	00.3	3,635,248	99.7	5.5	94.5
Total	7,438,009	436,193	11.6	3,315,786	88.4	35,199	00.9	3,650,831	99.1	6.3	93.7

in the percentage of the population mastering basic literacy skills. Even most working-class English men and women were able to read and write by the end of the nineteenth century. Likewise, Britons in Egypt were a relatively literate group of people. The majority of British subjects in Egypt in 1897 were literate (Table 1.17). Compared with the literacy rate of Egyptian males (who were mostly from agricultural and uneducated backgrounds) at 10.5 per cent, male British subjects had a very high literacy rate – 96 per cent in Cairo, 87 per cent in Alexandria, and almost 87 per cent in all of Egypt. Around 70 per cent of female British subjects in Egypt were also literate – a much greater literacy rate than that of Egyptian females during this time (0.3 per cent). Although the census of 1897 does not give specific information regarding the literacy rate of Britons from the British Isles, it is safe to assume that the high literacy rate among British subjects in Egypt reflects an equally high, if not higher, literacy rate among Britons from Britain. Their high literacy rate is reflected by their various occupations in the government and professional sectors.

The census of 1917 specifies the literacy rate of not only British subjects but Britons from the British Isles (Table 1.18). It appears that more than 85 per cent of British men and almost 80 per cent of British women (from the British Isles) in Egypt were literate. However, of the significant number of British men (673) and women (1,648) from the British Isles who were illiterate, a reasonable number of them may have come from the working-class and may have been less educated. Compared with the literacy rate of Egyptians (12.7 per cent for men and 1.2 per cent for women), Britons in Egypt were still highly literate and well educated. Surprisingly however, the literacy rates for both male and female British subjects declined significantly after 1897. By 1917, the literacy rate for male British subjects was only 71.5 per cent compared with 86.6 per cent in 1897 (Table 1.17) and the literacy for female British subjects was only 62.7 per cent compared with 70 per cent twenty years earlier. Perhaps similar to the lower literacy rate for Britons from Britain in the 1917 census, the lower literacy rate for British subjects may have been attributed to the arrival of a number of lower class British subjects into Egypt during this time. The literacy rate of French subjects is included in Table 1.18 as a benchmark to compare the literacy rate of Britons from Britain and British subjects with another group of Europeans (or European-educated people) who were highly literate. It seems that the literacy rate for Britons from Britain was marginally higher than that of

Table 1.18: Literacy rates and percentages (for those 5 years old and above) according to nationality and gender, 1917.[114]

Nationality		Sex	Total Population	Literate	Percentage Literate
Local Egyptian subjects		Male	5,418,476	688,238	12.7%
		Female	5,358,619	66,335	1.2%
British subjects	British (origin: British Isles)	Male	4,517	3,844	85.1%
		Female	3,685	2,037	79.5%
	Maltese	Male	3,617	2,436	67.4%
		Female	3,310	1,794	54.2%
	Other races	Male	3,724	2,204	59.2%
		Female	3,193	1,660	52%
Total British Subjects		Male	11,858	8,484	71.5%
		Female	10,188	6,391	62.7%
French subjects		Male	3,384	2,728	80.6%
		Female	4,780	3,798	79.3%

the French subjects in Egypt while the total population of British subjects were significantly less literate than French subjects. This demographic survey of the British in Egypt based primarily on the Egyptian census records provides some preliminary answers to the questions regarding the population of the British in Egypt, their locations of residence, their religious leanings, their ages, and their rate of literacy. The data also support some of the observations that subsequent chapters will refer to. First, the smallness of Egypt's British population compared to other foreign communities combined with the statistic that the majority of Britons in Egypt were between the ages of 20 and 50, suggests that the community was largely transient. Britons were primarily in Egypt to work. They did not see it as a home for retirement nor were children encouraged to stay for higher education or beyond. Therefore, succeeding chapters mention the anxiety faced when there was a threat to the granting of British nationality for children in Egypt whose British fathers were born outside Britain and the resentment caused when the purchase of tax-free bonds to help the British war effort meant that Britons in Egypt had to decide never to return to Britain. Second, the locations of residence for British railway workers in Boulaq and the more affluent Britons in Maadi, Zamalek, and Heliopolis point to the socio-occupational diversity among Britons in Egypt, a key theme in this study, which will be discussed further in a subsequent chapter. Third, the multi-cultural context in which the British in Egypt found themselves provided the backdrop to the formation and ambiguities of British identity and the need for symbols and institutions to galvanise the community – notions that following chapters will explore. In spite of the lack of differentiation between British subjects and Britons from the British Isles in some of the records, the census figures generally provide a helpful impression of the important demographic issues in question. Indeed, this data is vital to our understanding of Egypt's British community during the time of the occupation.

2

BOUNDARIES OF BRITISH IDENTITY

Current social and political discussions related to immigration and integration of various ethnic groups into British society often raise the question of what 'Britishness' or 'British identity' are.[1] This chapter contributes to this conversation by exploring the nature and nuances of 'Britishness' observed within a specific historical context – occupied Egypt. At first glance, distinguishing Britons from other ethnic groups in Egypt appears to be a straightforward exercise. Those in Egypt who were from Britain or born into British families were classified as 'British' and as part of the British community and those who were not, were excluded. However, research suggests that there was ambiguity about who belonged in the British community due to the fluid nature of ethnic identity – a notion shaped by historical changes and different points of view. The outset of this chapter aims to articulate this malleable nature of ethnic identity through briefly examining aspects of ethnic theory, British history, and the colonial encounter. After mentioning the boundaries that appear to separate those in the British 'camp' from those who were not, the bulk of the chapter will focus on the ambiguities of British identity and ethnic distinction in Egypt based on changing historical circumstances and divergent perspectives. It will explore the questions: To what extent were white-skinned Europeans of non-British origin ever identified as British? Were Australians and Maltese, by and large subjects of the British Empire, ever included in the British community? In light of the demise of the Capitulations, what determined the nationality of British offspring in Egypt? Over the question of intermarriage, what were the prospects for British nationals, especially women, who married Egyptian men? How did this affect their 'British' identities?

Before discussing these questions however, it may be helpful to define 'ethnicity' since the term appears to be used differently by cultural anthropologists, historians, political scientists, and sociologists.[2] Ethnicity, as used in this study, is the sense of belonging to a social group according to a perceived common ancestry.

Primordial and Situational Theories of Ethnicity

Although Max Weber briefly utilised the term 'ethnicity' in his work before his death in 1920 and was the only classical sociologist to do so,[3] the word 'ethnicity' did not enter the disciplines of sociology and anthropology until the 1960s and early 1970s.[4] Before the 1960s, ethnic diversity was examined in social science under the category of race.[5] However, due to the racist and discriminatory undertones associated with the word 'race', ethnicity emerged as the new label through which scholars explored the variations of colour, origin, and culture among human beings. In the 1960s, during the initial years of 'ethnic' studies, the word 'ethnicity' was understood to imply regimentally classified and rigidly conceptualised racial groupings. The functionalist theory, which permeated sociology in the 1950s and part of the 1960s, defined ethnicity as something primordial, sacred, and sustained by parochial ties. Ethnic communities were clearly segregated units characterised by cultural distinctiveness.[6] The notion of primordial ethnic ties meant that all members of the group shared the same unitary identity.[7]

However, by 1969, Norwegian sociologist Fredrik Barth's groundbreaking work, *Ethnic Groups and Boundaries*, established a new paradigm for understanding ethnicity. Barth was a key proponent of situationalism which argued that ethnicity was essentially not fixed or primordial but shaped by circumstances. Since ethnicity was dependent on situation, Barth argued that what was important were the boundaries that determined the parameters of each ethnic community. Far more crucial to the notion of ethnicity was the external form of organising social life rather than the inborn 'cultural stuff'.[8] In other words, the critical focus of investigation was no longer the aboriginal characteristics and culture of the ethnic group, but the boundaries that distinguished the group from other groups. These boundaries were highly situational and not primordial.[9] They were produced and affected by particular historical, economic, and political interaction and circumstances. By extracting the notion of ethnicity from that of a fixed primordial culture and presenting it as a fluid and malleable form of social organisation,[10]

Barth was responsible for the historic shift from a static to an interactional approach in the study of ethnicity. Therefore, Barth's situationalism or instrumentalism (as it was also called) introduced an approach to the study of ethnicity and ethnic communities which focused on boundaries and was defined in a constantly changing historical, social, and cultural context.
Even though Barth's work was groundbreaking, he was not without critics. Eickelman argues that

> as logically elegant as Barth's approach to ethnicity is...it is limited in understanding ethnicity because it lacks an adequate notion of how social processes are related to the production of the cultural conceptions with which people distinguish themselves from 'other' categories and with which they account for, evaluate, and weigh the importance of these distinctions.[11]

Eickelman suggests that missing from Barth's work is an explanation of how conceptions of distinctiveness within an ethnic group are formulated by social processes. The contemporary sociological notion of constructionism provides a solution to Eickelman's misgivings about Barth's dearth of conceptual formulation of ethnic distinctiveness.

The Constructionist Theory of Ethnicity

The 'constructionist turn implies a shift of relative emphasis from ethnicity as an aspect of social organisation to ethnicity as consciousness, ideology, or imagination.'[12] Constructionism ascertains that the individual consciousness and perception are pivotal to the realisation and continuation of ethnic boundaries and identification. What is paramount in the understanding and formulation of ethnic boundaries is what goes on in the imagination of the individual.[13] Rather than focusing on the broad ethnic classifications of the collective, boundaries created and perceived in one's own consciousness are more accurate in portraying the reality of ethnic categorisation and identification. Urging other social scientists to study individual consciousness, Cohen articulates this position by suggesting:

> Anthropology has been preoccupied with the boundaries between cultures. It has preferred to avoid the boundaries between minds,

between consciousness, because ironically enough...these are seen as being too difficult to cross...We have shied away from, have even denied any interest in, the boundedness of the mind, the limits of consciousness which separate one self from another. We have excused ourselves from such an enquiry on the grounds that it would be too difficult, and that our concept of culture enables us to invent people as being similar to each other. Instead of dealing with the individual, we have restrained our ambition and addressed ourselves instead to whole societies or to substantial parts of them. Yet, looking at individuals' boundary transformation may alert us to the qualitative nature of collective boundaries...[and] looking at the boundaries of selfhood must sensitise us to the qualities of bounded collectivities.[14]

Since 'ethnicity...is informed by self experience and self consciousness,'[15] one individual's boundaries may be very different from another's. As individual consciousness becomes the starting point to this constructionist approach to ethnicity, ethnic identities can be assumed to differ across space and change over time. Consciousness combined with the societal conditions and changes that groups encounter underpin a dynamic, not static, ethnicity. Identities and boundaries are in constant construction and reconstruction as they are being negotiated in the mind.[16] In constructionist thought, fixed boundaries give way to boundaries that are malleable and penetrable. Therefore, hybrid, mixed, and ambiguous identities emerge to form what Papastergiadis defines as the 'third space':

> Concepts of purity and exclusivity have been central to a racialised theory of identity...[But in] the last decade there has been barely a debate on cultural theory or postmodern subjectivity that has not acknowledged the productive side of hybridity, and described identity as being in some form of hybrid state...The positive feature of hybridity is that it invariably acknowledges that identity is constructed through a negotiation of difference, and that the presence of fissures, gaps, and contradictions is not necessarily a sign of failure. In its most radical form, the concept...stresses that identity...[is] an energy field of different forces...Its 'unity' is not found in the sum of its parts, but emerges from the process [as]...*a third space* within which other elements encounter and transform each other.[17]

The Fluidity of British Identity in British History

Not only does ethnic theory suggest that identity is fluid, but British history also supports this notion when it comes to British identity. Historian Linda Colley, well-known for her work on the 'Britishness' question, argues that though England and Wales are 'old countries', Britain, and still more the United Kingdom, are 'comparatively recent constructs patched together at different stages and in different ways.'[18] Parliamentary union between England and Wales took place in the 1500s while dynastic union between these countries and Scotland occurred only in the early 1600s. It was not until the Treaty of Union in 1707 that the United Kingdom of England, Wales, and Scotland – by the name of Great Britain – was formed. Ireland and then Northern Ireland were included in 1801 and then 1916 respectively. Colley contends that in the nineteenth century, though most Victorian Scots were Unionists and were willing to define themselves as British and Scottish, there was also a 'growing enthusiasm in Scotland for the cult of William Wallace as the champion of Scottish freedom from English conquest and invasion.'[19] Colley asserts that British identities 'in these islands have frequently been plural and shifting...[and have] been subject to centuries of contingencies and organisational flux.'[20] Paul Ward, another historian of 'Britishness', also affirms that British identity has been fluid and contested. He points to Jews in London who sought to train other Jews to be English in the Jewish Lads Brigade as well as black seafarers in the British merchant marine who fought for 'British justice' in their demands for improved working conditions in the opening decades of the twentieth century.[21] British national identity is constructed and not 'given': 'national identities are [not] primordial, they are continually being redefined.'[22]

Fluidity of British Identity in the Colonial Encounter

Besides ethnic theory and British history, the fluidity of British identity is also reflected in the colonial encounter. During the colonial period, Britons who lived abroad developed unique identities due to their 'distinct imperial experiences and understandings.'[23] Their identities were 'reducible neither to metropolitan nor indigenous colonised society but rather [characterised by] the transnational intermediate zone bridging them.'[24] Valerie Johnson, in her work on British expatriates in the Anglo-Persian Oil Company in the early 1900s, affirms that colonial encounter shaped and transformed British identity. Her research suggests that

'British identity was forged from transnational interaction with non-British peoples overseas, whose own cultures and identities influenced and helped to form ideas of Britishness.'[25] She points out that since many British expatriates worked in India prior to their assignment in Persia, they adopted Indian styles of housing, and Indian terms in their correspondences, so much so that the staff in London did not always understand their writing. Johnson argues that 'Britishness' was being changed and British culture reinvented through their colonial experience.[26] Britishness 'has historically been a hybrid that has always included in its very definition the different cultures to which it has been exposed.'[27] Ethnic theory, British history, and the colonial encounter suggest the fluidity of ethnic identity and correspondingly, the inclusiveness and malleability of ethnic boundaries. As Stoler assumes, 'colonisers...were [not] unified...[and] their boundaries – always marked by whom those in power considered legitimate progeny and whom they did not – were never clear.'[28]

Ethnic Theory and the British Community in Occupied Egypt

In light of constructionist theory, the task of defining the ethnic constituency of the British in Egypt is complicated. There seem to be situations to suggest a firm and clear boundary. Other circumstances and varying perspectives imply ambiguous boundaries. This chapter seeks to answer the following questions: What were situations that made ethnic boundaries appear clear and fixed? How were the ethnic boundaries that separated British nationals from the rest of the population blurred or ambiguous? How did changing historical circumstances challenge their definition of who belonged to the community and who did not? Is there a 'third space' constituting a hybridity that emanates from determining British ethnic identity out of unclear boundaries?

Clear Ethnic Boundaries

It seems that, for the most part, the British in Egypt clearly knew who belonged in their 'camp' and who did not. There was 'a rigorous system of exclusions for native Egyptians, including segregation or exclusion on buses and trams, and certainly from clubs, some bars and cafés, and many social [settings].'[29] Specifically, British officers were exclusive, insular, and seldom mingled with the local or non-British populations. Lord Cromer recalled that 'in Egypt [the English officer] mixes rarely in any society that is not purely English...[They] live their own insular exclusive lives; they neither know, nor care to know, anything about local politics.'[30] Even during the First World War, when the British military desperately needed volunteer nurses to help take care of its wounded soldiers, non-British women were not accepted because the military officers 'did not like people of foreign extraction...to be about [in their hospitals].'[31] Further, as will be discussed in more detail in chapter 6, it was clear that as the possibility of conscription loomed larger, only Britons from Britain were considered eligible. In other words, British subjects of other ethnic backgrounds were exempt from the prospective draft that never materialised.[32]

Besides British military personnel, British officials and teachers shared the same exclusive tendency. By the 1900s when a greater influx of British officials entered Egypt, they 'formed a colony of their own, and did not need to mingle with the natives. [They] had little knowledge of the Egyptians and even less contact with them.'[33] Likewise, British teachers, recruited from Britain to teach in Egyptian secondary schools 'referred...to their pupils as "walids" [and]...to their Egyptian colleagues as the "effendis". [British and Egyptian teachers] had separate common rooms.'[34] They were told to 'go about their business in a detached, clinical manner...which meant that [they] should avoid becoming too friendly with Egyptians.'[35] The teachers were also to have

> little or [nothing to do with] their pupils; as soon as...work was over, the English masters escaped...to the sporting club...[to play] games...or to sit and gossip at the Turf Club over tea or a whiskey and soda with their English friends.[36]

In other words, 'contacts between the British and Egyptians were usually limited to formal meetings between officials at various levels...Rarely were friendships formed beyond the call of duty.'[37] Indeed a sharp boundary distinguished the British community from Egyptians and other non-British residents.

What were the factors that created this firm divide? First, there was a significant language gap between most of the members of the British community and other Europeans and Egyptians at this time. 'Most... Englishmen...could not speak the [Arabic] language properly and therefore felt divorced from Egyptians.'[38] Even though a fair number of British officials had some proficiency in French and Arabic (they had to pass Arabic exams early in their careers), the 'ideal of creating and maintaining a corps of British officials fluent in the language of the country was never realized.'[39] The British military officer especially did not mix with 'any society which is not English...because of his ignorance of any language but his own.'[40] Even British civil servants, who were usually better linguists than military officers, socialised in primarily English-speaking circles.[41] Some departments, like the Ministry of Education even opposed the hiring of British teachers who knew Arabic for fear that they would 'waste their time explaining what they taught to natives in Arabic rather than making them learn English.'[42]

Besides language, cultural interests were by and large very different between the British and Egyptians and other non-British residents in Egypt. The Briton's

> social habits differ widely from those of the cosmopolitan society of the Egyptian towns. What does the Levantine, Frenchman, or Italian, [or Egyptian] care for horse-races, polo, cricket, golf, and all the other quasi-institutions which the English officer establishes where he goes?[43]

In other words, 'national tastes, interests, and leisure habits differed to such a degree that the lack of common ground severely restricted conversation and hampered the development of greater intimacy [between Britons and Egyptians].'[44] Not only did recreational interests divide Egyptians and Britons but the clubs in which the activities were experienced entrenched the lines of segregation further (though they allowed to some degree non-British European participation). In fact, one reason that the British started new clubs was so that they could pursue their interests in ways that suited their cultural sensitivities. For example, the English Club of Alexandria was established in 1904 because non-British expatriate members of the Old Khedivial Club objected to the bridge playing of British members in their shirt sleeves in hot weather while British members took exception to the non-British members' casualness of dress for dinners at the club.[45] At the Gezira Club in Cairo, 'Egyptians were excluded in 1886 when it was first opened as a playground for the British.'[46] By '1900, club and sporting society had taken shape, institutionalizing the separation of Egyptian and European. Egyptians were [still] barred from entry.'[47] The Gezira and Turf clubs were almost completely barred to the Egyptian population before the outbreak of the First World War. No Egyptian obtained membership in either of them in this period; additionally, it was regarded as being extremely bad taste for a British member to bring an Egyptian into the club as a guest.[48]

Moreover, British residents in Egypt were concerned that close contact with the majority of Egyptians would expose them to illness. It 'was clearly recognised at the time...that indigenous populations in particular succumbed to any number of fevers and poxes...It was also recognised that the British – migrants, military, missionaries – suffered and died from "alien" diseases in alien places.'[49] The perceived fear of infections from 'inferior races' compelled Britons to establish a 'healthy' physical distance from Egyptians who resided in 'crowded...dirty and unhygienic'[50] locations. Particularly during the cholera epidemics (in 1883, 1896, and 1906) when many Egyptians died, Britons in Egypt, like Oriental Secretary Harry Boyle, established stringent boundaries of quarantine, even on his own property, to prevent access or interaction with Egyptian domestic helpers.[51]

Another reason for the rigid boundary between Britons and Egyptians was the formula which Britons in the civil and military services utilised to maintain their powerbase in Egypt in light of the small number of Britons in Egypt.

> One method by which the British were able to control this population was that of extolling their own racial superiority, maintaining their isolation from the Egyptians, and treating the Egyptians as kindly, but inferior peoples. This attitude instilled fear and respect in the populace, so long used to having an alien minority rule by many of the same techniques. When supplemented with force or threat of it and coupled with genuine efforts to bring material and other benefits to the subject peoples, this technique enabled the British to maintain order with a minimum of drain on their military establishment.[52]

To uphold this authoritative distance, 'some senior officials even lectured young English recruits on the proper social conduct in Egypt...[which was] that the English were not expected to associate with Egyptians outside of work.'⁵³ Even football embodied a place of separation and power as British army units or other expatriates almost always played against Egyptians and never on the same side. British authority was 'perhaps best represented by the fact that...those who refereed matches... were always foreigners.'⁵⁴ British society in Egypt had become 'so narrow under Cromer and so excessively introvert that his successor, Sir Eldon Gorst, was almost ostracised by the local English [residents] when he tried to invite Egyptians to the British Agency.'⁵⁵ By keeping a firm distance away from Egyptians, particularly during the years under Cromer, British officials hoped to project and promote an image of respect, power, and authority in front of their Egyptian 'subjects'.

Although their exclusiveness and aloofness may have buttressed the British officials' aura of superiority and authority, this approach also generated a backlash of anger and resentment among Egyptians culminating in eventual nationalist action against the British. Inevitably, the Gezira and Turf Clubs 'became objects of envy and hatred for the Egyptian population.'⁵⁶ Mustafa Kamel, a prolific Egyptian nationalist writer and leader during the occupation, commented that the cold and unattached style of British rule in Egypt under Cromer, was heavy-handed and 'deprived the Egyptian [officials] of any influence or initiative.'⁵⁷ Around the same time, Egyptian author Muhammad al-Muwaylihi, in his novel *Hadith 'Isa ibn Hisham*, concurred that the British control of Egypt, which kept the Egyptians basically powerless, would result in a greater desire for Egyptian self-rule – 'to run our government with our own hands.'⁵⁸ Muwaylihi echoed the 'need for...reform [and the] sense of frustration and bitterness against the occupying power [that were felt by] many educated Egyptians at the time when *Hadith 'Isa ibn Hisham* was being written.'⁵⁹

However, not all Britons followed this strict scheme of social apartheid. As mentioned, many British officials were encouraged to learn Arabic and some were sent for long periods to the Egyptian countryside to work as inspectors for various government departments which meant that they had to mix frequently with Egyptians. Yet, when they returned to Cairo or Alexandria, they seemed to slip back into their comfortable English-speaking huddles. Nevertheless, there are a few records of young British officials who deliberately sought the friendship of Egyptians outside of the necessary obligations of work. A case in point was John de Vere Loder, a young upper-class lieutenant and Etonian, who, over a period of time, befriended the Wissa, Alexen, and Khayat families, wealthy cotton merchant clans who lived in Alexandria but owned plantations in Assiut.

He played tennis with the young people of the families and even went on a motorboat holiday in Assiut with them.⁶⁰

Another group of Britons who had significant contact with Egyptians were the missionaries. The Church Missionary Society (CMS), an overseas ministry arm of the Church of England, deployed missionaries to start clinics, hospitals and dispensaries, establish schools for Egyptian boys and girls, and lead evangelistic efforts to convert Muslims to Christian faith. Many of them were encouraged to live within Egyptian neighbourhoods (unlike the majority of Britons who lived in the European quarters) of Cairo, Alexandria, or other locations, and were very closely associated with Egyptians day-to-day. For example, Miss Eliza Bywater, leader of the CMS Girls' School in Bab-el-Luk in Cairo recorded how important it was for her to be living 'right among the Moslems...where we have very good hopes from these houses [for] new scholars [or pupils], as well as keeping on many of the old ones.'⁶¹ Miss Cay and Miss Jackson, who were also missionary teachers, lived in Old Cairo among lower class Egyptians.⁶² A male missionary was also urgently sought after to live in Old Cairo because he would have far more influence than the missionary doctors who had only visited occasionally, and 'could follow up...by inviting enquirers to his house.'⁶³ Missionaries like J. G. B. Hollins filled this need of living close to Egyptian Muslims by taking 'a flat in another quarter [of Cairo], so as to be nearer Mohammedans.'⁶⁴ Indeed, it seemed to the CMS that 'the most effective method of cultivating the Moslem field [was] to locate in the midst of distinctly Mohammedan communities...[which was] done very successfully in Cairo.'⁶⁵ In the inaugural years of the twentieth century, two of the most prominent CMS missionaries in Cairo, Douglas Thornton and Temple Gairdner, gathered large numbers of educated Muslims to open dialogues, debates, and lectures on topics of general interest that would lead to discussions on Christian themes. They also opened up a bookstore that attracted many Muslims to personal conversations about the Christian faith and published and disseminated a weekly English-Arabic magazine entitled *The Orient and the Occident* that dealt with contemporary issues from a Christian viewpoint. Pioneered in 1905, it quickly acquired a wide readership of about 3000 Egyptians.⁶⁶ Outside Cairo, other missionaries worked among the rural villagers bringing with them medical relief and the Christian message to adults and children.⁶⁷ Although Britons like de Vere Loder and the missionaries seemed to have considerable interaction with the Egyptians, it is fair to say that the majority of Britons in occupied Egypt rarely related to Egyptians. Their social connections were primarily with other members of the Egypt's British community. In other words, in most cases and for most of the time, there appears to be a substantial barrier between Britons and non-Britons, whether Europeans or Egyptians, at the time of the occupation.

British and Westernised Muslims

Though there were definite boundaries separating the British from the Egyptians, were there factors, like a common European education or preference for European culture, that may have integrated some Egyptians into the British community? In the case of Egyptians who experienced European education, Cromer points out that 'most Europeanised Egyptians [were] Muslims.'[68] These Muslim Egyptians were by and large from upper-class backgrounds and sought to imitate the lifestyles of Europeans 'not only by adopting their technology…but also by internalizing their attitudes'[69] and 'standards of desirability in dress, food, residence, [and] etiquette.'[70] As a result of this emulation for the European way of life, some Europeanised Egyptians began to acquire very positive opinions of Western secularism and individualism which consequently increased a certain apathy or lack of concern toward religion as whole.[71] This group of Egyptians, Cromer identified as 'de-Moslemised Moslems and invertebrate Europeans.'[72] He identified them as Franco-Egyptians and not at all as hybrids – culturally British yet physically Egyptian. Each Europeanised Egyptian was seen as: 'first… an agnostic…The term "Europeanised" when applied to the Egyptian educated in Europe, though not a misnomer, is lacking in precision, for the great majority of Europeanised Egyptians are, in truth, Gallicised Egyptians with the stamp of…French training on them.'[73] Cromer further argues that French education and administrative training have been more detrimental than helpful for the Egyptians.

> [And] among the obstacles which have stood in the way of the English reformer in Egypt none are more noteworthy than that the Europeanised Egyptian is impregnated with French rather than with English habits of thought…French education has exercised a deteriorating effect on the Egyptians. The tendency of every Egyptian official is to shirk responsibility. He takes little real interest or pride in his work. He thinks less of what should be done than of acting in such a manner as that no personal blame

can be attached to himself. This habit of thought makes the Egyptian official instinctively shrink from the English system of administration, for under that system a good deal is left to the discretion of the individual, who is, therefore, to think for himself. He naturally flies for refuge in the French system, and there he finds administrative procedures prescribed apparently made for everything, to the most minute detail, in a series of elaborate codes. Entrenched behind these codes, the Gallicised Egyptians is, to his joy, relieved in a great degree from the necessity of thinking for himself. The Gallicised Egyptian does not recognise emergencies and he spurns common sense.[74]

In Cromer's 'consciousness', even the Europeanised Egyptians were quite distinct from the British even though they aspired to Western lifestyles and, to some degree, secularism. No doubt, underlying Cromer's attitude was the colonial rivalry between the French and the British at this time. As a result of their Gallicisation (which in Cromer's view meant their French education, administrative passivity, and incompetence), Cromer characterised Europeanised Egyptians as a lesser race. However, according to one British resident in Cairo, 'Egyptians of all classes and shades of opinion...and the fallaheen in particular, [were weak and in need] of a strong mastermind [i.e. the British], without the influence of which they [were to] lose their bearings.'[75] Needless to say, a clear wall seemed to exist between the ruling British and the inferior Egyptians of every class and religious background, even those who adopted European lifestyles and secularism.

The British and the Copts

Was the position of the Copts any different than the Europeanised Muslim Egyptians? Though there were significant differences between Coptic Orthodoxy and the various denominations represented in Britain, did a common Christian heritage fudge the lines of ethnic distinctiveness? According to one British observer, the

> idea that the English, being a Christian race, should show a preference for native Christians was a fixed one and no amount of arguments could shake it (if a Christian could not help a Christian, what was the value of Christianity?).[76]

However, there was little doubt regarding the clarity of the ethnic boundary that divided the British and Egyptian Copts. This was clearly confirmed when, in 1919, much to the dismay and disappointment of the British, the Copts whom the British had assisted immensely, 'joined Moslems in the mosques and exhorted excited crowds to unite in driving the British from Egypt.'[77] Though the Copts may have received economic help from the British and shared some common Christian beliefs with them, it appears that their first loyalty was to Egypt. One British observer described this allegiance this way:

> But in the higher walks of life, the Coptic lady is both emancipated and enlightened. She blends intellectuality with education, being often highly cultured and possessed of literary gifts of no mean order. She, or her daughter, has been to an English public school and perhaps to an Oxford college besides – contacts from which she has learned to admire liberty and fair play, if from a somewhat one-sided viewpoint. The stirrings of patriotism have thrilled her with a long-dormant sense of inheritance; she is Egyptian to the core, and full of aspirations towards her country's resurrection and aggrandizement. She has its history at her fingertips and dreams of a Pharonic restoration.[78]

The British, the Turks, and the Levantines

Ethnic boundaries between the British and the Turks in Egypt may have been just as pronounced as the boundary between the British and the Egyptians. Even though members of the Turkish Court may have shared some semblance of power, wealth, and social interaction with the British, as in the case of Khedive Abbas Hilmi's wife who hosted foreign women such as British businessman Harry Barker's wife, Lena, whom she spoke to for forty-five minutes in Egyptian Arabic in 1896,[79] they were distinctly identified as Turkish. Perhaps, most poignantly, Rodd describes Ghazi Moukhtar Pasha, Turkish High Commissioner in Egypt,[80] as 'a sympathetic and dignified example of the *old-fashioned immutable Turk*,'[81] even though he spoke fluent French, was a brilliant military commander, lived in 'sumptuous quarters in Cairo...[with another] residence near the sea,'[82] and was honoured at dinner parties hosted by the European diplomatic elite.[83] Indeed, a clear boundary separating the Britons from the Turks existed as even the powerful, wealthy, and honoured Moukhtar Pasha was unmistakably labelled a Turk. Meanwhile, similar to the Turks, Syrians, Armenians, and other Levantine groups, also seemed to be clearly on the other side of the ethnic divide vis-à-vis the British. The most glaring example of this firm boundary was the reason behind the lack of attendance of British students in the Victoria College for boys in Alexandria.

> The school is not and never has been popular with the members of the British community here. The English themselves dislike the idea of having their boys educated with Levantines, and hence they think that the school never will be used by the better class of English boys. The argument that the school undoubtedly is and will be more and more of great use in increasing British influence here, unfortunately does not appeal to the average Englishman.[84]

It seems that many Britons in Egypt, particularly those from the upper and middle classes, did not want their children educated with other ethnic groups, especially from the Levant, out of fear that their children's educational standards would be threatened by the inclusion of what was seen as inferior 'Oriental' races. Their unwillingness may also have been due to the function of public schools – to form beneficial networking for future careers. This touches upon the British attitude that they did not see their children having careers in Egypt, so the networking at a school, albeit full of wealthy Levantines and Egyptians, was far less advantageous than in a public school in Britain. Therefore, Britons in Egypt tended to send their children to school in Britain if they had the resources. The interracial aspect of the boarding school never fully materialised.

Ironically, in spite of his preference for the segregation of Britons from other ethnic groups, Sir Evelyn Baring (later Lord Cromer), earlier in his administration, put forth the idea of a boarding school where British and Egyptians boys could freely mix.

> It is most desirable that the young Egyptians could not be too much separated from the English boys…The main object…in encouraging this scheme is not so much to teach the Egyptian boys such knowledge as can be learnt from books and by tuition – though that is also very important – as to afford them every opportunity

of acquiring the healthy moral tone which exists amongst English schoolboys. This, of course, can only be acquired if they mix freely with the English boys.[85]

Why did Baring advocate an interracial environment at Victoria College and yet at the same time support the aloofness of British officials in Egypt? The reason was that in order to combat 'Frenchness' in Egypt's education system, Baring sought to establish 'Britishness' among the children of affluent Levantines and Egyptians through this boarding school (Victoria College's symbolic significance will be discussed in the next chapter).

Ambiguous Ethnic Identity

After observing the fixed boundary that existed between the British and Coptic, Europeanised, and ordinary Egyptians, as well as Turks and Levantines, our attention now turns to the situations where ethnic boundaries seemed ambiguous. In other words, while ethnic boundaries appeared fixed, certain conditions seemed to have weakened or blurred the boundaries, resulting in the ambiguity of ethnic boundaries according to individual consciousness. These ambiguities are borne out in the attempt to determine the ethnic identities of 'white-skinned' Europeans and Australian soldiers during the First World War, British subjects of Maltese origin, children born in Egypt to British subjects in view of the demise of the Capitulations, and the British women who married Egyptian Muslim men.

White-skinned Europeans and Australians

Even though, as Lord Cromer articulates, 'there [was] little social sympathy between the English, and any class of Europeans in Egypt,'[86] there may have been certain instances that allowed individuals to cross ethnic boundaries due to their white skin colour. Those who shared white skin usually represented superiority and power.

> Being a 'white man' was not, according to the colonial literature, just a question of pigmentation. It was a moral condition. Belief in one's innate superiority was only half-belief. It had to be demonstrated. Superiority lay in deeds: it lay not just in power but in the way power was exercised. A white skin was held to be

an asset because it was associated with qualities...or order [and respect].⁸⁷

Rodd recalls one incident which illustrated a white European classified as 'British' in the limited context of a game of golf. He noted that 'the Austro-Hungarian Consul-General, Baron Heidler von Egeregg...had in Egypt become an enthusiastic amateur of golf, and as British as any of us.'⁸⁸ Similarly, the Australians, who shared a common skin colour, language, and heritage⁸⁹ with the British, were perceived as British by Britons during the First World War. Even though the Australian Imperial Force (AIF) was a distinct unit on its own right, one Australian soldier was told to be disciplined and astute as a member of the British armed forces when warned by British officers not to go out on this own.⁹⁰ What frustrated the British in Egypt was the lack of discipline among the Australian troops as they served alongside more disciplined British troops.⁹¹ One British observer critically suggested that Australian soldiers were different

> not due to their predominating numbers nor to their slouch hats. It was rather a matter of personality. Military discipline seems to run off an Australian like water off a duck's back. He will not only answer a question, but will favour you with all his views on that and allied topics, expressed in vigorous and unconventional language, as man to man. His well-known non-saluting pose in early days was only typical of his attitude towards the minutiae of military discipline in general.⁹²

Though the Australians were thought to be rude and undisciplined, they were still considered part of the British forces – unlike the Indian soldiers who were also under British imperial command but were never considered 'British' because they were not white-skinned. Thus individuals with white skin, and in particular certain Europeans and Australian troops, were labelled 'British' in particular situations, indicating a certain fluidity in the boundary separating Britons from non-Britons.

The Maltese

The ambivalence of the identity of Maltese British subjects also invokes the malleability of the British community's ethnic boundary. The Maltese were made British subjects as a result of the British occupation of

Malta, Gozo, and the Ionian Islands in 1814 (Malta remained a British dependency until 1968). Malta represented an important naval base for the British fleet to secure an accessible and profitable Mediterranean trade route and influence in the region. The Maltese formed perhaps the largest contingent of British subjects in Egypt during the late nineteenth and early twentieth centuries. At its peak, the Maltese population in Egypt may have reached as many as 25,000 during this time.[93] They were described as loyal, honest, and industrious artisans,[94] with a strong sense of community exemplified by the work of the Maltese Benevolent Society of Alexandria. Established in 1889, the Society's main object was 'to render moral and material help to Maltese British subjects residing in Alexandria and to assist the poor of the...community.'[95] Although the majority of Maltese in Egypt did not appear to be particularly rich, the Benevolent Society distributed E£28,000 worth of aid to the most urgent and deserving cases and an average of E£700 per year to the Alexandrian Municipality between 1890 and 1919. Nearly all the funds came from the initiative of private donors or members of the committee. In those 30 years, the Benevolent Society also created a band, a club, two artistic and dramatic societies and the Mutual Help Society for Artisans.[96]

Even though there was a strong nationalist movement in Malta that protested against British occupation in favour of Maltese independence,[97] certain members of the Maltese community in Egypt believed in the importance of defining themselves (and all the Maltese in Egypt) as loyal British subjects. Conte Mario de Villa-Clary, president of the Benevolent Society for almost 25 years (1895–1919) and later chairman of the Committee of the Maltese Colony of Alexandria, exemplified this pro-British sentiment. He came from the upper class, married an Englishwoman, and had a son who studied in Britain. He frequently referred to the pro-British aspirations of the Maltese community in his writings. Notably, he desired that the benevolence of the Maltese community would not only reflect its virtues but would honour the British Crown.

> I have always endeavoured to work in such a way as to make the society...a centre from which should shine all the best and most noble manifestations of our Community not only when our devotion to our Mother Island is concerned, but also as regards our loyalty towards the British Crown in the person of our most Gracious Emperor and King.[98]

According to de Villa-Clary, the Maltese were committed to the British Empire. Along with British subjects everywhere, the Maltese in Egypt zealously celebrated Queen Victoria's Diamond Jubilee in 1897. The Committee of the Maltese Colony in Alexandria also sponsored a free English course for young Maltese boys.[99] De Villa-Clary believed that 'the English and Maltese Colonies in Egypt [should] father together and form a solid and strong Colonial group of active and loyal British subjects.'[100] However, the British community was not ready to include the Maltese to such a degree. For example, Lord Cromer, when describing the British colony in Egypt spoke of 'the bona-fide English; not the Maltese and others who swell the list of British subjects in the census returns.'[101] It was likely that Britons saw the Maltese as a very different group with their own language, Mediterranean culture and largely Roman Catholic faith. Similarly, de Villa-Clary also wrote of the Maltese' general exclusion from the British community and noted that many Maltese in Egypt were disappointed that they were not treated as British subjects – with a special association with the British Crown. Instead, 'most of my compatriots complain of the fact that although they are British subjects... they are very often...treated by the English Community as if they were foreigners.'[102] Thus de Villa-Clary was heartened by Lord Milner's words, during a fund-raising dinner at Victoria College, which applauded the Maltese' generosity and suggested that closer ties between the British and Maltese communities would strengthen the British community.

> I think...a better understood and more intimate relationship, more fraternal feelings evidenced by true open-hearted mutual help between English and Maltese in Egypt, and a deeper acknowledgement of all the sincere efforts the latter are making to that purpose, *would certainly give a stronger appoint to the British Community both in Egypt and in the East.*[103]

The Maltese, like Conte de Villa-Clary, saw themselves as part of the wider British community, but the British by and large perceived them as outsiders. Yet Lord Milner, in the context of fund-raising for the British community, seemed to include the Maltese as members in wider community. De Villa-Clary noted that when it came to philanthropy, due to their generosity and experience of benevolence, the Maltese were not forgotten as fellow donors who cared for the needs and glory of the

British Empire: '[We] are never forgotten whenever it is a question of appealing to their generosity in the numerous subscriptions of British national interest of philanthropic works, to which we have always endeavoured to do our utmost according to our means.'[104]

Did the Maltese occupy the 'third space'? In the mind of someone like de Villa-Clary, they should have belonged more to the British community. Perhaps, in the minds of some of the Maltese who may have sided with the nationalists in Malta, they did not think of themselves as British subjects. In the view of Britons in Egypt, it seemed that the Maltese were recognized as members of the wider British community if they could financially assist the British but were otherwise excluded from the community. In this case, ethnic identity appeared to be negotiable according to the economic needs and circumstances of the time. Perhaps, this is the ambiguity that defines the 'third space'. The boundaries change according to the circumstances and the views of the perceiver. As Cohen argues:

> Not all boundaries, and not all the components of any boundary are so...apparent. They may be thought of...as existing in the minds of their beholders. This being so, the boundary may be perceived in rather different terms, not only by people on opposite sides of it, but also by people on the same side.[105]

British Nationality and the Demise of the Capitulations

The mutability of the British ethnic identity in occupied Egypt was also evident in the formulation of British nationality law when the Capitulations were under threat. The Capitulations refer to the system which granted extraterritorial rights to foreign residents in Egypt. Protection under the Capitulations (discussed further in chapter 5) was regarded 'as essential to the preservation of person, property, and profit'[106] without which foreigners and their businesses could not expect to succeed in Egypt. Originally, the Capitulations aimed to protect European traders from the arbitrariness of Oriental 'despots' and from local opposition to their activities. They can also be viewed as expressions of the Ottoman millet system that allowed a measure of self-governance to minority groups in Ottoman territories.[107] By the last quarter of the nineteenth century, the system evolved into an elaborate set of rules detailing the extraterritorial rights and privileges of foreign residents and governing their status in Egypt. For example, many foreigners were exempt from taxation and had virtual immunity from domiciliary search because many consuls were disinclined to respond to legal requests made by the Egyptian authorities.[108] Most notably, Europeans in Egypt were outside local jurisdiction. In civil cases, they were subject to the Mixed Tribunals and in criminal cases, to the Consular Courts of their own country of origin. This system was open to much abuse and resulted in many instances where law-breakers went unpunished.[109] The status and nationality of foreigners rested on the negotiated treaties between the Egyptian government and each individual country. So Greeks, Italians, Britons, and several other European powers in Egypt all acquired civil rights and privileges defined and enforced on the basis of their nationality.

By 1919, the emergence of the Egyptian nationalist movement combined with the British willingness to restore some form of independence to Egyptian authorities by the early 1920s placed the Capitulations and the status of the British jurisdiction over Egypt in jeopardy. A letter to the Foreign Office explains:

> So long as the capitulations continue to exist in Egypt it is evident that the position of the 2nd and later generations of British subjects who are born in Egypt is covered by…Clause I (1) of the British Nationality and Status of Aliens Act 1914, but assuming that the time comes when these capitulations are abolished and that His Majesty no longer exercises jurisdiction over British subjects in Egypt, the position at once changes.[110]

Due to the Capitulations, children born in Egypt to British fathers, who were born in Egypt or elsewhere, were made British subjects.[111] As one British observer noted, an 'Englishman born in an English protectorate should no less than an Englishman born in an English Colony preserve his birthright as an Englishman.'[112] Yet, the legal understanding at the time stated that 'if the capitulations [were] abolished and nothing intervenes to alter the strict operation of the [British Nationality and Status of Aliens] Act, the position would be that the son born in Egypt of an Englishman, who had himself been born in Egypt, would be *relegated to the status of a local Egyptian subject*.'[113] In this case, it appears that ethnic distinctions were determined by legal interpretations and by political circumstances.

> If or when the abandonment of British consular jurisdiction in Egypt becomes imminent...*children of British fathers* born in Egypt will no longer be able to rely upon the proviso to section (I) of the British Nationality Act of 1914, and claim to be regarded as having been born within His Majesty's allegiance. *They will be regarded as being born abroad.*[114]

In other words, according to the Nationality and Status of Aliens Act, a child of British parents, raised with British customs, manners, aspirations and the English language, was liable to be labelled, not only 'born abroad', but a 'local Egyptian subject' once the Capitulations came to an end. This outcome was tragic considering the aforementioned hope that British children born in Egypt were generally expected to return to Britain at some point or at the very least given the right to do so.

To ensure that the children born in Egypt to British fathers, who themselves were born in Egypt or outside Britain, would continue their status as British nationals, there was a series of discussions and correspondences between the President of the British Chamber of Commerce in Egypt, Victor Naggiar, and the Foreign Secretary, Earl Curzon. Naggiar, on behalf of the British community in Egypt, strongly urged the Foreign Office to amend the Nationality and Status of Aliens Act to guarantee that the children born to British fathers in Egypt would be made British subjects even after the demise of the Capitulations. What followed in the summer and autumn of 1921 were key recommendations from Naggiar and the British Chamber of Commerce to Curzon. First, to ensure that Britons would be given the opportunity to retain their official British nationality rather than having its termination imposed on them, Naggiar suggested that, 'provisions should be made...in the terms of the British Nationality and Status of Aliens Act (of 1914)...for British subjects until they arrive at the age of 21 years, when each shall declare whether he or she desires to retain British nationality or not.'[115]

Second, Naggiar recommended that children born into the same family (i.e. to the same British father), should all be identified as British subjects regardless of when the Capitulations would come to an end. This was to avoid the scenario whereby a child born in Egypt before the termination of the Capitulations would be considered British while his or her sibling, in the same family, born after the end of the Capitulations, would not be considered British but an Egyptian subject. The solution, according to Naggiar, was to guarantee that all children, born to a British father whose marriage took place prior to 1 January 1915, would be considered 'British' by law.

> That in view of the hardship inflicted by the Act upon families by which the children are divided into different nationalities...the Act should be altered so as to include as British subjects the whole family of a British father of his marriage celebrated before the 1st January 1915, where a child of the marriage born before that date would have been a British subject by the law then in force.[116]

This recommendation would at least ensure that a generation of children born to British fathers, whose marriages would most likely have taken place before 1915, would remain British subjects in spite of the end of the Capitulations.

Naggiar's campaign was successful. By the summer of 1922, the British Nationality and Status of Aliens Act underwent a process of amendments. Its new provisions included the following:

> A British subject was any person born out of His Majesty's dominions whose father was, at the time of that person's birth, a British subject...
> i) This person must register within one year after birth or in special circumstances, with the consent of secretary of state, allow for two years.
> ii) This person must register within one year after reaching the age of 21 though there was some flexibility for special cases.[117]

To prevent any child born to British fathers from losing his or her status as a British subject in light of the Capitulations' demise, the British Nationality and Status of Aliens Act was amended. So long as the child's father was a British subject and his or her birth was registered with the British Consulate in the first year (or in some cases, two years) of birth, the child would be guaranteed British nationality, regardless of the date of birth.

From this legal process of maintaining the identity of those born in Egypt (to British fathers) as British subjects, the mutability or negotiability of ethnic identity becomes evident. Ethnic identity is, at certain times, dependent not on primordial or fixed distinctions, but on legal perceptions determined by political circumstances. One may argue, however, that precisely because British identity was primordial and so strong, laws had to be changed to protect British children from being 'disappointingly' labelled as Egyptian subjects and being denied British citizenship for the rest of their lives. Yet I argue that the threat of British children losing their identity, no matter how entrenched, as British subjects was real in light of the imminent demise of the Capitulations and of British control in Egypt. At that point in time, British ethnic identity seemed negotiable, ambiguous, and changeable for future generations of those born to the British in Egypt.

Intermarriage: A Threat to Identity

Perhaps, no issue exposed the ethnic boundary between Europeans and Egyptians as much as intermarriage. The 'typical European view of mixed marriages was that they were unspeakably abhorrent to Europeans and non-Europeans alike.'[118] For Europeans, this disdain for mixed marriages stemmed from the fears of producing genetically corrupted offspring, of surrendering European women to the alleged sexual appetites of non-European 'native' men, and of upsetting the sexist and racist ideologies of the time.

The fear of corrupting European offspring with non-white blood was based on the Social Darwinist assumptions of the time. From the 1880s until the 1920s, when sociology was just beginning to establish itself as a scholarly discipline and colonialism was at its height, Social Darwinism biologically classified human beings according to racial characteristics similar to the classification of plants and animals in the growing fields of botany and zoology. As Ernst explains: 'Nineteenth-century racial science attempted to...pigeonhole different indigenous groups of people (Bengali, Parsi, Sikh, and so forth)...in imitation of the schemes of botany and biology...Just as scientists and collectors pinned various sorts of butterflies and beetles on to their collection boards.'[119]

These evolutionist assumptions, with the doctrine of the 'survival of the fittest', established the natural hierarchy of human beings with the white man on top. Other non-white races were understood to be less evolved and were thereby 'child' races that were dependent on the more civilised race for social and intellectual development. Thus the thought of producing offspring with biologically inferior genes were abhorrent to most Europeans, especially at a time when the eugenics movement, which aimed to genetically reproduce the highest calibre of offspring through biologically engineering, was gathering momentum in European social thought. In other words,

> Social Darwinism...and Eugenics added fuel to the prevalent fear of racial mixing, since it warned against the dilution of 'pure racial stocks' and the decline of white civilisation...The horror of miscegenation...or 'race fusion'...or racial degeneration...was held to sap the fibre of white civilisation at its most vulnerable point.[120]

Consequently, intermarriage was discouraged in the colonies. In Malaysia, as Stockwell points out, British men who took Asian wives were marked as unconventional and thus failed to reach the highest levels of Malaysian civil service.[121]

Intermarriage was not only despised by Europeans, due to its genetic contamination of offspring, it was also loathed because indigenous men were thought to be uncontrollable sexual predators. 'European women's presence,' according to Strobel, 'it [was] thought, aroused [the] sexual appetites of indigenous men, and women had then to be protected from the latter...The presence of supposedly vulnerable women provided a reason to fear the alleged sexual appetites of indigenous men.'[122] Due to the European perception of the sexual prowess of indigenous male predators, intermarriage between indigenous men and European women was condemned as harmful to Western women and threatening to the Western male sexual ego. There was, of course, a double standard whereby Western men in certain colonies, particularly in Southeast Asia, had indigenous mistresses or concubines. However, in Egypt and in most predominantly Muslim contexts, local 'women [were] never allowed to form friendships of this kind'[123] with Europeans.

> Moslem women, as is well known, [were] never supposed to see any men except their husbands and immediate relations, and [were] kept strictly to their own apartments, or harem...[and even] Christian women...[were by and large] not supposed to speak to visitors.[124]

Due to the fear of indigenous men and the general seclusion of indigenous women, Europeans seldom had friendships with Egyptians of the opposite gender, let alone the opportunity to pursue marriage. Generally, there was a clear boundary separating the interracial interaction between the sexes. Besides the fears of contaminated progeny and the sexual appetite of indigenous men, intermarriage between 'native' men and European women was abhorrent to Europeans because it threw into question the very foundation of the interracial and sexual hierarchical beliefs of the time. 'Sexual liaisons between white women and indigenous men confounded the fundamental belief that women should be subordinate to men,'[125] since the white race was considered superior to indigenous races. Intermarriage between white women and indigenous men challenged the racial and sexual ideologies of the day. Protection of white women from indigenous men fit nicely into the racist and chauvinistic framework of that time.

Not only did Europeans fear the consequences of intermarriage for European women with indigenous men, some indigenous voices also discouraged intermarriage of indigenous men with European women. Although 'marriages between Mussulmen and Christian women are looked on with favour...as it is understood that the Prophet encouraged the habit, which evidently tended to the increase of the number of true believers,'[126] certain Egyptian women – like middle-class teacher and author, Malak Hifni Nasif – persuaded middle and upper-class Egyptian men to marry educated Egyptian women. She viewed that marrying European women, particularly of the lower-class, was 'a national danger that [produced] children with divided cultural loyalties'[127] and diluted intelligence. Hopwood mentions just such an example of a lower-class British woman married to an Egyptian man. He recalls Vice-Consul Thomas Rapp's encounter with the women, who, in his view, had an ugly Oxford accent and was a former assistant hairdresser from St. Giles, Oxford. She was living in Egypt after marrying one of the elite Egyptian graduates of Oxford University who had been a frequent customer to the hairstylists that she was working for.[128] To educated Egyptian women, this kind of marriage corrupted the genes of bright Egyptian men by mixing them with unintelligent foreign women. Further, Nabawiya Musa, teacher and inspector in the Ministry of Education, also discouraged Egyptian men from marrying European women because 'a man who marries a Westerner becomes with his children [a] Westerner... An Egyptian woman, who marries a foreigner...is capable of giving Egypt new Egyptians.'[129] Another argument used against intermarriage by certain Egyptian women writers is that offspring from marriages of Egyptian men and European women would produce disloyal Egyptians who would reduce the nationalist commitment of the next generation. Further, intermarriage between Egyptian men and particular working-class European women was 'threatening since they robbed [educated] Egyptian women of bright men.'[130] According to certain Egyptian women commentators, Egyptian nationalism combined with the fear of losing educated Egyptian men to foreign women (who may be of the lower class and thereby 'contaminating' the offspring of educated Egyptian men) consolidated the boundary separating Egyptian men from European women. Notably, both Europeans and Egyptians were afraid of intermarriage because it would corrupt their offspring. The loathing and restricting of intermarriage was a mutual concern and priority on both sides.

Protecting British women from polygamous men,
invalid divorces, and ill-treatment

On the basis of the general fears and attitudes against intermarriage of the time, Britons generally discouraged the intermarriage between Egyptian Muslim men and British women due to the polygamous practices of Muslim men, the uncertainty of divorce, and their ill-treatment and abuse of their wives.

Intermarriage between British women and Egyptian Christian men was not as loathed by the British as marriage with Muslim men. Though not looked upon as an ideal arrangement, a Copt could marry an Englishwomen by obtaining the signed permission of his patriarch, followed by two religious marriages (one in a Coptic church and one in an Anglican church).[131] Girgis Soliman, an Egyptian Copt, was given permission by the British authorities in Egypt to marry an English girl from Newcastle while studying there. The marriage was legal, both in the eyes of the Coptic Church and the British government, provided that the bride's parents agreed (if the bride was under 21 years of age) and that the couple sign a declaration of adherence to the Coptic church upon their arrival in Egypt.[132] Though not warmly embraced, marriage between a Coptic man and a British woman appeared to be tolerated.

However, marriages between British women and Egyptian Muslim men were largely despised by the British community. Mixed marriages were denounced to 'protect' British women from marrying polygamous Muslim men. The Foreign Marriages Act of 1892 and the Foreign Marriages Order in Council of 1913 outlined that:

The marriage of a woman of British nationality professing the Christian faith with a...Mohammedan, even...when it is valid in all respects in this country, is not necessarily so when the husband returns to...his own Mohammedan country...The marriage [may not] necessarily imply...the voluntary union for life of one man and woman to the exclusion of all others...and under Mohammedan law *the Mohammedan husband may, if he desires, take other wives in addition to the first, without consulting his first wife (whether Christian or otherwise)*. Even if the Mohammedan husband had entered into a covenant with his Christian wife not to take any other wife, such a covenant could not prevent him from taking another wife...in a Mohammedan society if so desired...The forms observed at a marriage under English law before a Registrar are not necessarily recognised by Mohammedan law...and afford no protection to the wife in a country where Mohammedan law is observed...A Mohammedan husband may...divorce his wife at will...while should he return to his own country leaving his Christian wife here, the fact of their being thus locally separated might be equivalent to divorce under Mohammedan law; in either case such divorce, while not dissolving the marriage in England under English law, would be operative in the Mohammedan country.[133]

Due to the polygamous nature of some Muslim marriages, one of the most prominent concerns for British women who married Egyptian Muslim men was that English law could not protect their marriages in a Muslim country. British women were unable to obtain divorces since their marriages, instituted under English law, seemed likely invalid under Muslim law in the first place. This would place them in not only a confusing but pitiful situation where their marriages would be recognised and protected under English law but would have no power to influence a Muslim husband from taking another wife or pursuing a divorce. In addition, their divorces would not be recognised under Muslim law because according to Muslim law, they were never married. In other words, according to Mrs. Edith Louisa Butcher, wife of Dean Butcher who for many years during the British occupation was Chaplain of All Saints' Church in Cairo:

Even if such marriages [between a Muslim man and an Englishwoman] are now recognised by English law, that does not make them binding on the Moslem. He can still, by his own law, marry three other women in addition to the first, or divorce his English wife at any time and on any pretext. I remember one poor Englishwomen who had gone through the ceremony of marriage with a Moslem Egyptian...After some years, unable to bear the misery of her position, she applied for a divorce by English law. She could easily have got one as far as her case against the man went. But taking legal advice it had to be explained to the poor thing that as she was not legally married, she could not be legally divorced.[134]

Similarly, Besley, Acting Judicial Adviser to the High Commissioner of Egypt warned:

Article 120 of the Code du Statut Personnel recognises the validity of a marriage between a Mohammedan and a Christian woman, provided that there are two Christian witnesses to the wedding. But, although these witnesses can bind the Christian woman, their testimony is valueless against the Mohammedan man. It seems to follow from this, that, in a case such...where the Mohammedan man denies the validity of the marriage, there will be no witnesses to prove it, and therefore...it will be null and void, as being a marriage contracted without witnesses...If there was no marriage in the eyes of Mohammedan law, there can obviously be no divorce.[135]

Even in spite of these concerns, some British women still chose to marry Muslim men. In 1911, Francis Cownie, a British woman, married A. D. Allam, an Egyptian Muslim. In response to Miss Cownie's decision, a British gentleman, G. E. Jeffes, wrote a letter to Arthus D. Alan of the British Consulate warning against the ill-treatment that Muslim men could lay on their British wives. He declared that Muslim husbands could not only marry up to four wives, but inflict corporal punishment on them, divorce them at any time, seclude them indoors, and enforce an Islamic upbringing on their children.[136] Jeffes' letter goes on to say that 'however much a native may be civilised, he is not, and cannot be, received in English society in Egypt,'[137] and that only 'unpleasantness... occurred [when] native gentlemen [were] allowed to associate with English ladies.'[138] He cautioned that an English woman would be 'cut off from the society of her fellow countrymen in Egypt and find herself obliged to associate with women of a far lower standard both morally and intellectually.'[139] Remarkably, Jeffes would rather 'see an Englishwoman [live] with a Mohammedan in open sin as his mistress than as his wife.'[140] Similarly, J. W. A. Young, a British official on one of his tax-inspections, was appalled by the ill treatment of an English woman who was married to an Egyptian in the village of Galubiyya in 1914. The house where she lived was poor with unbaked brick and a flat roof. Apparently, she had married the village leader's son when he was studying engineering in England. She was the daughter of his landlady in Britain. Young records:

> After I had waited for a little while, a young English woman and a small English boy walked in [who was her younger brother]. The woman appeared to be about twenty and the small English boy about eight years old...She said, 'My father-in-law [the 'Umdeh]...will be with you in a few minutes. How is the war going? They tell me that Germany is winning but I never see an English newspaper.'[141]

Young then began to speak to the 'Umdeh who confirmed to Young that his son had beaten his new bride of only two months. 'Of course he beats her,' said the 'Umdeh, 'I love my wife but I frequently beat her.'[142] Young was horrified by this young English woman and her brother's plight. He wanted to free them immediately from their desperate predicament.

> It seemed to me a most extraordinary case. Here was this young English woman captivated by the charms of an Egyptian Moslem of no class, who had probably given her an utterly false description of his rank in life and of her future home and she had now found herself in the mud hovel of her father-in-law in a remote village of the Egyptian Delta leading the life of a peasant and would, if she remained there, be in a few years a wrinkled hag, for fellaheen women are old before they are thirty. I picture her as time went on trudging down to the river every morning, afternoon and evening, with the other village women to scoop up water for washing and drinking, an empty petroleum tin balanced on her head and her long black garment trailing behind in the dust. And her young brother! What a life for him! He was to be brought up with the other village boys and to be educated in the Kuttab where no language was taught but Arabic. Later when I returned to Cairo I reported the case to the British Consulate and also to the British Agency, *when*

it was discovered that her marriage papers were not in order...she and her brother were sent back to England.[143]

Young's attitude tended to be typical of the British in Egypt who was concerned that Muslim men would beat up their British wives while perhaps less aware that certain British men in Egypt were also beating their British wives, as will be discussed in a later chapter. In this case, he was convinced that the British woman who married the Muslim man must have been deeply misguided and thoroughly regretful of her marriage. The only hope for her was to escape the situation. There seemed little ambiguity when it came to how the British felt about mixed marriages. The perceived ill treatment of British women by British men widened the boundary between the British and the Egyptians as the following observation suggests:

> English women who have lived in the East almost always attribute the Oriental conception of women as the reason for their shrinking from contact with natives, even from those who are intellectually cultivated...Englishmen also frequently give this as reason for disliking that their wives and daughters should meet natives in society.'[144]

Intermarriage and nationality

It appears that little ambiguity existed for the British (and most Europeans) when it came to intermarriage with Egyptians. European men were almost entirely secluded from Egyptian women – Copt or Muslim. For British women, it seemed that marrying a Copt was tolerable but marrying a Muslim was detestable. Yet, there were ambiguities when it came to the nationality of British women who decided to marry indigenous men. For example, the Irish-Australian woman who married the Turkish Prince, Said Tusun, was considered British by the Cairo elite. The Princess was a widow when she married the Prince. Both were not on the best of terms with their families. The Princess 'was not recognised by the Cromers and other leading English families, although she was accepted by most of the Continental element. The Prince accordingly was super-sensitive about her and accepted no attention to himself unless also offered to his wife.'[145] Considered 'English' by Europeans of the Continent but not accepted as 'English' by the English, the Princess represented the ambiguity that came from the various perceptions of differing groups.

Besides perceived ambivalence of the Princess' identity, the greater ambiguity of identity was rooted in the fact that British women who looked British, had British parents, and a British upbringing, were being denied British nationality once they married Muslim men. The Foreign Marriages Act stipulated that:

> a woman of British nationality, professing the Christian faith who marries a Mohammedan who is not a British subject, but is a subject or citizen of a Mohammedan state...*loses her British nationality on her marriage*, and when the husband and wife land in any Mohammedan country (not being in the Dominion or under the Protectorate of His Britainnic Majesty) they both become subject to the Mohammedan law. Further, *the wife having lost her British nationality, would appear to have become disentitled to the protection of assistance of any British authority – consular or otherwise*.[146]

The fluidity of ethnicity was visibly illustrated here. A British woman could suddenly become a mere foreigner immediately upon marrying a Muslim. Ethnicity here, instead of being fixed and primordial, was both situational and changeable – dependent on the viewpoint of the beholder.

British Prisoners

One final contrast can be brought to light. While British women were being stripped of their British nationality upon their marriage to Muslim men, British criminals in Egyptian jails were being 'honoured' as Britons and protected from having to share the same conditions as other Egyptian prisoners. British prisoners were originally 'made to consort with the lowest of native prisoners.'[147] At the Manshiyya Prison in Cairo, there were on the average 1200 prisoners. Three to five British subjects were imprisoned each year but their terms of imprisonment never exceeded three months.[148] Yet, even though their terms were short, there was considerable pressure to separate the British convicts from the indigenous prisoners as T. C. Rapp, the British Vice-Consul of Cairo, noted:

> Europeans are obliged to associate with natives and the taps from which washing and drinking water is drawn are directly opposite, and within two yards, of the latrine seats without any dividing

partition. *It is degrading for an Englishman, no matter to what depths he has sunk, to be obliged to come into such intimate contact with the dregs of the native populace.* This, to my mind, is the matter which most requires radical alteration.[149]

Although the jails were full of bugs, without hot water, and the Egyptian warders could only speak Arabic to the British prisoners, the crucial reason behind separating the British prisoners from the Egyptian prisoners was not the poor conditions of Egyptian jails. Rather, for the British officials responsible for prisons, it was 'particularly undesirable that British subjects should be herded together with natives of criminal classes...The arrangement of other accommodation for Consular [British] prisoners [was] a matter of pressing necessity.'[150] Hence, the evidence suggests that keeping British criminals in Egypt from sharing prison space with native Egyptians was an urgent priority for the British authorities. Yet, it appears that upright British women who happened to marry Egyptian Muslim men were torn from their British nationality, denied the rights and privileges of British citizenry, and 'relegated' to a lifetime of being ethnically and legally Egyptian. This seems to demonstrate an appalling double standard whereby law-abiding British women, who were perceived to be 'subjugating' themselves to the alleged ill treatment of polygamous Egyptian husbands, were seen to be committing a greater 'crime' than British male criminals.

This chapter began by outlining key paradigms related to the study of ethnicity and suggests that ethnic identity, rather than being solely fixed and unchangeable, is malleable depending on different circumstances and perceptions. The discussion attempted to show that there were some clear boundaries between the British community and Egyptians, Turks, and Levantines in occupied Egypt. Generally Britons, except for some officials and the missionaries, had little interaction with the Egyptians due to differences in language and cultural interests, their fear of catching diseases from the Egyptians, and their belief that their aloofness would project and maintain their sense of authority and power over the Egyptians. Related religious traditions, shared language or education seemed to have minimal impact in weakening the social boundary that existed between the British and the Egyptian Copts or Westernised Muslims respectively. However, the bulk of the chapter examines the ambiguity of ethnic identities that emerged from varying historical circumstances and perspectives. For example, the Maltese seemed to be included as part of the British community only when Britons pursued their charitable giving. Children born to British fathers (born outside of Britain) were denied British nationality when it appeared that the Capitulations were coming to an end. British women who married Egyptians lost their status as British nationals. Notably, the negotiability of British identity contributes to a key thrust of this book that underscores that there was diversity within Egypt's British community. The ambiguity of British identity also brings to light a previously underemphasised aspect of the historiography of Britons in Egypt during the prime of British imperialism.

3

SYMBOLS AND INSTITUTIONS

Roles of Symbols in Community

Every community of people is defined by certain features and commonalities that give it meaning and identity and distinguish it from other communities. Benedict Anderson, in *Imagined Communities*, asserts that the characteristics of community are articulated in the mind – similar to the individual 'consciousness' described in the previous chapter.

> All communities larger than primordial villages of face-to-face contact (and perhaps even these) are imagined…because the members of even the smallest [community] will never know most of their fellow members, meet them, or even hear of them, yet in the minds of each lives the image of their communion.[1]

Even though members of each community would actually meet only a small minority of their fellow members, they usually have 'complete confidence in their steady, anonymous, simultaneous activity.'[2]

This confidence in the reality and vitality of the community comes from particular constructs shared in the imagination of each member of the community. These constructs are what we call symbols. 'Symbols of community are mental constructs. They provide people with the means to make meaning. In so doing, they also provide them with the means to express the particular meanings which the community has for them.'[3] This chapter centres on identifying and examining the symbols of the British community in occupied Egypt since 'ethnic identity is expressed symbolically.'[4] In this discussion, the word 'symbol' refers to three aspects of representation. First, they serve as emblems to 'differentiate [one ethnic group] from other groups.'[5] They 'reinforce…the specialness,…

Fig. 2. Map of Central Cairo: Locations of important areas and buildings for the British community (map not to scale, only main streets indicated). Based on Map of Cairo, no. 64480 (4): Edward Stanford, 12, 13, 14, Long Acre W.C., 16 June: 1906, London and General Map of Cairo, no. 64480(6), Survey of Egypt 1920.

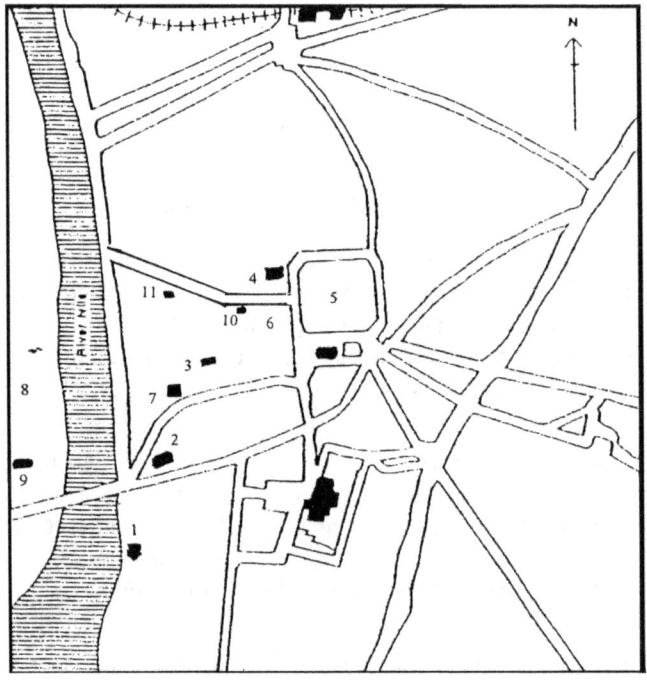

1. British Residency
2. Qasr el-Nil Barracks
3. Turf Club
4. Shepheard's Hotel
5. Ezbekiyya Gardens
6. European Quarter
7. Savoy Hotel
8. Gezira Club
9. Anglo-American Hospital
10. All Saints' Church
11. St. Andrew's Church

the exclusiveness,...[and] even chosen-ness of the group.'⁶ They define and give shape to the community's identity and act as the glue that keeps it together.

Second, symbols represent a common memory, heritage, or ancestry in a given community. Patterson refers to the inner concourse of ethnic identity as one which begins with the 'consciousness of shared crisis, one symbolically validated...with a common memory.'⁷ The crisis is normally one that creates a sense of isolation that is experienced collectively, not individually. Further, symbols validate myths.

> This is the myth of blood, the deeply held belief that the entire group has a common ancestry, common history, and sometimes a common fate. It is this myth – often having little or no basis in fact – that the...ethnic group...ritualises. The ethnic group...is not so much a moral community as is a religious group – a community of memory.⁸

French sociologist Barthes articulates this usage of myth in *Mythologies*:

> Myth is not defined by the object of its message, but by the way in which it utters this message...[Myths are created when an] object in the world [passes] from a closed, silent existence to an oral state, open to appropriation by society.⁹

Barthes states that objects can pass from a closed state to an oral state. It is in the 'speech' of objects that myths and messages emerge. Objects, monuments, buildings and rituals all tell a story within every community. Inanimate objects that point to and remind members of the group of a common history and shared crises, then, are the symbols which communicate a message or 'myth'. In light of this, this chapter will use the term 'institutions' since it implies buildings, structures, and traditions. Symbols and institutions construct the shared concepts and memories that identify and nurture commonality within an 'imagined' community.

Third, besides acting as the enforcer of common identity and curator of common memories, symbols elaborate, enhance, manipulate, and perpetuate the culture, ideas, aspirations, and significant heroes of an ethnic group in front of other groups.¹⁰ Symbols not only galvanize and unify the group from within but also radiate the group's identity (in the case of the British in Egypt – power, prestige, and influence) to other groups.

The following analysis attempts to identify and examine the symbols and institutions within Egypt's British community which reflected its distinctiveness and common history, and perpetuated the group's image to outsiders. With reference to British communities mainly in India, Mombasa, and Malaya during that time, this study explores the symbolic value and roles of the British flag, the English language, expatriate geographic locations, clubs and sports, military structures and activities, hotels, schools, hospitals, churches, and key occasions. It is also hoped that this discussion of British symbols and institutions will illumine previously underemphasised aspects of the history of Egypt's Britons such as the lack of funding for certain British institutions and its implications.

The British Flag

Although the flag usually acts as a clear symbol of a nation's presence and power in occupied territory, surprisingly, there seems to be little evidence to suggest that the British flag was a significant symbol in Egypt. H. F. Wood, British traveller during the 1890s, was the only observer, according the sources used in this study, who mentioned the presence (or the lack) of British flags in Alexandria and Cairo. He recalls:

> It might be inferred that above the [sign] 'Headquarters British Garrison', if nowhere else, the British ensign is to be seen at Alexandria. [But] I did not see the British ensign either there or anywhere else until reaching Cairo, and then only at the premises of private tradesmen and at the masthead of Nile excursion or pleasure-boats...The stars and stripes floated from the summit of the American Consulate adjacent to the English Church [in]... Alexandria; but neither upon ordinary business structures, nor upon private or official residences, nor upon the quarters of the British commander at Alexandria, nor at the headquarters of the garrison itself, was any British flag to be perceived.[11]

According to Wood, the British flag was not only absent on official buildings in Alexandria and Cairo, it was non-existent in informal events and occasions as well.

I supposed that, as the cities of the Continent where the British colonies form their clubs for outdoor recreation, the Union jack might have harmlessly adorned the ground of the local cricket, football and lawn-tennis club. It was not so, however...[In one particular] football match between the Alexandria Club and a crew of the gunboat Fearless...nothing of the colours [of the club jerseys and]...nothing in any of the usual decorations to a club-house or marquee suggested the British flag.[12]

From the evidence of the 1890s, it appears that the British flag was rarely seen. Therefore, one may conclude that the flag, as a basic symbol of presence and predominance, was not utilised by the British in occupied Egypt. This was most likely due to Britain's sensitivity to Egypt's official position as an Ottoman territory and to the need to restrain potential tension with France over Britain's standing in Egypt.

The English Language

English was not the most widely used language in education[13] or among the legal and business circles in Egypt during the British occupation, though certain Britons wanted to make English the official language of Egypt's mixed courts which would symbolise Britain's hold on power. The mixed courts tried civil cases for foreign residents while criminal cases were tried in the Consular Courts of their country of origin. To the chagrin of some in Egypt's British community,

> French was the language that most people in Egypt had in common... [The] easiest way for a foreigner, whether he was Italian, Belgian, Swiss or Russian, to converse with a local, whether he was Turkish or Egyptian, was through the medium of French. This was also the case if the foreigners wished to do business amongst themselves and often between Turk and Egyptian also. Added to France's cultural influence through legal writings and philosophy, and the French education that many Egyptians had enjoyed, this led to an easy assumption of the French language as a lingua franca.[14]

Not only was French the primary language of education (next to Arabic) and interaction between Europeans and Egyptians, it was the main language for the mixed tribunals, government newspapers and notices, official legal documents such as tenders, railway time tables, decrees issued by the Sultan of Egypt, and cab-stand notices.[15] Since French was the medium for the mixed courts in Egypt, the legal system was based on French codes. However,

> while using the vast amount of French legal thought as an aid where necessary, judges were clearly able to interpret the Codes in an Egyptian context, free from enactments not suitable to the Orient...Thus any influence of French law that may have transposed itself into the Codes was soon influenced itself by Egyptian surroundings.[16]

By 1917, the Capitulations Commission was appointed to deal with the abolition of the capitulations and to formulate the judicial reforms necessary to achieve this. Much to the displeasure of British lawyers, the minutes to the meetings of the Commission were written in French and the leading British judge in Egypt, Justice Grain, was not invited to participate in its proceedings; even though Egypt was firmly under Britain's political authority. Therefore, J. P. Foster, a British solicitor practising in Egypt, along with nine other British lawyers, strongly recommended to the Commission that

> English should be made, without delay, the judicial language of Egypt [and] that English criminal procedure and law be adopted. Justice Grain or someone familiar with English law and procedure... should [be] appointed [and] the minutes of the commission should be kept in English, and the voluminous minutes which have been hitherto kept in French should be translated into English...*English should no longer be relegated to a back seat.*[17]

To Foster and his legal colleagues, English as the official language of the mixed courts combined with English judicial procedure symbolised the rightful place of British dominance in Egypt. How appropriate was it to have French, and not English, as the primary language of the courts in a territory under British control? Disappointingly for Foster and his cohorts, the Foreign Office, though sympathetic, was dismissive of his recommendations. The Minutes of the Capitulations Commission and the Advisory Committee on Egyptian legislation continued to be recorded in French.[18] Most likely, the Foreign Office felt that the symbolic installing of English as the language of the mixed courts was not worth the risk of upsetting its European allies in Egypt during the war or destabilising Egypt unnecessarily. Even so, in 1918, William Brunyate the Judicial Adviser continued the campaign to implement English as the everyday language in the mixed courts. However, his recommendations were met with opposition, not least from French judges and lawyers and those who had been accustomed to French as the legal language of Egypt. After more than one hundred meetings with leaders of the mixed tribunals to discuss the introduction of English as the language of the mixed courts, Brunyate's plans were rejected.[19] It was likely that other European authorities in the mixed tribunals were reluctant to accept English as the main language of the courts because they already felt threatened by the establishment a formal British protectorate in Egypt. Though certain members of the British legal community undertook to formalise English as the official language of the mixed courts due to its symbolic significance as the language of the 'rulers' of Egypt, the effort was unsuccessful during the period of the occupation.

The Symbolic Significance of Location

Comparative studies show that spatial separation in colonial cities emerged, underlining and cementing social separation. Ross and Telkamp's work in comparing colonial cities reveals that,

> in Algiers…Saigon…and Dakar, there was from the beginning a spatial distinction between the 'white' town and the area inhabited by the local population, whether Algerian, Vietnamese or Sengalese; [and] the same phenomenon [occurred] not just in the French Empire, [but] in English cities [as well]…This encoded and determined social stratification and categorisation.[20]

Similarly, new residential neighbourhoods apart from the native quarters were established for the British community in Bengal. S. C. Ghosh writes: 'With the growth both of wealth and a new sense of security… new housing sprang up along the existing roads, the Avenue, Pilgrim Road, and row Bazer and by passing the native quarters of Dinga and Colinga.'[21] Jürgen Osterhammel observes that the 'basic organizing principle [for colonial cities] was a segregation of residential quarters along racial lines. This segregation was partly the result of deliberate policies and partly of unplanned developments.'[22] He mentions that eighteenth century Calcutta was divided between 'white town' and 'black town'. The British also laid out separate residential districts in Delhi, Dakar, Nairobi, Singapore, and Kingston in Jamaica. The European districts were almost always more spacious, with villas and bungalows on large lots and equipped with an elaborate sewage system. Indigenous quarters were usually cramped and lacked the sanitary structures and conditions of the European quarters.[23]

As already intimated in chapter 1, the segregation between Egyptians and foreigners was evident in occupied Cairo. The partitioning was comparable to that of Bengal, Calcutta, Delhi, and other colonial locations mentioned above. Mitchell points out that a key factor for this segregation was the perceived potential for disease and crime that originated from the poorly lit, tight and cramped quarters along the narrow streets of pre-colonial Cairo.[24] Motivated by his desire to create a healthier Cairo, Khedive Ismail implemented a wide-ranging construction scheme during the middle of the nineteenth century. He proceeded to build the 'Paris' of the Middle East with the help of European engineering expertise. Wider streets and more open areas were built in order to curb disease and to allow police to monitor 'dark' areas of crime more readily. Open spaces were created for new shops and entertainment. Cleanliness on the streets was encouraged.[25] As a result, these wider spaces became areas where Europeans were more likely to frequent, away from what they perceived to be the less developed, unsanitary, and unsafe areas where most native Egyptians dwelled. Construction of European buildings and institutions in Cairo, during the time of the British Occupation, by and large remained in areas that the Khedive had already developed as European.

An analysis of the maps of Cairo during from the 1900s testifies to this segregation. According to Edward Stanford's map of 1906,[26] the residential map of Gezira in 1907[27] and another map published by the Survey of Egypt in 1920,[28] most districts in Cairo were chiefly Egyptian while some areas vividly showcased European architecture. More specifically, within these predominantly European quarters, British buildings and institutions were situated on three main sites. The Gezira Island (which in 1906 was called Gezirat Bulak) featured a large residential quarter for British residents,[29] the Gezira Palace Hotel and Gezira Sporting Club. On the club's grounds were the racecourse and the Anglo-American Hospital. The Qasr el-Dubara quarter, just southeast of Gezira and east of the Nile River, was another leading residential neighbourhood for British residents of Cairo. It hosted the Semiramis and Savoy hotels as well as the British Residency – the office and home of the Consul General. According to Roger Owen, it became 'a symbol of Britain's...supremacy,'[30] and 'a major centre of power in Cairo, visited regularly by Egyptian cabinet ministers, the consuls-general of the European powers, the representatives of the various local European communities, and others.'[31] Finally, the Ezbekiyya area, northeast of the Qasr el-Dubara quarter, contained the often-frequented Shepheard's Hotel, Continental Hotel, Hotel Victoria, and the Anglo-Egyptian Bank. The All Saints' and St. Andrew's churches were also in the same vicinity in nearby 'Ataba. Although facilitated by earlier aforementioned Khedival policies, the pattern of segregation between the foreign rulers and native Egyptians emerged primarily during the British Occupation when more and more Britons settled in Cairo. British residents in Cairo chose to live, work, and relax in Gezira, Qasr el-Dubara (near Garden City) and the Ezbekiyya area; while Egyptians primarily inhabited regions like Boulaq, Shobra, and Old Cairo. On the outskirts of Cairo, Britons also resided in Zamalek, Heliopolis, Maadi, and Helwan. Abu-Lughod articulates this divide between the European quarter and the Egyptian parts of Cairo:

> By the end of the nineteenth century Cairo consisted of two distinct physical communities...The city's physical duality was but a manifestation of the cultural cleavage...The native city [was] still essentially pre-industrial in technology, social structure, and way of life, [with] the labyrinth street pattern of yet unpaved [streets];... the 'colonial' city [featured] its steam-powered techniques, its faster pace and wheeled traffic, and its European identification... [with] broad straight streets...flanked by wide walks and setbacks, militantly crossing one another at rigid right angles...[The native city] was dependent upon itinerant water peddlers [while the residents of the 'colonial' city]...had their water delivered through a convenient network of conduits connected with the steam pumping station near the river. [The native city was] plunged into darkness at nightfall while gaslights illuminated the thoroughfares [of the 'colonial' city along with] formal gardens, strips of decorative flowers beds, or artificially shaped trees. One entered the old city by caravan and traversed it on foot or animal-back; one entered the new by railroad and proceeded via horse-drawn [carriages]. In short...the two cities...were miles apart socially and centuries apart technologically.[32]

It appears that the symbolic value of the geographic location of European, and more particularly, British institutions, buildings, and residential neighbourhoods lay in their separateness from the native Egyptian quarters. Not only did this separation merely affirm the glaring ethnic and cultural difference between Britons and Egyptians, they also provided the British residents of Egypt with reminders of unity and commonality, in a shared heritage and tradition. One pertinent example was Gezira Island. It represented for the British community a place that reminded them of a common heritage in Britain and gave them a 'home' away from home as one astute British observer so poignantly comments:

> the little English colony seems very self-contained, with the inevitable golf course, tennis-club, and Anglican church. Cairo has an English quarter in the island of Gezireh inhabited by the more fortunate of our officials, and it is surprisingly English in its appearance. Some of the roads, with their neat tree-lined pavements, their wooden garden-gates and 'tradesmen's entrance', might be in Wimbledon or Beckenham or some other prosperous London suburb.[33]

The familiar universe of larger homes, infrastructure for water and electricity supply, 'imported British plants to make British gardens,... British sports and British food'[34] was a comforting attraction to British personnel in the military and civil services and in British companies. It was likely that this segregation also represented British power and aloofness for Britons themselves and the average Egyptian.

It may be helpful to clarify that the actual buildings in Cairo may not have reflected a specific 'British' predominance in Egypt. Though

> the inspiration for the Ma'adi district (built from 1906 by the Delta Company) came from the British style of sloping roofs and flower gardens [and that]...Garden City was also a British-style district following the same pattern as Ma'adi with its villas and gardens.[35]

Mark Crinson, in his work on architectural styles in Egypt, suggests that larger, more significant buildings and architectural landmarks were rarely representative of British design, labour, or pre-eminence. 'In Cairo, as in Alexandria, building materials were often imported. Most building work was in the hands of Italian architects and contractors, and British involvement was unusual.'[36] Of significant buildings in Egypt in the late nineteenth century, Crinson pinpoints that only St. Mark's church in Alexandria, the New Hotel in Ezbekiyya Gardens, the Post Office and the Hospital in Suez were constructed by British architects who stayed true to a distinct British style of design which featured pyramidal roofs and convex mansard roofs. Some British architects such as Robert Stephenson and Owen Jones were hired by the Egyptian authorities to design buildings which showcased neo-Islamic domes and pavilions.[37] Though the splendour and size of European architecture in specific areas of Cairo and Alexandria indicated to Egyptians a formidable foreign presence and power in their country, the buildings themselves rarely communicated a particular *British* pre-eminence. Most likely, the segregated British quarters acted more as a rallying point for their community solidarity and common heritage than the actual design of the buildings.

Clubs

Clubs were very important to the cohesion and expansion of the British Empire. In cities in Britain, clubs since the seventeenth century 'performed a vital social and cultural role...They promoted social integration...[and] generated a renewed consciousness and pride in urban community.'[38] Clubs enforced British culture and imperial prowess within Britain and throughout the Empire.

> There was a parallel expansion in membership of...public schools, the gentlemen's clubs, and the Empire. Clubs in London such as the Oriental, the East India, the Calcutta, the Madras, and the Bombay reflected in their very names the Imperial expansiveness. They helped to sustain its social structure.[39]

Clubs, established in nearly every major colonial centre, provided the space to cultivate imperial customs and ideals. The 'Empire depended on rulers who cleaved to others to constitute a fraternity who, belonging to the same club, wore the same mask, had the same manners, [and] the same heavy volition.'[40] For instance, the Mombasa Club nurtured a hidden code of conduct that accentuated British culture.

Club behaviour is, or should be, inbred; such passes from father to son; the rules are not written but the penalties for breaking discipline are usually understood by everyone…A woman's name was not to be mentioned in any derogatory sense; a wager was a debt of honour; a promise made was a matter of honour; swearing or over-drinking was a matter for the committee; to cheat at cards meant expulsion; blasphemy was a serious matter; derogatory remarks in respect of other members, slander of any kind, notoriety in personal behaviour; all to be deplored. These and so many other matters [were not]…included in [the] printed rules. It was expected that members knew the drill and kept to the unwritten tenets of Club membership and behaviour.[41]

Thus, clubs in the colonial era served as symbols of a common culture, mannerism, and conduct. They acted as reminders of imperialism and perpetuated the exclusiveness and supremacy of the Empire to both club members and outsiders.

Comparable to the Mombasa Club and other clubs in the British colonial territories were the clubs in Alexandria and Cairo. The Inspector-General of Prisons, Coles Pasha, created the Alexandria Sporting Club in 1890 which featured cricket, course-racing, and other forms of amusement for Alexandria's British community.[42] It was 'a symbol of privilege and power with the British community at the heart of the club's establishment…and representation on various committees.'[43] However, by far the most prominent club in Egypt was the Gezira Sporting Club in Zamalek – the island just west of Cairo's city centre. The Club was opened in 1886 for the purpose of providing recreation for the officers of the British military. British civilians were allowed to be members of the Club 'by courtesy' of the military.[44] The Club's property consisted of 150 feddans (close to 150 acres).[45] Its frequent activities and spaciousness fostered prestige, exclusiveness, and camaraderie among British military officers. Briggs points out: 'the favourite [of]…out-of-door resorts for officers is the Gezireh Sporting Club…while "other ranks" mainly patronise the Ezbekiyeh Gardens, with their fine trees, restaurants, banks and YMCA.'[46] The Club also acted as a place of refuge for other British professionals such as businessmen, government officials, and teachers. By 1909, there were 750 civilian members of the Club; most of whom paid the one-time life-long members' fee of E£50. The club, synonymous with the exclusivity of the British community, provided a haven for Britons to escape from Egyptians. Bimbashi McPherson describes this sentiment when he comments on the daily routine of his fellow British teachers:

> little or no friendly intercourse [existed] between them and their pupils, [since] as soon as their work as over, [they] escaped on their bicycles to the Sporting Club at Gezirah, there to indulge in their own games of golf or tennis or squash racquets.[47]

Egyptians were excluded when the Club first opened in 1886.[48] Very few non-Britons were ever allowed in. Eventually, a limited number of wealthy Egyptians who socialised with Europeans were permitted to enter.[49]

Moreover, the Gezira Club represented for members of Cairo's British community a place of recreation, rest, and relaxation in the way that Britons were accustomed to. It 'was...opened as a playground for the British.'[50] For instance, J. W. A. Young, an inspector of the Survey Department noted that the club had many acres of grounds featuring the usual 'British' recreation including polo and golf.[51] In 1909, there were 13 tennis courts; eight croquet grounds; four polo grounds; hockey, cricket, football grounds; six squash racquet courts, a 12-hole golf course, courses for races and steeplechases, training tracks, a horse-racing course, and excellent club house facilities.[52] Notably, with activities ranging from golf, tennis, cricket, field hockey, and football, to the well-attended horse races and polo matches[53], the Club symbolised British sporting culture – an important aspect of British identity.

Lastly, the Gezira Club represented the physical presence of British landscape design and gardening. Paul Rich points out that the style of architecture of colonial clubs like the Gymkhana Club in Bombay and the Alweyah Club in Baghdad 'favoured Cotswold and Tudor [and] seemed to represent gentle, pastoral [and] particularly English values.'[54] Similarly, the Gezira Club landscape, by featuring hollyhocks, defied the Middle Eastern climate and asserted its distinctiveness.[55] For Britons, the Club was 'charming, even if it had no sports, for its wealth of flowers, its broad stretches of turf, its southern trees and beauty.'[56] Essentially, the Gezira Club was a symbol of British exclusiveness, common traditions, customs, and recreation. It also reflected imperial power and privilege before Britons, Egyptians, and of other Europeans.

Besides the Gezira Club, the well-known Turf Club in Ezbikeyya, first on Shari'a Menakh and then on Shari'a Maghraby,[57] also served as a symbol of social interaction among the British residents in Cairo. Unlike the Gezira Club, the Turf Club lacked the British heritage cultivated by British sporting activities and the unique physical presence of a vast property featuring British landscaping. Yet, it did affirm the British ethnic distinctiveness and community identity that the Gezira Club underscored. Perhaps that was why a British officer described the Turf Club as both 'the only place...which has any feeling of home about it... [yet] reminds one very slightly of a British club.'[58] Primarily, it was a key place for British residents in Cairo to interact socially and politically as 'almost every Englishman in [Egyptian] society [belonged] to it.'[59]

Socially, the Turf Club was the centre for exchanging gossip and discussing business. According to Sir Richard Vaux, it was 'great centre of mutual admiration...gossip and good fellowship.'[60] Similarly, Lord Edward Cecil recalls that though

> [the English] talked scandal at the club,...discussed games, made future arrangements and plans,...argued about politics and...a little useful business at times...more harm is done in the hall of the Turf Club [due to gossip] than in the other rooms occupied by Englishmen in Cairo.[61]

On other occasions, the Turf Club was a forum for serious political decision making within the British community.

> In overseas clubs, as at home, the affairs of the Empire were often decided. In Cairo, the Turf Club occupied the old building of the British Agency, and it has been suggested that the kind of business transacted had not changed with the change in ownership.[62]

The Turf Club became the hub of administrative discussions for many British officials. During 'the ritual ablutions of drinks, men relaxed among familiar faces, talking shop...The Turf [Club] was important, for much of what passed as leisure was actually work.'[63] It might thus appear as no accident that one of the most significant political speeches of the British occupation was delivered at the Turf Club. Sir Eldon Gorst, British Consul-General of Egypt from 1907–11, made his influential 'Egypt for the Egyptians' speech at the Turf Club. He emphasised that the British government would eventually withdraw its political domination over Egypt. He suggested that Egyptians were ultimately going to fill the government positions that the British held. This direction created resentment and loss of sympathy for Gorst among the British officials of Egypt since Gorst was implying that their positions and careers were to be eventually replaced by Egyptians. No British official who heard the speech was happy to be told that his career prospects were in jeopardy.[64]

Indeed, Young was accurate when he described the activities and conversations in the Turf Club as both 'official' and social. For the initial years of the British occupation, conversations were primarily 'official' dealing with government projects, promotions, appointments, and salaries. Later, when members of the Turf Club came from the commercial or archaeological professions, chats in the Turf Club became anything but official.[65] Though not as symbolically significant as the Gezira Club, the Turf Club served as a rallying point for Britons in Egypt and symbolised British camaraderie in Egypt through the social and political discourse that took place in it.

Another popular club was the Jockey Club. It served as a place for the British, especially the military, to congregate and compete. It brought a thread of British heritage through the sport of horse-racing. The American diplomat Thomas Skelton Harrison reminisces: 'Yesterday afternoon were held the races...I hear that "all the world and his wife" were there, especially the English.'[66] The Jockey Club was so important that it, at times, demanded the attention of the most senior officials in the British administration in Egypt. For instance, when Brigadier General Sir George Macaulay recommended to the British High Commissioner of Egypt, Sir Reginald Wingate, in 1918 that the Jockey Club of Egypt assume overall authority for all racing matters in Alexandria, Gezira, and Heliopolis, Wingate responded by not only agreeing to this plan but by affirming the 'great interest taken by the Military in Racing.'[67] Macaulay then replied to Wingate by saying that 'there is so much money in racing now that a...much stronger control is needed over many things connected with it.'[68] Hence, the Jockey Club was not only an important symbol for British culture and social interaction; it even attracted the financial and administrative attention of British officials in Egypt.

As for clubs for lower working class Britons in Egypt, there appears to have been very few. One club, the Railway Institute Club, had tennis facilities. Though primarily for the use of lower working class railway workers, it seemed to also have allowed others like office clerks onto its premises.[69] Indeed, clubs became indispensable in the imperial landscape. They became, as Stockwell observed from his studies on the British in Malaya, [oases:] more than...recreational [centres]; the [club] was an emblem of exclusiveness [and acted] as a sanctuary providing temporary refuge from an alien world. For a dispersed and close-knit society...the corporate identity of the overseas Europeans was institutionalized, and ritualized...[in the club].[70]

Sports

Three sports which originated in Britain – tennis, football, and fox hunting – merit further mention as symbols of British culture. Lawn tennis appeared to be a popular activity for many Britons in Egypt.

> Lawn tennis, from a mere pastime, *had become part of the serious business of life*. Courts were laid down of the right dimensions and with due attention to foundations and drainage and the right way of the sun...Everybody played. Hostesses availed themselves of a popular form of entertainment by holding their 'at homes' in the form of tennis days...The crowd at these gatherings was often so great that a good game was out of the question; but on off days, we made up for hard practice and in time developed some admirable players.[71]

Football, played by British soldiers and other Europeans throughout the period of occupation, drew significant interest, even among Egyptians. It embodied a sport where the colonizer not only taught the colonized but also played against them, represented by the Anglo-Egyptian Cup tournament that began in 1916.[72] During the 1880s, fox hunting was popular among Britons in Egypt even though the hounds could not survive the Egyptian heat.

> Foxes having been sighted in the neighbourhood, the idea of getting up a hunt was started by some sporting members of the garrison. A pack of hounds was brought out from England and some meets were arranged [though not much was caught]...Unfortunately the hounds did not acclimatize and their summer in Cyprus, where they were sent to recuperate, failed to restore them to health. They died, and the hunting came to an end.[73]

However, in 1901, there was evidence of fox-hunting in Egypt again.

During a hunt, a few British officers were following their hounds in pursuit of foxes and inadvertently entered the property of Wilfrid Blunt – a prominent British resident. Four of Blunt's servants immediately assaulted the officers for trespassing and were subsequently given one to two month jail sentences.[74] Though not without its problems, fox-hunting along with lawn tennis and football were symbols of British sporting culture in Egypt.

Hotels

Like clubs, hotels were symbols for social interaction and enjoyment, particularly the hotel balls.

> The hotel balls are...the leading feature of our society. There are now very few big European houses where entertainments are given, and the increased size of our social world has rendered the small dances and parties of ten years ago impossible. The result is that nowadays nine-tenths of the entertaining is done at the hotels, and usually on ball nights...All the principal hotels give a ball once a week throughout the season; but the smart ones...are the Savoy and the Semiramis. Next, in order of merit, come the Gezirah, Shepheard's, and Heliopolis, and last of all, the Continental...As each hotel gives its weekly ball on a different day of the week, it is possible to go to a dance six nights out of seven for the five months of the season; and I really believe there are some people who do this and survive.[75]

Although the hotel balls catered to the entire European community during the time of the British occupation, they also offered social enjoyment for many British residents of Cairo. For example, the casino at the Gezira Palace Hotel regularly attracted 'three hundred to four hundred people... mostly of the English contingent.'[76]

Not only were hotels symbolic of British social activity, some of them were physically symbolic of British culture and lifestyle. The luxurious Mena House Hotel by the edge of the Pyramids symbolised – for British residents in Egypt – British heritage, tradition, and a common nostalgia for the homeland. Though influenced by Indian design, with mashrabiyya windows, brass-embossed doors, blue tiles, and mosaics of coloured marbles, the hotel featured a warm English country-house atmosphere boasting English breakfasts, great log fires, cheerfully furnished rooms, and quiet and unobtrusive service. An air of repose permeated the hotel,[77] symbolising the best of British comforts with 'Oriental' decor and a view of the Pyramids.

It appears that cafés were not symbolically significant to the British as the clubs and hotels were, since the British did not seem to entertain a strong 'café' culture as other Europeans, especially those from warmer Mediterranean climates. The cafés in Egypt largely did not maintain an exclusive British clientele and so rarely represented Britain culturally or decoratively. For example,

> apart from the hotels, the chief military resort in Cairo is Groppi's, a large café, with a garden, in the centre of the city…is much less exclusive…Colonels,…sergeants and privates,…nursing sisters,… civilians and effendis [likely of Turkish origin], all jostle together at the little tables in friendly confusion.[78]

Unlike clubs and hotels, cafés were not symbols that reflected British culture and exclusiveness to Britons and non-Britons in Egypt.

Military Structures and Activities

Perhaps the most obvious 'outward and visible sign[s] of the predominance of British influence,'[79] for Egypt's British and non-British residents were military structures and activities. These symbols were consistent with Lord Cromer's strategy. He was:

> a master psychologist of this imperial relationship, striking fear and at the same time instilling respect in the subject peoples… by establishing the image of the superiority – both military and moral – of the British and by punishing all efforts to challenge this position.[80]

The British military barracks at Qasr el-Nil symbolised British protection and power just next to the Cairo's town centre. Even more significant perhaps were the barracks in Abbassiyya. They were:

> the chief home of the British garrison in Cairo. The buildings near the main road – Red Barracks on the left, Zafaran Barracks on the right and the Talbot Block beyond – are somewhat antiquated, and not as

desirable in many respects as one could wish. But the magnificent new barracks beyond them are probably the finest structures of their kind in existence anywhere. They are characteristic of the British Army in their solid qualities, their effect of permanent stability, their absolute insistence on good materials and their fitness of the job in hand. *The new buildings at Abbassiya suggest that Britain has sat down very deliberately and heavily in Cairo, without any intention of moving during the next few hundred years.*[81]

These new barracks at Abbassiyya, built in the years leading up to the First World War, appear to symbolise Britain's intention of long-term rule over Egypt. Similarly, three British warships stationed in the harbour of Alexandria – the Monarch, the Invincible, and the Helicon (the admiral's flagship) – also provided a very visible reminder of British naval supremacy.[82]

Besides barracks and warships, activities such as British military marches acted as ritual displays of authority and superiority.[83]

No picture of Cairo that does not include the soldier can be considered complete...By company or regiment, soldiers are so frequently marched through the streets that the visitor might believe Cairo to be a vast military camp. Martial music is the adjunct of every function, and every anniversary, religious and festive...It is part of the scheme of administration to keep the soldier in evidence, *impressing the simple native with the importance of the army.*[84]

On ceremonial occasions like the Queen's birthday, the British military were also put on display at full strength and reviewed by leading members of the British and Egyptian communities. During the First World War, the drills of the Local Defence Corps symbolised for Britons in Egypt the importance of unity in fighting Britain's enemies.

British subjects were drilled by the Military Authorities at Kasr el Nil Barracks parade ground, and on a few occasions on which I was in Cairo and attended the drill it was an amazing sight to see school masters, judges and highly placed officials forming fours under the sharp word of command of a British sergeant.[85]

This 'chivalry and ceremony...were the means by which this vast world [of empire] was brought together, interconnected, unified and sacralised.'[86]

Hospitals

British hospitals in Egypt were intended to represent and symbolise British medical prestige. However, the Anglo-American Hospital failed to be a symbol of British medical success while the British Hospital experienced trouble in its initiation. Perhaps only the Kitchener Memorial Hospital had any symbolic success – as a memorial tribute to the life and work of Lord Kitchener.

Built in 1903, the Anglo-American Hospital was expected to serve as a symbol of British medical stature to compete with the success of the German Hospital. Founded in 1883, the German Hospital was the best hospital in Egypt by the turn of the century. It had an international standing and reputation. Its International Committee of Management consisted of two Germans, two Britons, two Swiss, and two Americans. Its matron and nursing staff were mostly German and there were some Italians.[87]

> [The] British community with customary laissez-faire was content to remain the only important European community in Cairo without a national hospital and upon the occasion of Queen Victoria's Diamond Jubilee (1901) subscribed a considerable sum which was handed over to the German Hospital for the building of additional accommodation.[88]

However, the turn of the century was also an intense time of imperial rivalry. In 1896, 'Kaiser Wilhelm II officially proclaimed Germany's pursuit of *Weltpolitik*...a renewed and enlarged interest in imperialism.'[89] Increasing German economic competitiveness, military and, particularly, naval prowess and colonial involvement were priorities of this policy. Needless to say, 'German *Weltpolitik* was...a cause of friction and much bad feeling with the British.'[90] In this charged atmosphere of imperial rivalry, Lord Cromer invited donations for a joint Anglo-American Hospital in 1901. Cromer and the American Consul-General in Egypt enthusiastically endorsed the project. King Edward, Queen Alexandra, and President William McKinley all agreed to become patrons of the hospital. Funds for the hospital came in easily; more than E£6,300 were raised in two years. By 1903, the hospital received its first patient and featured 22 beds. It contained special, private, and general wards costing respectively 100, 30 and 15 piastres per day. Two of the beds were available for the disabled or who were unable to pay.[91] Despite its encouraging start, the hospital encountered subsequent hardship. It was accused by some of Cairo's British residents of exploiting wealthy American tourists while not being able to exemplify the quality of a 'British' institution (since an Anglo-*American* institution can never be purely British in character and 'excellence'). Even more damaging to its success was its location on Gezira Island, meaning that only a small proportion of the British population, who happened to live on the island, could visit the hospital easily. The majority of British residents lived in other parts of the city and found it inconvenient to travel to the hospital due to the overcrowded route connecting the island to the mainland.[92] For these reasons, the hospital 'lacked the whole-hearted support of the Anglo-American community resident in Egypt [and had even] evoked considerable hostile feeling.'[93] This lack of support may have provided the backdrop to the hospital's poor hygiene and maintenance record which will be discussed in chapter 5. Though the hospital eventually functioned well under capable Egyptian physicians, the Anglo-American Hospital was an example of poor planning and foresight during the time of the occupation.

By the outbreak of World War I, there were hospitals under Austrian, French, German, Greek, and Italian auspices in Egypt. To address the problems of the Anglo-American Hospital and the need for an independent British Hospital in light of so many other countries with their national hospitals, High Commissioner McMahon supported the idea of building the British Hospital as a symbol of prestige.

> The time has now come, and indeed is long overdue, when the resentments and jealousies of the past should be mutually forgotten and the question of eliminating German influence and combining to establish a truly British Hospital should be taken up afresh in a new spirit.[94]

However, even until the early 1920s, the British Hospital remained only an idea in the minds of many Britons in Egypt. In the context of financial difficulties, they simply could not pay for the land, the architectural plans, and the construction of the hospital.

Another hospital, with ambitious aspirations, was the Kitchener memorial hospital named after Lord Kitchener, a prominent British military leader in the imperial era. When Kitchener died tragically in 1916, McMahon wrote to the Foreign Office suggesting that some lasting memorial of permanent benefit to Egypt be instituted. The Egyptian National Fund in Memory of the Late Lord Kitchener was established. It recommended that

> the best memorial was one which would perform the dual function of meeting the public need...of perpetuating [his] memory and that a monument erected from Egyptian funds should be of utility to Egypt and the Egyptians. [It] advised therefore that the memorial would be a hospital for women and a school of Gynaecology.[95]

By 1922, E£90,000 were collected to meet the E£250,000 target to build the hospital. Six Egyptian girls were sent to England to study gynaecology for the purpose of returning to teach at Kitchener's memorial hospital. The ex-Austrian Hospital was purchased in 1923 to accommodate the 50 beds that the hospital needed to start with.[96] By 1929, the School of Medicine for Women, the Training School for Nurses, and the Kitchener Hospital for Women and Children, established to serve the poor of Cairo, were firmly part of Egypt's medical heritage.

The Anglo-American Hospital and the ill-fated British Hospital were unsuccessful efforts to demonstrate British medical expertise and commitment to the health needs of the British and other communities. Only the Kitchener Memorial Hospital as a lasting monument to Lord Kitchener successfully reflected the British concern for the medical betterment of Egypt.

Schools

British education in Egypt symbolised British culture, tradition, and identity by providing a medium whereby young people would grow to be aware of their British heritage. Even if they were not from a British background, students were meant to understand and grow in sympathy and loyalty to the British political hegemony and culture in Egypt. Across the Empire, British parents and well-to-do indigenous families saw the benefits of a British education and in particular, the rewards of the English public school system.

Along with the effects of the hidden curriculum with its introduction to the rituals of success, there were obvious benefits from better facilities, better teachers and smaller classes. It was taken for granted that the public school was the best school, and that there would be one wherever there was an elite to be educated...In England or overseas, of British stock or native, aspiring families impressed upon their children the importance of public schooling. An ambitious native establishment wanted an educational system on public school lines.[97]

Besides schools which were dependent on religious associations like the Church Missionary Society (schools which accepted mostly Egyptian pupils), there were three other non-church-based English schools in Egypt during the British occupation: Victoria College in Alexandria (already mentioned in the previous chapter), the New English School, and Dean's Building School in Cairo. Before the establishment of these schools, Egyptian students from wealthier families and residents of European origin were instructed primarily in French and taught in a French curriculum resulting in the cultivation of French sympathies and interests among the pupils. Thus it was imperative for the British to establish their own schools especially in light of the fact that it was Britain that occupied Egypt at this time.

It seems a very pressing need that in view of the political situation in Egypt, British influence should be made predominant in the education of boys either belonging to the class roughly described as Levantine – Syrian, Greek, Maltese, Cypriot and Israelite or of the Egyptian nationality, who form the great mass of private scholars.[98]

Victoria College, opened in 1902, was established in memory of Queen Victoria. Britons in Egypt were encouraged to send their sons to Victoria College. Well-to-do boys in Alexandria and other parts of Egypt from every ethnic background were also encouraged to attend the school where they would receive an English public school education. The 'object of the College is to afford Egyptians and residents in Egypt the opportunity of giving their sons a liberal education in accordance with the principles of the English Public Schools.'[99] Hence, cricket and football were played and the Certificate Exams came from the Oxford and Cambridge Joint Board.[100] Moreover,

> English is the medium of instruction, the Headmaster and most of the staff are English and the whole system and curriculum, the atmosphere and the moral tone of the School are in accord with the traditions of English public schools...[The school aims to] foster liking for British institutions among its foreign pupils and succeeds admirably in cultivating good-will in the relations between the boys (many of whom are local subjects if not of Egyptian birth) and the representatives of the Protecting Power, after they leave school.[101]

Victoria College and other public schools in the Empire instilled British traditions in their students, British or indigenous, and integrated them into an old boys' network that fostered loyalty to and the ability to benefit from the British Empire.

> The public schools indirectly helped to provide the pattern for Imperial organisation...The dissemination of the public school was not only through British enthusiasts but by 'natives' fuelled by a desire for the knowledge of how to manipulate Imperial symbols and thus acquire power, an acknowledgement by the ruled that an expertise in ritualism conferred political status.[102]

The 'public school spirit became the spirit of British society and the Empire.'[103]

Although Victoria College aspired to become a symbol and 'centre of British culture...in the Near East'[104] and 'a very valuable stronghold of British culture in Egypt,'[105] the school was in serious financial trouble by 1911. Lord Cromer, who had ironically advocated the original establishment of the school, had refused to contribute to the school financially out of fear that the education of 'natives' would lead to equipping them for self-governance. Further, as previous mentioned, many upper middle class British parents disliked the idea of sending their boys to a school filled with Syrians, Greeks, as well as other Europeans and were sending their boys to public schools in Britain.[106] To make matters worse, only one British financier, Mr. Alderson, was backing the school and with the threat of the school closing, parents were even more reluctant to send their children there.[107] Miraculously, enough money was collected within the British community to keep the school afloat, but by 1920, it faced a rather severe financial shortfall once again. Thus High

Commissioner Wingate gave a fund-raising speech to the British business community in 1920. In his speech, Wingate stresses that although the college faced financial crises, 'Victoria College stands as one of the few unofficial monuments of British work in Egypt...[advancing] British interests in this country.'[108] The school survived and became the spawning ground for a generation of 'Etonians of the Middle East, amongst them many of Egypt's prospective businessmen and notabilities were brought up and educated.'[109]

As Victoria College symbolised British interests and culture, and accepted students from other communities of Egypt, the New English School and the Dean's Building School were established mainly for Egypt's British community. The New English School was

> intended exclusively for children of British...and American birth [which were few]. It has been thought necessary to make this rule absolute in order to keep out the Levantine element...[It was] started to provide education for the children of two distinct classes: those...whose parents cannot afford to send them to be educated in England; [and] those who require preparation for an English Public School.[110]

Essentially, the New English School, established in 1916, provided education for children of British parents who were not wealthy, but not poor enough to send their children to the Dean's Building School. The Dean's School, opened in 1903, was named after Dean Butcher, Chaplain of All Saints' Church in Cairo for many years. The school served the needs of the poorest members of the British community. Fees were minimal and the school depended on gifts from other British residents. Unlike the New English School, the Dean's School accepted children who had one British parent, so that British influence on their lives could be secured and even amplified.[111] The Dean's School closed in 1917 since by then, 'the large majority of children were neither English, nor the children of [British] railway workers, [and] it was difficult to continue... to appeal for a continuance of subscriptions.'[112] Even though Victoria College, New English School and the Dean's Building School all faced problems and financial difficulties, they were nonetheless key symbols for British heritage, influence and cohesion.

The Cairo Cathedral

If a building is to express its function, a church must be expressive of Christian worship. The function of a church having been defined in terms of an elaborate ritual, the building becomes a symbol of that ritual...The function of a church then becomes not just to provide for worship but overtly to express specific doctrine... religious symbolism comes to be justified.[113]

There were two main British churches in Cairo during the time of the occupation. The Scottish Presbyterian Church named St. Andrew's and the Anglican Church named All Saints. St. Andrew's was a symbol of home and spiritual familiarity particularly for the Scottish soldiers during the First World War. A church report recorded:

Always they come – the soldiers, mostly Scottish, in the morning a sprinkling but at night a great crowd from far and near, sometimes filling the church to the very front of the Nave. Their spirited singing of the old familiar hymns is a thing to be remembered. Were it only as the spiritual rallying-place of our Scottish soldiers...far from home, St. Andrew's more than justifies its existence.[114]

One officer commented that worship at St. Andrew's reminded him of 'a real old-fashioned Scotch service...[with a] sort of 'Day at Home' touch about it!'[115]

However it seems that no other endeavour involving an institution, site, or building provided a better glimpse of the British community's thirst for symbolic representation of their heritage and power than the quest to build the Cairo Cathedral from 1916 to the early 1920s. In 1876, All Saints' Church was opened as the first Anglican Church in Cairo. Though originally just a small parish church, it became the main centre of worship for many British residents in Cairo and in the surrounding areas. Evidence for its symbolic significance can be found on its interior walls, which displayed plaques recording the deeds of the British military and memorials inscribing the names of British soldiers and officers who had died for the Empire.[116] Unfortunately, the church faced many repairs at high costs over the next decades due to its ageing building. As the British community grew, the church proved to be more and more inadequate and enlargements were carried out in 1891, 1892, and 1899. By the 1900s, the structure of the building was beyond repair and the noise from the main street became increasingly unbearable to the point where worship was affected.[117] Moreover, the building could no longer accommodate the congregation:

> hundreds have been turned away every Sunday, for want even of standing room and the evening services have had to be held twice over to make room for all who wish to be present. Even in normal times it is evident that the accommodation of our present church will be quite insufficient.[118]

As Egypt became officially a British Protectorate in 1914, 'it became clear that something more was required than the mere rebuilding of a parish church.'[119] By 1915, the Bishop of Jerusalem, McInnis, suggested that 'the time had come for the construction in Cairo of a church worthy of our religion and our name.'[120] The argument he used was that the Egyptians might find it strange that there was not a bigger church for those who were Anglicans.

> To people who think so much of their religion as they do, it conveys the sense that we think very little of ours. It diminishes our prestige in their eyes, especially when our big memorial services, such as those after the death of King Edward and Lord Kitchener, have to be held in the open air, for lack of any church in which to hold them. Many hundreds of the leading natives in Egypt attend these services, and they cannot understand our taking no steps to remedy this state of affairs.[121]

It appears that the British community needed their own cathedral to commemorate special occasions and, by its mere physical presence, to symbolise British prestige and the importance of their faith. This was accentuated by the fact that Cairo, being the biggest city in Africa, hosted large Coptic, Greek Orthdox, Roman Catholic, and Armenian churches but not a British one. Bishop McInnis most passionately argued the need for this symbol in his letter to *The Times* on 29 June 1916:

> Such a church would be as much a witness and a symbol of our Christian faith to the people of Egypt as is the Cathedral of

Khartoum to those of the Sudan. To ourselves it would not only be a symbol, but the outward expression of our inward faith, the centre of our religious life, and a new and perpetual incentive to worship.[122]

The Cathedral would symbolise British religious commitment to Europeans and Egyptians, act as a mother church for other smaller Anglican congregations in Egypt, and, as McInnis states, serve as a memorial to Lord Kitchener and those who died fighting for the British Empire:

[We] had already decided that our Cathedral should enshrine the immortal memory of our brave dead...[we] call for a Cathedral in memory of Kitchener, in Cairo...to all in Egypt not merely the Secretary of State for War and hero of a hundred fights, but the man everyone of us – British or Egyptian – relied upon and loved as a friend.[123]

After the First World War, the need for the establishment of the Cathedral as a symbol for commemorating Britain's war-dead became even more crucial. One appeal for funding of the Cathedral read:

We appeal for funds for the erection of a Cathedral Church in Cairo. We make this appeal not only to the British and American Communities in Egypt, but also to the English-speaking peoples throughout the world. This Church is to be a Memorial to Lord Cromer, Lord Kitchener and all other men of our race who have devoted their lives to the service of Egypt; to all British residents in Egypt who have fallen in the war; and not least to those thousands of brave men from Great Britain, New Zealand, and other parts of the Empire who at Gallipoli, in the Western Desert, in Sinai and in Palestine have given their lives in the defence of Egypt.[124]

Other appeals included the efforts of the church parish council itself. The council's plan in 1921 was to 'increase the number of subscribers to All Saints' Church by means of personal canvass,...[with] the... Treasurer and Church wardens [allotting] spheres of action to individual members.'[125]

Although by 1917 the Khedive had given the site of the old Ismailiyya Palace at Qasr el-Nil to the British community, the site was deemed inappropriate for the building of the Cathedral. By 1922, the land was returned to the Egyptian government[126] and a new plan was established to erect the Cathedral on a strip of land north of the German Hospital.[127] Raising money to build the Cathedral continued to be a problem. However, the Cathedral was finally erected in 1938 on the east bank of the Nile just north of the Qasr el-Nil barracks after the church obtained E£70,000 from the sale of the old All Saint's Church site in Ezbekiyya in 1925 (the congregation met for 12 years, from 1925–37 in St. Mary's Church in Garden City) and from generous gifts to the Cathedral Building fund.[128] The Cathedral unashamedly represented the presence of Western Christianity in the heart of Cairo's city centre. By 1963, under Nasser's pro-Arab regime, the Cathedral was given its first notice of demolition in favour of the construction of a much needed flyover bridge connecting Gezira to Ramses in order to cope with Cairo's increasing traffic congestion.[129] With the Cathedral finally destroyed in 1978 and its new replacement tucked out of sight behind a fly-over in Zamalek, the Cairo skyline was no longer 'tainted' by any glaring symbol of imperial Christianity.

Egypt's British community struggled to establish the main institutions of hospital, schools, and church during the occupation. The fact that other nationalities like the French, Germans, Italians, or Greeks in Egypt had their own hospitals, schools, and churches meant a sorry state of affairs for the British community. The British Hospital in Cairo could not get off the ground. Using the Anglo-American Hospital was inconvenient for many in the British community. Victoria College, New English School, and the Dean's Building School all faced financial struggles. Victoria College, intended for English public school boys, was shunned by most of their well-to-do parents. The Cathedral, so grandiose and symbolic in the mind, was not erected until after the British occupation. Although the institutions aspired to lofty symbolic ideals of British prestige and community cohesion, they were also signs of failure. Sir Henry McMahon, in his frustration, writes:

> no attempt appears to have been made to meet the needs of the British community in a manner befitting the extent and importance of British interests in this country. In the important centres of Egypt, one sees large and imposing churches, hospitals, and schools belonging to other nationalities, but with two solitary exceptions.

British institutions of a similar character are either non-existent, or where they do exist are of very unimportant or inadequate nature. That such a state of affairs should have been allowed to continue for so long does not, I venture to think, [add] to our national credit in Egypt, even in the past when our position in the country was not so defined as it now is.[130]

Nonetheless, McMahon understood the reason for the lack of strong and viable British hospitals, schools and church buildings in Egypt:

> The contrast, so unfavourable to ourselves, is entirely due to one course: namely that while all British institutions have to depend solely in private effort and generosity, those of other nationalities have been set up and maintained largely, if not entirely, by the financial assistance of their respective governments.[131]

So the question begs to be asked: why did the British government refuse to fund the establishment of British institutions in Egypt when ironically, for all intents and purposes, it ruled Egypt politically and administratively? Whitehead sheds some light on this question by suggesting a reason for the lack of colonial educational funding.

> Prior to the First World War, the British Government took only a fitful interest in the development of schooling in its overseas dependencies, largely because education was considered a matter for local initiative and voluntary effort. Even within the colonies, local administrations were content, for the most part, to confine their educational activities to the routine and largely unimaginative disbursement of local revenues to voluntary agencies.[132]

Since education within British colonies, and to some extent, in Britain as well, was considered a local matter and did not warrant significant funding from the British government, education in Egypt, being a British occupied Ottoman territory and only later a protectorate, may have received even less attention, let alone funding. Moreover, British commitment to educating Egyptians was stifled by their fear of creating an educated class that wanted independence. So Douglas Dunlop, Education Adviser, engineered Egyptian education solely as a factory to produce submissive government clerks obedient to British authority.[133] In terms of the Empire as a whole, Whitehead asserts that it was only in 1923, past the timeline for this book, did the Colonial Office establish the Advisory Committee on Native Education in British Tropical Africa.[134] This brought new vision and finances to meet Africa's educational needs. The pragmatic nature of British colonial administration relied heavily on the judgement of local officials in preference to formal policy statements issued from the Colonial Office. Egypt was not even an official colony so was administered under the Foreign Office.

Perhaps this understanding of British colonial sentiment helps to explain why the British government during the occupation did not readily fund British institutions such as hospitals, schools and churches in Egypt. British policy favoured local initiatives such as in the approach to building schools. Perhaps even more significantly, the fact that Egypt was never a full-fledged colony may have made it even less likely to receive fiscal and long-term administrative attention from the British government. In other words, since British tenure in Egypt was always in doubt, long-term financial investment in British institutions in Egypt would have seemed less attractive to the British government and British financiers. Perhaps the difficulty in financing British public-service institutions is also symbolic of the British 'identity' that gloried in leaving much to self-help as opposed to supporting bureaucratic initiatives that stifled personal responsibility. Thus ironically, the poor financing of British institutions both expressed British 'identity' and yet limited the public assertion of it.

Dinner Parties and Home Theatre

Dinner parties and home theatre were symbols of British culture transplanted to entertain and strengthen the British community in Egypt. Dinner parties in homes not only brought together the British residents of Cairo but also re-affirmed their British identity and even power in Egypt. 'Victorian and Edwardian dining at times had less to do with eating than with the display of power…with a bias towards quantity rather than quality.'[135] Lots of food meant, to put it bluntly, lots of power.

Although he was American, Harrison writes extensively about the extravagant multi-course dinner parties of the British. On 8 August 1897, Mr. Money, the Chief of the Department of Public Debt in the late 1890s, hosted Lord and Lady Cromer, General Sir Francis Grenfell and Lady Grenfell, and General Money of the Scotch Highlanders and his wife, for dinner. Two days later, Sir Elwin Palmer, Financial Adviser of Egypt, invited the Cromers, Sir Herbert Kitchener, Major and Mrs. Kennedy, and Colonel and Mrs. Gordon for a meal featuring English pheasant. The next day, Mr. Dawkins, second to Sir Palmer in the Finance Department, invited other British notables for dinner.[136] These occasions fostered a sense of sharing in a common identity and power structure for the British administrative and military officials. Further, Margaret Strobel suggests that dressing for a dinner party, particularly for women – in corsets and stockings, symbolised 'civilised' behaviour and status. She asserts that 'British rituals functioned to elaborate the ideology of imperial rule. A regal and commanding style necessarily accompanied and aided political domination: pomp and ceremony portrayed the power of the colonial rulers.'[137]

On some occasions, private theatricals were held in restaurants and in homes. Harrison records a performance to which he was invited and which was sponsored by one of the most important British diplomats – Rennell Rodd, for many years the First Secretary of the British Agency in Cairo. The programme consisted of one short sketch called 'Breaking the Ice' performed by Miss Baring, Lord Cromer's niece, and Mr. Rodd himself; then a longer play entitled 'A School for Coquettes' featured Mr. and Mrs. Rodd, Lord Granville, and Captain Peel.[138] These private theatricals combined with dinner parties undergirded British culture, enjoyment, and sense of camaraderie.

Empire Day and Christmas Day

Empire Day, celebrated on Queen Victoria's birthday (24th May), was an annual symbol of British imperial greatness. The goal was to 'bring Britishers together and help them to feel that they [were] part of a great brotherhood, the greatest and...the strongest the world has ever known.'[139] Entertainment within the celebration was designed to promote British patriotism. For example, during an Empire Day event in Alexandria in 1916, seven tableaux (elaborate displays staged by actors not moving or talking) representing important events in British history were performed alongside musical recitals by well known Britons in the community and a speech from Mr. D. A. Cameron, Alexandria's British-Consul. Empire Day occasions were particularly important during World War I to raise the morale of all Britons in the Empire.

Besides Empire Day, Christmas Day symbolised British cultural and religious heritage more than any other occasion. It served as a focal point of gathering British residents together in different parts of the Empire. In Malaya, Stockwell mentions that some British Pahang District Officers travelled days and others for two weeks, on foot or by houseboat, in order to celebrate Christmas together in 1895.[140] Similarly, Christmas Day was a key opportunity for the British residents of Egypt to experience and cultivate their sense of togetherness and shared heritage as they met with and called on each other.

> It seems that when [Cairo's foreign residents] first came here, the [European] society of Cairo was much concerned to find that they had no day for all going round calling on each other, as Continentals do on New Year's Day, Levantine Christians on their New Year's Day, twelve days later, and Mussulmans at Bairam ['Festival' in Turkish]. On consideration, the society of Cairo, decided that [the] British ought to have such an anniversary, and fixed on Christmas Day as the most suitable. The British had to bear it, and with time it has grown to an institution. So the ladies sit at home all the afternoon dealing out tea, and the gentlemen go round, calling on everybody else, and Egyptian friends call on everybody after the same manner, so that the whole British colony, with native auxiliaries, rotates in a body round itself all Christmas afternoon.[141]

Not only was it customary for the British to visit each other on Christmas Day, but the other Europeans followed suit by calling on the British on Christmas Day.[142] Usually, many of the British residents attended church on Christmas morning. Some Britons in Egypt even travelled a hundred miles down the Nile River in order to take communion at All Saints' Church on Christmas Day.[143] Thereafter, some of them would take short excursions such as trips to 'Old Cairo' or to the Pyramids. In the evening, many would join other Europeans at the Shepheard's Hotel for a Christmas feast and celebration.[144] Besides Empire Day and Christmas Day, the colonial calendar featured other days of celebration for Britons such as the feasts of the saints (George, Andrew, Patrick, and David).[145] Likewise, Britons in Bengal celebrated and reunited for Christmas, the monarch's birthday and British victories in wars.[146] Special occasions ritualised with regularity 'reassured those who had doubts about their rule'[147] over land and people.

Conclusion

At the outset, this chapter suggests that due to the sensitivities related to official Ottoman rule and French influence and rivalry, the rarely used British flag held little symbolic value and English failed to become the main language and symbol of British authority in the mixed courts. With reference to similar British communities primarily in India, Mombasa, and Malaya, this discussion examines the symbolic importance of British events and institutions such as clubs, hotels, military structures and activities, hospitals, schools, churches, and special occasions, and of the locations of British neighbourhoods and buildings. Certain hospitals, schools, and churches struggled for funding, perhaps indicating to some extent the British government's promotion of self-reliance and reluctance to fund institutions that were not in formal British colonies. Nonetheless, it appears that many of these institutions and events signified British distinctiveness, presence and power for those inside and outside the British community in occupied Egypt.

4

SOCIO-OCCUPATIONAL DIVERSITY

As mentioned, studies regarding Britons in Egypt between 1882 and 1922 tend to focus on the lives and activities of upper and middle class British officials and military officers. There seems to be a strong assumption, as articulated in 1902 by a prominent British judge in Egypt Sir Richard Vaux, that 'the English Colony at that time was composed almost entirely of the Army of Occupation, and the civil servants, married and unmarried, attached in some capacity or other to the various Ministries – Finance, Education, Public Works, Interior and Justice.'[1] This chapter seeks to demonstrate that the British community in Egypt consisted of middle and upper class Britons outside the civil and military services, and also Britons from the lower working classes. Telling their story takes on particular significance considering that efforts were made to prevent the emergence of poorer working class Europeans in the colonies in order to preserve the European image of wealth and privilege.[2] This chapter and the next (on crime and misconduct) aspire to add to the study of 'history from below' during the colonial era. This study also contributes to 'imperial history' as it compares the income levels of Britons in Egypt with those in Britain in similar roles. The data suggests that, in many instances, financial gain was a significant factor for British migration to Egypt.

To highlight the socio-economic differences within the British community, this chapter explores the general salary differences between the upper, middle, and lower class Britons at that time and discuss the employment and salary arrangements of the British civil and military personnel in Egypt. Thereafter, a large part of the discussion will focus on the vocational orientation and income levels of upper and middle class Britons in Egypt, who worked outside the civil or military services, followed by those of the lower classes. To conclude this study on socio-economic contrasts, the chapter examines the snobbery and class distinctiveness inherent within Egypt's British community.

General Differences in Salaries

There was an enormous difference in income between the various classes of Britons in the British Isles during the latter part of the nineteenth century and the initial years of the twentieth century.[3] Within the upper class, seventeen landowners in Britain enjoyed an annual income from rental payments of £100,000 in the 1880s, which is equivalent to £5 million today.[4] Apart from landowners, the upper class industrial and professional elite, whose annual incomes exceeded £10,000, also included owners of large businesses, financiers, and the 'most successful barristers in Britain like Sir Edward Carson, Rufus Isaacs, F. E. Smith, and Marshall Hall...[who] earned...about £10,000 per year'[5] in 1901, which is equivalent to around £500,000 today. Middle class and upper middle class salaries of £300 to £1000 per year applied to many professionals such as most lawyers, physicians, engineers, administrators, teachers, and civil servants. The highest earning professionals tended to be solicitors and barristers whose average annual incomes ranged between £1,280 and £1,500 from 1881 to 1911.[6] The majority of the British population was from the lower classes,[7] whereas, in Egypt, the majority of Britons seemed to be from the upper middle classes. As for salaries, the lower classes in Britain tended to have incomes below £300 per annum. They were tradesmen and shopkeepers in family or individually owned businesses, certain self-employed artisans and craftsmen, clerks and minor civil servants, and more poorly paid schoolteachers and nurses.[8] Within the working class, the 'best-paid English adult male workers... earned between £80 and £100 per year',[9] policemen and postmen earned approximately £52 per year, and agricultural labourers earned only around £25 per year.

The British Civil and Military Personnel

Though this chapter primarily seeks to emphasise the diversity of occupations represented by the Britons in Egypt, a brief discussion of the significant body of Britons who worked in the civil and military services may provide a helpful context for comparison. Numerically, there were probably several hundred British officials in Egypt at any given time throughout the forty year span of the occupation. In 1883, there were 272

British officials in Egypt.[10] By 1896, there were 690 European officials in the civil service, and by 1906, there were 1,252.[11] Though it is unclear exactly how many officials[12] from this number were actually Britons from the British Isles;[13] the 1897 census data point to 635 British subjects who were civil servants in Alexandria and Cairo.[14] Since most of the civil servants resided in these two cities and only a few, if any, were British subjects of Greek, Maltese, or another ethnic origin, British civil servants (from the British Isles) represented the large majority of the European officials in Egypt.

Under the British occupation, Egypt was, for all intents and purposes, ruled by the British consul-general, assisted by British advisers, under an Ottoman figurehead named the 'Khedive' and the Egyptian ministers in different government ministries. British advisers to Egyptian ministers held the real power behind every government department, and every adviser was responsible to the consul-general and not to their Egyptian counterparts. Besides senior British officials acting as advisers to the Egyptian Ministries, there was also a growing contingent of young Britons who were recruited to Egypt to serve as under-secretaries and inspectors in each ministry. This system of employing British officials in all levels of government was designed to inspire Egyptian civil servants to imitate the conduct and competence of British civil servants in an efficient administration. The hope was that Egyptians would eventually be able to govern themselves, although British leaders like Sir Evelyn Baring (who became Baron Cromer in 1892, Earl of Cromer in 1901, and was consul general for the first 25 years of the occupation) believed that Egyptians were far from ready to be self-governing. To acquire the most competent and exemplary officials, Cromer recruited educated upper and middle class young men from select public schools and universities in Britain.

The young Britons recruited into the Egyptian civil service were highly qualified. Graduate engineers, medics, lawyers, and teachers[15] were recruited into the Ministries of Public Works, Health, Justice, and Education. The Ministries of the Interior and Finance welcomed outstanding graduates with less technical degrees such as History and Geography. They were expected to reach a certain level of proficiency in Arabic before they arrived in Egypt and were required to continue with more Arabic acquisition in their first years of work in Egypt. In the Interior Ministry, for example, new candidates were given the post of Assistant Inspector with a salary beginning at E£240–300 per year (the British pound was almost equivalent to the Egyptian pound during the occupation[16]). Combined with generous travelling allowances, their starting incomes drew near to a middle class level while their superior lifetime earning expectations likely enhanced their spending and lifestyle choices. The candidate was expected to travel twenty days of each month to other provinces to oversee the work of native officials, to examine registers, collect information, and report to the Ministry in Cairo. They were to give advice to Egyptian district governors and provincial governors, guided by instructions from the Interior Ministry. The first year of work was a probation year and the candidate was discharged if he was not likely to succeed. He would be automatically dismissed if found to be excessively ill or engaged in misconduct. With the exception of the first year, leave was given for two months every year on full pay. A third month of furlough was allowed on half pay. Leave could be accumulated though it was not permitted to last more than three and half months. Salaries were reduced by 5 per cent for a pension fund. Pensions were given to those who had served 25 years, were appointed before the age of 35, and were 55 years old or older. Those who served more than 15 years were entitled to a pension if forced to retire due to ill health. Those having served less than 15 years did not qualify for a pension.[17] A similar arrangement for salaries, dismissals, promotions, furloughs, and pensions existed in the other government ministries as well. After a significant length of service and experience, a British civil servant in Egypt could expect a respectable middle class salary of around £60 per month or £720 per year.[18] Salary increases were always welcomed especially for officials with families because the initial E£300 per annum was inadequate for supporting a family with an expatriate middle class lifestyle in Cairo. By the turn of the century, 103 British officials were earning between E£360 and E£840 per year while 47 senior officials were drawing above E£840 per year – near or within the range of upper class incomes. Although significantly above the average salary in Britain, some officials like Lord Edward Cecil, whose family refused to come to Egypt and thus needed to be kept at a certain status in Britain, suffered financially even with an income of about E£800 per year.[19]

Regardless of salary level, the British official in Egypt usually enjoyed a comfortable and well-rested lifestyle. In 1901, Sir Cecil Spring Rice, British Commissioner of Public Debt in Egypt, described his days in Cairo: 'I am enjoying the heat here – it isn't bad but tends to almost uncontrollable laziness: I get a long book…and every afternoon lie down to read til [sic] I sleep. Then play golf – then dine and even afterwards go to bed and get up at six for a ride.'[20]

Similarly, Hopwood suggests that the financial and recreational benefits for the British official in Egypt may have outweighed any disadvantages they experienced whilst living in Egypt.

For the British [official], life in Egypt was on the whole good... As in India, men served in Egypt with devotion and dedication, seeing it their duty to educate the Egyptian into British ways and standards, inured to the heat, the squalor and the flies, and looking with a fairly good humoured tolerance upon the 'natives'. The compensations were often a higher standard of living and higher positions than could have been expected in England. Life was eased by numerous servants, by polo, tennis and gossip at European clubs. Social life centred around the British residency and the honour of being invited to dine was much coveted.[21]

Another important contingent of Britons in Egypt was the British armed forces. The 5,000 strong British military, either serving in the Army of Occupation, or as officers in the Egyptian Army, included the officer corps who enjoyed many of the social and recreational outlets offered to the upper class Britons in Egypt, such as the Gezira Club. Military personnel who were not officers were not welcome onto the grounds of the Gezira Club or to upper class parties and dances, but were, instead, welcomed into places like the Soldiers' Club where the lower class rank and file relaxed, gossiped, and shared drinks together. Officers largely received middle to upper class salaries. The average annual salary for a soldier was around £40 to £50.[22] Further, the military provided for every soldier's costs in terms of lodging, medical care, clothing, education, and cash allowances.[23] Although members of the British rank and file were not from upper or middle class backgrounds, their presence in Egypt has been long acknowledged as part of the military apparatus. It is the Britons outside the government and armed forces from varying classes that this study attempts to describe within the context of the salary and lifestyle arrangements of those inside the civil and military service.

Census Records of British Vocations in Egypt

Although it is clear that a fair proportion of the Britons in Egypt worked in the civil or military services, what is less clear, from census records alone, is the exact number of Britons in other occupations. The reasons are twofold. First, only two of the four censuses (1897 and 1917, and not 1882 and 1907) recorded the different occupations that the British in Egypt were engaged in. In other words, over the forty-year span between 1882 and 1922, statistical information regarding British occupations in Egypt appears to be available only through two sources. Although census records at ten-year intervals may have given a greater amount of data on British vocations, even so the 1897 and 1917 censuses provide valuable information. Second, the records referring to the livelihood of British subjects in Egypt do not clarify whether these subjects were from the British Isles or from other British colonial territories, nor ethnic origins. Although the 1897 and 1917 censuses provide the exact figures for the number of Britons from the British Isles and the number of other British subjects of Indian and Maltese descent, these figures are not attached to work-related groupings. More precisely, the 1897 census indicates that there were 12,465 British subjects from the British Isles in Egypt, 617 of Indian origin and 6,481 of Maltese origin.[24] The 1917 census shows that there were 9,042 British subjects from the British Isles, 954 of Indian origin and 7,761 of Maltese origin.[25] However, by comparing the exact figures for the number of Britons from the British Isles in 1897 and in 1917 with the figures related to occupational categories, the records still suggest that Britons (from the British Isles) in Egypt were engaged in more vocations than just the military and the civil service.

In order to determine, as accurately as possible, the number of Britons who were not part of the military or civil service in 1897, one approach is to subtract the number of male British subjects in the military (very likely to be British soldiers from the British Isles; 4,887 in Table 4.1) and the number of civil servants (the vast majority of whom lived in Cairo or Alexandria; 635 in Table 4.4) from the total number of 12,645 Britons from the British Isles given in the previous paragraph. This calculation would leave 6,943 Britons from Britain who did not belong in the civil or military service. Taking into account that this figure included children and a good number of women who preferred not to work outside the home, the actual number of Britons from the British Isles who worked in other sectors besides the government or the military probably amounted to several thousand in 1897.

Though the census records do not give precise numbers for how many persons from the British Isles worked in which vocations, the data still reveal important occupational trends with regards to those who were British subjects, a large percentage of whom were Britons from Britain. Besides the civil service and the military, other key professions for male British subjects (Table 4.1) were navigation, iron-metal trade,

Table 4.1: Number of male British subjects in Egypt according to occupations.[26]

Occupation	Number of British subjects in occupation	Occupation	Number of British subjects in occupation
Agriculture	13	Various occupations	107
Food trade	324	Machines/skilled worker	180
Textiles	78	Employee	992
Woodworker	573	Teacher	542
Building trade	161	Clergy	35
Iron-metal	607	Freelance workers	473
Leather/hide	51	Military	4,887
Tobacconist	16	Domestic work	82
Merchant/banker	494	Total working men	11,312
Shopkeeper	93	Without work	417
Transport	16	Total population under 10	1,598
Navigation	1,583	Total male population	13,327

woodworking, and teaching. Table 4.2 indicates that male British subjects were also strongly represented in industry and commerce. The evidence firmly suggests that Britons from Britain were more than soldiers or civil servants. As Aldridge writes, there were '"English" booksellers, cigar importers,...sanitary engineers, confectioners,...drapers, dressmakers, florists, glovers, gunsmiths, hairdressers, hatters, livery stables, milliners, outfitters, photographers, saddlers, solicitors, tourist [agents] and tailors.'[27]

As for British subjects who were women, most of them may not have had an occupation. From Table 4.3, it appears that more than 85 per cent of female British subjects over the age of ten were not involved in any occupation. It may seem reasonable to project from this significant percentage that the majority of British females from the British Isles in Egypt were also not engaged in formal employment, though it appears likely that some worked as teachers, missionaries, maids, or employees in the textile industry.

Table 4.2: Percentage of male British subjects in Egypt according to occupational categories.[28]

Occupational categories	Percentage of male British subjects
Agriculture	1%
Industry & Commerce	35%
Machine/skilled worker	1.5%
Employee/civil servant	8.5%
Religion and Instruction	4.9%
Military	41.7%
Domestic	1.9%
Total	94.5%
Without declared profession	3.6%

Table 4.3: Number of female British subjects in occupations.[29]

Occupation	Number of female British subjects	Occupation	Number of female British subjects
Food trade	16	Religious nun/worker	26
Textiles	128	Total working women	549
Other professions	33	Domestic	135
Skilled worker	1	Total with domestic	684
Employee/civil servant	16	Without occupation over ten years of age	3,982
Commerce	51	Total including those without occupation	4,666
Profession – freelance	34	Children under ten years	1,570
Teacher	244	Total	6,236

Besides obtaining a general impression of the occupations taken up by British subjects in Egypt through the census of 1897, significant observations can be made from the census data (Table 4.4 and 4.5) regarding British vocations specific to the cities of Cairo and Alexandria. First, census data indicates that 15,028[30] British subjects lived in Cairo and Alexandria in 1897 out of a total of 19,563[31] in the entire country, meaning that around 77 per cent of the British subjects in Egypt resided in these two cities. If the same percentage is used to project how many Britons from the British Isles lived in these two locations, it seems that nearly 9,600 (77 per cent of 12,465) did. Second, the data appears to suggest that there were noteworthy occupational differences between British subjects in Alexandria and in Cairo. The British military personnel in Cairo seem to have outnumbered those of Alexandria by three times indicating that the bulk of Britain's military apparatus in Egypt was based in Cairo. Also, next to the military, male British subjects in Cairo seemed to be in the civil service and in merchant banking more than other occupations during this time. Three times as many male British subjects were merchant bankers in Cairo than in Alexandria. Surprisingly, it appears that more male British subjects were involved in the civil service in Alexandria than in Cairo even though Cairo was the nucleus of the British residency and key government ministries. Perhaps there was a sizeable contingent of male British subjects working for the government ministries in Alexandria who were not Britons from Britain. Perhaps the civil service in Alexandria was large due to the government moving there during the summers.

Third, whatever the vocational variations between British subjects in Cairo and Alexandria and the lack of clarity with regards to exactly how many Britons from the British Isles worked outside of the military and civil services, the data still indicates that a considerable number participated in a variety of occupations. According to Table 4.4, it appears that the number of male British subjects who served in the military and civil service in Cairo and Alexandria in 1897 was 5,243 or around 62 per cent of the 8,415 male British subjects of working age (not counting those with no declared profession who may have been children) in these two cities while 3,172 or 38 per cent worked in a diverse array of other occupations. They were civil servants, engineers, architects, designers, merchants, bankers, carpenters, cabinet-makers, students, sailors, mechanics, skilled workers, blacksmiths, butchers, bakers, café-owners, cooks, greengrocers, and shopkeepers. If one assumes that only Britons from Britain worked in the military and civil services, there would still

Table 4.4: Number of male British subjects in Cairo and Alexandria categorised by occupations.[32]

Occupation	Number of male British subjects		Occupation	Number of male British subjects	
	In Cairo	In Alexandria		In Cairo	In Alexandria
Gunsmith	2		Mason, marble layer		11
Lawyer, barrister	4	6	Shopkeeper	6	61
Barber	4		Magazine seller	1	24
Butcher	4	33	Farrier	1	
Baker	3	28	Sailor	1	221
Café-owner	10	22	Mechanic	17	151
Carriage driver	2	4	Doctor, surgeon, dentist	24	13
Stone-cutter	0	2	Carpenter, cabinet-maker	102	340
Candle-maker	1	0	Miller		1
Coal-worker	0	6	Military	3,385	1,223
Polisher		1	Musician, singer	3	7
Coachman	8	8	Merchant, banker	136	41
Shoe-mender/cobbler	14		Silversmith, goldsmith		5
Broker	5	29	Skilled worker	11	137
Cook	6	48	Confectioner, pastry cook	3	4
Hardware/merchant	2		Haberdasher, curtain-maker	10	
Clergyman	10	12	Painter/decorator	30	79
Entrepreneur	9	2	Pharmacist	5	7
Greengrocer	2	24	Door-to-door seller		7
Student	129	242	Professor, religious teacher	33	21
Tin-maker	4	10	Ironmonger, hardware dealer	7	5
Reader of Qur'an	2		Ironer	2	2
Civil servant	259	376	Seller	6	8
Foundry/metal worker	4	4	Locksmith	20	23
Blacksmith	20	108	Tobacconist	5	8
Fruit seller		5	Tailor	18	31
Guard/doorman	2	3	Tanner	1	1

Table 4.4 continued

Hotel/restaurant owner	2	4	Upholsterer	3	8
Printer	17	29	Turner/technician	3	9
Engineer, architect, designer	86	129	Veterinarian	6	1
Purse maker	6	68	Male workforce	4,475	3,878
Interpreter	9	2	Domestic worker	23	37
Gardener	2	3	Farmer	1	1
Milkman		1	With domestic workers/ farmers	4,499	3,916
Bookseller	4	2	No profession declared	451	1,127
Builder/bricklayer	1	7	Male population	4,950	5,043

Table 4.5: Number of female British subjects in Cairo and Alexandria categorised by occupations.[33]

Occupation	Number of female British subjects		Occupation	Number of female British subjects	
	In Cairo	In Alexandria		In Cairo	In Alexandria
Bath attendant		1	Milkwoman	1	
Laundress	6	19	Wine and spirits merchant	1	3
Singer, dancer		2	Doctor	2	1
Shopkeeper	24	25	Nun	14	9
Cook	4	3	Midwife	12	15
Dressmaker	25	97	British women with occupations	142	311
Greengrocer		1	Domestic jobs	34	85
Trainee	31	111	Total with occupation	176	396
Other employment	5	7	No occupation declared	1,601	2,862
Teacher	17	14	Total population of British women	1,777	3,258

be a sizeable group (9,600 total Britons in the two cities subtract 5,243 in military and civil service leaves 4,357) of British men and women from the British Isles involved in other occupations in Cairo and Alexandria.

As for female British subjects in Cairo and Alexandria in 1897, a large percentage did not have occupations outside of the home. From the data of Table 4.5, it appears that 90 per cent of female British subjects in Cairo and 88 per cent in Alexandria were without gainful occupations. Though again this data refers to British subjects in general and not to Britons from Britain in particular, the huge percentage of female British subjects who were without occupations indicates, in all probability, that most British women from the British Isles in Egypt were also not employed outside their homes in 1897. Similar to the general statistical information regarding the occupation of female British subjects in Egypt (Table 4.3) in 1897, it appears that some British women from the British Isles may have worked in shops, in dressmaking and in domestic service.

As for 1917 census (Table 4.6), it did not record any figure for the number of Britons in the military or the civil service. This may have been due to the transient nature of the British military during the First World War whose members were primarily in Egypt to recover from war wounds or to prepare for operations in Turkey, Palestine, or elsewhere and to the association of the civil service with the military as a key part of facilitating Briton's war effort. Also, in recording those with occupations, children and women without occupations were also omitted. Since Table 4.6 seems to refer to only 5,732 male and female British subjects in employment out of the total population of 24,354 British subjects, it is possible that it was referring primarily to the 9,042 Britons from the British Isles in this table. Whatever the case, a few helpful observations regarding occupational trends of British subjects in Egypt can be made. It appears that a large number of male British subjects (not necessarily Britons from Britain) in Egypt were engaged in marine transport, perhaps as sailors. Male British subjects were also significantly involved with trading (of textiles and food products), the communications industry (post, telegraphs, and telephones), the hospitality industry (hotels, restaurants and bars), the dress industry and financial services (banking and insurance). Female British subjects, with occupations, seemed to be most involved with the dress industry though similar to the situation in 1897, female British subjects, and in most cases, British women from Britain, were by and large not working outside of their homes.

Table 4.6: Number of male and female British subjects in Egypt and their occupations.[34]

Occupation	Male	Female	Total	Occupation	Male	Female	Total
Agricultural works	86	31	117	River and canal transport	4		4
Fishing and hunting	17	1	18	Transport (roads and bridges)	124		124
Nomads	1	0	1	Transport by rail	261	2	263
Living on private means	108	111	219	Post, telegraphs, telephones	397	40	437
Mining	37	1	38	Bank, exchange, credit, insurance	259	5	264
Salines	30		30	Brokerage, commission, exports/imports	179	5	184
Textiles	41	7	48	Trade in textiles	189	1	190
Leather, skins	1		1	Trade in dress	32	2	34
Wood-workers	15	4	19	Trade in leathers, skins and furs	3		3
Metallurgy	180	1	181	Trade in wood	8		8
Ceramics	3		3	Trade in metals	16		16
Chemical products	18	2	20	Trade in ceramics	1		1
Food products	228	6	234	Trade in chemical products, drugs, paints, and dyes	8	1	9

Table 4.6 continued

Dress industry	278	291	569	Hotels, coffee houses, restaurants, bars, and drinks	372	49	421
Furniture making	252	2	254	Trade in alimentary products	294	12	306
Building industries	171		171	Trading in furniture	43	2	45
Construction of vehicles	19		19	Trading in property	7		7
Production and transmission of power	221	2	223	Trading in fuel	69	1	70
Literature and art	135	5	140	Trading in means of transport	11		11
Other industries	9		9	Total with occupations	5,148	584	5,732
Transport by sea	1,021		1,021				

Although the census data on occupations in the 1897 census only refer to British subjects and not specifically to Britons from Britain (while the 1917 census does the same but seems to omit the British military and civil servants in its tallies for British subjects), the demographic evidence points to the impression that Britons from Britain worked in various vocations besides the civil and military services in occupied Egypt. Further, female British subjects and, in most cases, female Britons from the British Isles, were not involved with formal occupations. The rest of the chapter seeks to develop this theme of Britons working outside the upper middle class military and diplomatic network using evidence other than quantitative demographic data.

Upper Middle Class Britons in Various Occupations

Besides the civil service and the officer corps of the military, educated middle and upper class Britons (earning usually more than £300 per year) also worked as lawyers, doctors, engineers, and teachers. For example, there were eleven members of the English bar in Egypt in 1911 according to the private papers of diplomat Sir Milne Cheetham. Their names were J. Moss, A. S. Preston, and C. Halford, who were based in Alexandria; and R. Silley, J. P Foster, C. Perrott, G. E. Jeffes, Gottlieb, Devonshire, and Hershell, who were based in Cairo.[35] Foster's monthly income,[36] by 1920, was £62.8s.9d,[37] nearly £750 per year[38] and comparable to a senior government official. This information, along with data related to salaries and estates of various Britons who died in Egypt, is found in probate documents in the Consular Court records of Cairo and Alexandria. The probate records indicate that the physician Marc Ruffer, left an estate of £21,000[39] (equivalent to more than £1 million today); a considerable sum that suggests his middle class status.[40] Also, engineers like Charles Orr Campbell, of the Egyptian State Railways (ESR), earned £55 per month or £660 per year;[41] and after the First World War, Herbert Bunnell May, assistant auditor of the ESR, earned almost £67 per month, which amounted to about £800 per year.[42] Chief Draughtsman of the ESR, William Gledhill, whose monthly salary was £46.4s.4d per month or around £550 per year, also belonged in the upper middle class salary bracket.[43] The average salary for engineers in Britain during this time was significantly lower (around £287 in 1911)[44] which suggests that the higher earnings in Egypt were enticing. As for teachers, their average salary, around £300 per year (the minimum for the middle class), was twice as much as the average teacher's salary[45] in Britain – a clear incentive for teachers to work in Egypt. An example of a British teacher in Cairo was Charles Sherrard, who taught at the Coptic School in Cairo and earned £25.9s.9d per month or just over £300 per year.[46] The British authorities were particularly keen to recruit British teachers to teach English in order to reduce the linguistic and cultural influence of French in Egypt.[47]

Besides law, medicine, engineering, and teaching, educated upper middle class Britons were also working in the banking profession. In 1916, Sir Bertram Hornsby, who was fourth in command in the National Bank of Egypt, drew a lofty salary of £1900 per year,[48] well above the £1,000 per year generally associated with upper class salaries. However, it appears that other banks, like the Anglo-Egyptian Bank, paid its staff notably less. For instance, W. R. Carruthers, Manager of the Anglo-Egyptian Bank in Alexandria in 1916, complained that he was paid much less than Hornsby of the National Bank.[49] During the same year, A. Jessop, a cotton trade expert in the Anglo-Egyptian Bank in Alexandria, pleaded for a salary that would exceed £700 per year. Like Lord Edward Cecil who, as previously mentioned, found it difficult to raise a family with E£800 per year, Jessop too maintained that £700 per year was not sufficient. It was 'really the minimum on which a married man [could] live and keep up the position incumbent on him by his status in the Bank, especially [since] the costs of living [were] so high, and... expenses of leave to England every three years for [the] family'[50] were also considerable. Though at times challenging, overseas postings were generally comfortable and helped advanced careers. Not surprisingly, the financial status of the governors of banks was in a different league. Sir Edwin Milford Palmer, one-time governor of the National Bank of Egypt and former financial adviser to the Egyptian government, died in 1906, as the Chairman of the Delta Light Railways Company,[51] with an estate worth more than £144,037[52] which is equivalent to more than £7 million today.

Besides banking, upper middle class Britons ran other businesses in Egypt as well. For example, Robert Lang Anderson, son of a leading Scottish lawyer, and educated in agricultural studies at the universities of Glasgow and Edinburgh, worked in the agricultural, estate management, and engineering industries in Scotland before his arrival in Egypt in 1887. He eventually became Managing Director of the Aboukir Co., which was responsible for reclaiming 300,000 acres of Lake Abu Qir, east of Alexandria – by 1910, the property was worth around £300,000.[53] Educated in private schools in the north of England, Robert Johnson Moss was another successful upper class British businessman, who was based primarily in Alexandria for over 50 years. After arriving in Egypt in 1860, he built up R. J. Moss and Co., which exported cotton, sold steam cotton presses to the Egyptian market, imported agricultural machinery, and established an engineering repair centre that fixed imported ploughs, portable engines, pumps, cotton gins, corn mills, and corn shellers. After being educated in private schools in London, George Alexander Alderson, Director of Allen, Alderson and Co., established his business as the largest importer of machines into Egypt whose irrigation pumps were found all over the country.[54] Henry Barker and his son Harry were also well-to-do businessmen who spent decades in Egypt running Barker and Company, one of Egypt's largest shipping companies that transported mainly cotton, cottonseed, grain, and coal.[55] Yet, to illustrate the diversity of Britons represented in Egypt, there were successful businessmen who did not appear to be highly educated from exclusive private schools at all. For example, G. H. Stephenson, founder of the first and highly successful English pharmacy in Cairo (which dispensed drugs to the British military and the Citadel Hospital), started his apprenticeship after completing his education at Beverley Grammar School in Yorkshire.[56] Another respected British businessman in Egypt, Victor F. Naggiar, did not attend exclusive private schools but was educated at Chorlton High School near Manchester and immediately thereafter started working for Brooks' (which later became Lloyd's) Bank. He eventually became the founder of the import firm Borsali, Naggiar and Co., and was the President of the British Chamber of Commerce in Egypt during the latter years of the British occupation.[57] This suggests that some British businessmen stayed considerably longer in Egypt than military and civil officials, perhaps due to their ability to earn more in Egypt than in Britain.

Similarly, John Mason Cook, the most successful businessman in Egypt of his generation, did not have an exclusive upper class and private school background. Although he inherited his tour business from his father, Thomas Cook, the company's success did not occur until after John reached his adult years. Cook's business empire was remarkable. He saw himself 'as curator...to the world's largest outdoor museum... [and one who] subsidised restorations and excavations.'[58] He owned the largest fleet of cruisers in Egypt, including three fast mail boats, older towing steamers, specially built steel-hulled dahabiyyas, sailing crafts and barges, and the biggest steamer ever to have sailed the Nile at that time. By 1891, Cook had 24 steamers (of various classes)[59] and a practical monopoly over shipping on the Nile. By 1900, Cook's annual net profit soared to £82,000 prompting an American journal, the *US Excursionist*, to proclaim: 'Cook simply owns Egypt.'[60] Many Egyptians who lived on the Nile in Upper Egypt found that their livelihood depended on Cook. Their donkeys were subsidised by Cook; their vegetables were grown for Cook's steamers; their chickens were raised for Cook's tourists. And all of their boats were built by Cook's money.[61] As Hunter articulates, 'there were two empires on the Nile – Britain's military occupation, and Cook's Egyptian travel.'[62] So powerful had Cook become that *Vanity Fair* magazine in 1889 described Cook as:

> The chief person in Cairo...The nominal ruler [of Egypt] is Tewfik; but Tewfik takes his orders from Baring; and Baring, I suspect, has

to take his orders from Cook. The latter Sovereign becomes more and more potent as we get further up the Nile and here at Luxor, where a special hotel has arisen under the light of his countenance, he figures quite as a modern Ammon-Ra.[63]

Since it appears that Cromer and his officials had a stranglehold on power in every government ministry in Egypt, *Vanity Fair* was no doubt exaggerating. Nonetheless, Cook's extensive business empire illustrates the influence of a particular Briton in Egypt who was not in the civil or military service and who did not necessarily come from an exclusive public school background.

Often overlooked in discussions related to Britons in Egypt are clergymen and missionaries, many of whom were from educated upper middle class backgrounds. Chaplains to the church most frequented by the British establishment – All Saints' Church in Cairo – Rev. Charles Henry Butcher (chaplain from 1880 to 1907) and his successor, Rev. J. H. Molesworth, were both highly educated men with post-graduate degrees.[64] In 1909, the chaplain of the Anglican St. Mary's Mission in Cairo, Rev T. A. Branthwaite, even had two doctoral degrees.[65] Financially, the rector of All Saint's Church was adequately supplied. With housing provided, he was paid at least £350 (the rate that Molesworth was promised as Butcher's successor) per year; and Dean Butcher, as he was called, even acquired a generous £100 pension per year.[66] The total value of Butcher's estate was almost £3000.[67] Besides church ministers, missionaries also tended to be highly educated. A good number of British missionaries with the Church Missionary Society (CMS) served as educators and medical doctors. Rev. F. A. Klein, the first missionary sent to Egypt during the occupation, was a brilliant Arabic scholar. Two of the most educated, Rev. Douglas Thornton and Rev. Temple Gairdner, were both brilliant graduates from Cambridge University and developed a high proficiency in Arabic.[68] As mentioned in chapter 2, they created the magazine *The Orient and the Occident* which was published weekly in Arabic and in English.[69] The magazine was designed as an initiator of discussion featuring articles that provoked Egyptian intellectuals and students to consider perspectives and themes from a Christian angle.[70] As a result, Thornton and Gairdner were able to invite Egyptian scholars and students to various lectures and discussions related to the themes covered in the magazine.[71] Though highly educated, their salaries were most probably minimal since they were working for their faith and not for their bank accounts. For example, one missionary Mrs. Eliza

Bywater left an estate of only £33,[72] while another missionary doctor, Dr. Ernest Maynard Pain, an Australian with the CMS, may have received a monthly salary of a little less than £14.[73] British missionaries in Egypt, like many missionaries, tended to assume a financial status lower than their education or class backgrounds may have prepared them for.

Besides clergymen and missionaries, the British community in occupied Egypt included lawyers, doctors, teachers, bankers, and businessmen, and not just those in the government and military services. Educated and upper class Britons from Britain were not necessarily highly paid (such as in the case of certain missionaries) while businessmen like Stephenson and Cook were very successful even though they did not come from upper class backgrounds. However, Egypt's British community was even more diverse in vocational roles and composition due to the presence of lower class Britons at the time.

Lower Class Britons in Egypt

A superficial glimpse of Egypt's British community during the occupation may lead to the conclusion that it was monolithic, especially in its class representation. The upper class balls at the Shepheard's Hotel and lavish dinner receptions at the Consul-General's residence, frequented by British civil servants and military officers, are well known to observers of this period. The top of Cairo's British society (and for that matter, Egyptian society) included the Consul-General; the general leading the Army of Occupation; the five advisers to the Ministries of Finance, the Interior, the Judiciary, Public Works, and Education; the Chaplain of All Saints' Church; the heads of the British medical and law professions; and a few prominent bankers and financiers.[74] Rodenbeck, in *Cairo: The City Victorious*, illustrates that the pecking order of Egyptian society during this time included many other foreign residents with the British officials at the top.

> Down near the bottom – but still several notches above [Egyptian] day labourers – were the Maltese, south-Italian and Greek artisans: master masons, plasterers and ironmongers, and also the waiters, petty criminals and petty prostitutes whose trade flourished under consular protection…Next up the social scale came a clerical class of francophone effendis, Armenian tram conductors, Bosnian salesgirls and Bulgarian secretaries. Cairo's pharmacists and physicians, its engineers and its caterers and fancy jewellers came

from further north. The best photographers were German, the swankiest bespoke tailors English, the finest confectioners Swiss-Italian. The French and their speech dominated intellectual life. Jews from throughout the Diaspora took prominence in finance; Syro-Lebanese in trade. Behind the foil of the khedive and his cabinetfuls of landowning pashas, 2,000 British...bureaucrats managed affairs of state.[75]

Although Rodenbeck seems to recognise that there were some Britons, like the tailors, who may not have been at the top of the social order, he assumes that the noteworthy Britons in Egypt were government officials who were members of the upper middle classes, both in Britain and in Egypt. Though the upper middle class Britons in the civil service, military, financial, and professional sectors formed the most politically influential and numerically significant contingent within the British community, there were Britons in Egypt from the lower classes in a variety of occupations and situations. They 'traditionally [included] smaller tradesmen and shopkeepers, especially in individual and family-owned firms, clerks and minor civil servants, and certain self-employed artisans and craftsmen of the traditional type'.[76] Within the lower classes, the working class refers to those who were primarily manual labourers and domestic servants. While the upper middle class officials and professionals usually migrated to Egypt for better pay and work opportunities, the lower classes did as well. By the second half of the nineteenth century, according to Tranter, emigration (to many destinations) grew in popularity among the British lower classes and specifically among the working class, encouraged by the promise of higher earnings and improved standards of living abroad.[77] Therefore, in the 1880s, Hunt calculates that more than 150,000 working class Britons moved abroad each year.[78]

> [By] the early years of the twentieth century, the enthusiasm for emigration among the labouring populations had reached unprecedented levels...Despite the greater willingness of the charitable public to provide funds for emigration, almost without exception the various emigration societies received many more applications for assistance than they had funds to support.[79]

However, the destinations for British emigrants that Tranter and Hunt refer to were largely the United States and British dominions such as

Canada, Australia, and New Zealand, where Britons settled permanently. The case for emigration to Egypt was primarily due to shorter term job opportunities. Few Britons stayed in Egypt indefinitely. Motives aside, this chapter seeks to draw attention to some of the challenges that lower class Britons faced in Egypt during the time of the occupation.

Certain lower class Britons worked as office clerks. Guy Osborne Lion, aged 17, was hired to work in the office of James Francis Waterlow, an agent for the Remington Typewriter Company. Lion's job was to type Waterlow's letters from dictation or written drafts, make invoices, do bookkeeping, copy documents, and answer enquiries that came personally or by telephone.[80] Lion, who started working on a trial basis for Waterlow in April 1908 for £10 per month or £120 per year, experienced a significant earnings increase since his previous salary was only £2 per month or £24 per year (similar to annual salaries for teenage apprentice clerks in Britain that ranged from £16 to £20 since the mid-1800s).[81] For a 17 year old this was a huge income as starting salaries for clerks in Britain ranged only around £20 to £30 per year around the turn of the century.[82] Only more seasoned clerks, with twenty or more years of experience, earned more than £300 or £400 per year[83] whilst the average salary for a clerk in Britain in 1911 was around £230.[84] In light of Lion's earnings, it appears that there was ample incentive for young British lower middle class clerks to work in Egypt. Soon after hiring Lion, Waterlow found Lion's performance very unsatisfactory which suggests that Lion's employment record in Britain may have been rather poor and therefore, he may have been forced to work abroad. Although Lion had told Waterlow that he was familiar with the Remington typewriter, Waterlow found that Lion had no knowledge whatsoever of the machine. His 'typewriting was unpunctuated and the letters were all wrong...It was full of mistakes...[Waterlow] never saw anything so disgraceful in typing.'[85] Waterlow had to find someone else to finish the typing and apologised profusely to his customers for the mistakes. By the end of May, Lion had also been absent for six working days due to illness. On 30 May 1908, Lion was off work but according to Waterlow, Lion could not produce any kind of evidence to satisfy him that he was ill. Instead, he went to the Railway Institute Club – one of the few clubs for lower class members of the British community – to play tennis.[86] As a result, Waterlow dismissed Lion on 2 June. Since Waterlow did not pay Lion for his work in May, Lion sued Waterlow for the £10 in salary and claimed damages for wrongful dismissal. Lion was in no condition to pay court charges and argued that on the 31 May 1908, he had seen Dr Beddoe who told him to rest at home. However, Waterlow wanted a certificate from Dr Beddoe which Lion could not produce.[87] Eventually, the Court ruled that Waterlow was to pay Lion £10 for his salary in May and a further £40 in damages.[88] Upon Waterlow's appeal, the Court determined that the damages were excessive considering Lion's conduct and reduced them to £30.[89] This story is significant as it gives an example of British lower class workers (even delinquents) defying their superiors and even suing them.

Besides clerks, lower class Britons included artisans such as tailors.[90] James Henry Jones 'came out from England in December [1912] as Master Tailor to Messrs. Papdakis in Zagazig.'[91] Two months later, he died of a severe attack of bronchitis. The British Consulate arranged the funeral and discovered that the cost of his hospital, funeral and cemetery expenses were adequately covered by the small amount of cash that was found on him and by the sale of Jones' small revolver and two watches. The Consulate wrote to his widow saying that Jones had other possessions but that the sale of these items was 'not worth the amount of the freight as they [were] in a very bad condition.'[92] Therefore, it appears that, by virtue of their work as office clerks and tailors, the British lower classes in Egypt seemed to have earned more than their counterparts in Britain but were by no means well off. Policemen could be added to this category since Peter John Teskow of the Cairo Police earned about £10 monthly (£120 per year), at the time of his death in 1913,[93] more than an average policeman in Britain who earned just over £70 per year.[94]

Within the lower class, the working class engaged primarily in menial efforts. There appear to have been far fewer unskilled labourers from the British Isles in Egypt than in Britain itself, since there seem to have been ample unskilled labourers among the Egyptian population. Certain individuals of the working class, such as some in the building trade with specific skills and experience, seemed to have comparable salaries with the aforementioned clerks, tailors, and other skilled members of the lower class; while most working class members had more meagre incomes. Since there was a building slump in London in the early 1900s,[95] a national slump as the First World War emerged, and since 'new construction [fell] to negligible levels...[during] the war years,'[96] working class members of the building trade may have been lured to Egypt. A court case for wrongful dismissal, Chubb vs. Lovatt, documents the bittersweet story of a British foreman in the building trade in Egypt during this time. Sidney Chubb who worked for Henry Lovatt Co. in London accepted an offer to work for Lovatt in Cairo as a foreman carpenter for the construction of the new military barracks in Abbasiyya. Chubb initially agreed to work for £10 per month in January 1910. By March, his wage was increased to £14 per month; by July, it rose to £16; and by October, it inflated to £18. Compared to the salaries of lawyers and civil servants, at £60 to £70 per month, Chubb's income was low but his earnings doubled those of workers in the building trade in Britain at this time (with an average monthly wage of £9 per month in 1911).[97] Despite the fact that Chubb was required to pay for his passage out to Egypt, which cost £13.11s.0d, and for his wife's journey to Egypt – which amounted to £24.10s.9d, including excess baggage[98] – his earnings of £18 per month were still substantial in light of the building trade's downturn in Britain and the significantly lower incomes for workers in the building trade there. In contrast to Chubb's rapid wage increase since his appointment in January 1910, he was dismissed on 10 November 1910. Richard Woodley, the Manager of Henry Lovatt Co., fired Chubb because he was at times late for work. Further, according to Woodley's deposition, Chubb fought with one of the engineers and allowed certain masonry to be erected wrongly on 17 October 1910. By early November, Chubb took a break from work without permission one afternoon and left about 40 Egyptian men without supervision.[99] Woodley dismissed Chubb not long afterwards. In response, like Lion who defied his superior, Chubb sued Henry Lovatt Co. for wrongful dismissal. Despite his earnings, Chubb, at the trial's conclusion, was 'not worth £25 and [was] not able to pay...court fees of and incidental to [any] action in...Court.'[100]

Perhaps more representative of a British member of the working class than a foreman carpenter, were the many Britons in Cairo who lived in Boulaq and worked for the railway companies which also employed upper middle class engineers. Inaugurated in December 1900, the Boulaq shops were responsible for the building of rail carriages and nearly all the repair and maintenance work of the trains as well.[101] The British workers served as firemen, mechanics, and other maintenance staff[102] and received relatively low wages (less than half of Chubb's salary as a foreman). For instance, James Campbell, a mechanic in the ESR, appears to have had a monthly wage of just under £5 (or £60 per year) in 1910,[103] comparable to the annual wage of £74 for lower class workers in Britain in 1911.[104] Since the railway workers were poor compared to other members of the Egypt's British community, they were objects of charitable donations and legacies of wills. In 1898, Mrs. Edith Hector McClean, donated £1000 of her will for a church to be built for the poor Britons in Boulaq who were working on the railways.[105] By 1898, tramways had provided convenient transportation for the railway workers to travel to All Saints' Church in Ezbekiyya, thus there was no longer a need to build a separate church building for English workers in Boulaq. It was decided that Mrs McClean's donation be used to enlarge the existing church and that a separate portion of pews would be dedicated for the usage of the workers from Boulaq. To commemorate Mrs McClean's gift, a brass plate with the following inscription was created: 'This chapel was set apart for the use of the residents at Boulak [sic] in fulfilment of the wishes of the late Edith Hector McClean who laboured for their spiritual welfare during her life and did not forget them in her death.'[106] Similarly, other funds were designated to the British poor in Cairo such as the Antoun Yousif Charity Fund of E£1000 in 1892[107] and E£30 from the St. Andrew's Church jumble sale in 1915.[108]

Besides builders and railway workers, working class Britons in Egypt, particularly women, served also as maids. In Britain, 'domestic service was...a main source of work for women.'[109] More than 42% of employed women were working as housemaids.[110] By the end of the nineteenth century in Britain, 'one girl in every three between the ages of fifteen and twenty was a domestic servant. Altogether there were over one and a half million.'[111] In Egypt, a smaller proportion of women worked as maids. From Table 4.3, about 19.7 per cent of employed female British subjects were maids in Egypt. More specifically, from Table 4.5, 21.5 per cent of employed female British subjects were maids in Cairo. Although not desperately poor because their board and lodging were usually provided for, their income appears to be minimal. For instance, Elizabeth Chadwick worked as a maid for 20 years for Caroline de Willbois (although for some of these years, her work and travel with de Willbois may have been outside Egypt). At the time of Chadwick's death in 1906, de Willbois wrote to Mr. Alban, consul to the Finance Ministry, to inquire as to the time of the funeral.

> My poor maid's name was Elizabeth Chadwick but I do not know her age. I presume it must be about 60 years as she was for more than 20 years with me and was not young when I took her...I think it best that the funeral be a 3rd class one; but I would like to know what hour tomorrow it will be, because the girls and I will go to the cemetery...I will give over her two boxes to the Consulate, whenever you wish and the wages that are due to her. She has no money whatever, because she used to send every farthing home to her sister.[112]

Chadwick's monthly salary from Madam de Willbois was £3.11.3 (just over £40 per year). Chadwick was even poorer because even the little she earned, she sent it back to England to her sister. Poor British women also worked as nannies for wealthy Egyptian families.[113] Yet, still others arrived in Egypt destitute. 'One woman was actually sent out by some Board of Guardians in England with four penniless little girls under twelve.'[114] As for prostitution, though there were as many as 100,000 prostitutes in London alone during the mid-Victorian era,[115] the records of occupied Egypt point to a very limited number of prostitutes who were British. Out of 280 police raids on 175 brothels in 1914, not one British prostitute was found. Similarly, out of the 931 women minors in the white slave trade who were arrested at disembarkation in the same year, only seven were British.[116]

Class Inequality, Snobbery, and Conflict

In a discussion that includes class, it may be helpful to conclude by suggesting that the British class structure was not only a system of wage brackets and occupational categorisation. The notions of inequality and deference were deeply entrenched in the psyches of British men and women. Two examples from the British community in occupied Egypt demonstrate this psychological and social reality. First, during a Sunday service at All Saints' Church in 1891, Lord Dunmore and his family arrived at 'church ten minutes before the bell stopped ringing but could not get into the seat usually occupied by them and had in consequence to be dispersed [to different seats in]...the church.'[117] Although it was customary for residents to have their regular seats at church, it was understood that 'such allotted seats [would]...only [be]...reserved until the beginning of the [reading of the] Psalms.'[118] In this case, the Church Warden declared that Lord Dunmore and his family did not regularly occupy any seats and Lord Dunmore was even asked to be removed from a seat that one Miss McCarthy had occupied for the past year and a half.[119] Consequently, Lord Dunmore complained to Sir Evelyn Baring, the Consul-General, with regards to his ill-treatment by the Church Warden. In response, Mr. Crewe the Church Warden resigned, though he was recognised by the church council for 'his long and devoted [service] to the church'.[120] Needless to say, this incident illustrates the deeply ingrained snobbery and deference inherent in the British class culture. Not only was being denied one's desired seating arrangement inexcusable but to be turned out of a seat occupied by a 'lesser' being of a lower class, even if only slightly lower, was unacceptable to someone of the upper class. No church committee member dared to defend the Church Warden's actions or speak against his resignation.

The second example concerns the attitudes of British privates in the military with regards to their upper class superiors. One lower class soldier wrote an article published by the *Egyptian Gazette* as to how deeply he was enamoured with the rightful superiority of his officers:

> The officer's uniform, his education and social gifts, his exemption from physical toil, the law that forbids a private to approach him without the intermediary of a N.C.O. and even the officer's better food – all these conspire to make the ordinary private regard him as a kind of superior being. The normal soldier is ripe for hero-worship: his nature demands some one whom he can admire and be proud of. If he is given a typical Public School boy or university man as an officer, his happiness as a soldier is complete...Officers are officers; men are men.[121]

With this commitment to honour the class system from soldiers, officers, and church leaders alike, the British in Egypt constructed a social framework whereby they were classified according to wealth, education, occupation, and background. Examples of lack of deference and class conflict among Britons in Egypt are difficult to find. However, Robert Tressell's classic account of the British working class in the early 1900s, *The Ragged-Trousered Philanthropists*, suggests that there may have been working class labourers who felt that, underneath the polite deference, they were actually much more resentful and disrespectful towards the upper class. Frank Owen, the main labourer in the story, castigated the upper class by asserting that

> We...[the working class] are working and suffering...in order that the rich people...may live in luxury and do nothing...[and who] are the wretches who cause poverty...[as] they devour or waste or hoard the things made by the workers. Most of these people do not deserve to be called human beings at all. They're devils!...They are indulging in pleasures of every kind, all around them men and women and little children are existing in want or dying of hunger.[122]

There appears to be only one incident of a working class Briton being involved in, and even leading, a strike against the authorities – not directly against the government of British upper class officials in Cairo but the Egyptian-run municipal government of Alexandria. In February 1906, as part of wider Egyptian protests against Alexandria's municipal government, coachmen or carriage drivers went on strike (Table 4.4 indicates that there were 16 British subjects who were coachmen in 1897). They petitioned for a stop to a new taxation scheme on vehicles and horses, change of fares and regulations concerning stables, and a more accurate way to confirm the sickness of a horse before it was required to be hospitalised.[123] The strikes outside the office of the municipal government eventually turned violent. Interestingly, 'the leadership [of the strike]...was predominantly foreign, with a British subject...named Edward Fabry...arrested as the ringleader of the militants.'[124] Though it is unclear whether Fabry was from the British Isles, this is nonetheless a noteworthy account of a British working class subject who dissented against the established authorities of the time and even leading other Europeans and Egyptians to do the same.

By using court, census, and business records, this chapter has demonstrated that, beyond the obvious upper middle class group of officers and officials, the British in Egypt engaged in many other occupations and professions and that there was a significant number from the uneducated lower classes. Besides the military and civil services, upper middle class Britons worked as lawyers, doctors, engineers, teachers, bankers, businessmen, and missionaries; lower class Britons were carpenters, office clerks, and tailors; and within the lower class, working class Britons served as railway workers and maids. Women tended to stay home and were not usually engaged in employment outside their homes. Snobbery and deference were the ground rules regulating the hierarchical framework of the community. Further, the chapter shows that Britons went to Egypt (and perhaps other British territories) because upward mobility was more likely there than it was in Britain. It was also likely that the cost of living in Egypt was less than that of Britain, meaning that the generally higher salaries that Britons obtained in Egypt (as compared with salaries for the same work in Britain) were able to give them greater purchasing power. Besides the economic incentive, some Britons went to Egypt with more altruistic motives, such as clergy, missionaries, or civil servants who wanted to serve in what they perceived as less developed societies (but some might well have been enticed by higher pay and good benefits as well). There might also have been a psychological factor behind this social mobility which allowed members of the British lower classes, looked down on at home, to be seen as superior compared to lower class Egyptians.

Plate 1: Entrance of the Shepheard's Hotel, frequented by members of the British and European communities in Cairo, circa 1890s (Charles Dibble archives, courtesy Ola Seif).

Plate 2: Members of the British community taking tea at the English military tournament in Cairo, 1896 (Rare Books and Special Collections Library [RBSCL], American University in Cairo [AUC]).

Plate 3: Members of the British community with other expatriates at the Grand Stand, Cairo, 1892 (Viscount Allenby collection, Liddell Hart Centre for Military Archives, King's College London).

Plate 4: The Ezbekiyya Square, important centre for banking, shopping, and hotel functions for Cairo's Europeans, 1921 (National Army Museum archives).

Plate 5: Playing field for British forces at Qasr el-Nil barracks, circa late 1910s (RBSCL, AUC).

Plate 6: British Soldier at Qasr el-Nil Bridge, Cairo, circa 1890 (RBSCL, AUC).

Plate 7: Harry and Lena Barker with Frederick and Mary Rowlatt at Stanley Bay, 1914, Alexandria. Sir Frederick Rowlatt was the Governor of the National Bank of Egypt (1906–1921) and Harry Barker was an influential British businessman. (Barker Family collection, Photograph Album 1914 to 1915 no.1, GB165-0493, at Middle East Centre Archive, St. Antony's College, University of Oxford).

Plate 8: British military parade with Egyptian onlookers, circa 1919 (Viscount Allenby collection, Liddell Hart Centre for Military Archives, King's College London).

5

CRIME AND MISCONDUCT

Until recently, literature dealing with crime has generally been less 'academic' but more 'popular' in genre, with a focus on notorious events and personalities. Traditional academic accounts tended to concentrate on political, economic, and social aspects and seemed to address the issue of crime sparingly. However, in the last thirty years, historians have increasingly explored crime-related questions (how it is understood, defined, and dealt with) in order to more fully comprehend a given historical context.[1]

Likewise, historical writing related to the British in Egypt has centred largely on the political, military, and financial players of the time from middle and upper class backgrounds. Without reference to much crime or misconduct, the existing literature seems to give the impression that such people were generally socially upright and law-abiding citizens, though it is likely that certain offences were never reported. However, this chapter seeks to indicate that Britons in Egypt, of various classes and backgrounds, were engaged in professional misconduct and negligence, and criminal activity. Highlighting misconduct and crime among Britons in Egypt contributes to the main aim of this book which is to bring to light aspects of the British community's diversity that have been previously underemphasised in historical literature. Throughout the analysis, observations will be made related to the frequency of certain crimes and their potential causes among Britons in Britain in order to deepen understanding of British criminal behaviour during this period of time.

The shorter discussion dealing with professional misconduct and negligence is primarily based on certain private papers, some official letters, and business and church archives. Professional misconduct can be defined as wrongful or improper behaviour that falls short of standards expected within a profession. Negligence alludes to the failure to apply reasonable care. However, much of this chapter refers to British criminal activity defined by behaviour, which, 'if detected, would lead to prosecution in a court of law or summarily before an accredited agent of law enforcement.'[2] Sources used to examine British criminal behaviour in Egypt are largely, but not exclusively, centred on the Consular Court archives of Cairo and Alexandria. These records, as they pertain to criminal behaviour among Britons, have not been used much, if at all, in the historical narrative of the British in Egypt. As stated earlier, due to the Capitulations, foreigners in Egypt were given special privileges and rights. One key privilege was their exemption from local Egyptian jurisdiction. All criminal cases involving a foreign defendant were tried in the Consular Court of the defendant's country of origin. Civil cases for foreign residents involving the plaintiff and defendant from two different countries were usually tried in the Mixed Tribunals, while civil cases involving the plaintiff and defendant from the same country of origin were tried in the Consular Court[3]. In Egypt, the British Consular Courts were in Cairo, Alexandria, and Port Said. Appeals were made to the Supreme Consular Court in Cairo with the final authority resting on the Supreme Consular Court of the Sublime Ottoman Porte in Constantinople. For the Briton in Egypt, the Consular Courts offered important judicial protection from 'native' laws and provided the security of familiar British legal proceedings in the English language.

> In the British Consular Courts the Englishman in Egypt has a solid guarantee of security and efficiency. If he be accused of a crime he is tried under English law and according to the notions of fairness that animate English Criminal Procedure. In civil cases between British subjects, the parties' rights are determined by British law. In either case the proceedings come before a British judge and are conducted in English.[4]

It is hoped that by reviewing the cases in the British Consular Courts of Cairo and Alexandria from 1882 to 1922, a clearer profile of British criminals and their crimes will reflect the diversity within the British community in Egypt and challenge the traditional portrayal of principally law-abiding Britons in the civil and military service.

Before launching into the bulk of this discussion, it may help to note its limited scope. First, although British subjects of Maltese, Greek, or

CRIME AND MISCONDUCT   147

other origins were also tried in the British Consular Court, the main focus of this chapter is on the criminal actions of Britons from the British Isles. Some court cases point out clearly that the plaintiff or the defendant was of 'British' origin, as opposed to 'Greek' or 'Maltese', while others do not record the plaintiff or defendant's ethnic background. In the latter cases, since there were few residents in Egypt who had English last names and were tried in the British courts, they were most likely to be from the British Isles. There were relatively few Irish (though they were included in the same tallies as the English, Scottish, and Welsh in the 1907 census) and Canadians in Egypt at the time. The small number of Americans had their own tribunal. Australians and New Zealanders primarily arrived in Egypt after 1914, during the war effort, and their crimes tended to be restricted to rioting and prostitution. (More will be said towards the end of this chapter and in the chapter on World War I.) Second, British tourists, who committed crimes, were also tried in the British Consular courts. These temporary residents have not been included in this chapter. The Britons that are referred to in this discussion generally had a distinct role, profession, or vocation, meaning that they were not visitors but were longer-term residents in Egypt. Third, given the population distribution of Britons in Egypt during this time, this chapter will refer to misconduct and crime largely based in Cairo and Alexandria with only one exception in Port Said. Fourth, it is likely that a significant proportion of misconduct or crime among Britons in Egypt faced low detection and prosecution rates similar to those in London during this time.

> Only a tiny proportion of crime committed in London actually led to a trial. The vast majority of crimes went undetected or at least unpunished. Taking someone to court was both time consuming and costly and many victims accepted informal 'satisfaction' from the culprit, for example by securing the return of their stolen goods in exchange for dropping the charges. The relatively primitive forces of policing were simply not up to the task of preventing or effectively investigating crime, and the burden of detection and prosecution fell overwhelmingly on the victim.[5]

Lastly, for organisational expediency, this chapter is divided into particular areas of misconduct and crime: professional misconduct and negligence, personal/domestic crimes (domestic abuse, abortion, and suicide), social crimes (assault and libel), financial crimes (fraud, embezzlement, theft, and extortion) and sexual crimes (rape, bigamy, and prostitution).

Professional Misconduct and Negligence

By and large, many Britons in Egypt were competent administrators and professionals. There were few incidences of professional misconduct during the period of the British occupation. However, there were exceptions where professional judgement was questionable leading to resignation or dismissal. One such situation occurred in 1910 at Port Said. Dr. E. H. Ross wanted to go on leave but just before his scheduled departure, two patients who came to him were misdiagnosed. Though they had cholera, Ross concluded that they did not. Thus Dr. Ross was suspected of intentionally ignoring these two cases of cholera so that he could go on leave. If there was any hint of a cholera outbreak, then his leave would have had to be cancelled.

> There appears to be a strong case against Dr. Ross for grave negligence with regard to plague complicated with the suspicion that he did not carry out the usual routine of examination in two particular cases because if proved to be plague, they would have prevented his taking leave.[6]

The British authorities in Egypt made clear that 'if a charge of concealing plague could have been proved, [they would] have proceeded with it.'[7] However,

> after careful consideration of the evidence against Dr. Ross and after hearing his defence it became clear that the serious charges could not be driven home by a Council of Discipline however unpleasant the impression which must be left by his conduct. If he could not be dismissed there remained no doubt that he was, a most undesirable type of official.[8]

Though he was not dismissed, Dr. Ross resigned from his post in Port Said and 'received and accepted a severe official reprimand for negligence and disobedience to routine orders.'[9]

Besides this incident in Port Said, negligence in medical services was also evident in Cairo. As mentioned in the chapter on 'symbols', the Anglo-American Hospital was built in 1903 primarily for British residents and American visitors as a rival to the German Hospital in the charged atmosphere of imperial rivalry. Largely funded by upper class Britons and some Americans, it eventually lost the support of many Britons because of its inconvenient location on Gezira Island (due to the overcrowded route from the rest of Cairo to the island) and the sense that the hospital, by virtue of its American partnership, could never become an institution of pure British excellence. It seems likely that this lack of support contributed to the multiple shortcomings in the maintenance of hygiene and supplies, documented in a key report on the Anglo-American Hospital. Regarding hygiene standards, the laundry was in deplorable condition. The stove required repairing. The gearing was broken. Taps were leaking. Urgent repairs were needed to drain the accumulated soakage. The special washhouse for the washing of the soiled linen from maternity cases were locked up and used as storage for mattresses. No precaution was taken to separate the washing of the soiled linen of typhoid patients from the rest of the patients. The dirty linen from maternity, typhoid and other cases were all thrown into one common room where Sudanese women, who were both sceptical of the need for cleanliness and careless of infection, did the work. The report urged the immediate re-opening of the maternity washhouse and strict procedures to separate the linen of typhoid patients from those of other patients. With regards to supplies, the report noted that the system in place to manage the household supplies of the Hospital tended to wastefulness and extravagance. Proper inventories of stock combined with a clear recording of accounts were not kept. Small quantities were being frequently ordered as required. The quantities of stationery, china, and kitchen utensils were all running low, and certain items were missing entirely. There was no system in place for the inspection or repair of the Hospital linen, the supply of which was depleting. There were not enough mosquito nets for the number of beds, and a large number of the nets were full of holes and needed repairing. The report urged the Hospital to start re-stocking, ordering, inspecting, and repairing all the necessary items.[10] It seems likely that the negligence evident in the Anglo-American Hospital discouraged the Britons and others in Cairo from using it. Whatever the case, the Anglo-American Hospital was one exception to the stereotypical image of competence and reliability found in British administration and management.

Besides medical negligence, the controversial case of Charles Robert Ashbee may have been identified as professional misconduct to some and forward thinking to others in the educational arena. Ashbee, an architect by trade, came from Britain to teach in the Sultaniyya Training College in Cairo during the First World War. He was accepted by the Ministry of Education because male British teachers in Egypt were 'being taken for military service'[11] and desperately needed to be replaced. Soon after Ashbee started working in Cairo, certain British officials began to severely criticise his teaching style. Sir Ronald Graham, of the Residency in Cairo, suggested that 'Ashbee [was] a socialist without sense of discipline; and his theories and attitude in general [had] a deplorable effect on the boys he [was] called upon to teach.'[12] Major C. F. Ryder, Assistant Director of the Eastern Mediterranean Special Intelligence Bureau, labelled Ashbee an 'ultra-socialist…[who spoke] unfavourably of the Allies saying that they waged the present war…to satisfy their cupidity.'[13] He was also accused of passing the contents of anti-Governmental English newspapers to his Egyptian nationalist friends.[14] A few years later, Commissioner for Egypt to the Foreign Office, Henderson, claimed that Ashbee's 'methods were subversive of discipline. He openly ridiculed regulations and authority and his method of conducting examinations rendered the proceedings ridiculous…He was an advanced socialist and showed no discretion in airing his views, both in and out of college.'[15] Therefore, with other British officials supporting him, Douglas Dunlop, Education Adviser, proceeded to expel Ashbee.

However, actual proof of professional indiscretion or illegalities was hard to come by since Ashbee seemed to have only offered a perspective that was more sympathetic to Egyptian culture. Ashbee disliked the ordinary expatriate lifestyle of most of the Britons in Egypt. He loathed the 'fancied officials and "schoolmasters-managers" who think merely of getting through their work as quickly as possible so that they may go on with the usual English club life and amusements.'[16] Instead, he tried 'to get at the oriental side of [things] and avoid the British "official" side which is of course tediously familiar.'[17] He explains further:

> The oriental point of view is so different from ours and so valuable in fixing our judgement on the great issues of life – religious, aesthetic, [and] political that we ought to study it much more than we do. I study history and devote one whole day in the week to going through the mosques and native workshops…So where do you think I was last night? At a college of Dervishes listening to a Turkish Dervish – making music and singing. He was a wonderful musician.[18]

In Ashbee's thinking, the British education system was 'false' in that Egyptian boys were being examined according to British standards, which were mainly clerical. But what Egyptian students needed was character training and not skills to memorise facts and then regurgitate them on a piece of paper. He was critical of the harshness of British teachers towards Egyptian students exemplified by a situation where a student was disqualified from taking his final exam because he was a few minutes late. As a result, the student lost his whole year's work and a chance of a government appointment.[19] He hoped that Egyptian students would 'develop their own national capacity and...not assume that everything British is necessarily better than everything Egyptian. It is not.'[20] Ashbee appeared to hold views that were sympathetic to Egyptian nationalism.

Consequently, Dunlop was concerned that Ashbee's return to teaching in any school in Egypt for the autumn term of 1917 would increase his students' nationalist sentiments and turn them even more opposed to Britain's occupation of Egypt. So desperate was Dunlop to get rid of Ashbee that he tried to get the military authorities to stop Ashbee from entering Egypt after a summer in Britain. Further, he arranged an alternative post for Ashbee in England; and if he refused, Ashbee was to be given a full year's salary without employment.[21] In the end, Ashbee rejected the offer in Britain. He returned to Egypt denying that he was ever 'political' in the classroom. He asserted: 'I wish it put on record that there is no foundation whatever for [believing that] I had been discussing questions of a political nature with my students.'[22] However, he lost his post at the Sultaniyya Training College and tried unsuccessfully to acquire a post as a professor of English Literature. According to Dunlop and certain British officials, the story of Charles Robert Ashbee was one of professional misconduct. To others, notably Egyptian nationalists, Ashbee was a courageous anti-colonial liberal gadfly who was a long way ahead of his time. It seems probable that the British authorities dismissed Ashbee primarily because of his sympathy with Egyptian sentiments against British rule under the guise of his alleged incompetence or 'socialist' leanings.

In addition to the medical and educational fields, professional misconduct was also evident among those who practised law in the British community of Egypt. In 1911, there was an official reception to celebrate the coronation of King George V. However, Sir Milne Cheetham, who was responsible for inviting members of the British community to the event, was warned against inviting three lawyers named Reginald Silley, J. P. Foster, and Perrott.

> I am told by His Majesty's consuls, the judges of the Courts where these men practise, that their conduct is a danger to the prestige of the British Courts in Egypt. On one occasion, Silley and Foster were only prevented by force from coming to blows in Court. Foster is known chiefly for his violent temper. Silley and Perrott will take business offered them however dubious. The former was recently rebuked in Court for proceedings which in England constitute a serious offence for which he must have been disbarred. Both Silley and Perrott have had to be of the British Court in Cairo more than once if my information is correct. Members of the English bar who are Egyptian Civil Servants...strongly disapprove of [Perrott's] conduct and consider that it ought not to have been allowed to pass unnoticed.[23]

Cheetham, having met Silley and Perrott, was warned by 'several competent persons...to be very careful in dealing with them.'[24] According to Cheetham, all three lawyers 'could [never] be received at the Agency'[25] and they would have been removed if they came to the reception on their initiative.[26] Their conduct suggests that Egypt, and other occupied territories, may have been a refuge for some professionals who in Britain were regarded as undesirable or unsuitable. It appears that although the British in Egypt were usually professionally reliable, there were examples of negligence among medical, educational, and legal professionals such as Dr. Ross, the British management of the Anglo-American Hospital, Ashbee, and lawyers like Silley, Foster, and Perrott.

Personal/Domestic Crimes

Domestic abuse

Brutality at home was not uncommon in Britain during the late nineteenth century and early twentieth century even though 'women were reluctant to take their family's principal breadwinner to court...recognising the impact that even a short spell of imprisonment or a small fine could have on the family budget.'[27] British 'newspapers...frequently [recorded] cases of inhuman cruelty to wives and children.'[28] For example, in 1889, there were 8075 cases of assault on women in Britain and Ireland.

Penalties were often lenient, since only 43 of these cases resulted in the offenders receiving two or more years' imprisonment.[29] Similarly, among the relatively small number of Britons in Egypt during the occupation, there were a significant number of court cases dealing with domestic violence within British households. Only a few are highlighted here. In nearly every case, men were found guilty of beating their wives. This is noteworthy since 'many jurists and magistrates [in British courts] continued to believe that battered wives had provoked their husbands and refused to allow maintenance or separation orders.'[30] In light of the 1878 amendment of the Matrimonial Causes Act which secured maintenance and separation for women from violent husbands, the remedy sought by the Egypt's Consular Courts for domestic violence included imprisonment, fines, legal separation, eventual divorce, and alimony depending on the needs of each family and the earnings of the father. For example, in 1904, 'Thomas Lane of Cairo, [a] Fitter [possibly a turner/technician], is…convicted before this Court…that he on the 8th day of October…at Cairo, did assault and strike Adelaide his wife and threaten to kill her.'[31] The Court asked Thomas Lane to pay a fine of £2.0s.0d or otherwise be imprisoned for one month and ordered that Adelaide Lane 'be no longer bound to cohabit with [her husband] and that he shall pay her £2.10s.0d per month.'[32] Six years later, Olga Campbell took her British husband William Campbell to court for judicial separation. After eight years of married life, primarily in Alexandria and Cairo, she accused her husband of violent and drunken behaviour and also of neglecting to provide for the family. One particular incident prompted her to seek the legal and financial help of the British Consul in Cairo:

> On the 14th day of July 1908, [he] threatened to cut the throats of myself and of our children. [Even though he] was continually absent for long periods from the house…[he] would return from time to time…and take my earnings [as a dressmaker]…and spend them in drink leaving me and our children destitute.[33]

Later in 1910, Alice Stephens sued her husband Frederick Bowring Stephens for assault and 'causing her bodily harm…[She] further request[ed] that an order for separation be made and that…[he]…pay her an allowance for maintenance.'[34] That same year, Suzanne Bailey took her husband, William Henry Bailey, to court after 17 years of married life in Egypt. Mrs. Bailey had trained as a nurse and by 1910 was employed in Cairo. Mr. Bailey, an engineer, first worked for the British government in Egypt, then toiled for the Delta Light Railways, but, thereafter, kept getting dismissed from employer after employer.[35] Even as early as their first year of marriage, Mr. Bailey had already started beating Mrs. Bailey. In April 1899, she was beaten so badly that she went into hospital for treatment. Mr. Bailey also began to leave Mrs. Bailey and their children (they had four by 1901) for days without food or money. In 1902, according to Mrs. Bailey, Mr. Bailey wilfully gave her a venereal disease. Thereafter, she denied him sexual intercourse whenever he managed to return home to visit his family. After being severely beaten in September 1907 by Mr. Bailey, Mrs. Bailey sought the protection of the law. Even after being convicted, Mr. Bailey continued to ask Mrs. Bailey for money and started to send obscene letters to her. By 1910, Mrs. Bailey sought a judicial separation, custody of their children, and her husband's payment for the costs of the court case. The Court obliged and granted Mrs. Bailey each of her requests.[36]

Six years later, Robert Steven Leslie, an engineer of the Egyptian State Railways was charged with aggravated assault after 'striking and beating [his wife, Emilie Leslie,] with his fists and knocking her down.'[37] Mrs. Leslie was no longer obliged to live with her husband and he was ordered to pay her £6.13s.0d. per month.[38] As a result, the Egyptian Expeditionary Force cancelled the appointment of Robert Leslie to the Egyptian Labour Corps.[39] In the same year, Walter Quinn, a dentist with practices in Cairo and Alexandria, got off extremely lightly for violently assaulting his French wife, Thérèse. For 'causing her serious bodily harm',[40] Dr. Quinn was ordered to pay only £2 and Court fees or otherwise face one month's imprisonment.[41] However, since they lived in Alexandria, another court ruling two years later in Alexandria, dealt with Dr. Quinn much more severely. He was accused of frequently abusing his wife physically and mentally. He called her 'bloody prostitute, bloody French woman…[and said] he would kill [her].'[42] In May 1917, Mrs. Quinn testified:

> In the course of a violent scene my husband seized me, struck me on the body, tore my dress, broke various articles in the house and generally cruelly ill-treated and insulted me. [He] struck me with a knotted towel on the body and threatened to strike me with an Indian dagger…[I] took refuge in the Windsor Hotel [and sought] medical help.[43]

Finally, by 1919, after already living apart, the Court ordered Dr. Quinn to pay certain sums to his wife to maintain the rent on her home and to allow her to take all the furniture that was worth £150 altogether. Further, he was ordered to pay Mrs. Quinn's court fees, six instalments of E£25 per month as well as monthly payments of E£30.[44]

The aforementioned cases of domestic violence were a few examples of a sizeable problem among British families in Egypt though some of the cases involved British men married to women from other European countries. Although there are neither uniform reasons nor excuses for domestic violence, it seems that in the case of the British men in Egypt, alcohol, unemployment, and the pressures of securing work in a foreign context may have played a part in stirring them to violence. In Britain during this era, 'violence frequently ensued when wives refused husbands additional funds...to go drinking'[45] or when husbands arrived home drunk. It appears that for Britons in Egypt, domestic violence often led to the breaking down of marriages and families as the offended wife sought separation and alimony. Notwithstanding inflationary pressures, the above cases demonstrate the connection between earning potential and alimony payments. For example, Mr. Lane, a fitter, was ordered to pay £2.10s.0d per month in 1904. Mr. Leslie, an engineer, was sentenced to pay £6.13s.0d per month in 1916 while Dr. Quinn, a dentist had to pay E£25 to E£30 each month in 1919. Usually, domestic violence led to poorer fatherless families and fathers became less affluent due to the upkeep of children not in their custody. Though men were usually at fault when it came to violence, women were also, at times, responsible for creating domestic strife. In 1907, Alfred Griffith won custody of his daughter due to his wife's yearlong absence, negligence, and abduction of their child.[46] In 1911, James Duncan, who worked in the Sewage and Water services and, before that, had served in the British military in Egypt since 1896, won custody of his daughter after his wife left him.[47] Mr. Duncan suspected that Mrs. Duncan might have been leading an improper and immoral life. Though usually painful and traumatic for the families involved, fortunately, a large majority of British families in occupied Egypt did not face domestic violence that resulted in separation, divorce, alimony, and custody battles. It is important to note that often Britons were critical of Egyptian and Muslim men being violent towards their wives.[48] The evidence above suggests the hypocritical nature of these claims.

Abortion

During the late nineteenth and early twentieth centuries, abortion was 'frequently referred to as the "illegal operation" because it was the only operation specifically prohibited by statute law.'[49] Enshrined in the 1861 Offences Against the Person Act, the penalty for an attempt to procure abortion in Britain was life imprisonment – the most severe in Europe. However, the law was impossible to enforce when more and more women in the late nineteenth century proceeded with abortions in order to limit family size. By the turn of the century, approximately 2 per cent of live births in England resulted in death from prematurity due to the rising use of 'pernicious abortifacient medicines.'[50] Moreover, self-induced abortions were often unsafe and the law became a means by which women were protected from dangerous life-threatening procedures.

As well, abortion, its dangers and penalties were evident in the British community in Egypt. In 1911, Sergeant Harry Canning, of the 4th Battalion Rifle Brigade, was sentenced to six months' imprisonment for assisting his wife in an abortion procedure.[51] It is likely that many abortions escaped detection, but this abortion came to the attention of the authorities because Mrs. Canning died of septicaemia as a result of the procedure. Being new to Cairo (Mr. Canning had been in the city for 15 months, while Mrs. Canning only for 3 months) and overwhelmed with the work involved in taking care of two children, one of whom was an invalid, Mrs. Canning desperately did not want any more children. Moreover, Sergeant Canning was facing the prospect of being sent to Khartoum, leaving Mrs. Canning to take care of their children alone. A third child was most unwelcome. When the couple suspected that she might be pregnant, they sought the help of a Greek midwife named Helen Panajotopoulo. The belief at the time was that the abortion procedure would be relatively simple – carried out by applying a little water and cotton wool. After three visits to the midwife, on 11, 12, and 13 May 1911, Mrs. Canning became very ill. For ten days, Mrs. Canning begged Mr. Canning not to call a doctor because they did not want anyone to know about the abortion. But, by 23 May, her condition was so bad that there was no choice but to call Dr. Alexander Morrison,[52] a well-known doctor in the British community in Cairo.[53] Mrs. Canning was rushed to the Deaconesses' Hospital with a severe case of enteric fever, congestion of both lungs, enlarged spleen, a brown and dry tongue, rapid pulse, pain in her right groin, and drowsiness. In the next few days, she vomited most of her foods and medicines, developed severe pains in all her joints, acquired a very high fever and pulse, and became unconscious.[54] She died on the 29 May of septicaemia.[55] Sergeant Canning and the Greek midwife were immediately charged with using 'unlawful...instruments or other means with the intent to procure [a] miscarriage.'[56] Since Sergeant Canning had an excellent service record over a long period of time in the military, the Judge imposed the most lenient sentence he could – six months' imprisonment without any hard labour. Since he was a sergeant in the Army of Occupation, he was not confined in a prison with Egyptians but was sent to the Military Detention Barrack. This practice of keeping apart certain British inmates from Egyptian prisoners reinforced the segregation between Britons and Egyptians. The British Judge Grain hoped that the sentence would not affect Sergeant Canning's future military service or his pension arrangements.[57]

Not only does this incident illustrate the illegality of abortion in the British community in Egypt, but also the dangers involved in procuring abortions. In terms of the appropriate punishment for abortion, this case gives an example of the potential for tough penalties as well as the possibility of leniency depending on one's previous record. Perhaps it also alludes to the difficulty and loneliness experienced by certain British families in a foreign land away from their familiar social network of friends and relatives back in Britain.

Suicide

Before the passing of the Suicide Act of 1961, it was a crime to commit suicide under British law. Anyone who attempted and failed was liable to be prosecuted. The British community in Egypt witnessed its fair share of suicides. Nearly all of these suicides seemed to have been due to an 'unsound' mind – referring to a severe emotional, mental, and psychological crisis. For example, in 1892, Frederick John Barlow, a long-time fitter in the Government Railway shops of Alexandria, shot himself after getting into 'a fit of temporary insanity.'[58] Ten years later, in the same city, Sergeant Martin Doyle of the Leicestershire Regiment, as a result of an unsound mind, threw 'himself under a passing train, the wheels whereof passed over him and crushed him.'[59] In 1905, Dora Blake, a 25 year old domestic servant based in Alexandria, 'not being of sound mind...did kill herself by the administration...of a fatal dose of cocaine.'[60] Jessie Brown, a 26 year-old stewardess of Nile ships, 'being temporarily of an unsound mind...[killed] herself by taking...a dose of poison – carrosine sublimate.'[61] In 1911, Thomas Brown, a chemist in the Egyptian Salt and Soda Co. near Alexandria, committed suicide by shooting himself. His suicide note explained his intentions. 'Between sickness and loneliness my nerves are destroyed and my mind turned... My life in the last few months has been most unhappy, and I can bear it no longer.'[62] His depression was due to having a serious venereal disease.[63] That same year, Mrs. Eugenie Phillips, wife of Alfred William Phillips, an engineer in Alexandria, became psychologically unwell and developed delusions that her husband was being unfaithful to her. As a result, she violently attacked him one night and was eventually admitted to hospital for her illness.[64] Soon thereafter, she 'committed suicide by throwing herself from the top (3rd) floor verandah [sic] of the [Deaconesses'] Hospital while in a state of unsound mind.'[65] Lastly, in Alexandria in 1918, an Anglo-Egyptian Bank employee named Martin, who was the founder of the Alexandria Swimming Club, took his own life because 'his mind had for some...time [become] unhinged.'[66] Major Stowe, who was living with Martin before his death, noticed that Martin 'complained [that] he was being watched and that he was drinking very heavily.'[67] Martin was fearful that he was going to get blamed for stealing £3000 that was despatched from his branch in Alexandria to Zagazig in 1917. This made no sense to Martin's boss, Mr. Blunt, who would never have doubted Martin's honesty in any way. Martin's suicide was due to an unstable mental state characterised by paranoia and fear.

What do all of these suicides and domestic crises say about life in the British community in Egypt? They point to the sadness and depression that existed in the lives of British men and women in Egypt, mainly from the lower middle and lower working classes and from a variety of professions (fitter, sergeant, domestic servant, stewardess, chemist, wife of an engineer, bank official). Underneath the stereotype of being the comparatively prosperous and ruling constituency in Egypt, the British community also consisted of men and women who suffered physically (as in the case of domestic violence), mentally, emotionally, and psychologically.

Social crimes

Assault

Although Lord Cromer referred to the British mission in Egypt as a 'civilising' one, Britons in Egypt were not only guilty of domestic abuse but of assaulting Egyptians and non-Egyptians as well. In 1885, John Alfred Brown, an English engineer, was accused of assaulting an Egyptian named Georgi Zakhoora. Severely beaten, Zakhoora needed five days in hospital thereafter.[68] Months later, Mr. Brown's doctor described him in this way:

> Mr. Brown is a man of a highly nervous excitable temperament and subject to violent fits of temper on the least provocation. These fits of temper amount sometimes to actual frenzy, during which he seems to lose control over himself...On one occasion, I found him...unmanageable in hospital – so violent and noisy that I was obliged to summarily dismiss him.[69]

Brown seemed always drunk as well.[70] In 1901, Scottish professor of Firearms and Shooting, George Fowler, was accused of assaulting an American, Douglas Walcott in Cairo.[71] Five years later, the Cairo Police sued William Houghton (a journalist) and his wife Marguerite for beating an Egyptian Police Sergeant named Mohamed Ibrahim Saafan. They were each fined £5.[72] In 1910, Sidney Alfred Chubb, a foreman carpenter (mentioned in a previous chapter) was found guilty of assaulting Alfred Young, Superior of the Works Department.[73] Though the traditional image of the English 'gentleman' may have been intact in governmental, diplomatic, and business circles, there were nonetheless examples of violent and abusive Britons in occupied Egypt. Also notable was the fact that, at times, Britons were perpetrators of violence against Egyptians and other foreigners in Egypt.

Libel

Valuing credibility in both the private and business spheres, British residents in Egypt fought bitterly against those who sought to damage their reputations. For example, in 1883 in Alexandria, Edwin Barber called Messrs. John Ross and Co., cheats and robbers in front of witnesses with regard to the conduct of Ross' firm. Charles Boyle, Ross' lawyer, directed a statement to Mr. Barber that demanded

> an immediate apology [that] should contain a retraction of the statements made...at [his] expense in...the local papers as my clients may choose. Should no such apology be forthcoming, it will be my duty to advise my clients to take immediate legal proceedings against yourself.[74]

Barber refused to admit his guilt, so Ross took him to court and won – 'the jury having decided in favour of the Plaintiffs and awarded the sum of forty shillings as damages.'[75]

In 1905, John William Congdon, a British merchant accused William Houghton, a journalist in Cairo, of writing 'a false, malicious, defamatory and libellous article...in the..."Egyptian Graphic" thereby holding [Congdon] up to public hatred, contempt and ridicule.'[76] Houghton's article in the *Egyptian Graphic* asserted:

> *I desire to hold up to public hatred and contempt a person named Congdon*, said to be Auctioneer to the Army of Occupation, agent for several British firms of manufacturers and, in short, fully provided with the means of earning an honest competence, and yet who has taken to building houses for mosquitoes, or, at least [in] his advertisement in the 'Egyptian Gazette', – selling them. 'For sale'...this *conscience-less Congdon*...announces, a 'Mosquito house, apply Congdon, Cairo'...*His Britannic Majesty's Consul should see whether or not he is a registered British subject and warn him that between such reprehensible ways of money-making and expulsion there is but a short step.*[77]

In the Supreme Consular Court in Cairo, the 'Plaintiff claimed...for £500 damages for a malicious defamatory and libellous article written by the defendant.'[78] However, the defendant successfully proved that the article entered into the newspaper by accident. According to Houghton, the article was removed from the 'deferred' file into the 'active' file without his knowledge so he had no control over its publication. Congdon duly withdrew the court action against Houghton.[79]

Six years later, Wallace Daniel Hawkes, a merchant and commission agent, sued Charles Coulston Porri, a Wesleyan Methodist minister and a chaplain of the British Army of Occupation in Egypt, for libel. The Plaintiff argues that in 1911, the Defendant

> falsely, wickedly and maliciously spoke and published at Cairo to Herbert Stuart Wilson...his wife, and the wife of the Defendant the following words: He dresses up poor boys in expensive suits of clothes and gives them jewellery and takes them about with him on condition they occupy the same bedroom. [He] is guilty of the same crime as that of Oscar Wilde.[80]

In another letter, not only did Porri accuse Hawke of sodomy, he claimed that Hawkes was engaged in financial wrongdoing as well.

> Hawkes is running away from his creditors...he is not a fit man to associate with, and his character is [the] worst I have ever known. [He] had been guilty of dishonesty in his business and...committed or endeavoured to commit sodomy.[81]

Porri continued to write in yet another letter that Hawkes '[was] in a state of insolvency. His creditors will prevent him leaving the country...[He is] guilty of fraudulent or dishonest dealings in relation to his business.'[82] In response, Hawkes claimed that 'his character and reputation [had] been brought into public hatred and contempt and [he had] also severely suffered in his trade.' He sought £500 in damages. In the end, Rev. Porri, the Defendant, won. The Supreme Consular Court dismissed the case and no payment was made to Mr. Hawkes, the Plaintiff.[83] Although there were other libel cases tried by the Consular Courts in Alexandria and Cairo, these three cases give us a glimpse of the importance of reputation and credibility in the British community in occupied Egypt. Depending on one's perspective, particular libel cases may not have been 'criminal' in nature (since they may have been tried as civil cases) but were certainly representative of an area of misconduct. As for common causes behind libel actions, it appears that being accused of financial misdealing or sexual impropriety provided the most ammunition for taking an accuser to court for libel. It seems that, similar to today, financial and sexual scandals were most likely to damage a person's character and reputation in the British community in Egypt.

Financial Crimes

Financial crime was not unusual in Britain during this period.

> For most of the Victorian period, the English banking system was riddled with fraud and mismanagement. Commercial dishonesty [was]...widespread. By the late nineteenth and early twentieth centuries, improvements in bank management and accountancy had reduced the level of fraud, though by no means had eliminated it.[84]

Given 'the stereotyped image of the respectability of the Victorian... middle class,'[85] it is also noteworthy that financial crimes such as fraud, embezzlement, and theft were increasingly being committed by this group.[86] Similarly, the British community in Egypt was home to con artists, swindlers, and thieves. However, there seems to be little evidence exposing prominent members of the British middle class as perpetrators of financial crimes in Egypt. Rather, it appears that common thieves, a fair number of clerks, a policeman, and a matron of a hospital were guilty of these crimes. Perhaps middle class financial crime among Britons in Egypt went largely unreported. It was far easier for law enforcement bodies to avoid bad publicity and expensive proceedings than it was to pursue lower-class criminals who were already considered threats to the social order.[87] Although by no means exhaustive, the following describes some significant criminals among the Britons in Egypt during the occupation and their related crimes of fraud, embezzlement, theft, and extortion. In light of the close relationship between these crimes, clarification may be needed. Fraud involves deliberate deception or false pretence of some sort. Embezzlement may be a form of fraud, though it refers specifically to the taking of funds that one has been entrusted with. The crime of theft includes embezzlement and may be committed fraudulently or deceptively. In this chapter, the term is used to refer particularly to acts of stealing goods in a manner that is not fraudulent. Extortion, perhaps another form of theft, refers to the deliberate and coercive overcharging of customers and clients for goods or services.

Fraud

According to Consular Court records in Cairo, Charles Helfield was perhaps one of the more daring crooks in the community due to the number of his attempts at fraud over a short period of time. In 1900, Helfield was charged with obtaining money by false pretences at the Grand Continental Hotel in Cairo. He introduced himself to Alfred Petry, the hotel receptionist, as Baron A. Calendu di Tavani and told Petry that he had tried to withdraw money from the bank but it was closed. So Helfield, alias the Baron, asked Petry if he could borrow £7 and return the money to him after dinner on that day. Petry obliged. When Helfield did not return for dinner, Petry got suspicious and went to the train station to see if he could catch Helfield before the departure of the 11pm train to Alexandria. When Petry reached the train station, Helfield saw him and walked to another platform. Petry caught up with Helfield and demanded the payment of the £7. Helfield gave Petry only £4 and insisted falsely that Petry had only lent him £5. Thereafter, Petry took Helfield to the stationmaster and unsuccessfully tried to get the police to arrest Helfield. The police declined since 'there was no warrant and the accused had a ticket in his hand.'[88] While they were waiting, Helfield pulled off 2 rings, threw them at Petry and said, 'Are you satisfied?' And immediately, as the train started to move, Helfield jumped into the last carriage and escaped.[89] Eventually, having been reprimanded later, Helfield received his sentence – 'not exceeding twelve months imprisonment with hard labour.'[90]

After his release from prison a year later, Helfield committed two more similar crimes of obtaining money under false pretences. In August 1901, while at Pension Villa Margherita in Ramleh, Alexandria, Abdul Rahim Khan, along with his cousin Mir Alim Khan, who was ill at the time, met Charles Helfield. Helfield introduced himself as Captain Charles Alexander Hartford of the Royal Army Medical Corps. Helfield, as Hartford, showed interest in Mir Alim's illness and offered to see him as a patient. After giving a brief examination and taking Mir Alim's temperature, Hartford suggested that Mir Alim should be sent to hospital. As the British military doctor at the German Hospital in Alexandria, Helfield told Abdul Rahim Khan that he could easily secure a room for his cousin in the hospital. It was agreed that 'Dr. Hartford' would hire the room and Khan would pay him back. Hartford then went to 'hire' the room and came back to the Pension to tell Khan that the room cost four pounds and ten shillings for a fortnight and that he would return with an ambulance to transport his sick cousin in two days time. The patient, Mir Alim, paid the amount with a cheque and Hartford cashed the cheque at the Pension. Two days later, Hartford did not return and Abdul Rahim Khan went to the hospital to enquire. The hospital authorities told Khan that they did not know Hartford and that no room was booked or paid for. Hartford had also given Captain Vernon Jarvis of the Alexandria Police as reference, but when Khan asked Jarvis about Hartford, Jarvis said he knew nothing of Hartford. With his suspicions aroused, Jarvis sought the help of the Cairo Police and discovered that Dr. Hartford was indeed Charles Helfield, who had just completed a one-year sentence for obtaining money under false pretences.[91]

During that same month, Helfield was busy swindling another victim. By deceiving jeweller Angelo Cerfoglia into believing that he had clients and a new job in Aswan for £10 a month, Helfield was allowed to be Cerfoglia's middleman in August 1901. In other words, as Cerfoglia explained in his deposition in court, 'I gave [Helfield] the jewels as he told me [he] was going to sell them to people who asked him for them. If he had not promised me "employment" I would have never trusted him such an amount.'[92] The jewellery that Helfield received was worth £35 and included two gold watches, a pair of gold earrings, two lady's gold watches, and a diamond ring.[93] Helfield fled with the goods but was eventually arrested and brought to trial. He was sentenced to prison and penal servitude in the Island of Malta for three years.[94]

Similarly, the unemployed John Arthur McLaughlin, a former clerk in the British War Office in Sudan,[95] tried to defraud Rachel Dentes, of probable Italian origin, under false pretences a decade later. In April of 1912, McLaughlin introduced himself to Rachel Dentes and her two sons Morris and Raphael, as someone who 'was earning...£25 per month,...had inherited considerable personal property from his father and mother,...had large savings placed in Credit Foncier Bonds, Panama Bonds and Ottoman Railway Bonds,...and was entirely free of debt.'[96] Consequently, he was able to maintain a wife and family and asked Rachel Dentes for her daughter's hand in marriage. Mrs. Dentes, as a guarantee of the marriage, was required to give McLaughlin a sum of £500 in cash and two months later, gave McLaughlin an additional E£570 in cheques drawn on the Banco di Roma. In reality, McLaughlin earned much less than £25 per month, did not possess any of the savings that he claimed to have, and was in debt to various people. Soon after, Dentes discovered McLaughlin's fraudulent actions, took him to court and sought his immediate divorce from her daughter.[97]

John Hayes, a former British Army sergeant, who was discharged whilst with malaria, was by 1920 a penniless habitual drunk[98] and charged with the crime of obtaining under false pretences goods from Davies Bryan and Co. in Cairo to the value of E£146.14.[99] On 26 November 1920, John Hayes entered Davies Bryan's shop claiming that all his personal effects were stolen whilst he was returning from Khartoum and that he was about to stay for two months in Cairo.[100] He asked for an expensive valise worth E£40, an expensive dressing gown, an overcoat, six neckties, three pairs of gloves, a dozen 'Viyella' shirts, and six pyjamas. Hayes then said that he would take all the items and asked someone from the shop to collect a cheque from him the following day at the Qasr el-Nil Barracks. Since he purchased such a large amount, the shop manager thought it best that one of the shop's employees, Simon Axelrod, accompany Hayes to the Qasr el-Nil Barracks with the purchased items the following morning. Thereafter, the manager expressed his concern that if Hayes paid by cheque, Axelrod may not be able to discern whether Hayes's cheque was false or not in the dark. Hayes, pretending to be insulted, said that he would pay by cash, so the manager allowed Axelrod to accompany Hayes that evening.[101] When Hayes and Axelrod, along with a farash (porter), arrived at the Barracks, Hayes went to the mess room for drinks and urged Axelrod to drink excessively since Hayes planned to flee with the goods once Axelrod became drunk. However, Axelrod refused to drink a lot; whereupon Hayes eventually sneaked outside and told the farash that he had already paid Axelrod (though he had not) and drove off with the goods. After being arrested, Hayes was sentenced for larceny to six months with hard labour in prison.[102]

Embezzlement

A significant number of Britons in Egypt embezzled money from their bosses through false entries of accounts or mishandling of their employers' finances. In 1906, Thomas Frazer Thomson, chief corresponding clerk to Superintending Engineer Thomas Knight Sibbald at the Engineering Department of Thomas Cook & Son Ltd. in Boulaq,[103] embezzled E£267.95 from his employer. Thomson was responsible to seek a payment from Messrs. Cangos and Co. who were contractors to Thomas Cook and Son. After obtaining the cheque from Cangos and Co., he cashed it at the Anglo-Egyptian Bank for the amount of E£267.95.[104] Immediately thereafter, he fled to Port Said where he was arrested, taken to court and charged with embezzlement.[105]

Similarly, two years later, Rainey Munro Ross, a clerk in the Nile Cold Storage Co., embezzled money from his employer by making a series of false entries in the Butcher's Cash Sales Book. On 28 June 1908, he entered 'the amount of 62 okes of mutton meat and bones as having been sold for 60 piastres whereas in truth...[he only] sold...33 okes of meat and bones for 70 piastres.'[106] On 19 August, Ross entered 90 okes of beef and bones that were sold for 140 piastres but in fact, he sold 72 okes for 155 piatres. Further on two occasions in 1908, Ross omitted the recording of certain sales of bones and cuttings. Once, on 13 June, he omitted the sale of 53 okes for 106 piatres; and on 25 July, he omitted the sale of 63 okes for 140 piastres. He was charged with unlawful and wilful intent to defraud.[107] A year later, James Nadrett Jays was also charged with cheating his employer, the Gezira Club in Cairo, by stealing a cheque for E£39.40 and then by 'forging an endorsement of the name of the payee,...converted the...amount to his own use.'[108]

In 1910, in Alexandria, the case of British Constable F. W. Wood was brought to Court. Wood, of the Alexandria City Police, was found to have been 'systematically misappropriating small sums from...various funds...for a period of over three years. On comparing the Bank Balance Sheets with the [account] books, the total amount of his defalcations [amounted to] about E£800.'[109] Since Wood had destroyed old vouchers and documents, only a fraction of the actual misappropriations was traceable. The embezzled funds were found to have originated from a cheque for E£25 paid to the Police Funds by the Municipality of Alexandria, the salary of E£9.480 paid to a police officer on leave, whose power of attorney was held by Wood, and E£10 from Mr. Serelli for the entertainment of the Police Band at his establishment. When he sensed that he would be investigated, Wood arranged for a day's leave of absence and promptly disappeared. It was reported that he may have fled to Italy to join an actress whom he had an affair with whilst she was in Egypt. He was never found in Italy or anywhere else.[110]

Three years later, William Henry Baisty Skaife, chief clerk in the Shipping and Forwarding Department of Thomas Cook and Son Ltd. in Cairo embezzled '£488 [from] the property of Thomas Cook and Son (Egypt) Ltd. [by making] false entries in the accounts and books of the... Firm.'[111] He was subsequently imprisoned for six months.[112] In 1915, John Henry Johnson, a British foreman in the Lighting Department in the Egyptian State Railways and Telegraphs, was charged with having 'embezzled forty tins of petroleum belonging to the State Railways.'[113] He was given a fifty sterling fine.[114] In 1918, Richard Warbrick, son of a washerwoman at St. Anne's (northwest of Manchester) and employed as a clerk in the Cairo office of Alexandria businessman Joseph Smouha,[115] was sued by his employer. Warbrick, brother of the governess for Smouha's children, was initially hired in 1915 to help take care of the children. Later, he started working for Smouha's business at a very low salary of two and half piastres a week and lived in accommodation provided by the firm. Eventually, his salary went up to 10 piastres a week.[116] In September 1918, Smouha found Warbrick in possession of £50 in Bank of England notes and another draft for £10 drawn on the Imperial Ottoman Bank in London. Warbrick declined to tell Smouha how he acquired the funds; so Smouha suspected that Warbrick had taken some of the company's profits and may have even had more money hidden elsewhere.[117] Thus Smouha took Warbrick to court. As a result, the defendant was charged 'with intent to defraud, omit or incur in omitting in or from certain accounts belonging to...Joseph Smouha... with particulars of profits derived from the exchange of gold and other coins, banknotes and other securities.'[118]

Theft

During the second half of the nineteenth century, more than half the crimes in Britain were small-scale thefts and the majority of offenders were men in their teens or early twenties.[119] Michael Ellis may have been a good example of this among Britons in Egypt. According to Consular Court records, he was repeatedly guilty of theft. Born in 1892[120] and son of the owner of S. S. Ellis and Co, Merchants and Contractors,[121] he was taken to court for theft four times in the course of six years. Each crime was committed against members of his immediate family. In 1916, he was found guilty of stealing the 'jewellery of his mother Rebecca Ellis of the value of about £86.'[122] Two years later, 'he did steal, take and carry away from the house of Rebecca Ellis at Zeitoun several goods to the value of £34 on the 12th December 1918.'[123] In February 1921, he forged his brother's signature twice in order to obtain £30 and £40. The first time he was successful; the second time he was refused.[124] In 1922, he was sentenced to three month's imprisonment for stealing two pieces of material used for women's clothing from his wife Esther and then claiming that he had acquired them from a pawn broker so that his wife would give him 180 piastres for the items.[125] Besides theft, Michael Ellis was imprisoned for one month in 1919 (since he could not afford the £5 fine) for 'wearing a British Military Uniform with [the] rank of 2nd Lieut., though he was not entitled to it.'[126] Further, he was guilty of assaulting his wife Esther and throwing her to the ground on 26 February 1920.[127] Characterised by theft, deception, and assault against members of his own immediate family, the story of Michael Ellis offers a glimpse into not only the criminal history of one person but the inner turmoil that occurred within the life of particular families in the British community in Cairo.

Military officers were not immune from committing theft. In 1916, Major Buckland and his wife stole money from the Garden Team account. The Garden Team was a charitable show established to raise money for the medical care of the Bucklands' dying child. Since the Bucklands 'had done a lot [in Alexandria] in the way of theatricals for the troops,'[128] Lady Carnarvon and others set up the Garden Team show to help them. The show failed to bring in substantial funds but its costs were underwritten by Lady Carnarvon for £50. Bewsher, an employee of the National Bank of Egypt, authorised the overdrawing of the Garden Team account by Mr. Buckland, who had promised that he only needed the money for a day or two and then would return it. Buckland fled to the French front and left the overdraft with the National Bank of Egypt.

Although Lady Carnarvon sought to find Buckland in order to recover the money, Bewsher believed that the money was lost forever – especially since Major Buckland knew how to deceive through his years as a stage actor before joining the military.[129]

Extortion

Miss James, the Matron of the Anglo-American Hospital in Cairo, was found to have committed the crime of extortion twice in May 1911. Miss Sturge entered the hospital as a second-class patient at ten shillings a day. When it was time for Miss Sturge to leave, Miss James tried to get her to pay twice the agreed amount – £1 per day. A compromise was reached at 15 shillings a day and Miss Sturge proceeded to pay Miss James in gold. Miss James promptly recorded in the hospital accounts that Miss Sturge had paid only ten shillings a day and kept five shillings to herself. Similarly, Miss Allen also entered the hospital as a second-class patient at 10 shillings a day. When it was time for her to leave, Miss James asked her to pay £1 per day because Miss Allen had stayed in a first class room. Miss Allen protested and said that she should have been informed of this change of payment from the outset but agreed to pay the compromised rate of 15 shillings a day. (There was actually no such thing as first class rooms, the only difference between first and second class patients was the rates that patients paid.) Miss Allen, however, paid by cheque, which made it impossible for Miss James to keep the balance. 'The cheque was passed to the Secretary [of the Hospital] and the excess payment…of five shillings a day…was explained by the Matron…as a donation from Miss Allen for the Hospital.'[130] Three months after committing these crimes, Miss James was suspended from nursing, but was still given six weeks of full pay. Though the British official may have been known for his astute handling of finances, the British community in Cairo and Alexandria also consisted of swindlers, embezzlers, thieves, and extortionists.

Sexual Crimes

Rape

In Britain during this period of time, 'the overwhelming majority of incidents of sexual…violence…took place between people who were directly known to each other.'[131] This was true for Britons in Egypt as well. A British Christian missionary in Alexandria raped his housemaid – one of the few cases of rape committed by a British person recorded in the court records. The missionary was named Job Gammage, a British subject born in England, the manager of the Merchant Sailors' Home in Alexandria and Harbour Missionary of the Church of Scotland. In 1901, Job was convicted for raping Elisa Ann Cuff, his English maid in Alexandria.[132] Gammage was married with children. According to Cuff's testimony in court, Gammage gave her some cough medicine, which had a peculiar taste, just before she went to sleep on the evening of 8 or 9 February 1901. After having slept heavily, she was awakened by Gammage who was in bed with her and in the act of intercourse. Cuff struggled and pushed Gammage off and threatened to tell Mrs. Gammage. Mr. Gammage persuaded Cuff not to do this and assured her that no harm was done. After Gammage left her, Cuff barricaded the bedroom door and went to sleep again. After sometime, she began to develop signs of pregnancy. Having been accused by Cuff for getting her pregnant, Gammage denied any responsibility and threatened her if she attempted to tell anyone. At the same time, Gammage promised to help Cuff if she did not tarnish his name and duly sent her to missionary friends in Jerusalem on his own expense. When her pregnancy became more advanced, Cuff went to Syria where she told her story to missionaries and then to the British Consul. The latter sent her back to Alexandria and soon after arriving, Cuff presented herself to the Consular Court and made a sworn accusation against Gammage. Gammage avoided certain arrest by voluntarily presenting himself to the court. After the birth of Cuff's child on 17 October and a trial in which Cuff's story appeared truthful and consistent amidst Gammage's denials, Edward B. Gould, Consul-General in Alexandria, ruled that Gammage was the child's father. As the father, he would have to pay five shillings per week for the child's maintenance and education until he or she reaches the age of thirteen. Gammage was also ordered to pay Cuff the sum of £2.2s.0d for the expenses related to the birth of the child and the sum of £1.11s.0d for legal costs incurred.[133] Ironically, a British missionary, expected to uphold the highest moral standards, committed rape and then lied to cover it up.

In 1915, Edward James Harran, who worked in Delta Light Railways, was charged with 'feloniously and unlawfully ravish[ing] and carnally know[ing] Sophie Sardani, 14 years old, against her will.'[134] In March 1915, Sophie Sardani had been in the service of the Harran family in Helwan for eight months. One night, while Mrs. Harran was out, Mr. Harran called Sophie into his bedroom and abused her. She wanted to flee but he would not let go of her. When Mrs. Harran returned, Sophie wanted to leave the house. She gathered her things together and left five days later after telling Mrs. Harran what had happened.[135] In her deposition in court, Sophie admitted that Mr. Harran had actually abused her twice but she did not leave the house since he threatened her with death if she left or told anyone what happened.[136] Though Mr. Harran denied any wrongdoing and Mrs. Harran testified that Mr. Harran was never alone with Sophie because she 'did not leave [her] husband alone in the house during that week,'[137] Edward Harran was nonetheless charged and convicted of raping a teenager.

Bigamy

Bertram Ley Roberts, a British subject resident in Alexandria, was charged with bigamy in 1921. He had left his wife Edith in Victoria, British Columbia, Canada, with approximately £1000 in debt (which she was forced to pay), borrowed money from her relatives in England, and refused to contribute to any support for his wife and children.[138] After investigating his whereabouts, Mrs. Roberts' suspicions were confirmed. Mr. Roberts was living with a Greek woman named Angele Venizelos. They had been married in Cairo since 1918.[139] At the urging of Mrs. Robert's lawyer in Canada and the cooperation of the Acting Consul General in Alexandria, criminal proceedings were initiated against Mr. Roberts for bigamy[140] from which he received a sentence of six months' imprisonment with hard labour in Malta.[141] Since it took three years between his second marriage and his conviction, it appears that bigamy may have been difficult to prosecute especially if one's first spouse lived far away in Britain or Canada.

Prostitution

Prostitution in Cairo and Alexandria particularly during World War I posed a serious problem for the British community and the authorities. Although the actual number of British prostitutes and pimps was minimal, the adverse effects of prostitution on British neighbourhoods, soldiers, and the authorities were extensive.

Actual figures on the number of British prostitutes in Egypt are sparse. In a 1914 statistic based on 280 raids on 175 brothels in Cairo, it appears that no British prostitute was found. Along with the 100 Egyptian prostitutes that were arrested, there were 31 Italians, 23 French, 12 Greeks, four Austrians, three Russians, one Romanian, and one Japanese.[142] In another statistic based on a disembarkation of minors in the White Slave trade most likely during the same year, 931 girls were found. Though many of these were of 'local' origins like Greek Orthodox, Syrian Catholics, Maronites, Jews, and Armenian Jews, among them were also 11 Italians, eight French, eight Americans, 16 Austrians, six Germans, three Maltese, two Russians, two Belgians, one Spanish, and seven British.[143] This seems to be one of the few pieces of evidence indicating the number of British prostitutes in Egypt.

Even though there may not have been many British prostitutes, there were Britons running brothels and living off the proceeds of prostitutes. Gordon Ainslie Ness, an ex-lieutenant of the Lancashire Fusiliers, was appointed a constable in the Cairo City Police upon his demobilisation from the army. On 21 October 1921, the Cairo City Police charged him with living on the proceeds of a prostitute named Sophie Moltezaki from 15 March 1921 until 14 April 1921.[144] However, after a trial by jury, he was found not guilty and was deported under Martial Law.[145] Similarly, John Charles Shalders of Cairo, ex-sergeant of the military police, was charged with living on the proceeds of a registered prostitute named Rosa Lieben, a Jewish Russian subject, from 22 August 1920 until 28 October 1921.[146] Like Ness, Shalders was tried in 1922 before a jury, found not guilty, and was subsequently deported. Although Ness and Shalders were both found not guilty in court, their deportation pointed to the method adopted by the courts to rid the British community of Egypt of those engaged in undesirable behaviour and practices. Another former officer, Charles Frederick Boardman, ex-captain of the 3rd Royal Munster Fusiliers, demobilised on 11 October 1920, was charged with assisting in the management of a brothel from sometime after his demobilisation until the summer of 1923. He was tried, sentenced to two months' imprisonment, and later deported.[147]

Although limited in number as prostitutes and pimps, Britons in Egypt were, to a much greater degree, guilty of procuring prostitutes. Though there seems to be little evidence indicating the exact number of British civilian men who procured prostitutes during the time of the occupation, there is some evidence indicating the minimum number of British troops who procured prostitutes during World War I. The Cairo Purification Committee established to improve the welfare and health of British troops during this time published a report in 1916 detailing the number of British military personnel infected with venereal disease (VD). The following table gives a glimpse of the number of British troops in Egypt during the first five months of 1916 and the number who, due to their involvement with prostitutes, were admitted to hospital for VD during those months. The last column suggests the number of troops (out of a thousand) that would contract VD over the course of that year based on the ratio between the number of British troops and those with VD.

Table 5.1: Number and ratio of British troops infected with venereal disease in 1916.[148]

Month (1916)	Actual no. of admissions	No. of British troops	Annual ratio/1000 troops
January	324	126,963	30.6
February	497	173,147	34.4
March	607	160,607	45.2
April	696	155,016	53.2
May	524	145,836	43.2

Based on the above table, it appears that in the first five months of 1916, the number of British servicemen infected with VD was 2,648, which suggests an average of 530 infections per month. Projected on to an entire year, there may be as many as 6,360 men infected with VD. Given that the average number of British troops from the first five months of 1916 is 152,314, the annual ratio per 1000 troops of infected servicemen is 41.8 or 4.18%. Therefore, the minimum number of British troops guilty of procuring prostitutes over the course of 1916 is around 6,360 (the number which contracted VD), which represents approximately 4.18% of the total number of British troops present in Egypt during that year. Of course, there may have been many more British troops who were involved with prostitutes but were fortunate not to have acquired VD. Figures from 1918 indicate that even more soldiers, 4,490 in six months, meaning perhaps 8,980 for the year, acquired VD.[149]

As for how prostitution affected the British community at large, the sheer volume of prostitutes diminished the tranquillity and propriety of certain neighbourhoods inhabited by Britons, Europeans, and locals alike. There were approximately 3,000 registered prostitutes (and many unregistered) in Cairo's red light districts alone.[150] Native prostitutes populated the Waili and Sayeda Zeinab areas and the largest number was situated in the Wassa quarter, known in English as the 'fish market'. European prostitutes were in Wigh el Birka, Clot Bey, and the Ezbekiyya quarter.[151] Inevitably, certain British residents detested the influx of prostitutes in their neighbourhoods. Arthur T. Upson, of the Nile Mission Press, wrote to High Commissioner Allenby, complaining that 'as a British resident, [he was] disgusted at the Military and Civil Police allowing demonstrations from balconies of both low-class and better-class places, to draw in the soldiers by means of "suggestive" signs.'[152] Upson pointed out that naked women were being displayed in the windows overlooking the Russell Soldiers' Home since 1908.[153] He also complained of obscene dancing and processions of prostitutes in front of the Soldiers' Home.[154] Though Upson's perspective comes most likely from his identity as a member of a mission society, other Britons felt similarly. For instance, G. Andrews, resident in the Qasr el-Nil area, expressed his frustration in a petition signed by five other Englishmen to the High Commissioner:

> In the above road [Rue Tashtumar], there are three or four other English families, who likewise endorse what I say below. The road until lately was...very quiet and respectable...and situated in one of the best quarters of the town. Now unfortunately I regret to say it is the reverse. In this road there are houses of ill-fame of the worst kind and the scenes and noises that daily and nightly occur are disgraceful – in fact it is gradually being turned into a second Ezbekieh and the police seem to turn a deaf ear to any complaint. Until the early hours of the morning shouting and singing and quarrelling continue and it is very difficult for the persons round to get proper rest. One house in particular, opposite Cecil House Pension, is a meeting house of the military and others, who come to drink...Sometimes, even in daylight...women, or creatures, display themselves on their balconies in a state of nudity! And being family men, it is not nice for our children to be subjected to such sights...What redress is there? One cannot be continually moving into another house...we the residents both English and others think something must be done.[155]

However, depending on where one lived, the activities of prostitutes were not obviously visible from the street. For Mrs. Anne Moore Charlian, 'she can look directly into certain rooms occupied by these women... from her windows...but she admitted that from the street there was very little, if anything, to be seen that [was] objectionable.'[156]

Not only did British residents appear to resent prostitution at their doorsteps, it was a major headache for the British authorities as well. First, the British-led police forces in Cairo and Alexandria found it almost impossible to drive out prostitutes from their brothels due to the difficulty of acquiring Consular consent to do so.

It was not possible to drive these women out of the houses they have selected as, owing to the Capitulations, the Police cannot act without the consent of the Consulates who invariably refuse their consent to their removal as there was no other quarter to which they could be sent.[157]

Even if Consular consent were obtained, 'judicial delays and inadequacy of penalties [would] hamper [police] action at every turn.'[158] Second, even if the police and medical inspectors were successful in organising weekly medical tests for licensed prostitutes (registered prostitutes who were discovered to be infected would be sent to hospital until cured),[159] a large number of unlicensed prostitutes evaded these tests and thus were not necessarily treated for VD. This posed a very real danger to the health of the troops.[160] For example, during the month of January 1915, 660 of Cairo's registered prostitutes were tested and 103 (15.6 per cent) had gonorrhoea while 57 (8.6 per cent) had syphilis. Out of 1,154 registered native prostitutes, 128 (11 per cent) had gonorrhoea while 85 (7.5 per cent) had syphilis. However, during a 14-month period, in 1915 and 1916, 537 unlicensed prostitutes were arrested in Cairo and 234 (43.5 per cent) – a much higher percentage than the licensed prostitutes – were found to have some form of VD.[161] Hence, a significant number of British troops were most likely infected with VD through unlicensed brothels and prostitutes. Third, soldiers, sympathetic to the work of prostitutes and pimps, often interfered with police action. During police attempts to arrest prostitutes or order them into their houses, soldiers would immediately interfere and prevent the police from taking any action. Further, when pimps were arrested, they would appeal to passing soldiers who would immediately force the police to free them.[162] Eventually, special constables and reinforcements were assigned to arrest pimps and to deal with them severely.[163] In spite of the obstacles, the British authorities fought valiantly and, to some extent, successfully against prostitution and the threat of VD through a strategy of registering prostitutes, regular medical tests of prostitutes and troops,[164] hospitalisation of VD-carrying prostitutes, and arresting pimps. Early evening closing of bars in hotels and clubs along with tight control on the quality of drinks were enforced as well.[165] Though British prostitutes and pimps were few in number, a large number of British troops procured prostitutes during the First World War. As a result, the British community and authorities were locked in a serious battle against venereal disease, increasingly distasteful neighbourhoods, and unruly soldiers in support of prostitution.

Conclusion

Historical writing tends to present the British in Egypt as middle class, law-abiding citizens largely within the civil and military services. However, certain private papers, government correspondences, business and church archives, and primarily court records demonstrate that Britons in Egypt engaged in crime and professional misconduct. In other words, apart from the honest and gentlemanly typecast of the British in Egypt, there were those who were guilty of violent assault, seditious libel, professional negligence, fraud, embezzlement, theft, extortion, living off the proceeds of prostitutes, and procuring prostitutes. Even a British missionary, sent to Egypt to live an exemplary life, was guilty of rape and subsequent deception in covering up his tracks. Beyond the stereotype of hotel-hopping, party-going, ballroom dancing, 'Gezira-clubbing' upper middle class dinner guests of the Consul-General, there were Britons in Egypt struggling with domestic violence, alcoholism, unemployment, and severe depression that led to suicide. Examining the diverse array of crimes and criminals among Egypt's Britons contributes to an important goal of this book, which is to draw attention to their diversity and to previously underemphasised aspects in their historiography.

A short discussion on the causes and implications of crime may add to this analysis. First, what may have caused Britons in Egypt to commit these crimes? Were there common situations or problems that encouraged criminal behaviour? The evidence seems to suggest that unemployment and alcoholism tended to provide conditions for violent crimes while personal economic struggle encouraged financial crimes. Restlessness from inactivity offered an environment for British soldiers to procure or profit from prostitutes. Yet, regardless of their situation or financial status, certain Britons of almost every profession or sector of society – factory workers, technicians, engineers, dentists, doctors, teachers, lawyers, bank officials, businessmen, missionaries, and military personnel, were guilty of crime and misconduct.

Second, did crime and misconduct shed light on the ethnic boundaries that existed in Egypt at that time? Besides committing crime against fellow Britons, the court records show that certain Britons carried out fraud and rape against other foreigners, assaulted Egyptians and Americans, and lived off the proceeds of foreign prostitutes. Unlike the general segregation that existed between Britons and non-Britons in Egypt, it appears that some Britons were not shy to interact with members of other ethnic groups when it came to violence and unlawful financial or sexual gain.

Third, what impact did crime and misconduct have on the reputation of Egypt's British community among Egyptians, especially in a predominantly Islamic environment, and other expatriates? The contradiction between the realities of crime and Britain's civilising mission and image clearly pointed to Britain's hypocrisy. Not surprisingly, Egyptians were not impressed with the crime and misconduct committed by Britons in Egypt. For example, the British troops' unruly behaviour during the war 'added to [the] indignation and accelerated [the] alienation…[of] the native town-dwellers…from the protecting power.'[166] What may have angered Egyptians even more was the system that protected British and other foreign culprits. The Capitulations were

> consistently abused by certain foreigners in connection with drug-smuggling, the drink trade, prostitution, and gambling houses. Virtual immunity from domiciliary search and the leniency of many consular courts meant that these…activities could often be carried on by foreigners with comparative immunity and at considerable profit.[167]

British criminal activities and their frequent escape from justice (with no or little penalties) combined with the harsh punishment that Egyptians received at the hands of the authorities, as demonstrated in the Denshawai incident,[168] seems likely to have contributed to the rise in Egyptian nationalist sentiments. Understandably, nationalist writers such as Mustafa Kamil lost 'no opportunity throughout [his] work to vent his distrust, even hatred, of the British.'[169]

6

THE FIRST WORLD WAR

The story is well known. Nationalism, militarism, and colonial jostling plunged the European powers into the First World War (known at the time as the Great War). On 28 June 1914, six weeks after the assassination of the Austro-Hungarian Empire's heir to the throne Archduke Ferdinand, Germany and Austria declared war on Russia and France and invaded Luxembourg and Belgium, provoking Britain's entry into the war. By November, Turkey was also drawn into combat against Britain, France, and Russia. The War lasted four long years causing untold tragedy to millions and altering the political and economic landscape of significant parts of Europe and the Middle East.

Although primarily fought on European soil, the sheer scale of the war engulfed other nations. Egypt was no exception due to the Suez Canal's vital role in the transport, trade, and communications of Britain's empire. The security of the Canal was paramount for the smooth passage of British ships, supplies, and troops from the Empire to the European front. Since the Ottoman Empire had allied itself with Germany and Egypt, by 1914, was still officially Ottoman territory, the British Government moved quickly to dismantle Ottoman influence in Egypt and to protect the Suez Canal. First, the British military in Egypt announced that it had assumed total control of the country and implemented 'martial law [which] empowered the General in command to issue proclamations with the force of law...without consent of the Capitulatory powers.'[1] Second, on 17 December 1914, Britain declared Egypt an official Protectorate, formally terminating the Ottoman Empire's suzerainty over Egypt and any ambiguity that Egypt was still 'enemy' property – though it did not annex Egypt outright (as a colony) due to fears of nationalist backlash.[2] The following day, the pro-Turkish Khedive Abbas II Hilmi was deposed by the British administration and Hussein Kamil Pasha, Khedive Ismail's pro-British son, was appointed Sultan over Egypt. 'Sultan', rather than 'khedive', was the new title given to mark the new 'independence' of Egypt from the Ottoman Empire. Moreover, the supreme British representative in Egypt was upgraded from Consul-General (implying only a mere agent of only one of many 'consulates') to High Commissioner.[3] Third, to combat the threat of a Turkish invasion of the Suez Canal, troops were sent to Egypt and the Suez region to repel potential attacks. As it turned out, British troops faced only one direct threat to the Suez Canal, in February 1915, and they successfully repelled the Ottoman aggression. Thereafter, Britain's strategic attention in Egypt turned to the dangers of enemy submarines in the Mediterranean and the eventual campaign to capture Ottoman territory in Palestine, Syria, and Lebanon.[4]

This chapter and the next aim to chronicle the responses of Egypt's British community during two periods of crisis – the First World War and the revolutionary period of 1919–22. In line with a central aim of this book to demonstrate the diversity among the British in Egypt, this chapter centres on the differing responses and responsibilities of British men and women in Egypt during the war followed by the various activities that rallied the community's involvement to serve the war effort. The divergence within the community is also evident in the conflicting views that certain members of the British community had about official government policies of the time. Lastly, it discusses the various economic effects brought about by the war for Britons in Egypt in the context of the economic struggles that many Egyptians faced as a result of the war. Since there seems to be little written on the British community in Egypt during the First World War, it is hoped that this will add to the historiography of British imperialism and of Egypt.

Before launching into the crux of this account of the British in Egypt during the First World War, it may help to mention the demographic challenge of determining the exact population of Egypt's British community at this time. According to the 1917 census, there were about 3200 Britons from Britain in Cairo, a slightly smaller number in Alexandria, and around 9000 in all of Egypt.[5] As mentioned in chapter 1, military personnel were not accounted for in the 1917 census, most likely because of their temporarily status and their enormous number in Egypt at the time. As one statistic suggests, by the end of the war, there may have been as many as 400,000 troops under Britain's imperial[6] command in Egypt, though not all were in Egypt at any one time[7] and not all were ethnically British (many were from countries under Britain's colonial tutelage, such as India). The problem of ascertaining the exact number of Britons in Egypt during the war is due to the fact that many of the newly arrived British troops and nurses became part of the community of longer-term British residents. This group of British military and support personnel were new to Egypt because the troops that were in Egypt prior to the war had almost all been sent to fight in Europe. A fair number of British officers participated in balls, dances, and events and became prominent members of Egypt's British community. The lower class rank and file, though excluded from the high society events, attended British church services and were regularly invited into homes of British residents. Since the community included British civilians and new military and support personnel, simply narrowing the British population to around 3000 in Cairo and a total of 9000 in Egypt may not be the most precise depiction of community's size. Though it may not be possible to determine the exact population of the British community at this time, it is possible, from private diaries and memoirs, newspaper archives, and other records, to observe the community's roles, activities, viewpoints, and economic challenges.

Deployment of British Men

In 1914, there were two British-led armies in Egypt – the Army of Occupation headquartered in Cairo, led by Major-General J. H. C. Byng, and the Egyptian Army, based in various posts in Egypt, the Sinai, and the Sudan, led by General Sir Reginald Wingate. The 5000 soldiers in the Army of Occupation consisted of mostly Britons from Britain, except for one Indian mounted battery,[8] and occupied the Qasr el-Nil barracks and the cantonments in Abbassiyya and in Mustapha, northeast of Alexandria. The Egyptian Army consisted mainly of Egyptians but was led primarily by British officers. However, after the declaration of war, almost every regiment of the Army of Occupation withdrew from Egypt and returned to Britain to fight in Europe since they were already well trained and ready for battle. British officers of the Egyptian Army joined the war effort in Europe as well, though the bulk of the Egyptian Army's rank and file remained at their posts.[9] This sudden exodus of British military personnel affected the British community in Egypt. Many of these officers had regularly attended the British churches, participated in British sporting and recreational activities, and frequented the clubs and hotel dances of Cairo and Alexandria during the winter season. Perhaps more painfully for their families, the hurried withdrawal of these troops meant that their families were abandoned in Egypt, and left to wait for their return to Britain. One British soldier, who came to Egypt to replace the departed forces, recorded that the families of these men who were now fighting in Europe

> were left behind here...There were 15 or 20 English folk... mostly wives of the Northamptons (We relieved the Northampton Regiment)...[These] married women and children still occupy a large section of the barracks, and that is why some of us are in tents...[one family] takes up quarters that accommodate 19 of our fellows.[10]

For British men in Egypt who were not part of the Army of Occupation or the Egyptian Army and were eligible to fight, they were urged to join the war effort. After Britain declared war on Germany, Lord Kitchener, who left his post as the British Consul-General of Egypt to become the Secretary of State for War, issued a call for 100,000 new soldiers to reinforce the 200,000 already in the regular army.[11] Initially, only British men with previous military experience or who were 'athletic and well-educated English gentlemen'[12] from public schools were encouraged to participate in the war effort. Many of them volunteered because 'theirs was an interest well worth protecting.'[13] The British upper and middle classes, whether made rich by inheritance, London-based commerce, or manufacturing in the North of England, accumulated vast amounts of wealth during the last decades of the nineteenth century through the booming export trade and overseas investments.[14] Since many of the men in Egypt's British community belonged to the privileged classes, their volunteering for the war effort was natural and immediate. Defeat at the hands of Germany not only threatened the Empire but their wealth and livelihoods as well. Besides economic concerns, a sense of urgency, securing the well being of their families, and the nationalistic fervour of the time motivated them. One appeal for British volunteers articulated the importance of this victory.

> Not only the future of England, or of the British Empire or even of Europe, but that of practically the whole world will be affected by this great struggle, and in these circumstances the man who is considering how he can afford his passage money home or what his employers or his family are to do without him should preserve some sense of proportions, and should also bear in mind that, if

the Germans win, his firm may shortly find itself unable to pay his salary and his family may fall into the hands of the most blackguardly soldiering that has disgraced the civilised world for centuries past; the Germans have their eye on Egypt...They will not win, they cannot;...there are very few Englishmen worthy of the name who will hang back from the fighting line if it is at all possible for them to get to it...England is more important than any of her sons.[15]

However needed was their victory over the Germans, some Britons were not willing to join the war at all costs. Upon Britain's entry into the war, the British government in Egypt did not publicly acknowledge that it would facilitate the volunteering of British government officials by retaining their jobs and giving them paid leave. As a result, many aspiring volunteers did not join the war effort at the risk of losing their jobs. They also kept quiet in fear of embarrassing the government by highlighting its lack of commitment to the war evident in its unwillingness to guarantee their jobs. Finally, two months after Britain's declaration of war, 'the announcement that the Egyptian Government [had] decided to grant leave to Anglo-Egyptian officials who wish to join the British army and will keep their posts open for them...led to...a rush of volunteers from Egypt.'[16] Moreover, they were given a full paid leave of between three and a half months to six months.[17]

Besides the government's delay in providing paid leave and job guarantees to its employees, another financial factor hindered the initial deployment of British volunteers from Egypt to the war in Europe. A small number of these willing volunteers could not afford the passage home to Britain and initially, 'no steps [were being] taken...by the British community'[18] in Egypt to help. Unlike the British community in Constantinople that provided a travel fund and an additional allowance for young men to return from Turkey to Britain to fight in the war, the British community in Egypt did nothing.[19] Although the military authorities granted a successful applicant third class passage from Egypt to Britain, there was initially no concerted effort by Egypt's British community to financially assist poorer volunteers with immediate transportation to Europe's battlefields. However, by the summer of 1915, Mr. Birley, acting President of the British Chamber of Commerce, announced that if there was 'anyone unable to get free passage home from the Government or get accepted by the Army',[20] he and the Chamber of Commerce would make sure that there was funding for that person.

With the promise of paid leave and jobs at the end of the war for government officials and funding for the passage to Europe for all willing volunteers, many Britons in Egypt joined the battlefront in Europe. They were from a diverse array of 'Government services,...banks, and other commercial undertakings.'[21] For example, Mr. Willoughby of the Alexandria City Police; Mr. P. Sutton Page of the *Egyptian Gazette*; Mr. Thomas Henry Warwick and Mr. Douglas Charles Warwick, sons of H. S. Warwick of Cairo; Mr. Cooper, Director-General of the Blue Nile Barrage Projects; Mr. J. H. Scott of the Egyptian Law School; Mr. Stevenson, son of the Director-General of the Telephone Company; A. G. Mitchell, E. A. W. Plumptre and T. P. Williams of the Ministry of Education; and Mr. McCoughlin along with twenty four others joined the war effort from the Public Works Department. From the banking sector, eighteen from the staff of the National Bank of Egypt joined British military in Europe.[22] Others joined from the Anglo-Egyptian Bank, greatly reducing the number of its British staff, as expressed here in a letter by the bank's interim manager in Alexandria to his manager in London.

Cairns has gone to the Dardanelles as 1st Lieutenant...Our English staff is much reduced, and we have nobody available to replace any of the men at the agencies, should any of them go sick. But I suppose that you cannot send us anyone and that we must rub on as best we can. Birch from Khartoum is in Alexandria at present and I gather that he rather wants too to join the army.[23]

Other volunteers included members of the British Rifle Club in Egypt[24] and Church Missionary Society missionaries such as Rev. W. W. Cash, Rev. R. F. Neale, and Rev. A. J. Mortimore, who became chaplains.[25] Altogether, several hundred Britons joined the British military from Egypt.[26]

How about the Britons who were not eligible to fight in the war? British men who wanted to join the war effort but were beyond military age or who were indispensable in their employment in Egypt created a small military unit named Pharaoh's Foot. They believed that there was something very indecent about British men in Egypt hurrying daily to a club to play purposeless games while their compatriots were engaged in a life-and-death struggle in Europe. The unit aimed to assist the existing forces under the supervision of General Maxwell. They modelled themselves after the Special Constabulary Force in Britain that was also founded by patriotic men who were hindered by business commitments, age, or other reasons from joining the military. The Force helped to provide police services during the war since many policemen, being ex-soldiers, were called into the Army. Since the Egyptian police was already providing an adequate service, the Pharaoh's Foot became another military regiment. However, they were not given any weapons since the regular army were already short on rifles and General Maxwell wanted to wait and see whether their early voluntary enthusiasm would survive the drudgery of monotonous drills and living in barracks. As Maxwell anticipated, many well-to-do middle-aged men and senior government officials of Egypt's British community refused to join the Pharaoh's Foot. They refused to march without arms and face the ridicule and peremptory commands of younger sergeants, and presumed that the daily discipline and drilling of army life were below their dignity. Yet others did join the Pharaoh's Foot and patriotically marched and drilled regularly until the end of 1915 when a volunteer military unit in Egypt became unnecessary due to the mass influx of troops by that time.[27]

Why conscription of British men in Egypt was unnecessary

Besides the Pharaoh's Foot, there were many volunteers who were accepted and dispatched to various battlefields in the earlier stages of the war both in Britain and in British territories. However, there was still a need for conscription in Britain. The Military Service Act, passed in January 1916, conscripted all single men and childless widowers aged 18 to 41 in Britain. Later, the Military Service Act passed in May 1916 conscripted all men aged 18 to 41. By July 1917, the Military Services Act (Conventions and Allied States) was passed allowing the drafting of British subjects living abroad and of Allied citizens in Britain. By April 1918, still more soldiers were needed, so men between the ages of 41 to 50 were conscripted in Britain.[28] But as far as the British community in Egypt was concerned, conscription was never applied though the British government did consider it. In 1916, when the need for British soldiers was increasing, the General Officer Commanding in Chief in Egypt published a demand for an urgent census that indicated Britain's consideration of the question of conscription in Egypt. The military order required that all the male British subjects in Egypt from age 18 to 41 were obliged to answer questions regarding their name, address, profession, health condition, marital status, language skills, qualifications, and willingness to serve in the military free of pay or not.[29]

Besides the British military considering whether British men in Egypt should be conscripted from the results of this survey, British parliamentarians also pursued the question of whether Britons in Egypt should be drafted towards the end of the war. During a parliamentary debate in June 1918, Major Earl Winterburn asked Under-Secretary of State for Foreign Affairs Lord R. Cecil,

> if he is aware that there are large numbers of civilians of British... nationality in Egypt and the Sudan of military age; and if steps can be taken...to impose conscription upon all such persons...subject to the safeguarding of the efficiency of the Egyptian Civil Service and Egyptian industries.[30]

However, Earl Winterburn was mistaken. There were actually very few British men in Egypt of military age. A letter from the Judicial Adviser Amos stated that according to the 1917 census, the total number of male British subjects (including men of Maltese, Greek, and Indian descent) between the ages of 20 to 49 was around 3000. Even if they were all conscripted, the number was still relatively small compared to the multitude of men needed at the time.[31] However, the attitude of the time was that if conscription was ever 'applied to British subjects in Egypt, it would no doubt be limited to Englishmen.'[32] British subjects of non-British descent were exempt. This meant that only 840 men of military age with British parentage were eligible for conscription but many were indispensable in the civil service or were medically unfit to fight, leaving only about 200 men suitable for conscription.[33] The

> authorities [eventually]...ordered all British subjects of military age to record their names at the Consulate...[as] a precautionary measure in case the information is asked for later on from England... *There are so few genuine Englishmen here of military age* who are not doing indispensable work of some sort that anything like general conscription seems very unlikely.[34]

Since the 'number of British subjects remaining...in Egypt...who...could be obtained for military service by the adoption of such a measure, [was] insignificant, [it] would not justify the passing of special legislation and the setting up of the necessary administrative machinery.'[35] Not only was conscription of British subjects in Egypt not worth the logistic effort, it would have, in the view of the British Government, signalled its weakness and desperation to the Egyptian nationalists. This disadvantage would have appeared to outweigh any advantage gained by the conscription of a few hundred men.[36]

British men who stayed in Egypt

After Eldon Gorst became Consul-General in 1907, more opportunities were given to Egyptians in government jobs, yet certain Britons were still indispensable to the civil service. The government struggled to reconcile the requests of male staff to join the war effort 'with the imperative necessities of administration, and to hold the balance as evenly as possible.'[37] Also, certain businesses like the Anglo-Egyptian bank prevented specific personnel from joining the war effort in order to maintain its viability, as expressed by the bank's interim manager with his superior in London.

> Murray and Birch have been disputing as to which of the two has the prior right to go – I have told Birch that *he cannot possibly be spared* and I think he now understands this…As regards Moulson if you particularly wish him to go to Khartoum we will arrange to send him but we shall absolutely need someone to replace him. He is the *only* English man left on our staff, apart from the Chief Accountant and Cashier…The military work is now so heavy that we have had to re-open the Bank in the afternoons and return to winter hours – so please don't think we have nothing to do in Alexandria.[38]

Though conscription was never carried out in Egypt, the 1917 Military Services Act made it possible for British men between 18 and 41 living abroad to be drafted. As a result, indispensable employees of government departments and other businesses had to be issued with consular certificates in order for them to be exempt from the draft. This exception was allowed only if their

> retention in the country in which they are at present…[is] considered of greater advantage to the common cause and to British commercial interests [according to]…His Majesty's Consular officers…He

should remain in the above employment until instructions to the contrary are issued by His Majesty's Government...A change of employment must be at once reported...This certificate may be reviewed or withdrawn at any time.[39]

Despite this exemption, there was still a significant shortage of British workers in Egypt due to the many who had left to join the war effort. For example, the Ministry of Education was left desperately low on teaching staff since 'about fifty per cent of the English staff...served in His Majesty's forces. Most...were teachers in secondary schools.'[40] Further, 'to fill the places of those who left, Egyptians were appointed to teach English in the lower forms and a few Englishmen were found locally... [and] were for the most part...exceedingly poor.'[41] The anxious search for staff was expressed in Education Adviser Douglas Dunlop's appeal to High Commissioner Wingate for more passports for teachers from Britain to enter Egypt and also in his pursuit of a 53 year old teacher, named Charles Ashbee, who was beyond the age of military service.[42] This desperate hiring, as mentioned in the previous chapter, later turned out to be a grave mistake in Dunlop's view.

Besides the Ministry of Education, the Alexandria City Police was 'anxious to enlist Englishmen...owing to vacancies caused by the war,'[43] as immediate replacements. The Church Missionary Society also lost key missionaries particularly to military chaplaincies and 'these sacrifices, willingly made,...were heavy enough considering [their] none too great strength before the war.'[44] Moreover, with the potential changes in the mixed courts due to the possible abolition or downgrading of the Capitulations in light of Egypt's new identity as a British Protectorate, it was

> necessary to recruit more English lawyers...[However the Judicial Adviser Malcolm McIllwraith] scarcely knew how [he] could get men...during the war [since] nearly all the best of the younger men are away from their work and in [a military] camp, somewhere or other.[45]

In spite of the effort to retain as many key workers as possible, the war severely crippled the British workforce in Egypt and created job vacancies in many different sectors.

The Roles of British Women

Like the men, British women had various roles during the war as well. Although women did not engage in combat, they were instrumental as volunteer nurses, hostesses, and organisers of events to help convalescing or restless soldiers pass their days in Egypt.

The Gallipoli campaign

In order to understand the significance of the work that the British women in Egypt did during the war, it is important to realise the enormity of the task that they faced as the casualties from the Gallipoli defeat inundated Egypt. Much has been written about this failed Allied effort. It is suffice to say here that the military advance on the Gallipoli peninsula was an attempt to divert Turkish pressure on the Russians in the Caucasus, move beyond the stalemate of trench warfare in the European front, and open a supply route through the Dardanelles Straits into the Black Sea to aid Russia against Germany and the Austro-Hungarian Empire. The Allies assumed that a victory at Gallipoli would increase momentum and morale. During the first half of 1915, Allied forces – including Britons, Canadians, Australians, New Zealanders, and Frenchmen – stormed the Turkish defences along the Dardanelles. After an initial setback of losing six battleships against an Ottoman division that was extremely low on resources, the Allies allowed a month's time to pass in March 1915 before striking again. By this time, the Ottoman command had sent fresh men, equipment, and supplies to the region and in the following months, the 'hastily planned, ill-coordinated, inadequately supplied, and badly led'[46] Allied campaign at Gallipoli was crushed. Casualties on both sides were staggering. The Ottoman casualties amounted to more than 250,000.[47] Out of the 500,000 men in the Allied force,[48] 45,000 Britons lost their lives.[49] More than 150,000 were wounded or captured. Many of the 90,000 sick and injured were evacuated by ship to Alexandria, turning Egypt into one vast hospital and rallying many of the women of Egypt's British community to active charitable service.

Egypt as one big hospital

The Gallipoli casualties meant that Cairo and Alexandria became key centres for receiving ill or injured imperial soldiers.

> Few places presented greater facilities than Cairo and Alexandria for establishing hospitals in suitable buildings, and it was fortunate

that this was so, as otherwise hospitals would have had to be pitched under canvas, exposed to the sand and dust of the desert, as was the experience in Sinai and Palestine.[50]

The requisition of buildings for hospital usage increased exponentially as the Gallipoli struggle raged on during 1915. In April 1915, only 200 beds were available for British officers while 3,780 were available for men of lower ranks in all of Egypt. By January 1916, there were 870 beds available for officers and 32, 262 beds available for those in lower ranks.[51] A similar pattern of growth occurred for the facilities available to Indian soldiers as well.[52] These hospitals were established in existing hospital buildings, hotels, and schools. They were equipped with general hospital equipment. Other improvised hospitals were also established with bedsteads made of palm wood and mattresses stuffed with wool.[53]

A mass programme of requisition took place in Egypt to alter existing buildings into hospitals. In Cairo, Princess Fatima's Palace in Boulaq was made into a hospital for 500 to 600 British convalescents.[54] The old palace of the Citadel was transformed into a hospital of 543 beds.[55] A gentleman's college was transformed into the Nasriyya Hospital for Officers.[56] The German Agency in Garden City became the Red Cross Hospital.[57] Large and recently built Egyptian government schools such as those in Abbassiyya became hospitals, such as the Number 15 Hospital. Number 19 Hospital was in the Deaconess Hospital and Number 21 was at the Ras el-Tin barracks.[58] In Heliopolis, Lady Beatrice Rochdale recalls that a new and luxurious Heliopolis Palace Hotel, made with marble steps and pillars and brass fittings had

> hardly ever been used and [was] now taken as a hospital…It was like a palace…in fairy tales. One expected people in dazzling robes to be carrying gilt trays of lovely fruit about, but there were only a few hospital nurses and a few sick men in bed…It will take so many people to keep the place clean.[59]

Hospitals that were already in place were expanded or transferred to other buildings. The Number 2 Australian Hospital moved from the Mena Hotel to the Gezira Palace Hotel and increased to a capacity of 1000 beds. The Austrian Hospital in Shubra was taken over for the treatment of infectious diseases. Other existing hospitals were prepared to receive extra patients such as the Egyptian Government Hospital at Qasr el-Aini. Further from the heart of Cairo, the al-Hayat Hotel in Helwan and the Mena Palace Hotel in Giza, used as an overflow hospital, were requisitioned as well.[60] Certain hotels like the Shepheard's Hotel and the Continental were not taken over for military purposes and became focal points of dances, dinners, and parties for officers.[61]

In Alexandria, the Egyptian Government Hospital was placed on alert. The British Red Cross supplied the hospital ships entering Alexandria with food and comfort items. Three convalescent homes for officers with a total of 125 beds were established in Alexandria. In Montazah, just east of Alexandria, a hospital for non-commissioned officers and ordinary soldiers was set up with 1000 to 1400 beds.[62] Throughout the country, the British Red Cross established 13 auxiliary hospitals[63] and the Public Health Department set up tent hospitals as well.[64] As 'transport followed transport, each filled to overflowing with mangled humanity,'[65] the military authorities in Egypt were trying desperately to transform nearly all suitable buildings into hospitals, acquire the services of existing hospitals, maximise the number of beds for the patients, and mobilise personnel to care for them. Egypt had truly 'now become one vast hospital'.[66] Though initially, 'it was evident that the estimated accommodation in Egypt for the sick and wounded off Gallipoli was far short of the actual requirements...in time, every wounded soldier had a bed.'[67]

Hospitals and hospitality:
British women as volunteers, nurses, and hostesses

Not only were the sick and injured from Gallipoli given hospital beds, they were taken care of by many of the women of the British community in Egypt. These volunteers followed the pattern of British women in Britain who joined the Voluntary Aid Detachments (VAD) and had to finance their own way through courses and exams on nursing, first aid, and hygiene. They funded themselves through the period of training in hospitals and were eventually paid only £20 per year – even less than some house servants who were paid, on average, £25 to £30 a year.[68] They learned to cram stretchers into makeshift wards; build successful rest stations; convert railway trucks into storehouses, packing-cases into furniture, and condensed milk cans into mugs; and supply endless drinks and cigarettes to the dying, wounded, and ill British soldier.[69] Likewise, the British women of Egypt who volunteered and formed Egypt's VAD in the wake of the Gallipoli campaign also demonstrated this level of initiative and dedication but were unable to cope as the large numbers of the dying, wounded and ill flooded into Egypt from the Gallipoli in the summer of 1915. The need to recruit more women was clearly evident.

When the terrible and unexpected Gallipoli casualties began to be brought back to Egypt, week by week...[the] Colonial and Voluntary Aid Detachment nurses...were far from proving sufficient. The requirements of the situation had, therefore, to be met by voluntary recruitment among the ladies of Cairo, Alexandria, and other towns and chiefly among the wives and daughters of the official and business classes. And most devotedly and whole-heartedly were these appeals to their patriotism and spirit of self-sacrifice responded to, though many of these ladies had plenty of domestic occupation at home.[70]

As a result of these appeals, more women of the British community in Egypt, mainly from Cairo and Alexandria, increased the ranks of the VAD to about 1000 volunteers. Since military doctors were already overwhelmed with clinical and surgical duties, the women in the VAD were responsible for minor medical and non-medical needs of the patients from Gallipoli.[71] Instruction in Cairo and other centres was given to teach the art of bandaging and other elements of first aid. Many women, after a few weeks, became fairly proficient. Non-medical tasks included 'making beds, and serving in overheated canteens';[72] cooking, preparing snacks and afternoon tea in the hospitals; and handing out cigarettes, writing paper, envelopes, pencils, handkerchiefs, books, pillows, and walking sticks from hospital comfort stores which were managed by the British women volunteers.[73] An example of someone who provided non-medical help in 1915 was shipping merchant Harry Barker's wife, Lena, who 'went round the hospitals to visit the blind, and in several cases had the hard task of breaking the news to the men that they would never see again.'[74] Also 'when organizational breakdowns...prevented the patients from receiving petty luxuries like picture-postcards and cigarettes, or basic necessities like razors, toothbrushes, and clean clothes, the...Englishwomen helped to supply the deficiencies.'[75] Outside the hospitals, the women worked in tea kiosks on the quays, met the ships bringing in the sick and wounded from Gallipoli, and, like shipping magnate Harry Barker's fourteen year old daughter Beryl, went 'to the Docks at weekends to hand out tea and sandwiches to the men coming off the transport ships,'[76] and assisted in hospital trains between Alexandria and Cairo. They provided 'tea and recreation rooms, entertainment, games, [and] literature,'[77] organised tram rides provided outings for 6000 patients each month in Alexandria,[78] and helped to trace the whereabouts of missing soldiers from Gallipoli.[79] In their mission 'to assist in alleviating as much as possible the suffering of the sick and wounded, and to assist the authorities in promoting the [soldier's] wellbeing,'[80] the British women of Egypt served admirably and tirelessly.

Besides their hard work in the hospitals, British women were also indispensable in offering hospitality in their homes. In addition to the injured soldiers in hospitals, as many as 84,000 to 152,000 imperial troops were also assembled in Egypt during the war waiting to be deployed to the battlefront.[81] The first contingent of troops from Australia and New Zealand totalled 39,000 and the East Lancashire Territorials plus the Indian Army made the total count of troops around 84,000. By January 1916, after the final evacuation at Gallipoli, more than 64,000 troops from Australia and New Zealand were added, making the total force in Egypt about 150,000 strong.[82] Since there were so many idle soldiers in Egypt, hospitality was desperately needed and a fair number of British homes obliged. Some families strongly encouraged church attendance as well. For example, Mrs. G. M. A. Horsford's memoirs record the weekly Sunday dinners that were organised for a few soldiers at her childhood home in Cairo. Her eventual husband 'W. H. Horsford became one of the many wartime soldiers who were made welcome in [her] home and who were regular visitors on Sunday afternoons and evenings.'[83] Those who visited for dinner were rigorously urged to attend church too.

> There was one stipulation, whatever their denomination, if any, they were expected to go to church. This meant a long journey back into the town and then up again to the Citadel on time for 8 o'clock dinner. For many of them, these visits were their only touch of home life.[84]

Besides Sunday dinners, some British women entertained soldiers to tea or organised parties for them at the Continental Hotel or garden clubs near Qasr el-Aini.[85] Other women opened their homes for convalescent soldiers.[86] Though Australian troops 'had few opportunities to enjoy private hospitality or develop personal contacts with [British] civilians,'[87] as British homes were more likely to welcome British officers, many British families did provide hospitality for the Australians. One Australian drew 'attention to the graceful way in which the kindness...[and] hospitality [were] given' by the British in Egypt.[88] Another Australian soldier praised 'the splendid work for the soldiers'[89] carried out by the British community as a whole. This effort to host imperial soldiers followed a pattern established in Britain where 'with every inch of space taken up and with thousands of men sleeping in the open...private citizens [helped] in housing the overflow of recruits.'[90] For example, many servicemen passed through Preston, an important railway junction, and slept in gardens and accepted breakfasts in private homes.

When the weather deteriorated, the people of Preston welcomed soldiers into their homes, transformed schools and clubs into dormitories and provided entertainment...and hotpot suppers for the men. *These gestures were repeated in towns and cities throughout the country.*[91]

Although men were involved, British women were instrumental in the task of caring, catering, and providing hospitality for the troops both in Britain and overseas.

British Men and Women in High Society

However, were British men confined to the battlefield, government offices, or banks? Were British women restricted to hospitals and kitchens? Many British men and women during the war frequented the hotel ballrooms of Cairo. Cairo high-society had by no means declined during the Great War except for an initial slowdown during the first months of the conflict. In fact, as the 'big hotels [had] become the quarters of the...officers,'[92] Cairo high society gained momentum with the influx of British officers and their wives. The British 'community...absorbed them warmly [and] welcomed their help in the maintenance of those pleasures [which] the war had threatened to curtail.'[93] These officers, warmly accommodated at the best hotels at a reduced tariff, were admitted to membership in the elite Gezira Club on a special low subscription rate. Officers were offered hot baths, flowers to decorate their tents and messes, and help to purchase presents to send home. Invitations for quail shooting, tennis, polo, dinners, races, and dances were never in short supply.[94] Mothers of young British women were eager to introduce their daughters to these officers while some high society women (not only British) were desperate to be seen with them in hotel lounges and ballrooms. Captain R. B. Gillett of the Second Battalion Hampshire Regiment, convalescing at the Anglo-American Hospital, recalls an amusing example of this desperation when he was chosen to 'appear' with one of these women.

> It was fashionable for society ladies to be seen taking officers out in their cars. One day during the siesta when no one was about, two Egyptians entered through the French door, lifted me out of bed and carried me out to a large car occupied by a very opulent looking lady. After driving round Cairo we stopped at Shepheard's Hotel, where we had tea in a large lounge on two floor levels. This hall-like room was divided by clumps of palm trees and fountains played among them. I maintain that I am the only person who ever had tea in Shepheard's Hotel clad only in pyjamas.[95]

Not only were the officers welcomed into Cairo society, their wives also brought added colour and elegance as their 'frocks…brightened… the lounges of the principal hotels and the pavements of the shopping streets in the European quarter.'[96] For a British bank manager, the sight of a British woman 'in a hotel [in] pretty frocks [was] as satisfying as anything in Cairo.'[97] As the population of British women grew, an embargo was put upon this category of 'unnecessary luxuries'[98] for the interests of military efficiency. While wives were barred from entering Egypt, those already in Egypt were ironically forbidden to leave. As the armed forces moved eastward to fight in Palestine, the wives were left in Egypt. Despite the duties of war, British men and women were instrumental to the advancement of high society in Egypt.

Organised Committees and Associations

During the war, British men and women also functioned on various committees and associations to serve the war effort. They raised funds for needy Britons in Egypt and the wounded from Gallipoli, and sought to alleviate the idleness of the troops. The British Benevolent Fund was established to gain regular subscriptions from the generous British community in order to help Britons in Alexandria who were in distress during the war.[99] Similarly, Dr. Lucinda Forster set up the British Refugees Fund to collect money and clothing for poorer Britons.[100] Others raised funds for existing organisations like the British Red Cross. For example, Dr. and Mrs. Creswell lent their house and garden in Cairo for a home arts and crafts exhibition. There were 100 exhibits and the cost of materials was limited to half a piastre. Sideshows and teas were served and prizes were given to different exhibits which best represented 'utility', 'beauty', and 'originality'. Many attended, a good number of exhibits were sold, and £53 was raised for the British Red Cross on that day.[101] The British Chamber of Commerce also raised money to help injured Indian soldiers, who were part of the Allied effort in January 1915. The Chamber called a meeting of the British community in Cairo 'to consider the best way in which to help the Indian Military Hospital'.[102] As a result, £100 per month were pledged to the hospital to help the military defray costs and hire more nurses. The Patriotic League of Britons Overseas was founded to raise subscriptions and organize events to fund the construction of military hardware like warships and aeroplanes. To do this, it arranged cinema showings and orchestras for the entertainment of the troops. For example, in 1916 the League sold tickets for the 24 May Empire Day celebration featuring entertainment at the Alhambra Theatre in the presence of the Prince of Wales and the High Commissioner. Tickets were priced from 2 to 300 piastres, depending on the seat. All Britons in Alexandria were urged to attend.[103]

Britons in Egypt also organised committees with the hope of curbing the disruptive behaviour of troops from Australia and New Zealand during the war. As a result of boredom, high salaries, excessive consumption of alcohol, and youthful bravado, they turned Cairo into a resort for prostitution (as explained in the previous chapter) and drunkenness.[104] As the economy thrived, many new bars and taverns were opened to cater to this clientele.[105] The activities of brothel keepers and purveyors of cheap alcohol were not sufficiently restricted by the authorities. Other recreational facilities were few.

Several first-hand accounts vividly depict the alcohol-induced violence instigated by these troops. The Mancunian Sergeant Hopwood records:

> Though there are good fellows among the Australians, there are a lot of the other sort as well, [and] on the whole they have been a nuisance in the town. On this occasion they resided in a certain quarter of the native section of Cairo going in a lot of houses and throwing all the furniture out in the street where they set fire to it. They broke all the windows, and stole a lot of whiskey, wine etc. from various bars and other places. The redcaps were called out and were pelted with bottles etc., and then rushed. In defence, they

opened fire with their revolvers and...a lot of the 'Australians' got hurt, about eighteen I believe.[106]

As a result of the Australians' misbehaviour, the British troops (from Britain) in Cairo 'were confined to camp, except in case of men going out of town on special passes. Of course, this has spoiled the weekend altogether and it has raised some [negative] feeling between [the British troops] and the gallant Kangaroos.'[107] A year later, the outbursts were just as violent and even more frequent. The penalties of losing privileges remained unchanged. As one Australian officer describes:

> The soldiers' riots...until lately have been an everyday or rather night occurrence in Cairo. Some of our fellows are over the odds when they get loose, with the result that our leave and privileges have been greatly restricted in the city. They have burnt houses and motors and thrown pianos, beds and beer bottles into the streets from upstair windows. *On one occasion I passed through a street about two minutes before a piano came down.*[108]

Further, intoxicated Australian troops sometimes wandered for days through the streets of Cairo in a stupor causing trouble for other civilians. The *Egyptian Gazette* records one incident whereby a drunken soldier was harassing a British family. At Sault's restaurant, a first class French establishment, a young man was dining with his betrothed and her family. At midnight, a drunken Australian trooper came into the restaurant, walked up to the table, and wanted to offer a bottle of champagne to the brother of the betrothed. Then the soldier offered champagne to the whole table and turned to the bride-to-be's brother, saying, 'I want to marry your sister.' The brother of the engaged young lady replied immediately, 'She is already betrothed.' The drunken Australian then responded, 'Never you mind...I will pay all the damages for a breach of promise,' and then threw down a pile of banknotes.[109] Though there was certainly misbehaviour on the part of troops from Britain, there seems to be more evidence of violence, drunkenness, and lack of discipline on the part of troops from Australia. Due to their behaviour, the British community in Egypt set up committees to coordinate entertainment, clubs, sports, and lectures to steer them away from destructive activity. These activities were also for the enjoyment of soldiers from Britain who were waiting for deployment to the battlefront or who were recovering from injury and illness.

Entertainment and concerts

One of the most appreciated committees was the Soldiers' Entertainment Committee set up by Lady McMahon and Lady Maxwell in January 1916. The mission of the Committee was to spread out the concerts and entertainment regularly so that hospitals or military camps could fairly share the services of all the performers. As a result, just between April and May of 1916, concert parties staging 80 different performances visited 13 hospitals and rest camps. Thirteen concerts were organised in Ezbekiyya at the YMCA (Young Men's Christian Association) Soldiers' Club.[110] The Shepheard's Hotel hosted weekly concerts performed by military bands on Saturday afternoons.[111] Organ and violin recitals at St. Mark's Church in Alexandria were also performed in front of packed audiences.[112]

Besides organising concerts, members of the Egypt's British community actively participated in plays and theatricals. The Cairo Amateur Repertory Players performed short plays at the Soldiers' Club in Ezbekiyya Gardens in Cairo,[113] in the Opera House,[114] and at the YMCA in Ezbekiyya in front of large audiences consisting of military personnel of all ranks, hospital nurses, and civilians every Thursday evening. 'Standing-room only' was the usual scenario at the start of each performance.[115] In certain cases, even children of members of the British community were recruited to perform. In 1916, the daughters of Canon Gairdner, the missionary leader; Sir Malcolm McIllwraith, the Judicial Adviser; and Frank Rowlatt, the President of the National Bank of Egypt; all performed in a musical entitled 'Mrs. Jarley's Famous Waxworks.'[116] Canon Gairdner played the leading role of Mrs. Jarley. In addition to amateur performances, professional theatre companies also came to Egypt like Miss Ada Reeve's London Company – a first-class theatrical ensemble.[117]

Circuses and various get-togethers were also arranged. One corporal recalls his delight in the circus: 'The other night I went to see a circus at the Kursaal in Cairo and enjoyed myself very much. It was a splendid performance.'[118] The Rev. and Mrs. James Gillan organised sociable afternoons held at the Continental for soldiers to relax and enjoy more luxurious facilities, food, and atmosphere.[119] To entertain the idle troops in hopes of stirring them away from trouble making, the Soldiers' Entertainment Committee, the Cairo Amateur Repertory Players, and others in the British community facilitated plays, concerts, circuses, and social events.

Clubs

Egypt's British community established social and recreational clubs where soldiers were encouraged to read, write letters, participate in games and sports, and interact with fellow soldiers. They were also encouraged to seek the counsel of more mature women 'mother figures'. Such was the case at the British Soldiers' Café. Managed by a small group of British women, the café was designed as a place for soldiers to read, write, talk, play games, eat simple meals at reasonable prices, and seek the listening ear of a sympathetic 'mother figure'.

Recognising the fact that many men appreciate intensely the touch of home that is secured by the presence of a lady gifted with ready sympathy and a cheerful spirit, the Committee of the Café utilised a small room near the entrance in which the Lady Superintendant should spend her afternoons and evenings...there has streamed to and from this room a procession of soldiers from the homeland and from the Colonies, eager to ask for help and advice, or even to hear some friendly words of encouragement.[120]

Besides the British Soldiers' Café, women of the British community also gave their time, sympathy, and energy to the Maadi Soldiers' Club and Tea-Room.

Perhaps the most prominent club established and frequented by the British troops was the Cairo Soldiers' Recreation Club, run by the YMCA in Ezbekiyya. It provided them with a venue for boxing matches, cinematograph shows, hockey games on a skating rink, concerts, and lectures frequently given by a well-known preacher named Oswald Chambers. Soldiers were given free use of writing paper, tables, and games. They had to pay for refreshments but the proceeds were used to improve the club. Showers and plunge baths were also available at the Club and the Australian Comforts Fund supplied the soap and towels.[121] On one night, the 'largest crowd of soldiers yet seen...assembled to enjoy...[a] boxing contest, exhibitions of wrestling,...cinema pictures, and...free distribution of 16,000 cigarettes [donated by]...a friend...of the YMCA.'[122] One soldier wrote, in the book for visitors, 'Cairo is hell, but the YMCA in Ezbekieh is nearly as good for us as the other place.'[123]

Whatever the case, no account of the clubs in Egypt during the war would be complete without a glimpse at the work of the YMCA. There were 19 YMCA centres in Egypt and six of them were in Cairo. They provided tent shelters, a monthly supply of 300,000 sheets of paper for writing, an abundance of envelopes and ink in gallons, plus pens and pencils by the thousands. It was 'not the fault of the YMCA if mothers, wives or sweethearts were without the news of the boys.'[124] For recreation, there were quiet games like chess, dominoes, and cards. Every tent had a lending library and a piano and there was no restriction of when or who could use it. Lectures were given on a variety of topics. Concerts were given by the men themselves or from visiting concert parties.[125] There were also educational classes on a range of topics and various chess and draught competitions.[126]

> The work of the YMCA in Egypt was...worth that of all the chaplains put together. Their huts provided a home for homeless men, and they were the only homes they had. The troops lived in their thousands out in the desert...The ideal kept before the men by the workers in Cairo was the ideal of a home away from home... [T]he YMCA was doing a work that perhaps no other organisation could have done.[127]

The British Soldiers' Café, the Maadi Soldiers' Club, the Cairo Soldiers' Recreation Club, and the extensive work of the YMCA across the military camps in Egypt, established bases of recreation for the British troops and effectively turned many away from loneliness, boredom, drunkenness, and misconduct.

Outings and sports

Britons in Cairo also established the Convalescent Outings Society in order to promote 'excursions to the various beauty spots and show places of Cairo and the neighbourhood, for the benefit of the sick and wounded soldiers'[128] as well as diverting idle soldiers from drink and violence. The excursions included visits to the Delta Barrages, Zoological Gardens, Aquarium, Pyramids, Citadel, Ezbekiyya skating rink, the Egyptian Museum, and the Ostrich Farm.[129] The Society even 'erected a canteen, with stores and accommodations for as large a number as 300 men, at the Delta Barrage, where good food is provided for them during the day.'[130] However, sports seemed to be more preferred than outings. Judging by the vast numbers of soldiers who played or watched football, the sport was probably the most popular for the rank and file; perhaps because football was an important part of working-class culture.[131] Football tournaments were arranged regularly between British, Australian, and New Zealand military divisions.[132] At times, proceeds from ticket sales to football matches were used to raise funds for soldiers in need. For example, a big football match between expert players from England and Scotland was held on 16 March 1916 at the Egyptian State Railway Institute in aid of the Convalescent Outings Fund.[133] Fourteen teams formed the Military Football League. Each team represented a different department within the military apparatus such as the headquarters, military police, hospital staff, Australian troops, Welsh troops, and the Royal Army Medical Corps.[134] A cricket league also brought together sportsmen from Britain, Australia, and New Zealand and other countries of the Empire. Boxing matches, rugby, field hockey, horse races, and athletics tournaments were arranged as well.[135] Outings and sports were able to divert some of the troops from vice whilst they recovered or waited for their next military assignment.

Lectures

Regular lectures were organized by the YMCA and hosted by its most successful club, the Cairo Soldiers Recreation Club. Topics included 'A 1000 miles on horse-back through Asiatic Turkey,'[136] 'The Nile: From Central Africa to the Mediterranean,'[137] 'General Gordon and the siege of Khartoum,'[138] and 'Christianity in Egypt during the First Six Centuries.'[139] Usually well-received, lectures by specialists and prominent members of the British community, combined with plays, concerts, clubs, outings, and sports were organised to entertain idle and convalescing soldiers and diverting them from alcohol and unruly behaviour.

Conflict between the British Community and Government Policy

Requisitions

Besides the various roles of British men and women during the First World War, the conflicts between certain Britons and official government policy also reveal noteworthy diversity within the community. The British military authorities requisitioned many large buildings during the war and the Victoria College of Alexandria was no exception. As explained in a previous chapter, the Victoria College attempted to import the best of English public school education into Egypt. At the outset of the war, Mr. Lias, the headmaster, was adamant that the school should remain on its premises since any alternative would damage the success of the school. Even before the official request for requisition, Mr. Lias, wrote to Sir John Maxwell, commander of the military forces in Egypt, to plead his case against the requisition of the college.

> I do not think it is generally understood how difficult it would be to carry on a boarding school (we have 53 boarders) in a provisional building. First of all there are the dormitory arrangements, then there is the question of a dining hall, not to mention the difficulty and perhaps impossibility of arranging for games, which are necessary for the boys' health, and such lessons as physics and chemistry, which need special classrooms.[140]

Mr. Lias wrote further to Sir Henry McMahon, British High Commissioner in Egypt, on the eve of the requisition of Victoria College.

> Until it is shown that there are not equally great and perhaps even more suitable buildings available for a military hospital in Alexandria; I do not think that we ought to forget that we are morally bound by our engagement to the parents of our pupils.[141]

Lias sent his final demand to the Victoria College Council urging its members not to allow the military to requisition its building.

> It is impossible to find buildings in any way comparable to those that we now occupy. Nothing can be found in any respect equal to the present dormitories (with their sanitary installations and arrangements for supervision), classrooms, physical and chemical laboratories, reading-rooms and kitchen. It will be equally impossible to find suitable playgrounds...The Council should not spontaneously offer our buildings to the military authorities as a hospital...On the contrary, that before this is done, every other available building should be submitted for their approval.[142]

Even with Lias' articulate argument against the requisition, Victoria College was taken over by the military. Sir Maxwell confirmed to McMahon from the Army Headquarters that 'I am afraid we must take up...Victoria College...[It] is the only possible building in Alexandria which will take 1000 beds.'¹⁴³ And as expected, the requisition was very damaging to the continued success of the school.

Victoria College was moved to the Egyptian Survey Department building near the Ramleh Railway Station in Alexandria. As Lias anticipated, the Survey Department building did not have enough room for the various classrooms that the school required. For example, the college sought the use one of the sheds outside the main building as a chemistry classroom. Yet, the Survey Department refused this request stating that the sheds were needed for the storage of heavy iron and other articles. Although the chairman of the college urged the High Commissioner to 'invite the Survey Department to find some other storage accommodation,'¹⁴⁴ the ongoing problem of lack of quantity and quality of facilities persisted. Chemistry and physics were taught elsewhere as Headmaster Lias explained a year after the requisition:

> Our difficulties have not diminished and new ones have been added. I understand the necessity of providing proper accommodation for the sick and wounded, but I much regret that at our temporary buildings, which we have now occupied for more than a year, we have had to abandon almost entirely two such important subjects as chemistry and physics. [Our] application for a loan from the Ministry of Education for science laboratories [was] unsuccessful... [but] with the kindness of the Headmaster of St. Mark's Coptic School, two of our boys are getting lessons in chemistry and physics [there].¹⁴⁵

Besides the lack of space, the school also suffered financially. By the spring of 1916, it had a deficit of E£200 to E£300 largely due to the reduction of student boarders. There were 64 boarders in March, 1914; yet only 40 boarders in 1916. Though there was a slight increase in the number of day-only students, the resulting financial increase could not cover the monetary shortfall from losing nearly a third of the boarders due primarily to the requisition of the old building and the inadequacy of the new premises.¹⁴⁶ Besides the conflict that arose between Mr. Lias and the British military authorities due to the requisition of Victoria College, the decision not to requisition the Gezira Club also stirred conflict within the British community. One observer blamed this on the selfishness of British military and political leaders who were keen to reduce the quality of education at Victoria College but unwilling to give up their sacred playground.

I cannot understand why this great area in Gezireh has not been requisitioned by the military. What a splendid hospital camp or convalescent camp it would make. What an improvement it would be on a place like Luna Park. However, there is no hope of the members of the Club making such a sacrifice; were they ladies it would have been offered long ago, but men are selfish...I understand that the cream of the members have gone home to join the army and that only the old, infirm, and don't want to fight members are left. Are they not ready to sacrifice something to save wounded men being accommodated in places like the verandahs of Luna Park or the dormitories of the Citadel?[147]

The issuing of tax-free war bonds

To raise money for the war effort, the British authorities issued the sale of British Government Exchequer Bonds (tax-free investments for patriotic buyers to profit from interest accrued) which provoked antagonism from members of Egypt's British community. Although the government and the British Chamber of Commerce in Egypt highly recommended the purchase of these bonds, small investors among Britons in Egypt found the investment limiting and disadvantageous. The first problem for the small investor was the restriction of the amount of his purchase from outside Britain. One prospective investor wanted to buy bonds worth only £5 or £10 and was willing to pay through a standing order to the British government each month. However, bonds were not available in Egypt in such small amounts, though they were available in Britain. Overseas investors were invited to buy bonds ranging at least from £50 to £100. Since this investor only had £5 or £10 per month for the purchase of the bonds, he could not pay for them outside British soil. Only two arrangements were open to him. He could either pay a bank in Egypt to send his £5 home every month or he could pay a bank in England to purchase his £5 bond. Either way, he needed to pay again for postage and insurance on his bond to be sent safely to England.[148] Needless to say, this investor was unhappy with additional spending on postage and insurance and found the purchase of smaller bonds from overseas an inconvenient and expensive burden. In his own words,

> If the 'old country' [Britain] needs money surely she could put bonds in her Dominions – Protectorates or what you will – that I and many, many thousands, and tens of thousands of individuals,

may step into a consulate, a Post Office, or a Bank, and exchange cash for bonds...[I appeal to readers to explain how] an individual with a small monthly income (exceeding by...say...£15 his actual out of pocket requirements) – can obtain bonds, loans or anything else that the Chancellor or Exchequer has for sale.[149]

Unfortunately, the reply that this prospective investor received from K. P. Birley of the British Chamber of Commerce was simply to take the trouble and invest anyway for the good of Britain's war effort. Birley argues, 'Does not the patriotic nature of the call appeal to all Britishers and encourage them to take a little trouble where necessary, in which I am sure, their bankers will help them.'[150]

Even more disheartening for Britons in Egypt who wanted to invest in Exchequer Bonds was a response from the Chancellor himself hinting that they were not allowed to invest in foreign accounts or economies:

> I regard it as contrary to the national interest that, during the war, remittances should be made from this country for investment abroad in any form whatever. Monies accrued abroad to British subjects and firms...[should be] brought back...to invest in British securities.[151]

Thus any British investor who wanted to utilise the interest gained in bonds in Britain for his business in Egypt would be told by the banks that he was not allowed to do so; further stifling the purchase of bonds in Egypt.

Most disappointing to Britons in Egypt who hoped to invest in the tax-free bonds was the requirement imposed by the British government that if they wanted to purchase the bonds, they would have to declare their intention of never returning to Britain again. Only a permanent non-resident of Britain was allowed to obtain the tax exemption on the bonds. One potential investor explained his frustration over the need to assure the authorities that he was in perpetual exile in Egypt in order to obtain tax-free status and forever denying him the greatest longing he had in life, which was to return to Britain to reside in retirement. By purchasing tax-free bonds, he 'must never again indulge in the hope, which ninety-nine out of every hundred Anglo-Egyptians cherish, that the happy day will come when he can spend his declining years among his relations and friends at home.'[152] To renege on permanent non-resident status in

Britain meant that one had to end up paying the tax accrued over the years with interest to the British Government upon one's return to Britain for retirement or whatever reason. Therefore, to declare one's permanent non-residency and then to return to Britain was probably a fate even more punishing than not being allowed to retire in Britain. The same British resident in Egypt described this frightening prospect in this way:

> after having invested in these Bonds, should he go back on his declaration and after many years decide to make his home in England either in order to retire or because he has obtained an appointment at home, the unfortunate and patriotic investor in such securities will, as soon as he lands on his native shores, find himself called upon to pay a quarter of his capital probably representing the arrears of income tax on these Bonds extending over years. He may have very little money and may have spent all his interest from such investments on educating his children, or he may have lost it through unprofitable business transactions, and then he will find the inexorable Income Tax gatherers selling him up and reducing him to ruin. This is the alternative to perpetual exile which will await the poor Britisher, who out of patriotism has invested his money in these Bonds. The Government will have no pity in taking its pound of flesh.[153]

The prospect of never living in Britain again was to be avoided at all costs for most Britons overseas. Even K. P. Birley of the British Chamber of Commerce asked, 'However patriotic we may be, are we to declare that we will never live in England again as a price for such an investment?'[154] Not surprisingly, this predicament discouraged many Britons in Egypt from investing in Exchequer Bonds and put them at odds with the British government over the permanent non-residency required to be eligible for purchasing the tax-free bonds.

The War's Economic Effects on the British in Egypt

Economic boom

In this discussion of the diversity of challenges and responses that the British in Egypt faced during the war, it is important to refer to the wide range of economic effects that they encountered – prosperity, missed opportunities, and hardship due to inflation, within a context of increasing economic struggles for most Egyptians. The mass influx of imperial troops at the outset of the war created an economic boom in Egypt. The significance of the boom, however, can be more clearly appreciated in light of the short yet severe economic depression that preceded it. At the outset of the war, there was a sudden cessation of the large influx of visitors to Egypt during the winter tourist season.

> The streets of Cairo, at the beginning of November 1914, when the early winter visitors [would normally] begin to arrive [were empty]…and the 'Savoy' and other of the more luxurious hotels… [had] the mournful and deserted appearance [as if it was]…the height of summer. Numbers of the best shops and hotels remained barred and shuttered, and scarcely any motors or other vehicles were observable in the streets…The whole town…seemed hushed and deadened.[155]

Almost overnight, 'the numerous large hotels of Cairo and Alexandria, the expensive shops, the principal dealers in oriental…rugs, and wares of various kinds [were] confronted with the possibility of ruin.'[156] Though the Greeks, Levantines, and other non-British Europeans ran many of these businesses, it is fair to assume that British businesses suffered as well. However, just as abrupt as the economic decline was the speed and enormity of the unprecedented boom that followed. By the spring of 1915, the departed troops (to the European theatre of war) were replaced by two infantry divisions[157] and a cavalry brigade, dispatched from India, whose task was to defend the Suez Canal. At the same time, three divisions of infantry, the 42nd East Lancashire Territorial Force, and two divisions from Australia and New Zealand, were given the task of undergoing training to prepare for battle. Lord Kitchener, Secretary of War, had originally intended to use the Australasian troops to fight in Europe but there was not enough accommodation for them in Britain. Thus they were assigned to train in Egypt instead and were later directed to fight in the Middle Eastern theatre of war.[158] The British 'turned Egypt into an immense transit camp, supply and training ground.'[159] Under the central command of Lieutenant-General Sir John Maxwell, who was ultimately accountable to Lord Kitchener,[160] the troops, numbering 40,000[161] by the spring of 1915, poured into Cairo, Alexandria, and Port Said. Huge camps were set up for them. They not only saved hotels, shops, tourist and transportation businesses from bankruptcy but compensated for the losses incurred in the initial months of the war. This economic boom was accompanied by the enormous spending power of the soldiers. Egypt 'acquired an army of military tourists that [spent] E£3000 to E£5000 a day.'[162] Certain 'English regiments contained some of the greatest peers, and richest men in England [and]... wealthy Australians and New Zealanders, too squandered their money in profusion.'[163] Lady Rochdale records that the Australians all seemed 'very rich, [and did not] mind what they paid.'[164] An average Australian trooper was paid two shillings per day whilst the entire monthly salary of a private in the Scottish infantry was only four shillings and two pence.[165] The Australians received the 'highest pay given to privates in any army...[and] on top of that each man had seven and half pence over and above the British scale of rations.'[166] For all the suffering and pain that the Gallipoli campaign brought about for the British and Australasian armies, it was partially offset by the ongoing payment of large salaries for many soldiers and the subsequent spending of this money in Egypt.

> All the accumulated arrears of money that were paid out to the Anzacs [Australian and New Zealand forces] and the British troops who had been fighting for months at Gallipoli came in a great windfall to Cairo and Alexandria...They had come out of the jaws of death, they might be returning there at any moment, and they made the most of the present, as only soldiers can...Egypt must have reaped a rich harvest from the Army...most of the money [was] spent in Alexandria and Cairo.[167]

The imperial troops, particularly the Australians with their free spending attitudes, filled the streets of Cairo and Alexandria with 'a good deal of spare time and plenty of money, [and] monopolised every bar, music-hall, picture palace, and dancing hall, and almost wholly replaced the civilian element.'[168] They 'squandered enormous sums on worthless 'souvenirs,' on trinkets and handkerchiefs for their lady-loves, and in interminable drinks and drives.'[169] They bought huge amounts of 'food for themselves and fodder for their animals.'[170] The economic boom also facilitated the opening of many new businesses. Some 'fifty new bars and taverns were opened...in [just] six weeks'[171] and many new English bookshops were established during this period.

The large quantities of English books for sale and the number of new bookshops that have sprung up, mostly stocked with light literature in English...[are] one of the most patent signs of the presence of English troops in Egypt...Van loads of...novels and other popular books...are ordered at regular intervals...The hundred of thousands of British and overseas troops in Egypt are insistent upon a supply of light and readable literature.[172]

To refresh the tired shopper, tea gardens such as Alexandria's New English Tea Gardens, under British management, were established to provide a place of respite away from the heat and dust.[173] For the British, European or native businessman in Egypt, times were better 'than any he [had] ever known'[174] and 'for the most part, the inhabitants, both native and foreign, [made] profit out of the war.'[175]

Missed opportunities

Despite the economic boom, British businessmen in Egypt missed the opportunity to capitalise on new restrictions imposed on German and Austrian businessmen during the war. Soon after war was declared on Germany, the Austro-Hungarian Empire, and the Ottoman Empire, the British authorities implemented martial law to

> override the Capitulations...which would otherwise have kept the [British controlled] Egyptian government as powerless as before to take effective action against European foreigners. Under the umbrella of martial law, however, it could control the businesses of firms suspected of trading with the enemy [and] take over firms of enemy nationality.[176]

The imposition of martial law also allowed the British authorities to sequester German and Austrian homes for military service[177] and to freeze German and Austrian assets.[178] There were also prohibitions on 'German ships entering Egyptian harbours; Egyptian ships entering German harbours; [the] import of German goods into Egypt; [and the] exports of all goods [from Egypt] to German ports.'[179] British forces were permitted to capture enemy ships in Egyptian harbours and all Egyptian ports were closed to German shipping.[180] In light of these restrictions on German and Austrian assets and businesses and the anticipation of more favourable economic conditions due to the establishment of the British

Protectorate, British businessmen were hopeful that the new political realities would translate into greater profitability. Early in 1915, the British Chamber of Commerce in Egypt issued a statement articulating this newfound confidence and hopefulness.

> With the change in the status of Egypt and the approaching abolition of the Capitulations...the establishment of better conditions for traders in this country may be awaited with confidence...Under the new order of things it is to be hoped that British manufacturers will take every opportunity to consolidate their position in the Protectorate, and those who have been deterred in the past from doing business in Egypt...will make further efforts to gain a footing in this country.[181]

This new energy and buoyancy among the British businessmen of Egypt produced several new initiatives. The minutes of the 1915 annual meeting of the British Chamber of Commerce in Cairo clearly stated that 'active measures [were] now being taken...to render itself more useful than in the past to businessmen in this country as well as to English manufacturers.'[182] One such action, initiated by the Chambers of Commerce in Cairo and Alexandria, was the establishment of two committees, one in each city, 'to study the question of how best British interests in Egypt [were to] be promoted and developed'[183] under the new Protectorate. To improve British business interests in Egypt, a committee was established to form a business reference library in Egypt to assist British businessmen. The group consisted of the most experienced members of the British Chamber of Commerce – J. W. Eady, W. D. Hart, W. E. Kingsford, M. Setton, J. B. Mason, and Legal Adviser J. Grech Mifsud.[184] Lastly, after hosting a banquet every few years, the Chamber committed itself to increase the frequency of the banquets by hosting them annually. This would draw 'the official and commercial communities into closer touch',[185] since the Chamber felt that its members, with their knowledge of local methods, people, language, and specialized area of business, would be most competent to advise the government on commercial matters.[186]

In spite of these aspirations, the British sense of fairness manifested by the reluctance to destroy German and Austrian businesses seem to have hindered British businesses in Egypt from accumulating greater profit. For instance, although High Commissioner McMahon's speech in 1915 stated that 'British prospects...were very bright and...that he was ready to render...every reasonable assistance and support'[187] to the British Chamber of Commerce, he also argued that a fair trading environment was crucial to economic credibility and growth.

> The British Protectorate would not be used to push unduly British interests at the expense of...other nations. It would benefit all interests by assuring a greater security and other advantages... This would attract British capital and so give a fresh impulse to British trade in the country. Egypt has now the advantage of an able and enlightened ruler, who was anxious to promote all industrial interests.[188]

Besides the government's commitment to fair play, British manufacturers did not take advantage of the loss of German and Austrian trade. As one British businessman lamented:

> Unfortunately, English commission houses in Egypt are not numerous; therefore, no great pressure can be brought upon the British Chamber of Commerce, which is content to go on in the same old drowsy manner and does not seem to realise that German and Austrian trade, which had a very strong footing in Egypt before the war, must be substituted by British trade, and *not find the market open to them immediately after the war*.[189]

Due to Britain's position of power, it seemed likely that 'a preference would be given to British goods if some energy were displayed by the British Chamber of Commerce and active steps were taken to put the British manufacturer in close touch with the responsible commission houses.'[190] However, instead of turning to British firms, the commission houses began to look to America to replace German and Austrian goods.

Remarkably, though much of German and Austrian business activities and assets were frozen, some continued to engage in trade. The Government permitted certain German companies to carry on trade, though only if they were locally controlled by non-German partners, allowed to trade only in Egypt with Britain and its Allies, and licensed only to trade for the purpose of liquidation.[191] The Courts allowed non-German partners of companies with German owners in Egypt to continue the business so as not to hurt the businessmen of non-enemy states – Egyptians or other Europeans.[192] Astonishingly, one such company, whose capital was mainly German and whose directors were mostly German, was allowed 'to make profits out of contracts with the British Army.'[193] Ironically, this may have economically benefited Germany and thus strengthened her viability in the war effort. When asked whether the British Chamber of Commerce in Egypt had 'taken any steps in the matter of bringing pressure to bear on the authorities on the scandal of enemy firms,'[194] one prominent British businessman replied, 'the Chamber had done nothing in this matter...it was inconceivable that [it] would ever think of such a daring and audacious policy.'[195] Given the opportunity at the time to suppress German and Austrian businesses in Egypt, the British government (with its commitment to fair-play) and the British Chamber of Commerce seemed to have done little to take economic advantage of Britain's position as sole protectors of Egypt during the First World War.

The high standard of living and the rise in cost of living

As Egypt prospered during the war, the standard of living inevitably rose. One British child in Cairo commented after a trip to Khartoum:

> Cairo...was cool and fresh...It was heavenly to get home at last... to find a well laid table with cold ham and tomatoes for breakfast with butter in a gleaming silver dish with an ice compartment in it. Real butter! In Khartoum, it came up once a week on the mail train, was in a tin and was always semi-liquid by the time it reached us and it always tasted rancid.[196]

Another visitor observed that 'of all the various war centres, [Egypt] is decidedly the safest and most comfortable...and of all the capitals within the war zone, Cairo [is the best] for order and comfort.'[197] The missionary Temple Gairdner also affirmed this by saying: 'Egypt has been one of the safest and quietest lands on earth during the war, thanks to the overwhelming nature of the defence which the British Government saw right to bestow on the key of the Empire.'[198] Good food, safety, comfort, and a high standard of living characterised Egypt during the Great War.

However, coupled with a high standard of living was an unfortunate high cost of living. A report by the National Bank of Egypt claims that the cost of living index doubled from 1914 to 1918, from 100 to 202.[199] Due to the increased cost of fuel and food, the Turf Club significantly raised its prices in 1917. The Club raised the cost of its dinners by 2 piastres while the cost of tea rose by 1 piastre. A fee for use of a table was 2.5

piastres, charged to non-members of the Club. The Club's normal annual expenditure for coal in 1914 was E£200, but by 1916, it was E£500 and by 1917, it was E£800.[200] During the war, rents increased from 20 to 50 per cent (in some cases by 85 per cent),[201] and foodstuffs by 92 per cent in Cairo from July 1914 until May 1918, and by 116 per cent in Alexandria during the same period.[202] Did income keep pace with these increases? Salaries of government officials went up only on the average of 10 to 20 per cent.[203] After paying out all the essential costs, a government official and his family were left with little money for recreation and amusement which they deemed 'necessary for these hard times.'[204] The sharp price rise presented grave challenges for British businesses in Egypt as well. Arthur Blunt, the interim manager of the Anglo-Egyptian Bank, in his letter to his manager in London, gave a glimpse of how businesses responded to the high cost of living facing their employees.

> Our Minet el Basal staff (near Alexandria)...[are] complaining of the difficulty of making both ends meet owing to the further rise in the cost of living. Some of the lower paid married men must be feeling it and I suggested that I...give the most deserving men up to £10 each. I have since heard that special war bonuses have been granted in several offices...Everything has gone up tremendously of late.[205]

Though the Great War provided Britons in Egypt with great economic benefit, many also suffered due to 'the...exceptionally high...cost of living.'[206]

The hardship of Egyptians throughout the war

During the war, Britons in Egypt experienced prosperity, missed opportunities, and inflation in a context where many Egyptians suffered. Besides the high cost of living, they resented the immoral behaviour of the Australian troops and considered them 'wild beast[s] and only partially human'.[207] Egyptians also faced serious food shortages due to the increased food exports, decline in food imports, lack of nitrate fertiliser imports for crops (since the production of explosives for the war effort needed nitrate),[208] and the mass requisition of local food for the imperial forces.[209] Their camels, horses, donkeys, and mules needed for haulage, transportation, and industry were also requisitioned by the Imperial troops.[210] Worst, by 1917 Egyptian men were being conscripted into the Egyptian Labour Corps and the Camel Transport Corps to serve in Palestine. By the end of the war, 1.5 million Egyptians had been recruited into the British military machine. The Egyptian recruit 'was being forcibly taken away from his land, home and family to serve as a labourer for troops fighting a war in defence of a foreign king and country and against the Ottoman Sultan and Caliph of Islam.'[211] As the notable Egyptian historian, Abd al-Rahman al-Rafa'i observed:

> From the [British] soldiers came hurtful and disreputable behaviour against the [Egyptian] people – their possession, their persons and their livelihoods. So much that there was a deep effect of hatred towards the occupation and patronage…In the four years [of the war], the military authorities impounded the buildings, took over the grains, the harvest, the cotton, the food for the animals, the cattle, the trees (for firewood) and everything else. The English and Australian soldiers performed deeds against the Egyptians which caused them hatred and anger. The military authorities drafted a million workers in the Egyptian army and in their military campaigns, and many of them died in the killing fields.[212]

However difficult some of the economic challenges that faced the British community in Egypt, they paled in comparison with the hardship that many of the Egyptians faced. Their resentment and bitterness towards their British rulers likely increased their resolve to remove British rule in Egypt in the post-war years.

Conclusion

This chapter contributes to two key aspirations of this book by demonstrating the diversity among Britons in Egypt during the occupation and to bring to light previously underemphasised aspects of their historiography. To express this variety, the study examines the different roles and reactions to the challenges posed by the First World War. Men joined the war effort in Europe or stayed behind in key jobs while women served as volunteers, nurses, and hostesses. This diversity is also seen in the opposition that some Britons had towards certain government initiatives such as the requisitioning of Victoria College and the criteria to forgo retirement in Britain in order to purchase tax-free war bonds. Egypt's Britons also experienced diverse economic realities during the war – prosperity due to the economic boom, missed opportunities in light of restrictions on German and Austrian firms, and hardship due to inflation. Since the writing of Egypt's British community during the First World War appears to be largely overlooked, it is hoped that this effort will add to the historiography of British imperialism and of Egypt. Within this context, many Egyptians faced great suffering in the course of the war, which contributed to their resentment of British rule and longing for independence. It is to this period of revolutionary change that this study now turns.

7

THE REVOLUTIONARY PERIOD, 1919–22

The Origins and Nature of the 1919 Revolution

After introducing the context with a brief glimpse at the causes and events of the revolutionary period of 1919–22, this chapter addresses the two focal themes of this book by bringing to light the diversity within Egypt's British community and previously overlooked aspects of the community's history. It explores the range of challenges that encountered Egypt's Britons during the revolutionary period of 1919–22, and their varying responses to them. These challenges include the delay in demobilisation, the imminent abolition of the Capitulations, the pursuit of compensation in lieu of deaths or injuries, the threat of violent attacks, and the accompanying economic downturn of the time. Since little appears to have been written related to the British community during the revolutionary period, this chapter aspires to add to the histories of British imperialism and modern Egypt during this era.

By the end of the First World War, 'nearly every segment of Egyptian society had reason to resent British rule and be receptive to renewed nationalist agitation.'[1] The Muslim majority in Egypt resented the defeat of the Ottoman Empire that resulted in British domination over Muslim holy sites in Arabia.[2] Large landowners were irritated by the British authorities' curtailing of cotton production for the sake of cereals and foodstuffs which resulted in greater food supply for the British war effort but smaller profits for the landowners. Large landowners

> saw their interests as being further eroded…when a Cotton Control Commission was formed and given wide-ranging powers, including the right to fix cotton prices and control the purchase of

this crop from the producers. In early 1918 the Commission set the price of cotton at £42 per kantar, an act which infuriated the landowners, especially when the price of cotton in England began to rise significantly.[3]

Besides alienating landowners, educated Egyptian administrators and professionals deeply resented the British government's preference for younger, less experienced, and less able British officials in the civil service. Sir Valentine Chirol, the foreign editor of *The Times*, concurred by highlighting the growing number of British personnel in the civil services, even in subordinate ranks, and their perceived decline of efficiency, industry, and manners.[4] Egyptian administrators were also angered by the amount of money channelled for the salaries of these second-rate British officials. One Egyptian articulated this frustration:

> a different class of Englishmen [has come] here to earn a living by competing with the educated Egyptians for posts and for work in which we have no need for them. Egypt requires experts only, and is not in need of such ordinary men, who arrive in crowds from England, and have no special abilities. Their presence here has been the cause of misunderstanding between the Egyptians and the English, and had the British Government known their real position, their bad acts and the prejudice they cause to British influence in Egypt, it would have sent them out of the country…The budget of the Government is now E£30,000,000 of which the authorities availed themselves, without any justification for those enormous salaries to men of commonplace abilities whom the country has no need for…*The Egyptians are therefore right in claiming independence with the object of having a representative chamber to control such foolish expenditure from the funds of the nation.*[5]

In 1919, reports from the Ministries of Education and Public Works, the Administration of Public Health in the Municipality of Alexandria exposed the inefficiency, alleged corruption, and dereliction of duty of British officials further angering the educated Egyptians who were overlooked for jobs in the civil service.[6]

However, most damaging for British rule in Egypt was not the resentment of the large landowners or the educated professionals, but the opposition of the peasantry.

Fractiousness and indiscipline among the political elite was a familiar feature of the Occupation, and the British had come to expect violent rhetoric from the press and the threat of riots in the towns. But the upheaval in the countryside and a revolt of the fellahin...was an unexpected and wholly unwelcome novelty. The rural cultivators had long been thought of as the bedrock of Britain's control of Egypt; their loyalty was thought to countervail the frothy nationalism of salon politicians in Cairo.[7]

Peasants were bitter against the British authorities for requisitioning their animals and crops and for conscripting their sons for forced labour to assist the British military in the Levant. A severe food shortage, due to heavy Allied demands for food exports coupled with the decrease in foreign imports, sent food prices skyrocketing while 'wages of skilled labour [had] only advanced slightly.'[8] The limited supply of food combined with rapid inflation meant that 'peasants had to tighten their belts and...had good reason to fear that they would go hungry in 1919.'[9] Political involvement now involved the massive group of peasants in Egypt and not just a small group of upper class men.

No longer were Egyptian politics confined to the narrow and predictable activities of the pashas and the dynasty [the descendants of Muhammad Ali]. No longer could the placidity and indifference of the urban and rural masses be relied upon to countervail the rhetoric of drawing-room nationalists. Instead, the ability of the pasha politicians to mobilise popular support had to be reckoned with.[10]

Nearly all sectors of Egyptian society had come to realise that during 'the war years...the policies adopted by a colonial elite [placed] Egyptian interests – peasant, worker, or elite – well below the interests of the empire as whole.'[11] They recognized that their interests would only be served with the end of the British occupation.

To move towards independence from Britain, Egypt's disgruntled population found its charismatic figurehead in Saad Zaghlul and its coordinating structure in his political party, the Wafd. The British government's exclusion of Zaghlul and his colleagues from the Paris Peace Conference in early 1919 ignited widespread opposition against British rule. Towards the end of the war in November 1918, American

President Woodrow Wilson announced his Fourteen Points, which was a list of recommendations for a more peaceful post-war world order. One of the points suggested that all subject peoples should be given the right of self-determination, although he was mainly referring to Central and Eastern Europeans.[12] In response, Zaghlul and his colleagues petitioned High Commissioner Reginald Wingate concerning Egypt's complete autonomy and sought permission to travel to London to negotiate Egypt's independence. Far from granting independence to Egypt, the British government planned to maintain Egypt as a protectorate or annex it entirely as a colony.[13] Zaghlul's demands were rejected and he and colleagues were prohibited from entering Britain. Not easily deterred, Zaghlul and the Wafd began to establish greater legal legitimacy for themselves by securing thousands of signatures throughout Egypt in order to obtain 'power of attorney' to act for the nation. Each signatory in effect 'commissioned Zaghlul and his adherents to seek the complete independence of Egypt through peaceful and legal means…based on the principles of liberty and justice for which Britain and her allies in the war had been fighting.'[14] As a result, support for the Wafd and its cause grew among every sector of Egypt's population. Its leaders continued to appeal, though to no avail, to Britain and France for the right to negotiate Egypt's independence at the Paris Peace Conference in January 1919. Fearing the potential of a violent encounter with Zaghlul and his supporters after hearing 'wild talk of raising an…army'[15] to overthrow foreign rule among some Egyptians, the British authorities promptly arrested Zaghlul and four of his colleagues and deported them to Malta on 8 March 1919.

The British authorities' refusal to allow the Wafd-led delegation to present Egypt's case for independence at the Peace Conference and the subsequent deportation of nationalist leaders became known to many students and proponents of independence the next day. Student marches in Cairo took place immediately and, as the police dispersed the crowd, over 300 arrests were made.[16] By Monday 10 March, a riot had broken out in Cairo. Transport workers also went on strike, trams were wrecked, windows were smashed in the European quarters, and violence and looting took place. An uneasy feeling that the British authorities and police were unable to cope permeated Cairo. By Tuesday, Egyptian lawyers from the Native Courts and clerks from Ministries of Public Works and Education joined the strikes. Although British troops restored order by Wednesday, after killing 11 and wounding 51 demonstrators, the police were by and large ineffective in preventing the extensive property damage that had already taken place. By Friday, with students travelling to many Egyptian towns and villages to spread the demonstrations combined with the involvement of the peasantry in the countryside, many of the country's main railway stations and junctions were sabotaged. In order to protect their food supplies during the food shortage, the peasants 'attacked the rail lines to prevent the transport of agricultural commodities to the cities.'[17] By Sunday 16 March, Cairo was completely isolated and sections of the main railway both to Alexandria and to Port Said were torn up. Train stations in both cities were also damaged. The main train line to Upper Egypt was ruined in many places and, on 18 March, several 'English people [were] dragged [off a train] and killed in cold blood.'[18] On that same day, demonstrators threatened to disrupt water works but were effectively dispersed. By this time, the trams had ceased running and workers from many important industries were called to strike. The unrest also curbed communication links as one bank official recalled on 19 March:

> We have been cut off from all communication with Cairo for four days now. The line is badly cut in several places, telephone and telegraph wires are down and even the motor road and bridges are cut. The disorders are generally all over the country and extend to Upper Egypt and Fayoum, being particularly bad in the latter district.[19]

To put an end to the situation, newly appointed High Commissioner Sir Edmund Allenby, the victorious British general during the war in Palestine, released Zaghlul and his associates on 25 March 1919. A large measure of order was restored in Egypt as armoured cars and trains travelled up the Nile to put down the revolt and mobile columns of infantry patrolled the Egyptian countryside.[20] By the end of March, transportation and communications began to recover slowly. Trains were beginning to run between Cairo and Alexandria, but not regularly. Postal service between the two cities had resumed the normal two-day service. Though telegraph and telephone wires were still not working, some telegrams were successfully sent by aeroplane.[21] Despite the return of order, the actions taken by so many Egyptians were taking effect. The British authorities were forced to consider the ramifications of continuing the occupation of Egypt and the possibility of allowing greater autonomy for Egypt.

From March 1919 until 1922, a pattern of disturbances, violence, disruptions to infrastructure, anti-British agitation, and arrests defined the social and political landscape of Egypt. Both Muslim and Coptic leaders supported demands for independence. Many Egyptian women from all social classes were also active in protesting British rule by demonstrating, distributing leaflets, boycotting British goods, and supplying food to anti-British militants.[22] The effectiveness of the protests was largely dependent on the fact that 'all classes of Egyptians seemed to be joining together to one degree or another in opposition to British authority in Egypt. The political leaders, students, lawyers, workers, street people, peasants and [even] bedouins played various roles in this revolution.'[23]

The Milner Mission, sent in the winter of 1919, was commissioned to 'investigate, examine and determine the future form of the British protectorate.'[24] The intention was that any recommendation from this body of six respected British dignitaries would still be determined on the basis of Egypt as a British territory. The Mission's boycott by the Egyptian populace (Egyptians were discouraged from speaking with any member of the Mission), proved successful since its eventual report to the British government in London discussed with candour Britain's shortcomings in Egypt and the possibility of abolishing the British protectorate.[25] As long as the actions of the British government were interpreted by pro-independent Egyptians as dithering or delaying Egypt's independence, demonstrations and disruptions followed. In sum, the origins of the Revolution came from the grievances against the British during the First World War and the continuing drive for independence in face of the British government's opposition, both at the time of the Paris Peace Conference and thereafter. The actions of the demonstrators included riots, strikes, violence, murdering Britons, and disrupting communication and transportation. Eventually, by February 1922, Allenby, tired of the ongoing impasse and instability in Egypt, announced the independence of Egypt – granted on the basis of four 'reserved' points. The four points were areas that Britain would retain control of until future negotiations: Egypt's defence and foreign policy, the security of the Suez Canal, the governing of Sudan, and the protection of foreign interests and inhabitants in Egypt (i.e. the Capitulations).

Delay in Demobilisation

After observing the causes and events of the 1919–22 revolutionary period, we now turn to the wide range of problems and challenges that the British community in Egypt faced during this time. Perhaps one of the immediate challenges was the severe delay in the demobilising of British troops to Europe after the armistice in November 1918. Compared to the 5000 men in the British Army of Occupation in 1914, there were around 400,000 troops under imperial command in Egypt at the end of 1918.[26] Though many of these troops were not ethnically British in origin because they included Indian soldiers and men from other colonies, there was still a significant percentage from Britain. British soldiers, and in particular the officers, were part of the Egypt's British community due to their social interaction with other British residents through participating in many dinners, dances, and church services as well as receiving hospitality, entertainment, and health care. Although many were demobilised within the first six months after the war (more than 250,000 were demobilised), close to 130,000 men were still left in Egypt in June 1919.[27] Though demobilisation may have been intentionally delayed since Egypt was undergoing a time of instability and upheaval soon after the war, it was still the main operation of the military authorities. Soldiers and officers, caught in the delay, suffered from impatience and inactivity. Though promised demobilisation six months after the end of the war, many had to wait a much longer period of time before returning home due to bureaucratic delays and extended strikes in Britain. In 'the case of those who [had] employment waiting for them at home, [or] in the case of married men and those who have had no U.K. leave for two years or more, impatience [was] as great as ever.'[28] Many of these soldiers, who were waiting to be sent home, became harsh critics of the British military command. According to one frustrated captain, the military authorities were untrustworthy and 'can break their word, [but] we break ours under pain of death.'[29] He wrote to his father saying:

> It is a typical bit of filthy wangling that makes the Army Red Tape and the authorities in general so loathsome in the eyes of every decent man. Over the demobilization of officers the Army has broken every bit of good faith it ever had. Out of 42 officers in the Div. 1 Artillery, 29 are being retained...One major is a solicitor, the only remaining in the firm. Another captain had one year to go before his final for the bar. His contemporaries will now gain a year over him...Incidentally, he is married...There is terrific discontent...You would have thought too that three and half years continuous service abroad would be something in my favour. I am

not only frightfully disappointed...I am thoroughly disgusted...I am fed up to the teeth with everything.[30]

As they waited, their discontent grew and their morale weakened as one soldier expressed, 'They can keep me I suppose, but I'm damned if they can make me work.'[31]
They unsuccessfully appealed to dispense with 'unnecessary' parades and increase their quota of amusements, concerts, and relaxation since they felt that they were largely a civilian army by this time, though some did see action in putting down the riots of March 1919.[32] Yet, perhaps their greatest source of despair and frustration was due to the scarcity of jobs back in Britain.

The...uneasiness – and it amounts to exasperation – is due to the almost certain knowledge that the best 'jobs' are being seized at home by those whom fortune has favoured with early demobilization, and worse still by the munition workers, 'shirkers' and the 'conchies' whose release is being petitioned for, so many of whom stayed at home when they should have 'joined up ' and gone out to fight.[33]

Even officers were not exempt from the prospect of unemployment.

With officers...the case is different and while many look to securing official posts in the Middle East, a greater proportion are wondering whether, on returning to civil life they will be able to get work and salaries that will enable them to continue to live at anything like the standard of the last few years. The common impression is that they will not, and they are worried about it.[34]

The delay in demobilisation caused great disappointment among British military personnel and provided an opportunity for British residents of the community to serve them. For example, funds were raised by members of the Alexandria's British community, under the auspices of the Alexandria British Benevolent Fund, for some of the soldiers' expenses[35] Money was also generated by Alexandria's Britons to provide a souvenir booklet for all the British troops in the city to take home with them.[36] Eventually, the demobilisation did take place. By March 1920, there were 100,000 troops under British imperial command in Egypt. By April 1921, there were 25,000; and by the summer of 1921 around 20,000 remained.[37] Although the number that lingered was still more than three times the size of the pre-war British garrison of about 5,000 men, their prospects back home were also limited since Britain was undergoing a sharp recession at this time.

Impending Abolition of Capitulations

Besides the delay in the demobilisation of troops, another area that aroused opposition to British authorities from members of the British community was the imminent abolition of the Capitulations. As explained in chapter 2, the Capitulations were an arrangement whereby Europeans were allowed to be tried under the courts and legal codes of their own countries in Egypt. However, toward the end of the First World War, there was the anticipation that the Capitulations would cease and that a new legal code represented by the draft laws may be implemented to replace the Consular Courts. Under the draft laws,

> an Englishman will be tried under a modified form of the Native Code, and in the Mixed Courts. The proceedings will be conducted in a foreign language. The judge who hears the case may be a foreigner, who knows no word of English, and whose training under a foreign criminal system will certainly have imbued him with ideas of criminal law fundamentally opposed to the British sense of fair play...Under the British system, the accused cannot be compelled to make any statement; under the new system, not only can he be compelled, but his answers in English may have to be interpreted by a person whose language the accused does not know, to a judge who does not know English. Further...the accused may be convicted on a statement drawn up by a foreign official without any opportunity to traversing the accuracy of the statement...In civil cases British subjects will have their rights determined under a polyglot Code instead of under English law.[38]

Therefore, the Council of the Non-Official British Community (discussed in more depth later) urged all Britons in Egypt to 'take every possible measure to prevent the final adoption of the laws [since] to allow them to come into effective force would be nothing less than a calamity to the community.'[39] Although the Capitulations were not officially abolished until the Montreux Convention in October, 1937 (and even then, the Consular Courts were given twelve more years of life),[40] the threat of the implementation of the draft laws was doubtlessly a significant concern for Britons in Egypt at that time.

Compensation for Death and Injury

Besides encountering the delay in demobilising and the imminent abolition of the Capitulations during the revolutionary period, the British in Egypt faced death, injury, and the challenge of acquiring compensation for the casualties. Britons killed during this period appeared to have been murdered indiscriminately as one observer pinpointed in his memoirs:

> Rioting and bloodshed, railway lines torn up, [and the] assassination of isolated bands of British officers, were now the order of the day... Sporadic assassinations occurred from time to time – here, a young corporal, on his way to spend an evening with his young lady, – there, a Professor in the Law School, riding home on his bicycle to lunch. Some twenty-two or twenty-three British subjects, several of them known personally to the writer, were either fatally, or at any rate, seriously, injured in this way.[41]

The death toll of British personnel in Egypt began to mount on 15 March 1919 when at Kailub Markaz, about 2000 rioters gathered near a train station carrying pieces of timber and sticks. The police tried to disperse the crowd but when British soldiers and passengers arrived at the train station, one British soldier was shot dead while three Egyptians were killed and some were arrested.[42] More significantly, seven Britons were killed in the events of 18 March 1919 near Deirut, between Assiut and Minia. The seven were Alexander Pope, Inspector of Prisons in Upper Egypt; Major Cecil Jarvis of 20th Decca House in the India Army; R. F. B. Willsy, Staff Lieutenant; plus Summersgill, Peacock, Culyer, and Private Reading. All were unarmed in the first class carriage on the train from Luxor to Assiut. Along the train line on that day, 'there had been much excitement...including greeting of trains with patriotic cries, free travelling by crowds, and demonstrations of hostility to...English inspectors.'[43] When the train arrived at Deirut, a large crowd attacked the train and some rioters entered the first class carriage and killed two of the Britons.[44] In response, the acting stationmaster at Deirut sent a message to the local police in Dier Molis. When the train arrived in

Dier Molis, the police officer came with just six unarmed men out of a possible forty armed men that were available, sent no further warning to other police stations, and did nothing while the crowd grew more and more violent. Sixty Egyptian soldiers returning from Sudan on the train cheered the rioters. In fear of the crowd and attempting to escape, two Britons reached the engine and together with the Egyptian driver, tried to start the train but the vacuum brake had been applied. The driver fled whilst the two Britons were overpowered and battered to death. Three other Britons made it to the engine but were killed as well. One British telegram recorded that 'five bodies battered beyond recognition were thrown on the platform, stripped and subjected to [the] worst indignities.'[45] Though many railway officials and employees did all they could to help, British sources asserted that the police and Egyptian army passengers did nothing: 'If police officials in Assiut did their job, the massacre would not have taken place.'[46] Eventually, 34 Egyptians were sentenced to death, six to life imprisonment, others to hard labour and fines, and some were acquitted.[47]

Britons in Egypt continued to face the threat of murder during this period. In April 1919, Egyptian State Railways employee Dykes was killed in Abdin Square. He 'was shot opposite to and 30 yards from [the] barracks of the Egyptian Army...and received two wounds.'[48] British witnesses saw two shots fired from the barracks while Egyptian witnesses say that British patrols also fired shots. A week later, a Reuters telegram reported that three British soldiers and two Indian soldiers were murdered.[49] Approximately 75 Britons were killed or injured during the violent uprisings in the spring and summer of 1919 while at least 1000 Egyptians died at the hands of British troops attempting to suppress the insurrection.[50] In November 1919, another British officer was killed.[51] Six months later, the *Egyptian Gazette* recorded the attack and murder of another British officer, 'shot by an unknown person in Sharia Boulac.'[52] In December 1921, Mr. Hatton, a British employee of the Egyptian State Railways, was killed by gunfire.[53] Two months later, Michael Jordan, a British resident, and Mr. Brown of the Egyptian Department of Public Instruction were also slain.[54] In May 1922, the Assistant Commander of the Cairo Police, W. F. Cunliffe-Cave, 'was shot dead in a quarter of Cairo where most of the Egyptian Ministries were situated.'[55] From February to May of 1922, 'attempts...[were] made on the lives of no fewer than seven British subjects in Cairo, but in no instance [were] arrests...made.'[56]

Besides the loss of life, British soldiers and civilians also suffered injuries as a result of the violence. For example, four British soldiers were fired at and wounded in November 1919. During the following month, four more were shot and injured in two separate occasions.[57] In May 1920, a Munster Fusiler officer and two Tommies (British privates) were shot on a main street in Cairo.[58] Besides soldiers, civilians such as 'railway officials...Mr. Price Hopkins and Mr. Peach [were]...shot in the streets of Cairo and [received] not very serious...wounds'[59] in February 1922. The deaths and injuries incurred by the Britons of Egypt both reflected and contributed to the hostile atmosphere between Britons and Egyptians at that time.

Not only did Britons in Egypt experience the casualties mentioned, they had to deal with the struggle for compensation from the authorities. Certain members of Egypt's British community found themselves at odds with the British authorities, similar to what some of them faced in light of the delay in demobilisation and the potential abolition of the Capitulations. A month after Mr. Hatton's murder, the Egyptian State Railways requested that the Ministry of Finance pay for his funeral expenses. The Ministry of Finance 'ruled that these expenses [were not to] be defrayed by [the] Government.'[60] The Cairo Station Manager's office records that this denial of funeral expenses caused widespread resentment among the more than 230 Englishmen who worked for the Egyptian State Railways.[61]

> This decision...caused widespread indignation amongst the English staff of the State Railways...As one high official said to me this morning: 'I have a wife and children who will be put into serious straits if I am murdered; if they have to pay for my funeral expenses I shall give orders that my body is to be conveyed...in the cheapest wooden box procurable, which will be an object lesson of the generosity of the Egyptian Government, as doubtless, the cortege would be followed by a considerable number of...officials and subordinates.'[62]

Eventually, the Financial Adviser allowed the Ministry of Communications to pay for Mr. Hatton's funeral expenses after much hard work and ill will on the part of the employees of the Egyptian State Railways.[63] Although Mr. Hatton had no immediate dependants,[64] his family was eventually awarded E£6171 in compensation for his death while working for the Egyptian State Railways.[65]

Though the process of acquiring compensation for Hatton's death was long drawn out, the outcome was desirable for his family and for the Egyptian State Railways. Similarly, the widow of Mr. Aldred Brown also had to wait before she was awarded compensation of any kind. Mr. Aldred Brown, of the Egyptian Department of Public Instruction, was killed on the eve of retirement, in February 1922, after 31 years of pensionable service. Shortly thereafter, the High Commissioner informed Mrs. Brown that she would be awarded Mr. Brown's pension of E£268 per annum regardless of what she may acquire in a capital sum in compensation. In the five subsequent months, the pension only reached Mrs. Brown in February and March but not in April, May or June – highlighting the government's inefficiency. By June, Mrs. Brown's compensation of E£10,000 was finally approved and she was given assurance by Lord Allenby that her pension would also be given her monthly.[66]

For Mrs. W. F. Cunliffe-Cave, who was younger, her annual pension consisted of E£600. However, if she remarried, it would decrease to E£212 per annum. Her son also received E£250 annually until the age of twenty-three.[67] Mrs. Cave's compensation was significantly smaller than Mrs. Brown because she was 'considerably younger...[and,] according to the rules which govern pensions,...her award ought to lapse in the event of her marrying again.'[68]

The Hatton, Brown, and Cunliffe-Cave families received, though sometimes after a considerable delay, substantial amounts in compensation for the loss of their loved ones. Naturally, compensations for the injured were not as generous, but appeared to be fair on the whole. Mr. Price Hopkins and Mr. Peach received hospital expenses and full pay during convalescence.[69] Though the British authorities initially denied that Hopkins and Peach were attacked by reason of their duties and classified them with normal illnesses or injuries,[70] the Foreign Office urged the government

> to accord them compensation...calculated on the basis of the rate of pay of the official concerned multiplied by the number of days during which he was prevented from resuming his work, exclusive of any ordinary leave granted after his wounds had completely healed.[71]

Subsequently, Mr. Peach's injury deemed him unfit for work and he was given a compensation of E£5,600 if he chose immediate retirement.[72] When it came to paying compensation to Britons in Egypt for the death of relatives and injuries incurred due to the violence of the revolutionary era, the British authorities appeared to oblige eventually though not without an arduous delay.

Threat of Violent Attacks and Plans to Counter Them

Though certain Britons faced death, injury, or the loss of a loved one, the entire British community in Egypt experienced a general sense of fear and danger. Some sought to develop plans to counter the threats of violence against them. George Swan, Secretary of the Egypt General Mission, wrote to the British Consul in Cairo requesting protection for his missionaries based near Cairo: Miss F. A. Langford and Miss S. W. Pim in Belbeis, and Mr. A. M. May, Miss Liblite, Miss Perkins, and Mr. and Mrs. A. Y. Steel and their two children, in Shebin el-Kanata. Swan wrote that he would 'be grateful if some steps could be taken for their protection…[as] the mob has given away to wanton murder and pillage.'[73] Further, he urged the British Consul to protect other missionaries in Alexandria, Ismailia, and the Suez.

In 1919, a telegram from a British employee of the Anglo-Egyptian bank also expressed the degree of risk and concern that the British community faced in Cairo.

> On Friday afternoon very serious rioting took place here just near the bank and three or four men were killed. The worst incidents were in front of the French Post Office which is at the corner of the street that runs beside the bank. The mob which numbered thousands…filled the whole of Sherif Pasha St. and the Mohamed Ali Square and behaved like wild beasts. They smashed open and sacked several shops…and the police only arrived when all was over. The acting Chief of Police, an Englishman, undertook to keep order…*All authority is openly defied and unless something is done, and done quickly, we may be faced with consequences of a very grave nature. What little prestige remained to us is gone, and the natives attribute our attitude to fear.* No one who was not an eyewitness of what took place can form an idea of the wild and unchecked disorder.[74]

More than a year later, British staff members of the Anglo-Egyptian Bank at Minet el-Bassal near Alexandria were warned not to leave their homes due to the rioting in that city. In the days that followed, they safely reached the bank and kept the property intact even though some members were harassed.[75]

Besides soldiers, missionaries, and bankers, senior officials also faced significant risks. One Foreign Office document revealed that death threats were made on the High Commissioner and members of the Milner Mission.

> Information of unknown origin has been received from source, purporting to be in touch with certain Egyptian nationalists…This information reports…the existence of [a] plot to assassinate the High Commissioner…and all members of Lord Milner's Mission as soon as they land.[76]

Other Britons were targeted by paid assassins as well. Abou Zaid, an official in the Ports and Lights Administration in Port Said had received a top secret message with instructions from the Egyptian Association in London to pay every Egyptian or Italian E£100 for shooting British officers, E£50 for British soldiers and E£25 for civilian women and children.[77]

> It seems clear that Englishmen [were] being shot at or assassinated simply because they [were] English and incidents cannot fail to greatly increase the uneasiness of British officials of Egypt whose faith in the Prime Minister's willingness and ability to safeguard their position [was] not…strengthened by the failure of the Government to prevent the perpetration of these political crimes.[78]

To confront the threats, the British community reacted by implementing various precautionary measures. First, a chain of communication starting from the most prominent members of the British community through which warnings of potential danger may be passed on to every British person in a given location was established in Cairo and then encouraged in Alexandria.

> The best procedure would appear to be that adopted in Cairo, namely, to warn the leading British residents in certain selected districts throughout Alexandria in a personal and confidential manner, making them responsible in their turn for the warning of those of lesser standing living in their respective neighbourhoods.[79]

Second, for Britons outside the main urban centres, James Morgan, Acting Consul of the British Consulate in Cairo, drew up a list of all British subjects living in places like Mansura, Zagazig, and Birket-es-Sab. Though not many Britons lived outside Cairo and Alexandria, the list included missionaries, engineers, inspectors, merchants, teachers, and officials of the Ministry of Public Works and Agriculture. The list allowed the military authorities to know who required protection or assistance.[80] A further precaution was the insistence that British residents in Egypt were to 'take refuge in certain places where they [were to] be under military protection...in case of a serious rising taking place.'[81] Thus security arrangements for buildings like the British Consulate in Cairo were assessed. Captain Heard, Acting Consul-General in Cairo suggested 'that a British officer should go over the Consulate with him, and discuss its vulnerability and how best it could be defended by the Staff in case of a sudden attack by a mob. The consulate [was] on the street and the lower windows [were] only protected by wooden shutters.'[82] Furthermore, the British were discouraged from going out alone.[83] Perhaps the most controversial safety measure was the bearing of arms. Heard suggested that 'the...[British] consulates and Consular Agencies in the country...should be given a stand of arms and a supply of ammunition which would be under the sole control of the Consulate and used solely for the defence of Consular Buildings and of such British Nationals as had taken refuge there in time of stress.'[84] He had in mind the protection of smaller consulates such as the ones in Monsura or Zagazig where British military assistance was not easily available. However, one obvious concern with this suggestion was that other consulates of other nations might also begin to arm themselves, setting an undesirable precedent that may further threaten the general security of Egypt and the authority of Britain. The British authorities responded by stating that only Britons were allowed to bear arms and that they were to be armed in consular agencies surreptitiously.[85]

To protect the vital line of communication represented by the Eastern Telegraph Company buildings in Suez, Sir W. N. Congreve, the Lieutenant-General commanding the Egyptian Expeditionary Force, proposed the idea of establishing a volunteer guard of forty British men 'for the defence of the Eastern Telegraph Company's buildings in the event of emergency when required by the Military Authorities...Such a force might be of great assistance in an emergency.'[86] Congreve pointed out that there were precedents for this idea in the Abu Zaabal wireless station near Cairo and the Civilian Rifle Club at Alexandria both of which had armed civilian guards.[87] General Clayton, Adviser to Ministry of Interior approved of the idea and suggested that the civil guard be called the Eastern Telegraph Rifle Club of Suez, following the precedent set by other rifle clubs in Cairo and Alexandria.[88]

Similarly, Captain H. E. V. Huggett of the Royal Fusiliers promoted the idea of establishing a volunteer army in 1922 consisting of British residents in Egypt. Recruits would be British residents of military age that had served in the Great War as officers or soldiers along with a proportion of non-commissioned officers. The proposal assumed the raising of four companies of men at headquarters, two in Cairo, one in Alexandria, and one in the Canal Zone. Like the Territorial Battalion in Britain, there were possibilities for pay and training in the new volunteer army.[89] However, the High Commissioner rejected the scheme due to fears that it may arouse other nationalities in Egypt to do likewise.[90] To counteract the threats of physical harm or death to many different groups within Egypt's British community during the revolutionary period, the British in Egypt devised various schemes such as communication trees and armed guards. Ideas were disallowed if they were seen to decrease British military control over Egypt or escalate violence such as permitting other foreign consulates to use firearms.

Economic Downturn

Sharp rise in the cost of living

Finally, this chapter aims to unravel the many economic setbacks, concerns, and responses that Britons in Egypt encountered as a result of the revolutionary period. One of the economic problems that they faced was the sharp rise in the cost of living. It was generally assumed that prices would drop after the war since high prices were regarded as a 'war measure'[91] due to the inflationary impact of the imperial troops' spending power, as discussed in the previous chapter. However, prices stayed high due to the shortage of raw material, the continuation of high wages, the need to clothe the demobilised men,[92] and the severe food shortages. In fact, the cost of living index increased from 1919 to 1920 even in spite of the nationalist disturbances that shook Egypt at the time. As stated in the previous chapter, the cost of living index had been 100 in 1914. During the war, the index doubled to 202 in 1919, and increased further to 237 in 1920. Although the index dropped gradually in subsequent years (196 in 1921, 176 in 1922, and 162 in 1923), it was still much higher than pre-war levels. [93] Although 'merchants, tradesmen and landowners had profited during the boom of 1919,...wage-earners and the salaried class were hard hit by the high cost of living'[94] and many in the British community were wage-earners and salaried. For example, British teachers suffered due to the high cost of living.

> The failure to improve the salaries of foreign teachers in accordance with the present cost of living in Egypt results in very serious hardship to them, and we view our future in this country with grave alarm. A married man with children will find the greatest difficulty in paying his household expenses. With the present low rate of salary and absence of any opportunity of obtaining promotion, he has no prospect of so improving his position as to be able to educate his children adequately. In case of an expensive illness he would inevitably incur debts which he would find it almost impossible to pay. Moreover, unless he has private means of his own, he will not be able to go on leave to Europe with his family, however urgent the need may be on account of health, family, business or other reasons.[95]

The teachers were also not awarded any expatriation pay and surprisingly started with an initial salary not much different from their Egyptian colleagues. They even had less seniority than their Egyptian colleagues with the same qualifications. Their salaries did not keep up with the rise in the cost of living which had gone up 100 per cent since 1914 and journeys home to Britain had increased nearly fourfold from the prices of 1913.[96] Remarkably, British teachers waited six to eight years for even a small rise in salary.[97]

British salaried bank officials also suffered due to the high cost of living. A letter drafted by a group of British Anglo-Egyptian bank officials urged for salary increases following the example of British officials in the civil service who were receiving substantial cost of living bonuses.

> The cost of living is extremely high, higher for all English requisites in every case than in England, and with a noticeable upward tendency. This has been realised and compensated by the Government for example, by the fact that they have increased the salaries of junior officials...by 20% (fixed) plus 60% compensation for the high cost of living (to be retained) during the present prevalence of abnormal prices...We trust that you and the

Board will take a favourable view of the fore-going remarks and ameliorate the somewhat severe conditions under which we are at present working in your service.[98]

Later, another senior bank official in Egypt also urged the management in London to consider the salary increases.

As regards to...the young Englishmen's automatic rises...these should not be withheld. The salaries which they are receiving, although perhaps appearing to be large on paper, do not leave them much margin over and above their living expenses. In any case, the rises which were given them...last...May, were granted purely in order to meet the present-day high cost of living, and as such, should not affect in any way automatic increases.[99]

The post-war period ushered in a difficult time of high cost of living for many Britons in Egypt. As one bank official laments, 'there is no doubt that the cost of living here is increasing almost daily...Food and clothing are at ridiculous prices and so far as one can see there is little hope of improvement despite talk about control.'[100]

Revolutionary violence and the British business community

Besides the sharp rise in the cost of living, revolutionary violence posed a major challenge to the British business community in Egypt. Looting and the threat of looting meant that certain shops or banks had to close or were damaged. Due to the halting of transportation links, as a result of violence and intimidation, trading and shipping were handicapped and imported goods were not able to leave customs. This caused severe loss for British businesses due to the accumulation of storage fees and the loss of sales. British manufacturers were also harmed because they were unable to obtain payments for shipments because customers could not receive the products. J. W. Eady, a British businessman and agent for thirty English firms in Egypt reported that 'business was completely paralysed, wholesale merchants could not meet their financial engagements as collections from the villages are precluded,'[101] and predicted widespread bankruptcies if the situation persisted.[102]

In light of the nationalistic uprisings, there was the fear that British products in Egypt would face a widespread boycott by Egyptian activists. To counter that possibility, British businesses created advertisements that urged Britons to 'make sure that [their] uniform or suit is made of the best British material obtainable in Egypt and [to] support British industry for [their] own satisfaction.'[103] Though the boycott would have hurt British businesses, it never attained the mass appeal needed to decisively harm British business interests because many Egyptians were committed to certain British products 'which were in...heavy demand for years, and which would continue to be sought.'[104] In certain circumstances, brand loyalty prevailed over nationalistic interests.

The widespread disruptions also hurt the process of reclaiming the Northern Delta and the British firms involved in this venture. Agriculture was the body and soul of Egypt and much of its further development depended on the reclamation of the Northern Delta, which required the on-site expertise and supervision of many British firms. But in light of the threats on Britons, 'all the work of reclamation now stopped due to fears of uprisings since Englishmen were not safe to visit remote districts.'[105] As a result, cattle were dying due to lack of water and the reclamation project came to a halt – not only harming the present and future prospects of Egypt's economy but many of the British firms involved in the completion of the project.[106]

The British railway companies

Closer examination of a few British businesses during this time may help in highlighting the diverse challenges that Britons faced during the revolutionary era. The Egyptian State Railways suffered the deaths and injuries of some of its British employees. The company employed 31,536 people in total, of whom 232 were British. The Britons were mainly engineering specialists and most of them were situated at the Boulaq shops. For some reason, few Egyptians were attracted to working as locomotive engineers and even if they were interested, it would have taken years to train Egyptian engineers to replace British ones. Thus the company consistently needed to recruit many more British engineers. Yet, with the inadequate salaries and the uncertainties of living in a volatile Egyptian regime, British engineers were hard to come by. When 'there [was] a chance of a man being maimed for life, or killed, at all events enduring considerable suffering, it [was] hardly supposed that [the company would] be able to attract the proper class of man.'[107] The only encouragement for prospective engineers was to inform them that if they were maimed or killed, they or their families would be generously compensated.[108] Even with the 'attraction' of compensation, drawing in new and much-needed British engineers was a major problem for the Egyptian State Railways. Not only did the British community in Egypt lose some key railway engineers due to death and injury, but the disturbances kept away potential British newcomers from entering Egypt and may have dampened the morale of those Britons who stayed.

Another company with substantial British shareholding was the Egyptian Delta Light Railway. In March 1919, a trail of damage to the company's railway lines and carriages had 'an immediate effect... upon [its] earnings.'[109] Windows of carriages were broken. Goods under transport were stolen. Trains were derailed. Lines were cut in many places. Several of the train stations were burnt and pillaged.

The company's train service was entirely suspended. For some days, the wreckage of the company's property continued. Many stations were wrecked, and very considerable damage was done...Rails were pulled up and bent, sleepers were burnt, embankments were destroyed, and the telegraph lines were practically wiped out of existence. The destruction of communications was evidently one of the chief aims of the rioters.[110]

At Mit Ghamr, where the company's main railway workshops were based, much credit was given to McKay who successfully defended the properties from attack.

Thanks to the courage and resourcefulness of Mr. McKay, [the] chief locomotive superintendent, who organised measures for [the] defence of his staff, the attack failed...Due to Mr. McKay's efforts, [the company] suffered no serious damage...Had these shops been wrecked, it [was] difficult to estimate the loss.[111]

Altogether, the Egyptian Delta Light Railways lost more than E£47,000 through the property damage and an additional £46,000 in earnings owing to the military authorities' prohibition of train services.[112]

The Anglo-Egyptian Bank

Another example of a British-run business that suffered as a result of the upheavals was the Anglo-Egyptian Bank. Arthur Blunt, manager of the Alexandria branch recalled in 1919 that business was 'at a complete standstill,...profits will be by no means brilliant this half-year [and]... no insurance policy covers the risk of loss from civil commotion.'[113] However, though the banks in Cairo and Alexandria struggled, 'it [was] never...necessary to close [their] doors.'[114] Another serious problem for the banks was the strikes of its Egyptian employees. C. W. Green, Blunt's successor, wrote to the bank's chairman in London to suggest that his employees were on the verge of a strike.

> The political situation is most unsatisfactory…Industrial unrest has spread to most trades, and it is a nasty feature of this movement that the strikes which have so far been settled have resulted in victories for the men. The Alexandria Syndicate of Bank Clerks held a meeting yesterday evening…which according to rumour it was definitely decided to strike. As soon as I have official information on the subject I will advise you.[115]

Since the Egyptian civil servants were given a pay rise of 20 per cent plus an additional war allowance, Egyptian bank clerks also felt that they were entitled to a substantial increase.[116] They were offered a 20 per cent bonus but they refused this 'on the grounds that [the] bonus [was] not salary and can be stopped at any moment.'[117] By October 1919, upon hearing that the Credit Lyonnais was to grant raises of 15 to 50 per cent to its employees plus a war allowance of 20 to 25 per cent plus bonuses, the Alexandria Syndicate of Bank Clerks voted 600 to 18 in favour of strike action.[118] Green felt that the syndicate 'was in irresponsible and bad hands.'[119] The strike took place on 16 October. All 'business was stopped [and]…a large crowd remained in front of the bank to impede the entrance of staff. Police protection…was present.'[120] Though the strikes eventually ended with Egyptian bank staff accepting the salary increases and bonuses which were slightly less than those awarded to the employees of Credit Lyonnais, these strikes proved to be a trying time for British bank managers and staff. Not only did British bank staff have to work harder when their Egyptian employees on strike, British managers also feared the decline of their authority over their Egyptian employees. One manager, Brewsher, asked for a transfer after he realised that 'the possibility of his authority being ignored [was] well-grounded…[when] only one member of the staff spoke in his defence.'[121]

The Non-Official British Community and its opposition to the government

The challenges of instability, violence, loss of profits, and strikes caused much suffering for British business interests during the revolutionary period and precipitated the forming of the Non-Official British Community. In April 1919, Mr. W. E. Kingsford, Chairman of the British Chamber of Commerce and resident of Egypt for over 33 years, met with High Commissioner Allenby to discuss the effects of the disturbances on the society and commerce. At this meeting, Kingsford suggested the enforcement of martial law, the suspension of the Egyptian Prime Minister's authority until the restoration of order, the arrest of the uprisings' key leaders, and the appointment of a non-official advisory board made up of experienced British residents.[122] This advisory board of non-official British residents was called the Non-Official British Community and later the British Union in Egypt.[123] It consisted of prominent members of the British community, primarily in the business world though some came from other professions as well. The members of the advisory board argued that their view and voice was needed in the governing body of Egypt (not only in any popular assembly but in the Executive Council as well) since they were far more experienced in understanding the commercial and social situation than government officials. Also, through their long-established relationships and intimate contact with the Egyptian population, they were more likely to know or have access to more information concerning trade and commerce in Egypt than any government official.[124] The Non-Official British Community saw itself as a counterweight to the poor quality of new British officials in Egypt, mentioned earlier, who contributed to the Egyptians' growing resentment against the British. Kingsford describes that:

> In recent years too many of an unsuitable class and character have been employed in some of the Government Departments, to the exclusion in many cases of qualified and capable natives. This had had a discouraging effect on the latter, and created a feeling of enmity and want of confidence in the stated good intentions under the Occupation. The feeling of trust and cooperation...[that] previously existed, has to a large extent been sacrificed. Young Englishmen though influence have been jockeyed into positions for which they were unfitted, attracted by an easy life, unwarrantably short hours of work, and a pension at the end of their service. Such men have been too frequently recruited from the Public Instruction Department...with too little regard to their suitability... Many of the Englishmen in Egypt are lacking in tact, courtesy and consideration. Owing either to antipathy, or absence of knowledge of native customs, they hold themselves aloof and fail to command the respect or sympathetic confidence of the native.[125]

Although there were sufficient reasons to form the Non-Official British Community due to its expertise and experience, linkage with the Egyptian population, and depth of insight and competence far exceeding novice British officials, the association was only formed when the revolution threatened British sovereignty over Egypt.

By establishing the Non-Official British Community, British business leaders in Egypt were concerned that the British authorities were not proceeding effectively in their governance of Egypt. They felt that the British authorities had not sufficiently appreciated that the governing of a Muslim nation by a Western 'Christian' nation was fraught with peculiar dangers and to govern well, with the least amount of problems, required utmost wisdom and circumspection.[126] The Non-Official British Community felt that the British Foreign Office lacked 'a definite policy in Egypt [and that its] direction of Egyptian affairs [was] deficient both in sympathy and knowledge.'[127] The Non-Official British Community seemed to have favoured a much more conciliatory approach to governing Egypt. It asserted that 'Egypt should become a self-governing country in close and friendly alliance with the British Empire, Egyptians [should be given] wider opportunities of showing their administrative capacities,...[and] the rights of British subjects now existing under Consular jurisdiction [should continue].'[128]

On the contrary, other businessmen such as Walton, a senior official at the Anglo-Egyptian Bank argued that 'this policy of "wait and see" on the part of Great Britain hardly seems to be the thing judging by results. I think...Roosevelt's advice to govern or get out would be a much better line to follow.'[129] Elsewhere, he stated that, 'we seem to have made things worse by our continued dilatory policy and to have lost another opportunity of settling things once and for all.'[130] Likewise, other businessmen 'believed that the nationalist movement could be extinguished if it was given a sharp blow by the British, but if the currently lenient and cautious policies were followed the nationalists would [grow] strong.'[131] If independence was given more quickly, activists would have had less impetus to engage in violence. If the uprisings were subdued more promptly, then the perpetrators of the hostilities would have been aggressively punished and their actions restrained. Businessmen, in favour of stability in order for their businesses to thrive, opposed the Foreign Office's policy of delay that allowed time and resolve to build among the nationalists.

Why then did British politicians adopt a policy of delay? In their opinion, giving in to demands for Egyptian independence was premature in light of Britain's strategic, political and economic interests in Egypt – notably the control of the Suez Canal, defence and foreign policy, and the advantages afforded by the Capitulations. Further they did not feel that Egypt was ready for self-governance. Also, to have crushed the nationalists with excessive force would have fuelled opposition propaganda and alienated more moderate supporters of British political involvement in Egypt. For the Foreign Office, to withhold force demonstrated Britain's peaceable administration of Egypt and prevented the issue of its independence from accruing more world attention.[132] The British government needed to exercise a delicate balance in handling of the strikes, the violence, and indeed, the revolution. It opted for the maintenance of order by suppressing criminal activity such as attacks on individuals and damage to property, but permitted protests to take place. However, by February 1922, considerable independence was accorded to Egypt in light of the failure of the Milner Mission and the nationalist fervour throughout the country.

Conclusion

After a look at the origins and the nature of the revolution until the granting of independence in 1922, this chapter examined the diversity of challenges that Britons in Egypt faced during this time and their varying responses to them. These challenges included the delay in demobilisation (alongside the paucity of job opportunities for returning soldiers in Britain), the imminent abolition of the Capitulations, and the arduous quest for compensation for deaths or injuries. They also consisted of the ongoing threat of attacks and the associated economic hardships which involved a sharp rise in the cost of living that provoked some British teachers and bank officials to seek salary increases, and the closure and bankruptcies of businesses due largely to the inability to transport goods as a result of the violence. The unrest hurt the railway business as tracks and carriages were damaged and goods stolen. Strikes by Egyptian employees also brought the Anglo-Egyptian bank to a standstill since there were not enough British staff members to cover for their Egyptian colleagues and certain British managers seemed to have lost authority over their Egyptian workers. As a response to the economic downturn of the time, the Non-Official British Community was formed. It argued for the enforcement of martial law, arrest for key leaders of the uprising, and the establishment of an advisory board made up of experienced British residents (as opposed to the 'official' civil and military services) to give input to the governance of Egypt. One central disagreement with the British authorities was the perceived lack of decisiveness in dealing with the disturbances. The members of the Non-Official British Community, many of whom were from the business world, favoured either granting self-rule to Egyptians or a heavy-handed end to the nationalist movement. Whatever the case, they wanted the immediate restoration of stability for businesses to resume trading. However, the British government felt that conceding self-governance to the Egyptians, whom they viewed as ill-equipped, would harm Britain's strategic and economic interests in Egypt, while forceful action against the nationalists would fuel more hostile opposition and alienate moderate supporters of Britain's involvement there. It is hoped that this discussion of the variety of challenges that Britons faced during the revolutionary period as well as their different responses to them contributes to a key theme in this book – to demonstrate the diversity that existed within Egypt's British community. As well, since little has been written about the British in Egypt who were not part of the civil or military services at that time, this chapter aims to address another key intention of this work – to uncover hitherto overlooked aspects of the history of Egypt's Britons during the colonial era.

CONCLUSION

On 28 February 1922, Britain issued a declaration announcing the end of the Protectorate and the beginning of the independence of Egypt. From that point onwards, the British community in Egypt started to decline in numbers.

As soon as the Anglo-Egyptian agreement was brought into force and it became known that the services of British officials would no longer be required, a liberal scheme of compensation for loss in pay and pension was prepared by the Residency and accepted with a generous gesture by the Egyptian government.[1]

By 'twos and threes, by tens and then by hundreds, British officials were being sent away.'[2] They received healthy packages of compensation. Men from 40 to 50 years old who earned £E1400 to £E2000 per year were being awarded £E4000 to £E5000 in compensation. Although these payouts were generous, the officials were giving up their life's work and few were qualified to work in other fields. Though the numbers of British businessmen did not dwindle as much as the number of British officials who were being 'forced' to leave,[3] a report on the finances of Cairo's All Saint's Church in 1922 illustrates the sizeable exodus of Britons from Egypt.

> Finance greatly preoccupies [our Church Council]. We are faced with the possibility of a deficit in 1923. Not only have many supporters left the country, but many more are leaving, and those who remain find the calls upon their generosity more than they can meet. Every effort is being made to increase the sources of revenue

but it should be remembered that the congregation has the solution of the difficulty in its own hands. Every member should scrutinise the accounts, satisfy himself that there is no waste, and then see to what extent he can not only increase his own contribution but induce any of his friends and acquaintances who do not contribute to do so...*No organisation of collectors could possibly vie in efficiency with such a mass movement of the whole congregation.*[4]

The declaration of Egyptian independence, the end of the British occupation in Egypt, and the accompanying numerical decline of Egypt's British community, mark the end of the forty year period that this book is concerned with.

As specified in the introduction, this book makes use of certain private papers, census and court records, and business, military, newspaper, missionary, and church archives, some of which have not been utilised before in the historical writing of the British in Egypt. In contrast with existing studies that seem to focus primarily on the lives and political involvement of upper middle class Britons in the military or civil service, this work brings to light previously underemphasised aspects in the history of Egypt's Britons during the occupation. These include their demographic profile, the boundaries of their identity, their symbols and institutions, socio-occupational diversity, criminal activities, and various responses to the many challenges that they faced during the First World War and the revolutionary period of 1919–22. In particular, the study addressed the population, residential locations, literacy rates, and growth rates in the context of Egypt's population and other foreign communities. It drew attention to conditions where the boundaries of British identity seemed rigid, but also to circumstances that suggest the ambiguity of British identity. These situations consisted of the inclusion of the Maltese for fund-raising purposes, the exclusion of British women due to intermarriage with Egyptians, and the potential denial of British nationality for offspring of British fathers (who were not born in Britain) due to the imminent abolition of the Capitulations. The work also examined the symbols and institutions that solidified and reflected the identity of the British community to those inside and outside the fold such as military structures and activities, and exclusive residential locations, sporting clubs, and hotels. Due to the diplomatic sensitivities of the time, two symbols of British dominance, the British flag and the English language, featured little in public display and in the mixed courts respectively. An interesting finding was the lack of state financing for

British institutions in Egypt. This scarcity of funds may have stemmed from the British value of self-initiative and the belief that government funding weakens individual responsibility. Ironically, the lack or ongoing delay of financing British institutions, such as the Anglo-American Hospital, Victoria College, or All Saints' Cathedral, may have expressed the British value of self-reliance but may have also limited the visible projection of Britain's power in Egypt.

Within the overlooked facets of the history of the British in Egypt, one dimension merits particular attention and that is the diversity that existed among Egypt's Britons during the occupation. Research of court, census, and business records reveals that Egypt's Britons were from a multiplicity of backgrounds, vocations, and incomes. Besides the military and civil services, upper and middle class Britons worked as doctors, engineers, lawyers, teachers, bankers, businessmen, and missionaries. Lower class Britons were office clerks, tailors, and carpenters; and within the lower class, working class Britons served as maids and railway workers. Exposing the lives, activities, and challenges of lower class Britons adds to the study of 'history from below' – a theme of historical research that seems to be uncharted territory with regards to the British in Egypt during the colonial era. Diversity among the British in Egypt was also evident in the array of motives of why they came to Egypt. As income levels were compared with similar occupations in Britain, it seems that many businessmen, professionals, officials, and lower class workers may have come to Egypt for financial reasons: higher pay, a lower cost of living, and perceived social mobility. Others such as missionaries came not for money but to help those they perceived as spiritually needy.

Criminal activities of Egypt's Britons have received very little attention thus far. However, court records and, to a lesser extent, private papers, government correspondences, and business and church archives, demonstrate that another dimension of variety among Egypt's Britons can be attributed to the range of misconduct and criminal activities that they engaged in. Britons in medicine, education, and law participated in professional misconduct. Crimes committed by the British in Egypt included domestic abuse, abortion, suicide, assault, libel, fraud, embezzlement, theft, extortion, rape, bigamy, procuring prostitutes, and living off the proceeds of prostitutes. This book has attempted to point out that besides the stereotypical image of the upper class British official enjoying lavish dinner parties and dances at select hotels, there were Britons who battered, raped, and stole, usually within the context of their unemployment, alcoholism, and feelings of dejection. Besides the range of factors that may have encouraged crime, those who committed criminal offences emerged from a broad mixture of vocations: factory workers, technicians, engineers, dentists, doctors, teachers, lawyers, bank officials, business people, military personnel, and even missionaries. British criminal activity in Egypt seemed to challenge their 'civilising mission' and added to Egyptian sentiments against British rule. Similar to the writing of 'history from below', the writing of the social history of crime among the British in Egypt during the colonial period appears also to be a pioneering effort.

The First World War and the revolutionary era of 1919–22 also confronted Egypt's Britons with different challenges, and elicited varying responses. In the war, British men and women in Egypt served in a number of capacities. Some men joined the British military in Europe while others remained in important posts. Women volunteered, nursed, and hosted soldiers. A good number of Britons in Egypt contested the British authorities' requisitioning of Victoria College and their insistence on them to relinquish plans of retiring in Britain in order to invest in tax-free war bonds. They also faced varying economic realities during the war – prosperity from the economic boom, lost opportunities due to constraints on German and Austrian businesses, and inflationary difficulties. During the revolutionary period, the diversity of challenges included the delay in demobilisation, the limited job prospects for returning soldiers, the impending end of the Capitulations, and the hardship of obtaining compensation for death and injuries. The ongoing violence and related economic struggles resulted in a sharp rise in the cost of living (that provoked some British teachers and bank officials to demand salary increases), the closing of businesses due to the disruption to transporting goods, the wounds to the railway business (owing to damaged tracks and carriages, and stolen cargo), and strikes by Egyptian employees that debilitated the running of the Anglo-Egyptian bank. As a reaction to these problems, the Non-Official British Community was established to give input to the British authorities regarding the governance of Egypt. It consisted of longstanding British residents who were not part of the 'official' civil and military services. It voiced various concerns to the government, not least the viewpoint that the disturbances should have been quenched much sooner, whether by force or by the granting of Egyptian self-rule, in order to secure stability for business interests. The diverse feelings among Egypt's Britons were evident as the British authorities refused to heed the advice of the non-official Britons. The authorities denied self-rule to the Egyptians, whom they deemed as unqualified, and refrained from heavy-handed steps against the nationalists which they considered would escalate violence and marginalise moderate supporters of Britain's involvement in Egypt.

Alongside unveiling underrepresented facets in the historiography of Egypt's British community and particularly its diversity, the book also contributes to Egypt's urban, business, and missionary histories. Among the issues addressed that seek to enhance Egypt's urban history are: the demographic profile and residential locations of Egypt's Britons within the context of the wider population and other foreign communities; British symbols and institutions in Cairo and Alexandria such as clubs, hospitals, hotels, schools, and churches; the way in which the two cities became 'hospitals' for the war injured; and how their residents faced the violence and strikes of the revolutionary period. Included in the observations that attempt to complement the business history of Egypt are: the litigation faced by the Remington Typewriter Company and the construction firm, Henry Lovatt Company; the fraud and embezzlement committed against the Nile Cold Storage Company, Thomas Cook and Son, and Davis Bryan and Co.; the inability for Egypt's British Chamber of Commerce to capitalise on the restrictions imposed on German and Austrian businesses during the First World War; and the losses suffered by the Egyptian Delta Light Railways and the Anglo-Egyptian Bank during the revolutionary period. By mentioning their attitude towards the religious commitment of other Britons, their close interaction with Egyptians, their socio-economic background and position in Egypt, their work as chaplains in the First World War, and one surprising conviction of rape, the book aspires to add to the study of missionary history in Egypt.

This monograph finds its place at the intersection of British imperial history and Egyptian history. It is one more treatise among increasing efforts to examine the history of British expatriate communities during the colonial age. However, it has not been written just to fill a gap in the historiography, but to tell a tale worthy of its own consideration and essential to the understanding of the history of modern Egypt and the British Empire. This important account is now the 'told' story of ordinary Britons in Egypt, the diversity of their community, the wide range of their criminal activities, and their multi-faceted responses to the crises of the First World War and the revolutionary period of 1919–22.

NOTES

Note: URLs were correct at time of writing.

Introduction

1. Notable studies by Peter Mansfield, *The British in Egypt* (London: Wiedenfeld & Nicolson, 1971), John Marlowe, *Anglo-Egyptian Relations, 1800–1956*, 2nd ed. (London: Frank Cass & Co., Ltd., 1965), Afaf Lutfi al-Sayyid Marsot, *A Short History of Modern Egypt* (London: Cambridge University Press, 1985), *idem*, *Egypt and Cromer: A Study in Anglo-Egyptian Relations* (New York: Praeger, 1969), and P. J. Vatikiotis, *The History of Modern Egypt* (London: Wiedenfeld & Nicolson, 1969) focus on the political relationship between the British government, its power-base in Egypt, and Egyptian politicians and nationalists. Other key monographs by Roger Owen, *Cotton and the Egyptian Economy, 1820–1914* (Oxford: Oxford University Press, 1969), David Landes, *Bankers and Pashas: International Finance and Economic Imperialism in Egypt* (New York: Harper, 1958), and Robert L. Tignor, *Modernisation and British Colonial Rule in Egypt, 1882–1914* (Princeton: Princeton University Press, 1966) examine Britain's economic administration of Egypt. Memoirs and biographies of British diplomats and travellers such as Clara Boyle, *A Servant of the Empire: A Memoir of Harry Boyle* (London: Methuen & Co., 1938), Lord Edward Cecil, *The Leisure of an Egyptian Official* (London: Hodder & Stoughton, 1921), Bimbashi McPherson and Barry Carman, *A Life in Egypt* (London: BBC, 1983), Alfred Milner, *England in Egypt*, 13th ed. (London: Edward Arnold, 1920), Sir Ronald Storrs, *Orientations* (London: Nicholson & Watson, 1937), Sir James Rennell Rodd, *Social and Diplomatic Memoirs, 1894–1901* (London: Edward Arnold & Co., 1923), Sir Thomas Russell, *Egyptian Service, 1902–194*6 (London: John Murray, 1949), Douglas Sladen, *Egypt and the English* (London: Hurst & Blackett, Ltd., 1908), *idem*, *Oriental Cairo: The City of the 'Arabic Nights'*

(London: Hurst & Blackett, Ltd., 1911), and William Willcocks, *Sixty Years in the East* (London: Blackwood & Sons, 1935) provide significant insight on the lifestyles of upper middle class British officials in Egypt. Works by Anthony Sattin, *Lifting the Veil: British Society in Egypt, 1768–1956* (London: Dent, 1988), Derek Hopwood, *Tales of Empire: The British in the Middle East, 1880–1952* (London: I.B.Tauris, 1989), William M. Welch Jr., *No Country for a Gentleman: British Rule in Egypt, 1883–1907* (London: Greenwood Press, 1988), Paul and Janet Starkey (eds), *Travellers in Egypt* (London: I.B.Tauris, 1998), Michael D. Berdine, *The Accidental Tourist, Wilfrid Scawen Blunt and the British Invasion of Egypt in 1882* (Oxford: Routledge, 2005), Archie Hunter, *Power and Passion in Egypt: A Life of Sir Eldon Gorst, 1861–1911* (London: I.B.Tauris, 2007), and Roger Owen, *Lord Cromer: Victorian Imperialist, Edwardian Proconsul* (Oxford: Oxford University Press, 2004) chronicle the lives and activities of British travellers, military officers, and prominent government officials.

2. Recent examples of scholarly usage related to the British history of Egypt from the British Consular Court records at the National Archives in London: Will Hanley, *Foreignness and Localness in Alexandria, 1880–1914* (PhD dissertation, Princeton University, 2007) and Shane Minkin, *In Life as in Death: The Port, Foreign Charities, Hospitals and Cemeteries in Alexandria, Egypt, 1865–1914* (PhD dissertation, New York University, 2009); The Church Missionary Society Archives at the University of Birmingham: Paul Sedra, *Textbook Maneuvers: Evangelicals and Educational Reform in Nineteenth-Century Egypt* (PhD dissertation, New York University, 2006); and the Egyptian census records: Kenneth M. Cuno and Michael J. Reimer, 'The census registers of nineteenth-century Egypt: a new source for social historians,' *British Journal of Middle Eastern Studies*, 24/2 (1997), pp.193–216, and Robert Mabro, 'Alexandria 1860–1960: The Cosmopolitan Identity,' in Anthony Hirst and Michael Silk (eds), *Alexandria, Real and Imagined* (Aldershot: Ashgate, 2004), pp.247–62.

3. Sir Milne Cheetham, in letter to Sir Arthur Nicolson, 23 June 1911, in Cheetham's private papers at Middle East Centre, St. Antony's College, University of Oxford.

4. The 1907 census included the Irish as part of the British community as discussed in the 'demographic overview' chapter.

5. The chapter on 'Boundaries' will discuss the rare moments when British subjects of Maltese origin were perceived to be 'part' of the British community.

6. The chapter on 'Boundaries' will consider the issue of who belonged to the community in more detail.

7. David Miller, 'Reflections on British national identity,' *New Community* 21/2 (1995), p.155.

8.. Britain's military occupation of Egypt began in 1882 while limited independence was granted to Egypt in 1922.

9. Hanley: *Foreignness and Localness in Alexandria*; Minkin: *In Life as in Death*; Mabro: 'Alexandria 1860–1960'; Khaled Fahmy, 'For Cavafy, with love and squalor: some critical notes on the history and historiography of modern Alexandria,' in Hirst and Silk (eds): *Alexandria, Real and Imagined*, pp.263–80; and *idem*, 'Towards a social history of Modern Alexandria,' in Hirst and Silk (eds): *Alexandria, Real and Imagined*, pp. 281–306.
10. Raymond E. Dumett, 'Exploring Cain/Hopkins paradigm: issues for debate; critique and topics of new research,' in Raymond E. Dumett (ed), *Gentlemanly Capitalism and British Imperialism: The New Debate on Empire* (London: Longman, 1999), pp.1–2: 'Editors of important scholarly journals in both British history and general world history report a great upswing in the popularity of imperial and colonial topics in articles submitted, . . . as ongoing research areas, . . . in new courses, postgraduate seminars, and on programme panels at scholarly conferences . . . in the United Kingdom, Commonwealth countries, and . . . in North America.'
11. Mrinalini Sinha, 'Britishness, clubbability, and the colonial public sphere: the genealogy of an Imperial institution in colonial India,' *Journal of British Studies* 40 (2001), p.521.
12. Elizabeth Buettner, *Empire Families: Britons and Late Imperial India* (Oxford: Oxford University Press, 2004), p.3. Buettner borrows this concept from Sinha's 'Britishness, clubbability' p.492.
13. *Ibid.*, p.2.
14. P. J. Cain and A. G. Hopkins, 'Gentlemanly capitalism and British expansion overseas II: new Imperialism, 1850–1945,' *Economic History Review*. 2nd series. XL/I (1987), p.19.
15. Ronald Robinson and John Gallagher, 'The imperialism of free trade,' *Economic History Review*. 2nd series. VI/I (1953) p.1.
16. Anthony Webster, *The Debate on the Rise of the British Empire* (Manchester: Manchester University Press, 2006), p.69.
17. Eve Troutt Powell, *A Different Shade of Colonialism: Egypt, Great Britain, and the Mastery of Sudan* (London: University of California Press, 2003), p.8.
18. Nicholas B. Dirks, 'Introduction: colonialism and culture,' in Nicholas B. Dirks (ed), *Colonialism and Culture* (Ann Arbor: University of Michigan Press, 1992), p.9.
19. E. P. Thompson first coined this term in an article entitled 'History from below' in *The Times Literary Supplement*, 7 April 1966, pp.276–80. His classic work *The Making of the English Working Class* (London: Victor Gollanz Ltd., 1963) centred on the working class and added a new dimension to historical research.
20. Christopher Kent, 'Victorian social history: post-Thompson, post-Foucault, postmodern,' in *Victorian Studies* 40/1 (1996), p.99.
21. E. J. Hobsbawm, 'History from below – some reflections,' in Frederick

Kranz (ed), *History From Below: Studies in Popular Protest and Ideology* (Oxford: Oxford University Press, 1988), pp.13–27.
22. Tim Hitchcock, 'A new history from below,' *History Workshop Journal*, 57 (2004), p.297. http://muse.jhu.edu/journals/history_workshop_journal/v057/57.1hitchcock.html
23. Stephanie Cronin, 'Introduction', in Stephanie Cronin (ed), *Subalterns and Social Protest: History from Below in the Middle East and North Africa* (London and New York: Routledge), p.1.
24. *Ibid.*, p.2. Cronin defines 'subalterns' as groups that have a subordinate social, political, economic, and ideological status. Subaltern studies appear to have found particular traction among scholars of postcolonial South Asia.
25. Robert Bickers (ed), *Settlers and Expatriates: Britons over the Seas* (Oxford: Oxford University Press, 2010) appears to be the first edited volume accounting for overseas British communities outside the Dominions.
26. Alexander Kitroeff, *The Greeks in Egypt, 1919–1937: Ethnicity and Class* (London: Ithaca Press, 1989), P. M. Glavanis, *Aspects of the Economic and Social History of the Greek Community in Alexandria during the 19th Century* (PhD thesis, Hull University, 1989), and Sotirios Roussos, *Greece and the Arab Middle East: The Greek Orthodox Communities in Egypt, Palestine and Syria, 1919–1940* (PhD thesis, SOAS, University of London, 1995).
27. Thomas Philipp, *The Syrians in Egypt, 1725–1975* (Stuttgart: Steiner-Verlag-Wiesbaden-GmbH, 1985).
28. S. C. Ghosh, *The Social Condition of the British Community in Bengal, 1757–1800* (Leiden: E. J. Brill, 1970), Veena Talwar Oldenburg, *The Making of Colonial Lucknow* (Delhi: Oxford University Press, 1989), Raymond K. Renford, *The Non-Official British in India to 1920* (Delhi: Oxford University Press, 1987), Damayanti Datta, *The Europeans of Calcutta, 1858–1883* (PhD thesis, Churchill College, University of Cambridge, 1995).
29. Robert Bickers, *Britain in China: Community, Culture and Colonialism* (Manchester: Manchester University Press, 1999).
30. John G. Butcher, *The British in Malaya, 1880–1941* (Oxford: Oxford University Press, 1979).
31. Valerie Johnson, *British Multinationals, Culture and Empire in the Early Twentieth Century* (PhD thesis, King's College, University of London, 2007).
32.. James Onley, *The Arabian Frontier of the British Raj: Merchants, Rulers and the British in the Nineteenth-Century Gulf* (Oxford: Oxford University Press, 2007).
33. John Paul Bailey, *The British Community in Argentina* (PhD thesis, University of Surrey, 1976).

34. Margaret Harvey, *The English in Rome: 1362–1420: Portrait of an Expatriate Community* (Cambridge: Cambridge University Press, 1999).
35. Damayanti Datta, *The Europeans of Calcutta, 1858–1883* (PhD thesis, Churchill College, University of Cambridge, 1995). p.i.
36. Georgina Sinclair, 'Book review for Barry Godfrey and Graeme Dunstall (eds), *Crime and Empire 1840–1940; Criminal Justice in Local and Global Context*, Cullompton, Willan Publishing, 2005,' in *Crime, History and Societies* 11/2 (2007), p.155.
37. Clive Emsley, *Crime and Society in England, 1750–1900*, 3rd ed. (London: Pearson Longman, 2005), p.1.
38. Tim Hitchcock, Peter King, and Pamela Sharpe, 'Introduction: chronicling poverty – the voices and strategies of the English poor, 1640–1840,' in *Chronicling Poverty – The Voices and Strategies of the English Poor, 1640–1840* (London: Macmillan, 1997), p.3.
39. James Aldridge, *Cairo* (London: Macmillan, 1969), Janet Abu-Lughod, *Cairo: 1001 Years of the City Victorious* (Princeton: Princeton University Press, 1971), Samir Rafaat, *Maadi: 1904–1962: Society and History in a Cairo Suburb* (Cairo: Palm Press, 1994), Michael J. Reimer, *Colonial Bridgehead: Government and Society in Alexandria, 1807–1882* (Cairo: AUC Press, 1997), Robert Ilbert, *Alexandrie, 1830–1930: Histoire d'une Communauté Citadine*, Vol. I and II (Le Caire: Institut Francais d'Archéolgie Orientale, 1996) and Max Rodenbeck, *Cairo: The City Victorious* (Cairo: American University in Cairo Press, 1999).
40. Recent examples of studies of the missionary experience in Egypt: Heather Sharkey, *American Evangelicals in Egypt: Missionary Encounters in an Age of Empire* (Oxford: Princeton University Press, 2008), Paul D. Sedra, 'John Leider and his mission in Egypt: the evangelical ethos at work among nineteenth-century Copts,' *The Journal of Religious History* 28/3 (2004), pp.219–39, Sedra: *Textbook Maneuvers* and Sedra, *From Mission to Modernity: Evangelicals, Reformers and Education in Nineteenth Century Europe* (London: I.B.Tauris, 2011). And a recent example of missionary history in the colonial context: Ussama Makdisi, *Artillery of Heaven: American Missionaries and the Failed Conversion of the Middle East* (London: Cornell University Press, 2008).
41. Valerie Johnson's work on the Anglo-Persian Oil Company in *British Multinationals, Culture, and Empire in the Early Twentieth Century* (PhD thesis, King's College, University of London, 2007) is a recent example of this kind of study.
42. The annual forum on the Economic and Business History of Egypt and the Middle East is one body that is drawing attention to more scholarship on British business history in Egypt during the imperial era.
43. Starkey and Starkey (eds): *Travellers in Egypt* and Sattin: *Lifting the Veil*, are useful sources for understanding the variety of European travellers who

went to Egypt during the eighteenth and nineteenth centuries.
44. Archives of Barker family, Special Collections, University of Exeter, EUL, 1850–1956, MS 238, Box 1, Section F, p.2.
45. The occupation itself occurred to a large degree for economic reasons in order to maintain the confidence of Suez Canal shareholders in face of the 'Urabi revolt. Paul Auchterlonie articulates this in 'A Turk of the West: Sir Edgar Vincent's career in Egypt and the Ottoman Empire,' *British Journal of Middle Eastern Studies* 27/1 (2000), p.56
46. Robert Tignor, 'The economic activities of foreigners in Egypt, 1920–1950: from Millet to Haute Bourgeoisie,' *Comparative Studies in Society and History* 22/3 (1980), p.423.
47. Letter from Granville to Sir Evelyn Baring, Consul-General, 4 January 1884, as quoted from Alfred Milner, *England in Egypt*, 13th ed. (London: Edward Arnold, 1920), p.27.
48. Wilfrid Scawen Blunt, *My Diaries: Being a Personal Narrative of Events, 1888–1914* (London: Martin Secker, 1932), p.84.
49. P. J. Cain, 'Character and imperialism: the British financial administration of Egypt, 1878–1914' *Journal of Imperial and Commonwealth History* 34/2 (2006), p.182.
50. Tignor: *Modernisation*, p. 416.
51. David Cannadine, *Ornamentalism: How the British Saw Their Empire* (Oxford: Oxford University Press, 2001), p.xiv.
52. Heather Sharkey, 'Muslim apostasy: Christian conversion, and religious freedom in Egypt: a study of American missionaries, Western imperialism, and human rights Agendas,' in Rosalind I. J. Hackett (ed), *Proselytization Revisited: Rights Talk, Free Markets and Culture Wars* (London: Equinox, 2008), p.142.
53. *Ibid.*
54. *Ibid.*
55. For a detailed description of literature related to the theory of cosmopolitanism, see Ulrike Frietag and Nora Lati, 'Cities compared: cosmopolitanism in the Mediterranean and adjacent regions,' project description (version 2, 2007), http://halshs.archives-ouvertes.fr/docs/00/14/93/27/PDF/Freitag-Lafi-Cosmopolitanism.pdf. For recent examples of writings on cosmopolitanism in Egypt during the colonial period, see Deborah Starr, *Remembering Cosmopolitan Egypt* (New York: Routledge, 2009), Robert Mabro, 'Alexandria 1860–1960: the cosmopolitan identity,' in Hirst and Silk (eds): *Alexandria, Real or Imagined*, pp.247–62, Sami Zubaida, 'Middle Eastern experiences of cosmopolitanism,' in Steven Vertovec and Robin Cohen (eds), *Conceiving Cosmopolitanism: Theory, Context and Practice* (Oxford: Oxford University Press, 2002), pp.32–41, and James Whidden, 'Cosmopolitan Egypt,' in Bickers and Louis (eds), *Settlers and Expatriates*.
56. Fahmy: 'For Cavafy, with love and squalor,' p.272.

57. Starr: *Remembering Cosmopolitan Egypt*, p.7.
58. *Ibid.*, p.13.
59. Will Hanley, 'Grieving cosmopolitanism in the Middle East studies,' *History Compass*, 6/5 (2008), pp.1346–67.
60. Hanley, 'Grieving Cosmopolitanism', p.1346.
61. Hanan Khouloussy, *For Better, For Worse: The Marriage Crisis that Made Modern Egypt* (Stanford University Press, 2010), p.5.

1: Demographic Overview

1. Kenneth M. Cuno and Michael J. Reimer, 'The census registers of the nineteenth-century Egypt: a new source for social historians,' *British Journal of Middle Eastern Studies* 24/2 (1997), p.194.
2. Roger Owen, *The Middle East in the World Economy, 1800–1914* (London: Methuen, 1981), p.216.
3. Jeffrey G. Collins, *The Egyptian Elite under Cromer, 1882–1907* (Berlin: Klaus Schwarz Verlag, 1984), p.18.
4. *Ibid.*
5. Cuno and Reimer: 'census registers', pp.194–5.
6. The percentage calculations are my own based on the census data.
7. *Ibid.*
8. *Recensement Général de l'Egypte, 1882, Tome Deuxième* (Le Caire: Impremiere Nationale de Boulaq, 1884), pp.xx–xxi. (Accessed at Centre d'Étude et de Documentation Économique, Juridique et Sociale, Cairo).
9. *Recensement Général de l'Egypte, 1897, Tome Premier* (Le Caire: Imprimerie Nationale, 1898), p.xviii, and lii (Accessed at Robarts' Library Government Publications, University of Toronto).
10. *Census of Egypt, 1907* (Cairo: National Printing Department, 1909), Table XVII, p.148 (Accessed at Rare Books and Special Collections Library, American University of Cairo).
11. This figure includes those of English, Welsh, Scottish, and Irish origin in Egypt. Technically, the Irish are not considered British, but because the data of Britons in the census of 1907 includes that of the Irish, I have little choice but to include the Irish in the British tallies in this chapter. That being said, the Irish population in Egypt seems to have been minimal.
12. 'Colonial' refers to those, not originally from the British Isles, who have become British subjects due to colonial arrangements (besides British subjects of Indian and Maltese origin).
13. *Census of Egypt, 1917*, Vol. II, from Ministry of Finance, Statistical Department, (Cairo: Government Press, 1921), Table VIII, p.513. (American University in Cairo Reference Collection).
14. Figures based on calculations from Table 1.1.

15. There is uncertainty as to whether this figure (6,118) represents the number of British subjects in Egypt (which would include British subjects from Malta, India, and other colonial territories) or the number of British subjects from Britain.
16. Figures based on calculations from Table 1.1.
17. Roger Adelson, *London and the Invention of the Middle East* (London: Yale University Press, 1995), p.78.
18. Keith Jeffrey, *The British Army and the Crisis of Empire, 1918–1922*, (Manchester: Manchester University Press, 1984), p.113, records that 400,000 troops under British imperial command were based in Egypt, but not all at the same time. I also comment on this in chapter 6.
19. Mike Reimer, *Colonial Bridgehead: Government and Society in Alexandria, 1807–1882*, (Cairo: American University in Cairo Press, 1997), p.85.
20. Arnold Wright (ed), *Twentieth Century Impressions of Egypt: Its History, People, Commerce, Industries, and Resources,* (London: Lloyd's Greater Britain Publishing Co., Ltd., 1909), p.401.
21. Soldiers under British imperial command positioned in Egypt after the start of the war were either convalescing after the Gallipoli defeat or waiting to be sent to Palestine and Syria to fight, as discussed further in chapter 6.
22. *Census of Egypt, 1917*, Table VIII, Population by nationality, p.513.
23. From my own calculations (number of total British subjects subtract number of British from British Isles).
24. *Recensement Général de l'Egypte, 1897*, Tome Premier, p.xviii.
25. *Ibid.*, Table for Professions et Métiers, Sexe Masculin, p.lxiii.
26. *Census of Egypt, 1907*, Table XXI, Occupations, p.170. Based on figures for Land Army in Cairo and Alexandria, the figure represents the total number of those in the Land Army, and may include a small number of military personnel who were not British from the British Isles or British subjects. Therefore, it may be a slightly higher estimate than the actual number of British men in the Army of Occupation in 1907.
27. *Ibid.*, based on the high estimate of 6835 British men in the Army of Occupation in 1907.
28. *Census of 1917*, Table VI, Groups of Occupations by nationalities, p.472.
29. *Census of Egypt, 1917*, chapter VI, 'Growth in population among certain nationalities and stagnation among other nationalities,' pp.129–30.
30. *Ibid.*
31. Suzanne Brugger, *Australians and Egypt, 1914–1919* (Melborne: Melborne University Press, 1980), p.48.
32. As mentioned in the 'Introduction', the term 'cosmopolitan', with its implied elitism and nostalgia, may not be the best word to describe a place where lower and working class Britons also lived.
33. Thomas Philipp, 'Demographic patterns of Syrian immigration to Egypt in the nineteenth century: an interpretation,' *Asian and African Studies*, 16

(1982), p.171.
34. Robert Mabro, 'Alexandria 1860–1969: the cosmopolitan identity,' in Anthony Hirst and Michael Silk (eds), *Alexandria, Real and Imagined* (Aldershot: Ashgate Publishing, 2004), p.253, explains that there were Syrians, Lebanese, and others from the Levant who adopted Egyptian nationality; whereas, others from the same ethnic groups opted for foreign nationalities under the provision of the Capitulations.
35. Thomas Philipp, *The Syrians in Egypt, 1725–1975* (Stuttgart: Steiner-Verlag-Wiesbaden-GmbH, 1985), p.82.
36. Philipp: 'Demographic patterns', p.182.
37. Philipp: *The Syrians in Egypt*, p.84.
38. Philipp: 'Demographic patterns', p.195.
39. Albert H. Hourani, *Minorites in the Arab World*, (London: Oxford University Press, 1947), p.48.
40. *Ibid.*, p.49.
41. Derek Hopwood, *Tales of Empire: The British in the Middle East, 1880–1952* (London: I.B.Tauris, 1989), p.11.
42. Gudrun Krämer, *The Jews of Modern Egypt, 1914–1952* (London: I.B.Tauris, 1989) and Joel Benin, *The Dispersion of Egyptian Jewry: Culture, Politics, and the Formation of a Modern Diaspora* (Berkeley: University of California Press, 1998) provide valuable insight on Egypt's Jewish community during the colonial era although they mainly focus on the time period beyond the scope of this book.
43. Alexander Kitroeff, *The Greeks in Egypt, 1919–1937: Ethnicity and Class* (London: Ithaca, 1989), p.23.
44. Hourani: *Minorities*, p.49.
45. Hopwood: *Tales of Empire*, p.11.
46. *Recensement Général de l'Egypte, 1882*, 15 Gamad Akher, 1299; Tome II (Le Caire: Boulaq, 1884), Ministry of Finance, Census Department, (Arabic version) pp.22–23.
47. *Recensement Général de l'Egypte, 1897*, Tome Premier, Basse Egypte (Le Caire: Imprimerie Nationale, 1898), pp. xvi–vii.
48. *Census of Egypt, 1907*, p.129.
49. *Census of Egypt, 1917*, pp.512–17.
50. Though the Greeks lived under Ottoman rule and may have been more culturally 'Near Eastern' rather than 'European' at that time, they are classified as 'European' due to their geographic origin in Europe.
51. Kitreoff: *The Greeks in Egypt*, pp.11–12.
52. Hopwood: *Tales of Empire*, p.11.
53. Mabro: 'Alexandria 1860–1969', pp.250–2, and Anthony Gorman, 'Foreign workers in Egypt 1882–1914: subaltern or labour elite?' in Stephanie Cronin (ed), *Subalterns and Social Protest: History from Below in the Middle East and North Africa* (London: Routledge, 2007), p.240.
54. *Ibid.*, p.21.

55. Janet Abu-Lughod, *Cairo: 1001 Years of the City Victorious* (Princeton: Princeton University Press, 1971), p.115.
56. Marius Deeb, 'The socioeconomic role of the local foreign minorities in modern Egypt, 1805–1961,' *International Journal of Middle East Studies* 9 (1978), pp.11–22 (p.16.).
57. Jeffrey G. Collins, *The Egyptian Elite under Cromer, 1882–1907* (Berlin: Klaus Schwarz Verlag, 1984), p.22.
58. Harold Toffelson, *Policing Islam: The British Occupation of Egypt and the Anglo-Egyptian Struggle over Control of the Police, 1882–1914* (London: Greenwood Press, 1999), p.184.
59. James Aldridge, *Cairo* (London: Macmillan, 1969), p.211.
60. Collins: *The Egyptian Elite*, p.22.
61. *Recensement Général de l'Egypte, 1882*, 15 Gamad Akher, 1299; Tome II, pp.22–3.
62. *Recensement Général de l'Egypte, 1897*, Tome Premier, Basse Egypte (Le Caire: Imprimerie Nationale, 1898), p.36.
63. *Census of Egypt, 1907*, pp.132–4.
64. *Census of Egypt, 1917*, pp.482–7.
65. *Recensement Général de l'Egypte, 1882*, Deuxième section, p.22.
66. *Recensement Général de l'Egypte, 1897*, p.lii.
67. *Census of Egypt, 1907*, Table XVII, 'Nationality', p.133.
68. *Census of Egypt, 1917*, Table VII, p.482.
69. Based on calculations from Table 1.1.
70. Based on the number of British subjects where number of Britons from British Isles is unavailable.
71. *Ibid.*
72. Justin McCarthy, 'Nineteenth century Egyptian population,' *Middle East Studies*, 12/3 (1976), p.27 as quoted from Collins: *The Egyptian Elite*. These figures are based on McCarthy's figures after adjustments due to inaccuracies of the 1882 census.
73. *Recensement Général de l'Egypte, 1897*, Tome I, Basse, Egypte (Le Caire: Imprimerie Naitonale, 1898), p.36.
74. *Census of Egypt, 1907*, pp.132–4.
75. *Census of Egypt, 1917*, pp.482–3.
76. Aldridge: *Cairo*, p.213.
77. Douglas Sladen, *Oriental Cairo: The City of the 'Arabian Nights* (London: Hurst and Blackett, Ltd., 1908), p.14.
78. *Ibid.*, p.13.
79. *Recensement Général de l'Egypte, 1897*, Population Classée selon la Nationalité, pp.6, 8, 10, 12.
80. Aldridge: *Cairo*, p.211.
81. Sladen: *Oriental Cairo*, p.37.
82. FO141/494/14268. General Manager's Office at Cairo Station to Ministry

NOTES 255

of Communications, Cairo, 15/09/1922.
83. All Saints' Church Archives, Minute Book 25, Sister Margaret Clare's report, 25 March 1915.
84. *Ibid.*
85. All Saints' Archives, Cairo, Minute Book 26, Dr. Page May to Cromer, responding to Germans' request to use St. Paul's Church, 24 December 1904.
86. Max Rodenbeck, *Cairo: The City Victorious* (Cairo: American University in Cairo Press, 1999), p.181.
87. Hopwood: *Tales of Empire*, p.13.
88. All Saints' Archives, Cairo, Minute Book 26, St. Paul's church committee meeting, 30 December 1904.
89. Certain Jews had European nationalities. Some Jews carried British nationalities. Though 'Britons and Jews' may not necessarily be two mutually exclusive groups, there appears to be only a small number of Britons with Jewish origins in Egypt.
90. Raafat, *Maadi, 1904–1962: Society and History in a Cairo Suburb* (Cairo: Palm Press, 1994), p.33.
91. Rodenbeck: *Cairo*, p.180.
92. Raafat, *Maadi,* p.33.
93. *Ibid.*, pp.34–5.
94. *Egyptian Gazette*, 'Dr. Macinnes's Diocese: Church Work after the War,' 13 May 1915, p.5.
95. *Residential Map of Gezira*, published by the Survey of Egypt, 1907, in F. T. Rowlatt, Hanging File in private papers, St. Antony's College archives.
96. *Residential Map of Zamalek* and 'Liste des abonnes de Zamalek, 1920', Ministry of Finance, Survey of Egypt, Cairo in Serge Weber, 'Zamalek depuis la période anglaise, caractéristique socio-économique, fonctions d'un quartier du Caire' Format 4, 1618 (Cairo: CEDEJ, 1994).
97. Raafat: *Cairo, the Glory Years,* p.135, mentions 52 British government and business leaders out of 84 long-term residents in total living in Gezira, based on a French-language Egyptian commercial directory in 1913. Of the 52 Britons, 'most of them [were] top executives in the Egyptian administration, major companies and banks. This...list includes directors of the Survey Department, the Prison Administration, the Irrigation Administration, and the Department of Health. Among the joint stock companies we find directors of the Menzaleh Navigation Company, the Egyptian Markets company, the Egyptian Dreging Company and Thomas Cook. Topping the banking list is the National Bank of Egypt, the Agricultural Bank and the Imperial Ottoman Bank.'
98. Aldridge: *Cairo*, p.218.
99. Rodenbeck: *Cairo*, p.180.
100. Chapter 3 will comment further on the British locations of residence.

101. *Recensement Général de l'Egypte*, 1897, on religious affiliations of British subjects in Cairo, p.38; in Alexandria, p.74; and in Egypt, p.lviii.
102. PRO: FO841/172. Joseph Smouha vs. Richard Warbrick, Depositions in Cairo, 2 November 1918.
103. *Census of Egypt, 1917*, Table XI, British subjects by religion, p.34.
104. St. Andrew's Church of Scotland, Cairo, Archives, Minutes of session meetings, 23 December 1921.
105. F. A. Klein, 'Letters from Egypt,' 22/01/1885, *The CMS Intelligencer*, X (September 1885), p.676.
106. CMS papers, letter from Douglas Thornton from Cairo to Rev. Baylis in London, 1 July 1900.
107. *Ibid.*, interview with Rev. D. M. Thornton, with Revs. H. E. Fox, B. Baring-Gould and F. Baylis, 17 June 1902.
108. St. Andrew's Church archives, minutes, 23 December 1921.
109. *Recensement Général de l'Egypte, 1897*, p.lxvii.
110. *Ibid.*, p.670.
111. Table VIII, *Census of Egypt, 1917*, p.520.
112. David F. Mitch, *The Rise of Popular Literacy in Victorian England: The Influence of Private Choice and Public Policy* (Philadelphia: University of Pennsylvania Press, 1992), p.xvi.
113. *Recensement Général de l'Egypte, 1897*, Literacy for persons 7 years and above, p.lx; for literacy rates of British subjects in Cairo, p.39; for literacy rates of British subjects in Alexandria, p.75.
114. *Census of Egypt, 1917*, Table IX, Nationality and Literacy, p. 530.

2: Boundaries of British Identity

1. Rogers Brubaker and Frederick Cooper, 'Beyond identity,' *Theory and Society* 29 (2000), 1–47, argue that 'identity' as an analytical category is not useful because it is too ambiguous. I suggest that the term is useful if it is qualified, in this discussion, by 'ethnic' identity. 'British identity' is a term used often in the discussion on 'Britishness.'
2. Alexander Kitroeff, *The Greeks in Egypt: 1919–1937* (London: Ithaca, 1989), p.4.
3. Max Weber, *Economy and Society: An Outline of Interpretative Sociology*, Guenther Roth and Claus Dittrich (eds) (Berkeley: Univerisity of California Press, 1968), p.389.
4. Nathan Glazer and Daniel Patrick Moynihan, 'Introduction', in Glazer and Moynihan (eds), *Ethnicity: Theory and Experience* (Cambridge, MA: Harvard University Press, 1975), p.1.
5. Stephen Cornell and Douglas Hartmann, *Ethnicity and Race: Making Identities in a Changing World* (London: Pine Forge Press, 1998), p.69.

6. Edward Shils, 'Primordial, personal, sacred and civil ties,' *British Journal of Sociology* 8 (1957), pp.130–45.
7. Cora Govers and Hans Vermeulen, 'From political mobilisation to the politics of consciousness' in Govers and Vermeulen (eds), *The Politics of Ethnic Consciousness*, (London: Macmillan, 1997), p.15.
8. Katherine Verdery, 'Ethnicity, nationalism and state-making: ethnic groups and boundaries past and future' in Cora Govers and Hans Vermeulen (eds), *The Anthropology of Ethnicity Beyond 'Ethnic Groups and Boundaries'* (Amsterdam: Het Spinhuis, 1994), p.54.
9. Fredrik Barth, 'Enduring and emerging issues in the analysis of ethnicity' in Govers and Vermeulen: *Anthropology of Ethnicity*, p.12.
10. Cora Govers and Hans Vermeulen, 'Introduction' in Govers and Vermeulen: *Anthropology of Ethnicity*, p.2.
11. Dale Eickelman, *The Middle East: An Anthropological Approach*, 2nd ed. (Englewood Cliffs, New Jersey: Prentice-Hall, 1989), p.210.
12. Cora Govers and Hans Vermeulen, 'From political mobilisation to the politics of consciousness,' in Cora Govers and Hans Vermeulen (eds), *The Politics of Ethnic Consciousness* (London: Macmillan, 1997), p.4.
13. This is consistent with Benedict Anderson's view that ethnic distinctions and nationalistic loyalties derive from one's imagination. Benedict Anderson, *Imagined Communities: Reflections on the Origin and Spread of Nationalism*, revised and extended ed. (London: Verso, 1991).
14. Anthony Cohen, 'Boundaries of consciousness, consciousness of boundaries: critical questions for Anthropology,' in Govers and Vermeulen: *Anthropology of Ethnicity*, pp.64, 66.
15. *Ibid.*, p.62.
16. Cornell and Hartmann: *Ethnicity and Race*, p.101.
17. Nikos Papastergiadis, 'Tracing hybridity in theory' in Pnina Werbner and Modood Tariq (eds), *Debating Cultural Hybridity: Multi-Cultural Identities and the Politics of Anti-Racism* (London: Zed Books, 1997), pp.257–8 (emphasis mine).
18. Linda Colley, 'Does Britishness still matter in the twenty-first century and how much and how well do the politicians care?' in Tony Wright, Andrew Gamble (eds), *Britishness: Perspectives on the British Question* (Chichester, Sussex: Wiley-Blackwell, 2009), p.21.
19. *Ibid.*, p.22.
20. *Ibid.*, pp.21–2.
21. Paul Ward, 'The end of Britishness? A historical perspective,' *British Politics Review* 4/3 (2009), p.3.
22. David Miller, 'Reflections on British national identity,' *New Community* 21/2 (1995), p.153.
23. Elizabeth Buettner, *Empire Families: Britons and Late Imperial India* (Oxford: Oxford University Press, 2004), p.2.
24. Cited from *ibid.*; Mrinalini Sinha, 'Britishness, clubbability, and the

colonial public sphere: the genealogy of an Imperial Institution in colonial India,' *Journal of British Studies* 40 (2001), pp.491–2, 521.
25. Valerie Johnson, 'British identity was forged by imperial overseas encounters', http://www.voxeu.org/index.php?q=node/1186, (June, 2008), p.2.
26. *Ibid.* p.2.
27. *Ibid.* p.3.
28. Ann Laura Stoler, 'Rethinking colonial categories: European communities and the boundaries of rule,' *Comparative Study of Society and History* 31 (1989), p.137.
29. Sami Zubaida, 'Middle Eastern experiences of cosmopolitanism,' in Steven Vertovec and Robin Cohen (eds), *Conceiving Cosmopolitanism: Theory, Context and Practice* (Oxford: Oxford University Press, 2002), p.37.
30. FO633/87. Cromer's papers, ch. 36, p.832.
31. Lady Rochdale, *Diaries*, Imperial War Museum, 19 March 1915.
32. FO141/644/2476. Letter from High Commissioner Sir Reginald Wingate to Judicial Adviser Amos, 22 June 1918.
33. Humphrey Bowman, *Middle East Window* (London: Longmans Green, 1942), p.140.
34. *Ibid.*, p.39.
35. William M. Welch, Jr., *No Country for a Gentleman: British Rule in Egypt, 1883–1907* (London: Greenwood Press, 1988), p.29.
36. Bowman: *Middle East Window*, p.39.
37. Hopwood: *Tales of Empire*, p.56.
38. Welch: *No Country*, p.25.
39. Robert L. Tignor, *Modernization and British Colonial Rule in Egypt, 1882–1914* (Princeton: Princeton University Press, 1966), p.189.
40. Lord Cromer, *Modern Egypt*, Vol. II (London: Macmillan, 1908), p.254.
41. *Ibid.*, p.255.
42. Welch: *No Country*, p.29.
43. FO633/87. Cromer: *Modern Egypt*, p.832.
44. Suzanne Brugger, *Australians and Egypt, 1914–1919* (Melbourne: Melbourne University Press, 1980), p.48.
45. Sir Henry Edward Barker, speech at a dinner on the occasion of the move to a new location for the English Club of Alexandria after being in one location since 1904, 14 December 1939, Box 14, Barker family archives, GB165–0493, St. Antony's College, Middle East Centre Archive, University of Oxford.
46. Magda Abu-Fadil, 'Gezira Club – still the "in" place to be,' *The Middle East* (September 1990), p.45.
47. Welch: *No Country*, p.43.
48. Tignor: *Modernization and British*, p.193.
49. Alison Bashford, *Imperial Hygiene: A Critical History of Colonialism,*

NOTES 259

Nationalism and Public Health, (New York: Palgrave Macmillan, 2004), p.14.
50. Tignor: *Modernization and British*, p.25.
51. Harry Boyle papers, St. Antony's College, 23 July 1902 as quoted in Hopwood: *Tales of Empire*, p.44.
52. Tignor: *Modernization and British*, p.194.
53. *Ibid.*, p.193.
54. Shaun Lopez 'Football as national allegory: Al-Ahram and the Olympics in 1920s Egypt,' *History Compass* 7/1 (2009), p.285.
55. James Aldridge, *Cairo* (London: Macmillan, 1969), p.213.
56. *Ibid.*, p.193.
57. Mustafa Kamel, *al-Liwa*, 12 April 1907 as quoted in J. C. B. Richmond, *Egypt 1798–1952: Her Advance Towards a Modern Identity* (London: Methuen & Co., 1977), p.156.
58. Muḥammad al-Muwayliḥī, *Ḥadīth 'Īsā ibn Hishām*, 3rd ed. (Cairo: Maṭba'at al-Sa'āda, 1923), p.245 as quoted in Roger Allen, *A Period of Time: A Study and Translation of Ḥadīth 'Īsā ibn Hishām by Muḥammad al-Muwayliḥī*, (Reading: Ithaca, 1992), p.85.
59. Allen: *A Period of Time*, p.93.
60. John de Vere Loder, private papers at St. Antony's College, 25 June 1916 and 1 July 1916, as quoted in Hopwood: *Tales of Empire*, p.56.
61. CMS papers: incoming letters from Egypt Missions, letter from Eliza B. Bywater to Rev. Baylis, in London, 29 June 1894 (University of Birmingham Special Collections).
62. *Ibid.* Letter from Rev. F. Adeney, secretary of CMS Egypt Mission to Rev. Baylis, CMS leader in London, 2 June 1894.
63. *Ibid.* Letter from Adeney to Baylis, 26 February 1894.
64. *Ibid.* Letter no. 65, report on J. G. B. Hollins in Cairo, 18 September 1897.
65. Charles R. Watson, *In the Valley of the Nile: A Survey of the Missionary Movement in Egypt* (London: Fleming H. Revell Co., 1908), p.193.
66. Lyle Vander Werff, *Christian Mission to Muslims – The Record: Anglican and Reformed Approaches in India and the Near East*, (Pasadena: William Carey Library, 1977), p.168.
67. CMS papers: incoming letters from Egypt Missions, letter from Bywater to Baylis, 9 July 1894.
68. FO633/86. Vol. IV, Part IV, ch. XXXV. Lord Cromer, 'Europeanised Egyptians, 1884–1898,' p.808.
69. Soha Abdel Kader, *Egyptian Women in a Changing Society, 1899–1987* (Boulder, CO: Lynne Reinner Publishers, 1987), p.70.
70. Magda Baraka, *The Egyptian Upper Class between Revolutions, 1919–1952* (Reading: Ithaca, 1998), p.141.
71. Kader: *Egyptian Women*, p.70.
72. FO633/86. Cromer: *Modern Egypt*, p.808.
73. *Ibid.*, p.813.

74. *Ibid.*, p.815.
75. FO141/581/9132. From G. R. Beasley, Land Expert, in report by Non-Official British Community, November 1919.
76. FO141/581/9132. General Memorandum: 5 July 1919: A. H. Hooker in report of Non-Official British Community, p.28.
77. *Ibid.*, p.29. The first time in history, Copts and Muslims threw off centuries of religious and racial prejudices, and presented a united front to the world that they were serious about expelling the British from Egypt.
78. Mabel Caillard, *A Lifetime in Egypt: 1876–1935* (London: Grant Richards, 1935), p.238.
79. Barker family archives, MS 238, Box 1, Section G, p.5.
80. Sir James Rennell Rodd, *Social and Diplomatic Memoirs, 1894–1901*, p.9: Moukhtar Pasha was originally appointed joint commissioner with Sir Henry Drummond-Wolff in 1885 by the Sultan Abdul-Hamid of the Ottoman Empire. The Sultan, however, refused to ratify the Drummond-Wolff Convention of 1887 nullifying Moukhtar Pasha's role. Yet, the Sultan kept Moukhtar Pasha in Egypt and allowed him the unofficial title of High Commissioner because the Sultan believed that Moukhtar had an 'evil eye'. The Sultan 'insisted on the maintenance of an honourable sinecure for this fine old soldier at a respectable distance from the Bosphorus.' Moukhtar Pasha had no official status in Egypt. H.F. Wood in *Egypt Under the British* (London: Chapman-Hall, 1896), p.62, further describes the Pasha's dubious role: 'The Ottoman High Commissioner has no intelligible attributes in Egypt. He is not an ambassador – for a sovereign cannot send an ambassador to a portion of his own dominions–and the Khedive himself is the representative of the Sultan of Egypt. Neither has Mukhtar any part or lot in the administration of the country...He is an anomaly...a nucleus...[for] Moslem fanaticism, or the intrigues of the old Turkish party. His presence is thus a perpetual nuisance.'
81. Rodd: *Social and Diplomatic Memoirs*, p.9. (Emphasis mine.)
82. *Ibid.*
83. Thomas Skelton Harrison, *The Homely Diary of a Diplomat in the East, 1897–1899* (New York: Houghton Mifflin Co., 1917), p.163.
84. FO141/512/608. Letter to Lord Cromer from President's office (of the Sanitary Maritime and Quarantine Council of Egypt), 20 May 1911.
85. FO633/5. Cromer's papers: Letter from Baring to Mr. Gerrard in reference to conversation with Yacoub Pasha regarding the educational system, 5 May 1889.
86. *Ibid.*, p.24
87. A. J. Stockwell, 'The white man's burden and brown humanity: colonialism and ethnicity in British Malaya,' *The Southeast Asian Journal of Social Sciences* 10/1 (1982), p.46.
88. Rodd: *Social and Diplomatic Memoirs*, p.67.

89. Brugger: *Australians and Egypt*, p.7. Australia had only obtained political autonomy from Britain in 1901 but was still closely bound to Britain by economic ties and mutual needs of defence.
90. Caillard: *A Lifetime in Egypt*, p.221.
91. Brugger: *Australians and Egypt*, p.17.
92. Martin Briggs, *Through Egypt in War-Time* (London: Unwin, 1918), p.26.
93. FO141/684/9445. Letter from Conte Mario de Villa-Clary, President of the Maltese Benevolent Society, to Viscount Milner, on his Special Mission on Egypt, 1 March 1920. The 25,000 Maltese were more numerous than the British community proper (including the military).
94. *Ibid.*
95. *Ibid.*
96. *Ibid.*
97. Mohammad al-Roumi, *Kuwait and Malta: British Imperial Policy, 1899–1939* (MA Dissertation, University of Malta, 1980), p.111.
98. FO141/684/9445. Letter from Conte de Villa-Clary.
99. *Ibid.*
100. *Ibid.*
101. FO633/87. Cromer's papers, p.831.
102. FO141/684/9445. Letter from de Villa Clary to Viscount Milner, 1 March 1920.
103. *Ibid.*
104. FO141/684/9445. Letter from de Villa Clary to Viscount Milner, 1 March 1920. (Emphasis mine.)
105. Anthony Cohen, *The Symbolic Construction of Community* (London: Routledge, 1993), p.12.
106. Michael J. Reimer, *Colonial Bridgehead: Government and Society in Alexandria, 1807–1882* (Cairo: American University in Cairo Press, 1997), p.87.
107. Will Hanley, 'Foreignness and localness in Alexandria, 1880–1914' (Ph.D. dissertation, Princeton University, 2007), p.2.
108. Mark Hoyle, *The Mixed Courts of Egypt* (London: Graham & Trotman, 1991), p.3.
109. Brugger: *Australians and Egypt*, p.5.
110. FO141/431/7838. Letter from Victor Naggiar, President of British Chamber of Commerce of Egypt to Under Secretary of State of Foreign Office, 4 November 1921.
111. Kitroeff: *The Greeks in Egypt,*, p.3.
112. FO141/431/7838. Arthur S. Preston, Legal Advisor: 11 May 1917 – Note for the Committee of the British Chamber of Commerce.
113. *Ibid.* (Emphasis mine.)
114. FO141/431/7838. Letter from Amos, Acting High Commissioner to Lord Curzon, 22 September 1921. (Emphasis mine.)

115. FO141/431/7838. President of the British Chamber of Commerce (in meetings with Committees of Alexandria and Cairo); two resolutions to Earl Curzon, Foreign Secretary, 28 July 1921.
116. FO141/431/7838. President of British Chamber of Commerce with (Alexandria and Cairo Committees) two resolutions for Earl Curzon, Foreign Secretary, 28 July 1921.
117. FO141/431/7838. The Amendment to the British Nationality and Status of Aliens Act 1922.
118. Stockwell: 'White man's burden', p.45.
119. Waltraud Ernst, 'Idioms of madness and colonial boundaries: the case of the European and 'native' mentally ill in early nineteenth-century British India,' *Comparative Study of Society and History* 39/1 (1997), p.162.
120. Saul Dubow, 'Race, civilisation and culture: the elaboration of segregationist discourse in the inter-war years' in Shula Marks and Stanley Trapido (eds), *The Politics of Race, Class and Nationalism in Twentieth Century South Africa* (London: Longman, 1987), p.76.
121. Stockwell: 'White man's burden', p.45.
122. Margaret Strobel, *European Women and the Second British Empire* (Bloomington: Indiana University Press, 1991), pp.1, 6.
123. E. A. Wallis Budge, *Cook's Handbook for Egypt and the Sudan* (London: Thomas Cook and Son, 1906), p.33.
124. Edith Louisa Butcher, *Things Seen in Egypt* (London: Seeley and Co, Ltd, 1910), p.41.
125. Strobel: *European Women*, p.6.
126. FO633/12; Cromer's papers, 2 December 1909; p.222, letter from Sir Cecil Spring Rice.
127. Malak Hifni Nasif, *Al-Nisa'iyāt* (Cairo: Al-Jarida, 1910), pp.10–11, as quoted in Mervat Hatem, 'Through each other's eyes: the impact on the colonial encounter of the images of Egyptian, Levantine-Egyptian, and European women, 1862–1920,' in Nupur Chaudhuri and Margaret Strobel (eds), *Western Women and Imperialism: Complicity and Resistance* (Bloomington: Indiana University Press, 1992), p.41.
128. Hopwood: *Tales of Empire*, p.70.
129. Nabawiya Musa, 'al-Muḥāḍarāt al-Nisa'ya fi al-Jami'āt al-Miṣriyāt' in al-Ahram (ed), *Shuhud al-'Asr* (Cairo: Al-Ahram, 1986), pp.40–1 as quoted in Hatem: 'Through each other's eyes', p.42.
130. *Ibid.*
131. Edith Louisa Butcher, *Egypt As We Knew It* (London: Mills & Boon, Ltd., 1911), p.170.
132. FO141/686/8747. 6 March 1919: W. Hayter responding to letters from Girgis Soliman in Newcastle-on-Tyne (26 January 1919) and from the Rev. Alfred Boote, Vicar at St. George's Vicarage at Newcastle-on-Tyne (25 January 1919).

133. FO141/463/1229. Marriages abroad and in the UK based on the Foreign Marriages Act 1892 and the Foreign Marriages Order in Council, 1913. (Emphasis mine.)
134. Butcher: *Egypt as We Knew It*, p.170.
135. FO141/686/8747. Letter E. F. W. Besley, Acting Judicial Adviser to the High Commissioner of Egypt to Residency, 31 August 1927.
136. FO287/2. Letter from G. E. Jeffes to Arthus D. Alan, HBM consul, 13 June 1911.
137. *Ibid.*
138. *Ibid.*
139. *Ibid.*
140. *Ibid.*
141. J. W. A. Young, unpublished papers, Vol. 1, ch. 8, p.7 (St. Antony's College, Oxford).
142. *Ibid.*
143. *Ibid.*, p.8. (Emphasis mine.)
144. FO633/12. Letter from E. R. Burn to Cromer, 10 November 1919, p.208.
145. Harrison: *Homely Diary*, p.128.
146. FO141/463/1229. Foreign Marriages Act. (Emphasis mine.)
147. FO141/470/1677. Rabino, British Consul in Cairo to First Secretary at the Residency...complaints from Europeans in Manshiyya Prison, 5 December 1922.
148. *Ibid.*
149. FO141/470/677. Vice-Consul of Cairo to First Secretary of Agency, reporting on complaints by British prisoner in Manshiyya prison, 1 December 1922.
150. *Ibid.*

3: Symbols and Institutions

1. Benedict Anderson, *Imagined Communities*, rev. ed. (London, Verso, 1994), p.6.
2. *Ibid.*, p.26.
3. Anthony Cohen, *The Symbolic Construction of Community* (London: Routledge, 1993), p.19.
4. Anthony Cohen, 'Boundaries of consciousness, consciousness of boundaries: critical questions for Anthropology,' in Cora Govers and Hans Vermeulen (eds), *The Anthropology of Ethnicity Beyond 'Ethnic Groups and Boundaries'* (Amsterdam: Het Spinhuis, 1994), p.62.
5. Cora Govers and Hans Vermeulen, 'Introduction', in Govers and Vermeulen (eds): *Anthropology of Ethnicity*, p.4.
6. Orlando Patterson, 'The nature, causes, and implications of ethnic

identification,' in Charles Fried (ed), *Minorities, Community and Identity* (New York: Springer-Verlag, 1983), p.31.
7. *Ibid.*, p.25.
8. *Ibid.*, p.31.
9. Roland Barthes, *Mythologies*, trans. by Annette Lavers (London: Granada, 1973), p.109. (Emphasis mine.)
10. *Ibid.*, p.32.
11. H. F. Wood, *Egypt Under the British* (London: Chapman-Hall, 1896), p.51.
12. *Ibid.*, p.52–53.
13. Roger Owen, *Lord Cromer: Victorian Imperialist, Edwardian Proconsul* (Oxford: Oxford University Press, 2004), p.242. Since the 1890s, the British Consul-General in Egypt (Sir Evelyn Baring, became Lord Cromer in 1892) had been attempting to reduce 'French cultural influence by recruiting British teachers' but faced limited success due to resistance by the French. The chapter on 'socio-occupational diversity' also refers to this recruitment of British teachers.
14. Mark S. W. Hoyle, *The Mixed Courts of Egypt* (London; Graham and Trotman, 1991), p.17.
15. Minutes of Manchester Chamber of Commerce, Middle East and North Africa section (1916–26), report after J. P. Foster's address, 12 November 1917 (Manchester Central Library, Archives Department).
16. Hoyle: *The Mixed Courts*, p.19.
17. Speech by J. P. Foster to the Manchester Chamber of Commerce, 12 November 1917, recorded in Minutes of Manchester Chamber of Commerce, Middle East and North Africa section (1916–26). (Emphasis mine.)
18. Minutes of Manchester Chamber of Commerce, 12 November 1917.
19. Hoyle: *The Mixed Courts*, p.116.
20. Robert Ross and Gerard J. Telkamp (eds), *Colonial Cities: Essays on Urbanism in a Colonial Context* (Lancaster: Martinus Nijhoff Publishers, 1985), pp.5–6.
21. S. C. Ghosh, *The Social Condition of the British Community in Bengal, 1757–1800* (Leiden: E. J. Brill, 1970), p.96.
22. Jürgen Osterhammel, *Colonialism: A Theoretical Overview* (Princeton: Markus Wiener Publishers, 1997), p.88.
23. *Ibid.*
24. Timothy Mitchell, *Colonising Egypt* (New York: Cambridge University Press, 1988), p.65.
25. *Ibid.*, p.67.
26. British Map Library, no. 64480 (4): Edward Stanford, 12, 13, 14, Long Acre W.C., 16 June 1906 (London); acquired by British Museum, 4 October 1906.
27. *Residential Map of Gezira*, published by the Survey of Egypt, 1907, in F. T.

NOTES 265

Rowlatt's Hanging File, (Middle East Centre, St.Antony's College, Oxford University).
28. British Map Library, no. 64480(6): *General Map of Cairo*, published by Survey of Egypt 1920.
29. Samir W. Raafat, *Cairo, the Glory Years: Who Build What, When, Why, and For Whom?* (Alexandria: Harpocrates Publishing, 2003), p.135. Raafat mentions 52 British government and business leaders out of 84 long-term residents in total living in Gezira, based on a French-language Egyptian commercial directory in 1913. Of the 52 Britons, 'most of them [were] top executives in the Egyptian administration, major companies and banks. This...list includes directors of the Survey Department, the Prison Administration, the Irrigation Administration, and the Department of Health. Among the joint stock companies we find directors of the Menzaleh Navigation Company, the Egyptian Markets company, the Egyptian Dreging Company and Thomas Cook. Topping the banking list is the National Bank of Egypt, the Agricultural Bank and the Imperial Ottoman Bank.'
30. Owen: *Lord Cromer*, p.185. The British Residency was also known as the British Agency.
31. *Ibid.*, p.184.
32. Janet Abu-Lughod, *Cairo: 1001 Years of the City Victorious*, (Princeton: Princeton University Press, 1971), p.98.
33. Martin Briggs S. *Through Egypt in War-Time* (London: Unwin, 1918), p.36.
34. Valerie Johnson, 'British identity was forged by imperial overseas encounters,' http://www.voxeu.org/index.php?q=node/1186 (June 2008), pp.1–2.
35. Magda Baraka, *The Egyptian Upper Class between Revolutions: 1919–1952*, (Reading: Ithaca, 1998), p.106.
36. Mark Crinson, *Empire Building: Orientalism and Victorian Architecture* (London: Routledge, 1996), p.171–2.
37. *Ibid.*
38. Peter Clark, *Sociability and Urbanity: Clubs and Societies in the Eighteenth Century City* (Leicester: Victorian Studies Centre, University of Leicester, 1986), p.22.
39. Paul J. Rich, *Chains of Empire* (London: Regency Press, 1991), p.145.
40. J. H. Grainger, *Patriotisms: Britain 1900–1939*, (London: Routledge & Kegan Paul, 1986), p.137 as quoted from Rich: *Chains of Empire*, p.145.
41. Edward Rodwell, *The Mombasa Club* (Mombasa: Mombasa Club, 1988), pp.24–5.
42. Coles Pasha, *Recollections and Reflections* (London: The Saint Catherine Press, 1918), pp.40, 158.
43. J-M. R. Oppenheim, 'Le sporting club: symbole et enjeu social,' *La Revue de L'Occident Musulman et de la Mediterreaneé (ROMM)*, 46, 1987, p.168.

44. Sarah Seawright, *The British in the Middle East* (London: East and West Publications, 1979), p.126.
45. Samir Raafat, 'Gezira Sporting Club milestones,' *Egyptian Mail*, 10–17 February 1996 from Samir Raafat's website: www.egy.com.
46. Briggs: *Through Egypt*, p.26.
47. Bimbashi McPherson and Barry Carman, *A Life in Egypt* (London: BBC, 1983), p.29.
48. Magda Abu-Fadil, 'Gezira Club – still the 'in' place to be,' *The Middle East* (September 1990), p.45.
49. Seawright: *The British in the Middle East*, p.126.
50. *Ibid.*
51. Young, unpublished papers, St. Antony's College, Oxford, Vol. 1, p.11.
52. Arnold Wright, *20th Century Impressions of Egypt: Its History, People, Commerce, Industries and Resources* (London: Lloyd's Greater Britain Publishing Co., Ltd., 1909), p.342.
53. Raafat: 'Gezira Sporting Club milestones.'
54. Rich: *Chains of Empire*, p.145.
55. *Ibid.*
56. Douglas Sladen, *Egypt and the English* (London: Hurst and Blackett, Ltd., 1908), p.505.
57. Young: unpublished papers, p.11.
58. William A. Douglas, *Letters and Memorials* (Edinburgh: Andrew Brown, 1920), p.36. Located in the Imperial War Museum. Douglas was a captain in the Royal Scots' 6th Battalion.
59. Sladen: *Egypt and the English*, p.504.
60. Sir Richard Vaux, private papers at Middle East Centre, St. Antony's College, Oxford University, p.32.
61. Lord Edward Cecil, *The Leisure of an Egyptian Official* (London: Hodder and Stoughton, 1921), pp.118–19.
62. Rich: *Chains of Empire*, p.169.
63. William M. Welch, Jr., *No Country for a Gentleman: British Rule in Egypt, 1883–1907* (London: Greenwood Press, 1988), p.33.
64. Peter Mellini, *Sir Eldon Gorst: The Overshadowed Proconsul* (Stanford: Hoover Institute Press, 1971), p.157.
65. Young: unpublished papers, p.3.
66. Thomas Skelton Harrison, *The Homely Diary of a Diplomat in the East 1897–1899* (New York: Houghton, Mifflin Co., 1917), p.90.
67. FO141/786/7553. Letter from Sir Reginald Wingate to Brigadier General Sir George Macauley, 15 August 1918.
68. *Ibid.* Letter from Macauley to Wingate, 16 August 1918.
69. FO841/102. Guy Osborne Lion vs. James Francis Waterlow, Civil Jurisdiction, Waterlow's deposition, 23 June 1908.
70. A. J. Stockwell, 'The white man's burden and brown humanity: colonialism

and ethnicity in British Malaya,' *The Southeast Asian Journal of Social Sciences* 10/1 (1982), p.48.
71. Mabel Caillard, *A Lifetime in Egypt: 1876–1935* (London: Grant Richards, 1935), p.47. (Emphasis mine.)
72. Shaun Lopez, 'Football as national allegory: Al-Ahram and the Olympics in 1920s Egypt,' *History Compass* 7/1 (2009), p.285.
73. Caillard: *A Lifetime in Egypt*, pp.49–50.
74. Command Papers relating to 'Assault on British officers near Cairo,' in Command Papers, 706, in Accounts and Papers, State Papers, no. 76. Vol. CXXX, 1902, Egypt, No. 3, 23 July 1901.
75. Cecil: *The Leisure*, p.145.
76. Harrison: *Homely Diary*, p.56.
77. Caillard: *A Lifetime in Egypt*, p.112.
78. Briggs: *Through Egypt*, p.26.
79. Lord Milner, *England in Egypt*, 13th ed. (London: Edward Arnold, 1920), p.29. Milner was at the time Under-Secretary of Finance in Egypt.
80. Robert L. Tignor, *Modernization and British Colonial Rule in Egypt, 1882–1914* (Princeton: Princeton University Press, 1966), p.195.
81. Briggs: *Through Egypt*, p.28 (emphasis mine).
82. Caillard: *A Lifetime in Egypt*, p.50.
83. David Kertzer, *Ritual, Politics and Power* (New Haven: Yale University Press, 1988), p.33.
84. Frederick C. Penfield, *Present-Day Egypt* (New York: The Century Co., 1903), pp.52–3. (Emphasis mine.)
85. Young: unpublished papers, p.1.
86. David Cannadine, *Ornamentalism: How the British Saw Their Empire* (London: Allen Lane, 2001), p.122.
87. FO141/680/4069. Letter from British High Commissioner McMahon to Lord Balfour, Foreign Secretary, 22 December 1916.
88. *Ibid.*
89. C. J. Bartlett, *The Global Conflict: The International Rivalry of the Great Powers, 1890–1990*, 2nd ed. (London: Longman, 1994), p.25.
90. *Ibid.*
91. Raafat, 'The Anglo-American hospital approaches its centennial,' *Egyptian Mail*, 13 January 1996; *Cairo Times,* 28 May 1998, as quoted from Raafat's website: www.egy.com.
92. FO141/680/4069. Letter from British High Commissioner McMahon to Lord Balfour, 22 December 1916.
93. Letter to Executive Committee of Anglo-American Hospital, summer 1911, All Saints' Church archives, Bundle 67B.
94. FO141/680/4069. Letter from High Commissioner McMahon to Lord Balfour, 22 December 1916.
95. FO141/607/3693. Letter from High Commissioner to Foreign Office, November 1916.

96. *Ibid.* Fathy Pasha's, President of the Kitchener Memorial Committee, report to High Commissioner Allenby, 13 July 1923.
97. Rich: *Chains of Empire*, p.111.
98. FO141/680/4069. Letter from Douglas Dunlop, Educational Advisor to High Commissioner McMahon, entitled: *Note on the Desirability of Encouraging British Educational Institutions in Egypt*, 26 October 1916.
99. FO141/512/608. Articles of the Constitution of Victoria College, approved by the General Meeting of Founders and Promoters, 28 March 1912.
100. FO141/680/4069. Letter from McMahon to Balfour, 22 December 1916.
101. *Ibid.* Letter from Dunlop to McMahon, 26 October 1916.
102. Rich: *Chains of Empire*, pp.59, 61.
103. *Ibid.*, p.36.
104. FO141/512/608. Speech by Sir Reginald Wingate, High Commissioner, at meeting of Victoria College Endowment Fund, 21 July 1920.
105. *Ibid.* Letter from Minister of Education in Egypt to Lord Allenby, 19 April 1922.
106. *Ibid.* Letter to Lord Cromer from Ruffer, 27 June 1911.
107. *Ibid.*
108. *Ibid.* Memo to High Commissioner, 1911.
109. Baraka: *The Egyptian Upper Class*, p.157.
110. FO141/680/4069. Letter from McMahon to Balfour, 22 December 1916.
111. *Ibid.*
112. All Saints' Church Archives, Minute book 25, 6 September 1917.
113. Chris Brooks, *Signs for the Times: Symbolic Realism in the Mid-Victorian World* (London: George Allen & Unwin, 1984), p.162.
114. St. Andrew's Church archives, May 1917 report.
115. Douglas: *Letters and Memorials*, p.60, letter on 15 October 1915.
116. Aldred Brown, 'All Saints' Church,' in Arnold Wright (ed): *20th Century Impressions*, p.202.
117. FO141/680/4069. Letter from McMahon to Balfour, 22 December 1916.
118. FO141/679/4117. Appeal for funds for Cathedral, 1919.
119. FO141/680/4069. Letter from McMahon to Balfour, 22 December 1916.
120. *Ibid.*
121. *Ibid.*
122. FO141/679/4117. Bishop's letter to *The Times* and other English papers, 29 June 1916.
123. *Ibid.*
124. *Ibid.* Appeal for funding for the Cathedral, 1919.
125. All Saints' Church archives, Cairo, minute book, 22, 16 November 1921.
126. FO141/679/4117. Letter from British Residency to the Egyptian Government, 18 July 1922.
127. *Ibid.* Letter from Financial Advisor, G. Vereker to Residency, 2 December 1922.

128. Arthur Burrell, *Cathedral on the Nile: A History of the All Saints Cathedral* (Cairo, Oxford: Amate Press, 1984), p.19.
129. *Ibid.*, p.78.
130. FO141/680/4069. McMahon to Balfour, 25 December 1916.
131. *Ibid.*, McMahon to Balfour, 22 December 1916.
132. Clive Whitehead, 'British colonial education policy: a synonym for cultural imperialism?' in J. A. Mangan (ed), *Benefits Bestowed: Education and British Imperialism* (Manchester: Manchester University Press, 1988), p.216.
133. Baraka: *The Egyptian Upper Class*, p.136.
134. *Ibid.*
135. Rich: *Chains of Empire*, p.109.
136. Harrison: *Homely Diary*, pp.77–83.
137. Margaret Strobel, *European Women and the Second British Empire* (Bloomington: Indiana University Press, 1991), p.10.
138. Harrison: *Homely Diary*, p.153.
139. 'Empire Day at Alexandria', *Egyptian Gazette*, 23 May 1916, p.4.
140. Stockwell: 'White man's burden', p.44.
141. G. W. Steevens, *Egypt in 1898* (New York: Dodd, Mead and Company, 1899), p.73.
142. Harrison: *Homely Diary*, p.110.
143. Brown: 'All Saints' Church', p.202.
144. Nina Nelson, *Shepheard's Hotel* (London: Barrie & Rockcliff, 1960), p.25.
145. Stockwell: 'White man's burden', p.48.
146. Ghosh: *Social Condition*, p.133.
147. *Ibid.*

4: Socio-Occupational Diversity

1. Private papers, Sir Richard Vaux, 1902, p.32, Middle East Centre, St. Antony's College, University of Oxford.
2. Ann Laura Stoler, *Carnal Knowledge and Imperial Power: Race and the Intimate in Colonial Rule* (Berkeley: University of California Press, 2002), p.25.
3. Not surprisingly, salary levels changed over the course of the 40-year span that this discussion is concerned with. It appears that inflation accelerated rapidly towards the end of First World War and even more so after the War. However, the relatively low level of inflation during the 15 years before the War provide a fairly consistent basis of comparing general salary figures over this time period.
4. W. D. Rubenstein, *Britain's Century: A Political and Social History, 1815–1905* (London: Arnold, 1998), p.281.
5. *Ibid.*, p.286.

6. B. R. Mitchell, *British Historical Statistics* (Cambridge: Cambridge University Press, 1988), p.153.
7. There are a number of ways to categorise and determine the various levels of class hierarchy in late nineteenth century Britain. Within the general categories of upper, middle, and lower classes, there are also a variety of sub-groups. For this article, the lower class denotes those who are not classified as upper class or as middle class professionals; and within the lower class, those who tended to be less educated, less skilled, and/or are involved in manual or domestic labour, are referred to as 'working class'. Also, incomes levels, wealth, and perceived wealth provide aspects of understanding class differences and categorisation but occupation, family ties, speech, and even mannerisms offer some of the other aspects. For the purposes of this study, incomes levels and occupations serve as the primary indicators for class designation.
8. Rubenstein: *Britain's Century*, p.290.
9. *Ibid.*, 294.
10. William M. Welch, *No Country for a Gentleman: British Rule in Egypt, 1883–1900* (London: Greenwood Press, 1988), p.21.
11. The Earl of Cromer, *Modern Egypt*, Vol. 2 (London: Macmillan, 1908), p.299.
12. Max Rodenbeck, *Cairo: The City Victorious* (Cairo: American University in Cairo Press, 1999), p.176, claims that there were 2000 British officials in Egypt during the time of the occupation without clearly identifying the source for this estimate.
13. 'British from the British Isles' refer to primarily Britons from the homeland and those of British parentage (besides the English, Welsh, and Scottish, census records included the few Irish residents of Egypt in this group). British subjects of Greek, Maltese, or other descent are not included. Children of mixed heritage tended to follow the nationality of their father.
14. *Recensement Général de L'Égypte 1897*, Tome Premier (Le Caire: Imprimerie Nationale, 1898), pp.46, 82.
15. Table 1 suggests that there were 542 British subjects who were teachers in Egypt in 1897 but Table 4 seems not to mention teachers in the list of vocations for male British subjects in Cairo and Alexandria at this time. Teachers were generally civil servants and were likely included in the 'civil servant' category whilst some may have been counted in the 'professor/religious teacher' category.
16. One Egyptian pound was equal to one sterling and six pence. See Roger Owen, *The Middle East in the World Economy, 1800–1914* (London: Methuen, 1981), p.8.
17. Peter Mellini, *Sir Eldon Gorst: The Overshadowed Proconsul* (Stanford: Hoover Institute Press, 1971), p.242.
18. FO 841/15. Probate Jurisdiction, Estate of Thomas Basil Etherington-Smith, 27 October 1915.

19. Welch: *No Country for a Gentleman*, p.36.
20. Letter to Sir Valentine Chirol, 13 August 1901, Sir Cecil Spring Rice private correspondences, Church College Archives, Cambridge University.
21. Derek Hopwood, *Egypt: Politics and Society 1945–1984*, 2nd ed. (London: Allen and Unwin, 1987), p.19.
22. Total for military salaries £249,827 approximately divided by total military personnel in Arnold Wright (ed), *Twentieth Century Impressions of Egypt: Its History, People, Commerce, Industries and Resources* (London: Lloyd's Greater Britain Publishing Co, 1909), p.401.
23. *Ibid.*
24. *Recensement Général de L'Égypte, 1897*, Tome Premier, pp.18, 52.
25. Ministry of Finance, *Census of Egypt, 1917*, Vol. II, Ministry of Finance, Statistical Department, (Cairo; Government Press, 1921), p.513.
26. *Recensement Général de l'Egypte, 1897*, Table for Professions et Métiers, Sexe Masculin, p.63.
27. James Aldridge, *Cairo* (London: Macmillan, 1969), p.214.
28. *Recensement Général de l'Egypte, 1897*, Table for Professions et Métiers, Sexe Masculin, p.24.
28. 29. *Recensement Général de l'Egypte, 1897*, p.27.
30. *Ibid.*, pp.18 and 32.
31. *Ibid.*, pp.46, 50, 82, 86, combining the populations of male and female British subjects in Cairo and Alexandria.
32. *Ibid.*; for Cairo, p.46 and for Alexandria, p.82.
33. *Ibid.*; in Cairo, p.50 and Alexandria, p.86.
34. *Census of 1917*, Table IV, Groups of Occupations by Nationalities, pp.472, 473.
35. Letter to W. G. Tyrell of Foreign Office, 20 June 1911, Sir Milne Cheetham private papers, Middle East Centre, St. Antony's College Archive, Oxford University.
36. Foster's annual income seems to be less than the average income for solicitors and barristers in Britain at that time (£1,343.50 in 1911. See Mitchell: *British Historical Statistics*, 153). It may be that very high earning lawyers escalated this figure for the profession's average income. As for Foster's motive to work in Egypt, there may have been a number of reasons including his inability to find equivalent work in Britain or his desire for experiences abroad.
37. The amount of British currency at the time is delineated by three categories: pound, shillings (20 in 1 pound) and pence (12 in 1 shilling). 1 Egyptian pound (E£) is worth about the same as £1. And there are 100 piastres in an Egyptian pound.
38. FO841/188. Estate of John Porter Foster, Barrister-at-Law, 26 February 1920.
39. FO847/67. Probate Jurisdiction, Estate of Dr. Marc Armand Ruffer, 15 April 1917.

40. Elite factory owners, manufacturers, and industrialists left fortunes of around £100,000, whereas middle class professionals left considerably less. Rubenstein: *Britain's Century*, p.285.
41. FO841/154. Probate Jurisdiction, Estate of Charles Orr Campbell, 10 July 1915.
42. FO841/190. Probate Jurisdiction, Estate of Herbert Bunnell May, 9 February 1921.
43. FO841/193. Probate Jurisdiction, William Gledhill, 30 August 1920.
44. Table of 'Nominal annual earnings – England and Wales, 1710–1911,' Mitchell: *British Historical Statistics*, p.153.
45. *Ibid.* The average teacher's salary in Britain was just over £147 in 1901 and £176 in 1911.
46. FO841/188. Probate Jurisdiction, Charles Sherrard, 13 June 1906.
47. Roger Owen, *Lord Cromer: Victorian Imperialist, Edwardian Proconsul* (Oxford: Oxford University Press, 2004), p. 242.
48. Letter from W. R. Carruthers, manager of Anglo-Egyptian Bank in Alexandria, to H. A. Richardson, chairman (1907–18) of AEB in London, 27 January 1916, letters from Anglo-Egyptian Bank staff, Barclays Group Archives.
49. *Ibid.*
50. *Ibid.* Letter from A. Jessop, Representative of the Anglo-Egyptian Bank at Minet-el-Bassal, to Carruthers, 8 September 1916.
51. Samir Raafat, *Maadi: 1904–1962: Society and History in a Cairo Suburb* (Cairo: Palm Press, 1994), p.15.
52. FO841/87. Probate Jurisdiction, Estate of Sir Edwin Milford Palmer, 12 February 1906.
53. Wright: *Twentieth Century Impressions*, p.326.
54. *Ibid.*, pp.326, 458.
55. Archives of Barker family, MS 238, Box 1, Section F, p.3.
56. Wright: *Twentieth Century Impressions*, p.372.
57. *Ibid.*, p.327.
58. Piers Brendan, *Thomas Cook: 150 Years of Popular Tourism* (London: Serber and Warburg, 1992), p.232.
59. *Ibid.*, pp.223–30. The steamers served more than 6000 visitors to Egypt each winter, among whom 1500 went up the Nile for three week voyages at £50 per head, two week trips for £25 per head, and eleven days for £20 each.
60. *Ibid.* Quoting *US Excursionist*, August 1897, p.230.
61. *Ibid.*, p.271.
62. F. Robert Hunter, 'Tourism and empire: the Thomas Cook and Son enterprise on the Nile, 1868–1914,' *Middle Eastern Studies* 40/5 (2004), p.44.
63. Brendan: *Thomas Cook*, p.232, quoting *Vanity Fair*, 23 February 1889 and 9 March 1889.

64. Wright: *Twentieth Century Impressions*, p.201.
65. *Ibid.*
66. Letter from Lord Cromer to Dean Butcher, 2 November 1895, minute book 32, All Saints' Church archives, Cairo.
67. FO841/91. Probate Jurisdiction, Rev. Charles Henry Butcher, 6 February 1907.
68. 'Our Frontispiece,' *CMS Intelligencer* 26 (1901), p.282.
69. *Ibid.*, 30 (1905), p.151.
70. *Ibid.*
71. *Ibid.*, 29 (1904), p.364.
72. FO841/188, Probate Jurisdiction, Estate of Mrs. Eliza Bannerman (Bywater) Knight, 1920.
73. FO841/146, Probate Jurisdiction, Estate of Ernest Maynard Pain, 23 January 1914.
74. Cheetham invites the most distinguished Britons in Cairo to discuss the proceedings of the Coronation celebration of George V. Letter to Sir W. Tyrell, 22 February 1911, Cheetham papers.
75. Rodenbeck: *Cairo*, p.176.
76. Rubenstein: *Britain's Century*, p.290–1.
77. N. L. Tranter, *Population and Society, 1750–1940: Contrasts in Population Growth* (London: Longman, 1985), p.132.
78. E. H. Hunt, *British Labour History, 1815–1914* (London: Wiedenfield and Nicolson, 1981), p.147.
79. Tranter: *Population and Society*, pp. 132–3.
80. FO841/102. Civil Jurisdiction, Guy Osborne Lion vs. James Francis Waterlow, 5 June 1908.
81. Gregory Anderson, *Victorian Clerks* (Manchester: Manchester University Press, 1976), p.14.
82. *Ibid.*, p.25. Chart of salaries of clerks at Liverpool's Sea Insurance Company, 1890–1914.
83. *Ibid.*
84. Mitchell: *British Historical Statistics*, p.153.
85. FO841/102. Civil Jurisdiction, Lion vs. Waterlow, Waterlow's deposition, 23 June 1908.
86. *Ibid.* Civil Jurisdiction, 23 June 1908.
87. *Ibid.* Lion's deposition, 22 June 1908.
88. *Ibid.* Court judgement, 24 June 1908.
89. *Ibid.* Appeal, 30 June 1908 and 30 November 1908.
90. Rodenbeck: *Cairo*, p.176.
91. FO841/133. Probate Jurisdiction, James Henry Jones, 24 February 1913.
92. *Ibid.* Letter to Mrs. Jones from the British Consulate, 20 March 1913.
93. FO841/143. Probate Jurisdiction, Peter John Teskow, 26 September 1913.
94. Mitchell: *British Historical Statistics*, p.153.

95. H. J. Habakkuk, 'Fluctuations in house-building in Britain and the United States in the nineteenth century,' in Derek H. Aldcroft and Peter Fearon (eds), *British Economic Fluctuations* (London: St. Martin's Press, 1972), p.265.
96. D. J. Coppock, 'The causes of business fluctuations,' in Aldscroft and Fearon (eds): *British Economic Fluctuations*, p.212.
97. Mitchell: *British Historical Statistics*, p.153.
98. FO841/115. Letter from Chubb to Barrister R. Silley, 22 November 1910, Sidney Chubb vs. Henry Lovatt Co.
99. *Ibid.*, Woodley's deposition, 5 May 1910.
100. *Ibid.*, Chubb's statement, 23 November 1910.
101. *Egyptian State Railways and Port of Alexandria, Report of the Board of Administration, 1900* (Cairo: Egyptian Railways Printing Office, 1901), p.16; *Report on the Egyptian State Railways and Telegraphs and Light Railways of Egypt, 1913* (Cairo: Printing Office of the Administration, 1914), p.18.
102. *Egyptian State Railways Report, 1900*, p.17.
103. FO841/110. Probate Jurisdiction, James Campbell, 2 March 1910.
104. Mitchell: *British Historical Statistics*, p.153.
105. Minute book 32, 11 September 1898, All Saints' Church Archives.
106. *Ibid.*, 27 October 1899.
107. *Ibid.*, 20 March 1892; *ibid.*, 19 October 1894.
108. Minutes, 23 March 1915, St. Andrew's Church Archives, Cairo.
109. Norman McCord, *British History 1815–1916* (Oxford: Oxford University Press, 1991), p.453.
110. Rubenstein: *Britain's Century*, p.320.
111. V. T. J. Arkell, *Britain Transformed: The Development of British Society since the Mid-Eighteenth Century* (London: Penguin Education, 1973), p.198.
112. FO841/89. Letter from Caroline de Willbois to Mr. Alban, Probate Jurisdiction, Elizabeth Chadwick, 25 December 1906.
113. Juan R. Cole, 'Feminism, class, and Islam in turn-of-the-century Egypt,' *International Journal of Middle East Studies*, 13 (1981), p.394.
114. E. L. Butcher, *Egypt As We Knew It* (London: Mills and Boon, 1911), p.151.
115. Rubenstein: *Britain's Century*, p.325.
116. FO141/466/1429. Prostitution and Bureau des Moeurs report, 1914.
117. Minute book 31, Cairo Church Committee minutes, 1870–90, 10 April 1891, All Saints' Church Archives.
118. *Ibid.*, 28 October 1887.
119. *Ibid.*, 10 April 1891.
120. *Ibid.*
121. 'The British Officer: From the private's point of view', *Egyptian Gazette*, 4 June 1918, p.7.

122. Robert Tressell, *The Ragged-Trousered Philanthropists* (London: The Richards Press Ltd, 1927), p.167.
123. Michael J. Reimer, 'Urban Government and Administration in Egypt, 1805–1914,' *Die Welt Des Islam* 39/3 (1999), p.301.
124. Helmi Ahmed Shalabi, *al-Ḥukm al-Maḥallī wa-l-majālis al-baladiyya fī Miṣr mundhu nash'atihā ḥatta 'āmm 1882* (Cairo: GEBO, 1987), p.132.

5: Crime and Misconduct

1. Clive Emsley, *Crime and Society in England, 1750–1900*, 3rd ed. (London: Pearson Longman, 2005), p.1.
2. *Ibid.*, p.2.
3. Will Hanley, 'Foreigness and localness in Alexandria, 1880–1914' (PhD dissertation, Prince University, 2007), p.3. Hanley devised a very useful chart to explain which courts (consular, mixed, native, or religious) are used depending on the type of case (criminal, civil, personal status) and the nationalities of the plaintiffs and defendants involved.
4. 'Draft laws for the reconstitution of the mixed courts,' *Egyptian Gazette*, 12 June 1920.
5. Tim Hitchock and Robert Shoemaker, *Tales from the Hanging Court* (London: Hodder Education), 2007, p.xxv.
6. Letter from Sir Milne Cheetham to Consul-General, Eldon Gorst, 31 July 1910, in Sir Milne Cheetham Papers, Middle East Centre, St. Antony's College, Oxford University.
7. *Ibid*. Cheetham to Gorst, 12 September 1910.
8. *Ibid*. Cheetham to Sir Louis Mallet, 18 September 1910.
9. *Ibid.*
10. All Saints' Church Archives, Cairo, Bundle 67B, E. M. Dowson, Chairman, Executive Sub-Committee, 'Notes of evidence of neglect in the recent administration of the hospital,' summer 1911.
11. FO141/669/4394. Letter from Douglas Dunlop (Education Adviser) to E. H. Cecil (Finance Adviser), 6 February 1917.
12. *Ibid*. Private letter from Sir R. Graham to High Commissioner McMahon, 1 July 1917.
13. *Ibid*. Major C. F. Ryder, Assistant Director, Eastern Mediterranean Special Intelligence Bureau, reporting on what certain Egyptian friends of Ashbee say, 22 June 1917.
14. *Ibid.*
15. *Ibid*. Henderson, Commissioner for Egypt to Foreign Office to Sir. Austin Chamberlain, 26 July 1926.
16. Private papers of Charles Robert Ashbee, King's College Archives, Cambridge University, letters from Ashbee to his wife, Janet Elizabeth Ashbee, 13 April 1917 and 1 May 1917.

17. *Ibid.*
18. *Ibid.*
19. *Ibid.*, 3 May 1917.
20. *Ibid.*, 4 May 1917.
21. FO141/669/4394. Major C. F. Ryder, writing about Dunlop, 24 June 1917.
22. Private papers of Charles Robert Ashbee, letter to Dunlop, 10 October 1917.
23. Private papers of Sir Milne Cheetham, Middle East Centre, St. Antony's College, letter from Cheetham to W. G. Tyrell, June 1911.
24. *Ibid.* Letter from Cheetham to Langley, June 1911.
25. *Ibid.* Letter from Cheetham to Tyrell, June 1911.
26. *Ibid.*
27. Elmsley: *Crime and Society*, p.103.
28. P. E. Moulder, 'The lives of working women – by one of them,' *Good Words* XXXIX (1898), p.638.
29. Matilda M. Blake, 'Are women protected?' *The Westminster Review* CXXXVII (1892), p.47.
30. Anna Clark, 'Domesticity and the problem of wifebeating in nineteenth-century Britain: working-class culture, law and politics,' in Shani D'Cruze (ed), *Everyday Violence in Britain, 1850–1950: Gender and Class* (London: Pearson, 2000), p.36.
31. FO841/81. His Britannic Majesty's Consular Court at Cairo (hereafter referred to as CCC), court order in Adelaide Lane vs. Thomas Lane, 17 October 1904.
32. *Ibid.*
33. FO841/64, CCC. Olga Campbell vs. William Campbell, 12 March 1910.
34. FO841/113, CCC. Alice Stephens vs. Frederick Bowring Stephens, Criminal Jurisdiction, 25 July 1910.
35. FO841/117, CCC. Suzanne Bailey vs. William Henry Bailey, 2 November 1910.
36. *Ibid.* Court Order, 6 December 1910.
37. FO841/156, CCC. Criminal Jurisdiction on Robert Steven Leslie, 18 July 1916.
38. *Ibid.* 29 July 1916.
39. *Ibid.* Letter from Egyptian Expeditionary Force, Headquarters, Lieutenant H. Norman Hardin to Arthur David Alban, His Britannic Majesty's Consul in Cairo, 25 July 1916.
40. FO841/155, CCC. Thérèse Quinn vs. Walter Quinn, His Britannic Majesty's Provincial Court at Cairo, 18 April 1916.
41. *Ibid.*, 7 June 1916.
42. FO847/64. Alexandria Consular Court (hereafter referred to as ACC), Quinn vs. Quinn, 26 August 1918.
43. *Ibid.*
44. *Ibid.*, 26 February 1919.

45. Shani D'Cruze, *Crimes of Outrage: Sex, Violence, and Victorian Working Women* (London: UCL Press, 1998), p.67.
46. FO841/92, CCC. Alfred William Griffith vs. Aline Griffith, Civil Jurisdiction, 4 May 1907.
47. FO841/120, CCC. Charlotte Duncan vs. James Duncan, 13 September 1911.
48. The notion that Britons considered Muslim men to behave violently against their wives is discussed in the chapter on 'boundaries' which quotes from a letter written by G. E. Jeffes to Arthus D. Alan of the British consulate, FO287/2, 13 June 1911, and from the unpublished papers of J. W. A. Young, from St. Antony's College, Oxford University, Vol. 1, ch. 8, p.7.
49. Barbara Brookes, *Abortion in England, 1900–1967* (London: Croom Helm, 1988). See the 'Introduction'. In fact, abortion remained illegal in Britain until 1967.
50. *Ibid.*, p.23.
51. FO841/122. CCC, Rex vs. Sergeant Harry Canning, 17 July 1911.
52. *Ibid.*, Sergeant Canning's deposition, June 1911.
53. Dr. Morrison was a prominent member of the British community in Cairo. J. E. Marshall, a judge in the Egyptian Court of Appeal, wrote in his book, *The Egyptian Enigma, 1890–1928* (London: John Murray, 1928), p.11, that Dr. Morrison was 'a man of great character,…a brilliant surgeon and a great public speaker in either French and English…He [spoke] Italian well, and [had] a very considerable working knowledge of Arabic.'
54. *Ibid.* Dr. Alexander Murison's deposition, 31 May 1911.
55. *Ibid.* Post-mortem exam of Mrs. May Canning, 29 May 1911.
56. *Ibid.* Criminal Jurisdiction, 31 May 1911.
57. *Ibid.* Letter from British Consulate, Cairo, to General Officer Commanding British Headquarters in Cairo, 17 July 1911.
58. FO847/32, ACC. Inquest into the death of Frederick John Barlow, 9 December 1892.
59. Ibid. ACC, Inquest into the death of Martin Doyle, 9 December 1902.
60. FO847/35, ACC. Statement with regards to Dora Blake, 25 April 1905.
61. FO847/36, ACC. Report accompanying the account of the Estate of Jessie Brown.
62. FO847/46, ACC. Inquest into the death of Thomas Brown, suicide note, Thomas Brown to Mr. Paterson, Manager in Egyptian Salt and Soda Co., 15 May 1911.
63. *Ibid.* Letter from D. A. Cameron, His Britannic Majesty's Consul-General in Alexandria to Judge of His Britannic Majesty's Supreme in Constantinople, 22 May 1911.
64. FO847/46. Alfred William Phillips' statement to His Britannic Majesty's Supreme Court for the Dominions of the Sublime Ottoman Porte, 2 September 1911.
65. *Ibid.* ACC, Inquest into the death of Mrs. Eugenie Phillips, letter by D. A.

Cameron, His Britannic Majesty's Consul General, 12 April 1912.
66. Arthur Blunt, Manager of Anglo-Egyptian Bank in Alexandria, to W. R. Carruthers, Manager in London, 5 September 1918, letters from Anglo-Egyptian Bank staff, Barclays Group Archives, Wythenshawe, Manchester.
67. *Ibid.*
68. FO847/12, ACC. Letter from Governor of Alexandria to His Britanic Majesty's Consular Court, 26 November 1885.
69. *Ibid.* ACC. Doctor's report on Alfred Brown, 9 January 1886.
70. *Ibid.*, H. de Coetlofou, Cairo Police, report, 31 January 1886.
71. FO841/53, CCC. Douglas Walcott vs. George Fowler, 6 April 1901.
72. FO841/87, CCC. Local Police vs. William and Marguerite Houghton, 26 January 1906.
73. FO841/114, CCC. Alfred Young vs. Sidney Alfred Chubb, 19 October 1910.
74. FO847/6, ACC. John Ross vs. Edwin Barber, letter from Charles Boyle, Ross' lawyer, to Barber, 23 October 1883.
75. *Ibid.* Judge Charles Alfred Cookson, conclusion of Ross vs. Barber, 30 November 1883.
76. FO841/83. John William Congdon vs. William Houghton, Criminal Jurisdiction, 14 February 1905.
77. *Ibid.* Article in *Egyptian Graphic*, 15 January 1905. Italics refer to Congdon's libellous words.
78. FO841/86. Congdon vs. Houghton at Supreme Consular Court, 8 March 1905.
79. *Ibid.*, 8 May 1905.
80. FO841/112. Wallace Daniel Hawkes vs. Charles Clouston Porri, Civil Jurisdiction, 2 June 1911.
81. *Ibid.* Letter to S. Duke, March 1911.
82. *Ibid.* Letter to George Frederick Hodgskins, March 1911.
83. *Ibid.* Civil Jurisdiction, His Britannic Majesty's Supreme Consular Court of the Sublime Ottoman Porte, 10 January 1912.
84. George Robb, *White-Collar Crime in Modern England: Financial Fraud and Business Morality, 1845–1929* (Cambridge: Cambridge University Press, 1992), p.56.
85. *Ibid.*, p.38.
86. Rob Sindall, 'Middle-class crime in nineteenth-century England,' *Criminal Justice History: An International Annual* IV (1983), p.27.
87. Robb: *White-Collar Crime*, p.9.
88. FO841/65, CCC. George Nungovich Hotels Company vs. Charles Helfield, Deposition of Mr. Milward, Assistant Station Master in Cairo, 3 July 1900.
89. *Ibid.* Deposition of Alfred Petry, 30 June 1900.
90. *Ibid.* Supreme Consular Court, Constantinople, verdict, 13 July 1900.
91. FO841/70, CCC. Abdul Rahim Khan vs. Charles Helfield, September 1901.

NOTES 279

92. *Ibid.* Angelo Cerfoglia vs. Charles Helfield, Cerfoglia's deposition, 9 September 1901.
93. *Ibid.* Criminal Jurisdiction, 2 November 1901.
94. *Ibid.*
95. FO841/127, CCC. Rachel Dentes vs. John Arthur McLaughlin, McLaughlin's deposition, 22 January 1913.
96. *Ibid.* Particulars of complaint filed, 19 December 1912.
97. *Ibid.*, 20 November 1913.
98. FO841/190, CCC. Edward Davies Bryan vs. John Hayes, letter from Sister Margaret Clare to Mr. Gout, 26 November 1920.
99. *Ibid.* Criminal Jurisdiction, 10 December 1920.
100. 'Davies Bryan swindled: A daring confidence trick', *Egyptian Gazette*, 25 December 1920, p.4.
101. *Ibid.*
102. FO841/195. Rex vs. John Hayes, His Britannic Majesty's Supreme Court in Cairo, Judge Peter Grain – sentence, 19 January 1921.
103. FO841/87, CCC. Thomas Cook and Son (Egypt) Ltd. vs. Thomas Frazer Thomson, deposition of Edward Aubrey Harrison, General Manager in Cairo, 13 January 1906.
104. *Ibid.* Deposition of Thomas Knight Sibbald, Superintending Engineer, 13 January 1906.
105. *Ibid.* Criminal Jurisdiction, 9 January 1906.
106. FO841/108, CCC. Rex vs. Rainey Munro Ross, Criminal Jurisdiction, 3 March 1909.
107. *Ibid.*
108. FO841/103, CCC. Keith Henry Marsham, Secretary of the Khedivial Sporting Club of Cairo vs. James Nadrett Jays, 26 January 1909.
109. FO847/45, CCC. Rex vs. Wood, notice from H. Hopkinson, Commandant of Alexandria City Police to Consul General in Alex, 30 August 1910.
110. *Ibid.*
111. FO841/132, CCC. Thomas Cook and Son, Ltd. vs. William Henry Baisty Skaife, Criminal Jurisdiction, 24 January 1913.
112. *Ibid.*
113. FO841/150, CCC. Egyptian State Railways vs. John Henry Johnson, from the General Manager's Office, 16 July 1915.
114. *Ibid.* Criminal Jurisdiction, 27 July 1915.
115. FO841/172, CCC. Joseph Smouha vs. Richard Warbrick, notes in Smouha's deposition: He was a very influential Jewish merchant/trader based in Egypt with operations in Manchester, Mesopotamia, Palestine and Persia.
116. *Ibid.* Smouha's deposition, 2 November 1918.
117. *Ibid.* Criminal Jurisdiction, 8 October 1918.
118. *Ibid.*
119. Emsley: *Crime and Society*, p.32.

120. FO841/198, CCC. letter from Rebecca Ellis, 13 July 1921, mentions ages of her children.
121. *Ibid.* Letterhead from assets of Isidore Ellis after his death, 18 August 1921.
122. FO841/155, CCC. Rebecca Ellis vs. Michael Ellis, Criminal Jurisdiction, 18 April 1916.
123. FO841/173, CCC. Rebecca Ellis vs. Michael Ellis, Criminal Jurisdiction, 9 January 1919.
124. FO841/197, CCC. Sydney Ellis vs. Michael Ellis, Criminal Jurisdiction, 11 May 1921.
125. FO841/206, CCC. Esther Ellis vs. Michael Ellis, Criminal Jurisdiction, 10 April 1922.
126. FO841/182, CCC. Provost Marshal vs. Michael Ellis, Provincial Jurisdiction, 21 August 1919.
127. FO841/188, CCC. Provincial Jurisdiction, 27 February 1920.
128. Letter from Carruthers to Coombs, Alexandria, 9 November 1916, Barclays' Archives.
129. *Ibid.*
130. All Saints' Church Archives, Bundle 67B, E. M. Dowson, Chairman, Executive Sub-Committee, 'Narrative of events connected with the resignation of the Late Matron of the Anglo-American Hospital,' summer 1911.
131. D'Cruze: *Crimes of Outrage*, p.30.
132. FO847/31, ACC. Report on case Rex vs. Gammage by E. B. Gould, sent to Judge of His Britannic Majesty's Supreme Consular Court in Constantinople, 13 August 1901.
133. *Ibid.*, Edward B. Gould, British Consul-General of Alexandria, sentence, 28 November 1901.
134. FO841/148, CCC. Victoria Ardani for her sister Sophie vs. Edward James Harran, Criminal Jurisdiction, 26 February 1915.
135. *Ibid.* Sophie's deposition, 1 March 1915.
136. *Ibid.*, 4 March 1915.
137. *Ibid.* Mrs. Josephine Harran's deposition, 4 March 1915.
138. FO847/74, ACC. Rex vs. Bertram Ley Roberts, letter from Alexander W. Staples, barrister-at-law in B.C., writes to Consular Agent, British Consulate in Alexandria, 12 July 1921.
139. *Ibid.* G. Gordon Ingram, Acting Commandant, Alexandria City Police, to His Britannic Majesty's Consul General, Alexandria, 25 August 1921.
140. *Ibid.* Acting Consul-General, Alex, to Acting British Consul, Cairo, 30 August 1921.
141. *Ibid.* Judge Linton T. Thorp's sentence, 8 November 1921.
142. FO141/466/1429. Prostitution and Bureau des Moeurs, 1914.
143. *Ibid.*
144. FO841/199, CCC. Cairo Social Police vs. Gordon Ainslie Ness, Criminal

Jurisdiction, 28 January 1921.
145. FO841/205, CCC. Rex vs. Shalders, memo. discussing those charged with living off the proceeds of prostitution, 17 November 1925.
146. FO841/199. Cairo Social Police vs. John Charles Shalders, Criminal Jurisdiction, 28 January 1921.
147. FO841/205. Rex vs. Shalders: memo. 17 November 1925.
148. FO141/466/1429, CCC. 'Actual infection rates on British troops,' in *Report of Cairo Purification Committee* (Cairo: Government Press, 1916), Appendix, Table IV.
149. *Ibid.* Arthur T. Upson, Nile Mission Press, Cairo, 16 July 1918.
150. Max Rodenbeck, *Cairo: The City Victorious* (Cairo: American University in Cairo Press, 1999), p.182.
151. FO141/466/1429. Annex 'B', of G. W. Harvey's (Commandant of the Cairo City Police) notes to the Cairo Purification Committee, 14 April 1916.
152. *Ibid.* Arthur T. Upson, of Nile Mission Press, to Allenby, 17 August 1918.
153. *Ibid.*
154. *Ibid.* Upson to Allenby, 31 August 1917.
155. *Ibid.* G. Andrews to High Commissioner, 24 June 1917.
156. *Ibid.* Major Garvice, Commandant of Alexandria Police to High Commissioner, report on perspective of Mrs. Anne Moore Charlian, 22 August 1918.
157. *Ibid.* Harvey to General Maxwell, 20 March 1916.
158. *Ibid.* Colonel H. Hopkinson, Commandant Alexandria City Police to Col. Beach, 21 September 1915.
159. *Ibid.* Alex Granville, Municipality of Alex, to General Maxwell, September 1915.
160. *Ibid.*
161. *Ibid.* Harvey, Commandant of Cairo City Police, to General Maxwell, report on native prostitutes, European hospitals, suppression of pimps and drink traffic, 20 March 1916.
162. *Ibid.*
163. *Ibid.*
164. *Ibid.* Cairo Purification Committee, minutes of 2nd meeting, 25 April 1916.
165. *Ibid.* Harvey to Maxwell, 20 March 1916.
166. J. de Vere Loder, letter to his father, 27 February 1916, private papers from St. Antony's College, Oxford) as quoted in F. Lissauer, *British Policy Towards Egypt, 1914–1922* (PhD Thesis, University of London, London School of Economics, 1975), p.90.
167. John Marlowe, *A History of Modern Egypt and Anglo-Egyptian Relations* (London: Cresnet, 1954), p.135 as quoted from Roger Allen, *A Period of Time: A Study and Translation of Ḥadīth 'Isā ibn Hishām by Muḥammad al-Muwayliḥī* (Reading: Ithaca, 1992), p.74.
168. Well-known in modern Egyptian history, the Denshawai incident refers

to the severe miscarriage of justice after a British officer was killed by sunstroke while escaping from villagers who were attacking him and his colleagues after the Britons were caught shooting at pigeons for sport. The pigeons happened to provide the livelihood of some of the inhabitants of Denshawai. The villagers were blamed for the British officer's death and after a show trial in which the leading judge was an Egyptian but was closely associated with the British administration, extremely harsh sentences were given. Four villagers were sentenced to death, two received life sentences while six others emerged with seven years imprisonment. Others were sentenced to lashing and the whole village, including women and children, were forced to watch the executions and the floggings.
169. Jack A. Crabb Jr., *The Writing of History in Nineteenth-Century Egypt: A Study of National Transformation,* (Cairo: AUC Press, 1984), p.158.

6: The First World War

1. Mark S. W. Hoyle, *The Mixed Courts of Egypt* (London: Graham and Trotman, 1991), pp.88–9.
2. John Darwin, *Britain, Egypt and the Middle East: Imperial Policy in the Aftermath of War, 1918–1922* (London: Macmillan, 1981), p.61.
3. Efraim Karsh and Inari Karsh, *Empires of the Sand: The Struggle for Mastery in the Middle East, 1789–1923* (Cambridge, MA: Harvard University Press, 1999), p.200.
4. Keith Jeffrey, *The British Army and the Crisis of Empire, 1918–1922* (Manchester: Manchester University Press, 1984), pp.111, 121.
5. *Census of Egypt, 1917*, Vol. II, Ministry of Finance, Statistical Department (Cairo: Government Press, 1921), Table VII, p.482.
6. In this study, 'Imperial' troops or forces refer to military personnel under the command of the British Empire (including Britons, Australians, New Zealanders, Canadians, and those from Malta and India, for example). 'Allied' forces refer to largely the same group defined by their military opposition against the Central Powers (Germany and the Austro-Hungarian and Ottoman empires) and would include French forces and later the Americans. 'British' troops refer mainly to Britons from the British Isles.
7. Jeffrey: *The British Army*, p.113.
8. W. G. MacPherson, *Medical Services General History*, Vol. III (London: His Majesty's Stationery Office, 1924), p.363; George MacMunn and Cyril Falls, *Military Operations: Egypt and Palestine* (London: His Majesty's Stationery Office, 1928), p.11, states the actual composition of the troops in the Army of Occupation just before World War I. It consisted of a regiment of cavalry (3rd Dragoon Guards), a battery of artillery ('T' Battery, Royal Horse Artillery), a mounted battery (7th Indian Mountain Battery, Royal Garrison Artillery), five battalions of infantry (1st and 2nd Battalion

Devonshire Regiment, 1st Worcestershire, 2nd Northamptonshire, 2nd Gordon Highlanders) and companies or detachments of Royal Engineers, Army Services Corp, Royal Army Medical Corps, and Army Veterinarian Corps.
9. Henry Keown-Boyd, *Soldiers of the Nile: A Biographical History of the British Officers of the Egyptian Army* (Hertsfordshire: Thornbury Publications, 1996), p.9.
10. Sergeant Harry Hopwood, Battalion orderly sergeant of the East Lancashire Brigade, also later of 2nd Volunteer Battalion of Manchester Regiment, in his private letters to his mother, 28 November 1914. National Army Museum.
11. John Keegan, 'Foreword', in Ian Beckett and Keith Simpson (eds), *A Nation in Arms: A Social History of the British Army in the First World War* (Manchester: Manchester University Press, 1985), pp.viii, ix.
12. 'Enemies in Egypt: British volunteers discouraged,' *Egyptian Gazette*, 28 September 1914, p.4.
13. Jay Winter, 'Army and society: the demographic context,' in Beckett and Simpson: *A Nation in Arms*, p.196.
14. *Ibid.*
15. 'Anglo-Egyptians and the War,' *Egyptian Gazette*, 1 June 1915, p.2.
16. 'Volunteers from Egypt: How to join Lord Kitchener's army,' *Egyptian Gazette*, 2 October 1914, p.3.
17. 'Anglo-Egyptian volunteers: the question of leaves of absence,' *Egyptian Gazette*, 3 October 1914, p.3.
18. 'Anglo-Egyptians and the War,' *Egyptian Gazette*, 1 June 1915, p.2.
19. *Ibid.*
20. 'Egypt and Conscription', *Egyptian Gazette*, 3 June 1915, p.2.
21. 'Egypt in wartime: Sir M. McIlwraith's views', *Egyptian Gazette*, 4 September 1917, p.5.
22. 'Egyptian Bank officials at the war,' *Egyptian Gazette*, 25 January 1916, p.5.
23. Arthur Blunt, interim manager in Alexandria of the Anglo-Egyptian Bank, to H. R. Coombs, Manager in London, 20 July 1915, Barclays Group Archives.
24. 'British rifle clubs and the war: members volunteer for service,' *Egyptian Gazette*, 6 August 1914, p.3.
25. Canon Temple Gairdner, Secretary of Egypt Mission, in *Church Missionary Review* (May 1919), p.70.
26. 'Anglo-Egypt's roll of honour,' *Egyptian Gazette*, 16 February 1916, p.7.
27. P. G. Elgood, *Egypt and the Army* (London: Oxford University Press, 1924), pp.147–8.
28. Ian Beckett, 'The nation in arms,' in Beckett and Simpson (eds): *A Nation in Arms*, p.14.
29. 'British subjects in Egypt: compulsory military service,' *Egyptian Gazette*,

3 May 1916, p.3 and 'British subjects in Egypt: opportunities for those over military age,' *Egyptian Gazette*, 19 August 1916, p.4.
30. FO141/664/2476. Parliamentary Debate, 11 June 1918.
31. *Ibid.* Letter from Judicial Adviser Amos to Residency, 22 July 1918.
32. *Ibid.* Letter from High Commissioner Sir Reginald Wingate to Amos, 22 June 1918.
33. *Ibid.* Report from General Headquarters of Egypt, 29 August 1916.
34. Letter from W. R. Carruthers, Anglo-Egyptian Bank manager in Alexandria, to Coombs, manager in London, 18 May 1916, Barclays Group Archives. (Emphasis mine.)
35. *Ibid.* Letter from Amos to Residency, 22 July 1918.
36. FO141/664/2476. Letter from B. B. Cubitt of the War Office to Lord Cecil, 6 July 1918.
37. 'Egypt in wartime: Sir M. McIlwraith's views', *Egyptian Gazette*, 4 September 1917, p.5.
38. Letter from Blunt to Coombs, 9 August 1915, Correspondences between Anglo-Egyptian staff and managers, Barclays Group Archives. (Emphasis mine.)
39. FO141/664/2476. Letter from Robert Cecil to His Majesty's Representative in Cairo, 18 May 1917.
40. FO141/503/1604. Letter from Egyptian Education Mission's Hebard to Lloyd Lord, 4 October 1926.
41. *Ibid.*
42. FO141/669/4394. Letter from Douglas Dunlop, Minister of Education to High Commissioner, 10 February 1917.
43. 'British subjects our of work: arrangements in Alexandria and Cairo,' *Egyptian Gazette*, 29 September 1914, p.4.
44. Temple Gairdner, 'The Nile valley in war-time: a word to the home base,' *Church Missionary Gleaner* XLVI 543 (May 1919), p.70.
45. FO141/621/321. Letter to Lord E. Cecil from Malcolm McIllwraith, 31 January 1916.
46. Roger Adelson, *London and the Invention of the Middle East: Money, Power, and War, 1902–1922*, (London: Yale University Press, 1995), p.118.
47. Karsh and Karsh: *Empires of the Sand*, pp.144–5.
48. *Ibid.*
49. Peter Liddle, 'The Dardanelles Gallipoli campaign: concept and execution,' in Peter Liddle (ed), *Home Fires and Foreign Fields: British Social and Military Experience in the First World War* (London: Brassey's Defence Publishers, 1985), p.110.
50. W. G. MacPherson, *Medical Services General History*, Vol. III (London: His Majesty's Stationery Office, 1924), p.382.
51. *Ibid.*
52. *Ibid.* In April, 1915, 235 beds were available for Indian officers and 5282

for lower ranks. By January 1916, 1131 beds were available for Indian officers while 34,874 was available for men of the lower ranks.
53. *Ibid.*, p.383.
54. *Ibid.*
55. *Ibid.*, p.362.
56. Lady Harkness, nurse sent to Egypt with the Queen Alexandra Imperial Military Nursing Service (QAIMNS), Dairies 1917, Imperial War Museum.
57. 'Egypt in wartime: Sir M. McIlwraith's views,' *Egyptian Gazette*, 4 September 1917, p.5.
58. MacPherson: *Medical Services*, p.377.
59. Lady Beatrice Rochdale, *Dairies*, entry 24 January 1915, Imperial War Museum.
60. MacPherson: *Medical Services*, p.377.
61. Henry Day, *A Cavalry Chaplain* (London: Heath Cranton, Ltd., 1922), p.72.
62. 'British Red Cross,' *Egyptian Gazette*, 16 August 1917, p.4.
63. MacPherson: *Medical Services*, p.377.
64. Elgood: *Egypt and the Army*, p.170.
65. *Ibid.*
66. *Ibid.*
67. *Ibid.*
68. Sharon Ouditt, *Fighting Forces, Writing Women* (London: Routledge, 1994), p.15.
69. *Ibid.*, p.13.
70. 'Egypt in Wartime: Sir M. McIlwraith's Views', *Egyptian Gazette*, 4 September 1917, p.5
71. Elgood: *Egypt and the Army*, p.144.
72. *Ibid.*, p.145.
73. Lady Rochdale: *Diaries*, 12 June 1915.
74. Archives of the Barker family, MS 238, Box 1, Section G, p.10.
75. Suzanne Brugger, *Australians in Egypt, 1914–1919* (Melbourne: Melbourne University Press, 1980), p.54.
76. Archives of the Barker family, MS 238, Box 1, Section G, p.10.
77. 'Women war workers in Egypt,' *Egyptian Gazette*, 13 July 1916, p.4.
78. 'British Red Cross,' *Egyptian Gazette*, 16 August 1917, p.4.
79. 'British Red Cross work in Egypt,' *Egyptian Gazette*, 22 January 1917, p.4.
80. 'Women war workers in Egypt,' *Egyptian Gazette*, 13 July 1916, p.4.
81. Brugger: *Australians in Egypt*, p.56.
82. *Ibid.*
83. Mrs. G. M. A. Horsford, memoirs, Imperial War Museum.
84. *Ibid.*
85. 'Women war workers in Egypt', *Egyptian Gazette*, 18 July 1916, p.5.
86. *Ibid.*

87. Brugger: *Australians in Egypt*, p.56.
88. 'The need of the moment,' *Egyptian Gazette*, 7 June 1915, p.2.
89. 'The social problem: Australian trooper's view,' *Egyptian Gazette*, 4 June 1915, p.5.
90. Peter Simkins, 'Soldiers and civilians: billeting in Britain and France,' in Beckett and Simpson (eds): *A Nation in Arms*, p.167.
91. *Ibid.* (Emphasis mine.)
92. 'Our khaki season: Cairo in war time,' *Egyptian Gazette*, 12 February 1915, p.5.
93. Brugger: *Australians in Egypt*, p.51.
94. *Ibid.*
95. Capt. R. B. Gillet, 2nd Battalion Hampshire Regiment, from transcript of BBC recording, from Imperial War Museum archives, date unclear.
96. Martin Briggs, *Through Egypt in War-Time* (London: Unwin, 1918), p.28.
97. W. R. Carruthers, Manager of Anglo-Egyptian Bank in Alexandria, letter to Secretary of Anglo-Egyptian Bank in London, 31 December 1915, Barclays Group Archives.
98. *Ibid.*
99. 'British Benevolent Fund', *Egyptian Gazette*, 2 March 1915, p.4.
100. 'British Refugees Fund', *Egyptian Gazette*, 22 February 1915, p.4.
101. 'Help for the Red Cross', *Egyptian Gazette*, 13 March 1915, p.3.
102. 'Indian Military Hospital San Stefano: A meeting of the British community', *Egyptian Gazette*, 6 January 1915, p.4.
103. 'Empire Day at Alexandria', *Egyptian Gazette*, 23 May 1916, p.4.
104. Brugger: *Australians in Egypt*, p.63.
105. 'Our khaki season: Cairo in war time', *Egyptian Gazette*, 12 February 1915, p.5.
106. Sgt. Harry Hopwood, 8 April 1915.
107. *Ibid.*
108. Second Lieutenant C. G. Meudell, of 1st Australian Artillery Unit and later, the Royal Flying Corps, *Diaries*, Imperial War Museum, 6 March 1916. (Emphasis mine.)
109. 'The Australians in Cairo: A Case of Love at First Sight', *Egyptian Gazette*, 7 January 1915, p.2.
110. *Ibid.*
111. 'The Egyptian Hotels, Ltd.: Shepheards Hotel', *Egyptian Gazette*, 12 January 1915, p.1.
112. 'St. Mark's Church, Alexandria: Organ and violin recital', *Egyptian Gazette*, 12 January 1917, p.6.
113. 'English plays in Cairo', *Egyptian Gazette*, 9 May 1916, p.5.
114. *Sphinx*, Newspaper, 13 January 1917.
115. 'Cairo's soldiers' entertainments', *Egyptian Gazette*, 24 November 1917, p.6.
116. 'Waxworks at Ghezireh Hospital: An enjoyable performance', *Egyptian*

NOTES 287

Gazette, 12 January 1916, p.6.
117. 'Miss Ada Reeve: First appearance in Cairo', *Egyptian Gazette*, 18 November 1916, p.6.
118. C. H. Rastell, 1st Worcestershire Yeomanry, letters, Imperial War Museum, 6 September 1915.
119. *Sphinx*, 11 March 1916.
120. 'British Soldiers' Café in Cairo', *Egyptian Gazette*, 1 April 1916, p.5.
121. 'Cairo Soldiers' Recreation Club', *Egyptian Gazette*, 20 March 1916, p.3.
122. 'Soldier entertainments at Cairo: Big night at the Ezbekieh Y.M.C.A.', *Egyptian Gazette*, 4 March 1916, p.4.
123. *Ibid.*
124. 'Y.M.C.A. in Egypt: A great years work', *Egyptian Gazette*, 25 January 1916, p.5.
125. *Ibid.*
126. 'Cairo Soldiers' Entertainments', *Egyptian Gazette*, 10 July 1917, p.5.
127. 'The Y.M.C.A. in France and Egypt', *Egyptian Gazette*, 26 April 1915, p.3.
128. 'The "Convalescent Outings" Society: Organised excursions for the wounded', *Egyptian Gazette*, 25 January 1916, p.5.
129. *Ibid.*
130. *Ibid.*
131. Winter: 'Army and society', p.196.
132. 'Football', *Egyptian Gazette*, 25 February 1915, p.5.
133. 'Soldiers' sports and entertainments at Cairo', *Egyptian Gazette*, 14 March 1916, p.6.
134. 'Football in Cairo: Cairo Military League', *Egyptian Gazette*, 6 November 1916, p.5.
135. 'Our troops in camp: Athletic sports at Zeitoun', *Egyptian Gazette*, 1 February 1915, p.3 and 'Boxing', p.6..
136. 'Our troops in camp: Lecture by Dr. Hargrave', *Egyptian Gazette*, 28 January 1915, p.4.
137. 'Our troops in camp: Lecture on the Nile', *Egyptian Gazette*, 1 February 1915, p.3.
138 'Egypt and the fair sex: Central Y.M.C.A. Alexandria', *Egyptian Gazette*, 8 April 1916, p.4.
139. 'Early Christianity in Egypt: Interesting lecture in Cairo', *Egyptian Gazette*, 12 May 1916, p.3
140. FO141/512/608. Letter from Mr. Lias to Sir Henry McMahon quoting letters from Lias to Maxwell on 10 December 1914 and 13 April 1915.
141. *Ibid.* Letter from Lias to McMahon, 13 April 1915.
142. *Ibid.* Memo from Lias to Council, 13 April 1915.
143. FO141/512/608. Letter from Maxwell to McMahon, 16 April 1915.
144. FO141/512/608. Letter from Arthur Preston, Chairman of Victoria College Committee, to General Wingate, High Commissioner, 12 June 1918.
145. FO141/512/608. Letter Lias to McMahon, 15 May 1916.

146. *Ibid.*
147. 'Our soldier guests: the example of the womenfolk,' *Egyptian Gazette*, 12 June 1915, p.5.
148. 'Exchequer bonds in Egypt: difficulties of small investors,' *Egyptian Gazette*, 9 May 1916, p.6.
149. *Ibid.*
150. 'Exchequer bonds in Egypt: a patriotic all worth some trouble,' *Egyptian Gazette*, 16 May 1916, p.4.
151. 'Exchequer bonds in Egypt: The difficulties of investors,' *Egyptian Gazette*, 10 May 1916, p.4.
152. 'Exchequer bonds in Egypt: Perpetual exile for British investors,' *Egyptian Gazette*, 23 May 1916, p.6.
153. *Ibid.*
154. *Ibid.*
155. 'Egypt in Wartime: Sir M. McIlwraith's Views', *Egyptian Gazette*, 4 September 1917, p.5.
156. *Ibid.*
157. Elgood: *Egypt and the Army*, p.115. The two Indian Infantry divisions were the 10th and 21st divisions of the Indian Expeditionary Force.
158. Marquess of Anglesey, *A History of the British Cavalry, 1816–1919: Vol. V: Egypt, Palestine and Syria, 1914 to 1919* (London: Leo Cooper, 1994), p.3.
159. Brian Porter, 'Britain and the Middle East in the Great War,' in Peter Liddle (ed), *Home Fires and Foreign Fields: British Social and Military Experience in the First World War* (London: Brassey's Defence Publishers, 1985), p.162.
160. MacMunn and Falls: *Military Operations*, p.13.
161. 'Our khaki season: Cairo in war time,' *Egyptian Gazette*, 12 February 1915, p.5; Porter: 'Britain and the Middle East', p.162. There were 70,000 Imperial soldiers in Egypt in 1915 (including Indians and other Westerners). By the end of the war, the figure approaches 300,000.
162. *Ibid.*
163. 'Egypt in Wartime: Sir M. McIlwraith's Views,' *Egyptian Gazette*, 4 September 1917, p.5.
164. Lady Rochdale: *Diaries*, 26 January 1915.
165. Anglesey: *History of the British Cavalry*, p.3.
166. *Ibid.*
167. Briggs: *Through Egypt in War-Time*, p.27.
168. 'Our khaki season: Cairo in war time,' *Egyptian Gazette*, 12 February 1915, p.5.
169. Briggs: *Through Egypt in War-Time*, p.27.
170. Nina Nelson, *Shepheard's Hotel* (London: Barrie and Rockcliff), p.76.
171. 'Our khaki season: Cairo in war time,' *Egyptian Gazette*, 12 February 1915, p.5.

172. 'Egypt and English books,' *Egyptian Gazette*, 10 November 1916, p.4.
173. Advertisement for 'English Garden Tea Room,' *Egyptian Gazette*, 22 April 1916, p.6.
174. 'Our Khaki Season: Cairo in War Time,' *Egyptian Gazette*, 12 February 1915, p.5.
175. Mabel Caillard, *A Lifetime in Egypt: 1876–1935* (London: Grant Richards, 1935), p.189.
176. J. C. B. Richmond, *Egypt, 1798–1952: Her Advance towards a Modern Identity* (London: Methuen and Co., Ltd., 1977), p.172.
177. 'Egypt in wartime: Sir M. McIlwraith's views,' *Egyptian Gazette*, 4 September 1917, p.5.
178. Samir Raafat, *Maadi:1904-1962: Society and History in a Cairo Suburb* (Cairo: Palm Press, 1994), p.47. For example, the German Luthy family and the Austro-Hungarian Lichtenstern and Scheynoha families had their assets sequestered and properties taken over by the British military.
179. Sir Alex William Keown-Boyd, memoirs 9 August 1914 records letter from R. H. Dunn, Legal Secretary in Khartoum to Private Sec of Governor-General in Khartoum (in St. Antony's College, Oxford University, Middle East Centre).
180. *Ibid.*
181. 'British trade in Egypt: the new order of things,' *Egyptian Gazette*, 11 January 1915, p.5.
182. 'The Chamber of Commerce: Annual Meeting of the Cairo members,' *Egyptian Gazette*, 27 February 1915, p.4.
183. *Ibid.*,
184. *Ibid.*,.
185. 'British Chamber of Commerce: dinner in Cairo' (speech by President H. K. Baynes of the British Chamber of Commerce in Egypt), *Egyptian Gazette*, 26 April 1915, p.3.
186. *Ibid.*
187. 'British Chamber of Commerce: dinner in Cairo' (speech by Sir Henry MacMahon, High Commissioner), *Egyptian Gazette*, 26 April 1915, p.3.
188. *Ibid.*
189. 'British trade in Egypt,' *Egyptian Gazette*, 25 January 1916, p.5. (Emphasis mine.)
190. *Ibid.*
191. 'Enemy firms in Egypt,' *Egyptian Gazette*, 22 February 1916, p.5.
192. Hoyle: *The Mixed Courts*, p.100.
193. 'Enemy firms in Egypt,' *Egyptian Gazette*, 14 January 1916, p.5.
194. *Ibid.*
195. *Ibid.*
196. Mrs. G. M. A. Horsford, memoirs, Imperial War Museum.
197. 'Food prices in Cairo,' *Egyptian Gazette*, 15 March 1916, p.5.
198. Temple Gairdner, *Church Missionary Review* LXIII (1916), writing from

Cairo, 26 August 1916.
199. *National Bank of Egypt, 1898–1948, 50th Anniversary Report* (Cairo: N.B.E. Printing Press, 1948), p.51.
200. 'The Turf Club: Annual meeting,' *Egyptian Gazette*, 3 May 1918, p.6.
201. 'House rent in Egypt: Continued protest against increases,' *Egyptian Gazette*, 1 June 1918, p.6.
202. 'Government officials' salaries: Increasing difficulties in meeting expenses', *Egyptian Gazette*, 26 July 1918, p.4.
203. *Ibid.*
204. 'House rent in Egypt: continued protest against increases,' *Egyptian Gazette*, 1 June 1918, p.6.
205. Letter from Arthur Blunt to Coombs, 7 June 1917, Barclays Group Archives.
206. Letter from Carruthers to H. A. Richardson, chairman of AEB (1907–18) 27 January 1916, Barclays Group Archives.
207. J. de Vere Loder, letter to his father, 27 February 1916, St. Antony's College, Oxford, as quoted in F. Lissauer, *British Policy Towards Egypt* (PhD Thesis, University of London: London School of Economics, 1975), p.90.
208. Ellis Goldberg, 'Peasants in revolt – Egypt 1919,' *International Journal of Middle East Studies* 24 (1992), pp. 261–80 (see p.264).
209. Lissauer: *British Policy*, p.80.
210. Goldberg: 'Peasants in revolt', p.271.
211. P. J. Vatikiotis, *The Modern History of Egypt* (London: Weidenfield and Nicolson, 1969), p.245.
212. Al-Rafa'ī, ʿAbd al-Rahmān, *Al-tarāja ʿ wa-l-intakās min al-iḥtilāl ila thawra 1919* (Cairo: Dar al-Ḥalāl, 1990), first published 1958, pp.113, 125.

7: The Revolutionary Period, 1919–22

1. Joel Benin and Zachary Lockman, *Workers on the Nile: Nationalism, Communism, Islam and the Egyptian Working Class, 1882–1954* (London: I.B.Tauris, 1988), p.84.
2. Sir Bertram Hornsby, of the National Bank of Egypt in Alexandria, private papers, Middle East Centre, St. Antony's College, University of Oxford, p.5.
3. John D. McIntyre, Jr., *The Boycott of the Milner Mission: A Study in Egyptian Nationalism*, (New York: Peter Lang, 1985), p.9.
4. 'The Egyptian peril: the nationalist case,' *Egyptian Gazette*, 16 December 1919, p.7.
5. 'The native press: the English in Egypt,' quoting from article in the Egyptian newspaper *Al-Ahram,,Egyptian Gazette*, 23 September 1919, p.4.
6. 'Anglo-Egyptian officials,' *Egyptian Gazette*, 17 December 1919, p.2.
7. John Darwin, *Britain, Egypt and the Middle East: Imperial Policy in the*

NOTES

     Aftermath of War, 1918–1922 (London: Macmillan, 1981), p.72.
8. CMS papers, letter from J. L. MacIntyre, Assistant General Secretary of CMS Egypt, to Rev. G. T. Manley, CMS leader in London, 26 April 1919.
9. Ellis Goldberg, 'Peasants in Revolt – Egypt 1919', *International Journal of Middle East Studies*, 24, (1992), p.262.
10. Darwin: *Britain, Egypt*, p.74.
11. Goldberg: 'Peasants in Revolt', p.276.
12. P. J. Vatikiotis, *The Modern History of Egypt* (London: Weidenfield and Nicolson, 1969), p.248.
13. McIntyre: *Boycott*, p.18.
14. *Ibid.*, p.20.
15. CMS papers, J. L. Macintyre to Rev. G. T. Manley, CMS leader in London, 26 March 1919.
16. McIntyre: *Boycott*, p.27.
17. Goldberg: *'Peasants in Revolt'*, p.262.
18. CMS papers: McIntyre to Manley, 26 March 1919.
19. Arthur Blunt, Manager of Anglo-Egyptian Bank in Alexandria, to W. R. Carruthers, Manager in London, 19 March 1919. Letters from Anglo-Egyptian Bank staff, Barclays Group Archives, Wythenshawe, Manchester.
20. McIntyre: *Boycott*, p.31..
21. Blunt to Carruthers: letter 26 March 1919.
22. Selma Botman, *Engendering Citizenship in Egypt* (New York: Columbia University Press, 1999), p.36.
23. McIntyre: *Boycott*, p.30.
24. *Ibid.*, p.32.
25. Elizabeth Monroe, *Britain's Moment in the Middle East, 1914–1971* (London: Chatto & Windus, 1981), p.68.
26. Keith Jeffrey, *The British Army and the Crisis of Empire, 1918–1922* (Manchester: Manchester University Press, 1984), p.113.
27. *Ibid.*
28. FO141/825/1132. From quarterly report on morale of troops, 31 March 1919, p.2.
29. *Ibid.*
30. *Ibid.*, p.3.
31. *Ibid.*, p.4.
32. *Ibid.*, p.2.
33. *Ibid.*
34. *Ibid.*
35. 'Alexandria British Benevolent Fund,' *Egyptian Gazette*, 12 April 1919, p.4.
36. 'The troops in Alexandria: British community's souvenir, *Egyptian Gazette*, 8 January 1919, p.6.
37. Jeffrey: *The British Army*, p.113.
38. 'British rights in Egypt,' *Egyptian Gazette*, 12 June 1920, p.2.
39. *Ibid.*

40. John Marlowe, *Anglo-Egyptian Relations, 1800–1956*, 2nd ed. (London: Frank Cass & Co, Ltd., 1965), p.303.
41. Richard Vaux, unpublished memoirs, Middle East Centre Archives, St. Antony's College, University of Oxford, pp.68, 70.
42. FO141/747/8972. Memo dated 30 March 1919, recording the events of 15 March 1919.
43. FO141/753/8940. Telegram from High Commissioner to Foreign Officer, 19 April 1919, recalling events of 17 March 1919.
44. *Ibid.* Telegram from High Commissioner to Foreign Office, 4 April 1919.
45. *Ibid.* High Commissioner to Foreign Office, 19 April 1919.
46. *Ibid.* Ministry of Interior Report, 22 June 1919.
47. *Ibid.* High Commissioner Allenby to Foreign Secretary Lord Curzon, 14 July 1919.
48. FO141/582/9116. High Commissioner to Foreign Office, 18 April 1919.
49. Reuters Telegram, 10 April 1919, in Anglo-Egyptian Bank staff letters collection, Barclays Archive.
50. Darwin: *Britain, Egypt*, p.79.
51. Marlowe: *Anglo-Egyptian Relations*, p.240.
52. 'The state of Cairo: outrages on British soldiers,' *Egyptian Gazette*, 17 May 1920, p.6.
53. FO141/494/14268. Minutes from Residency, 16 July 1922, General Manager's Office of Cairo Station to Ministry of Communication, Cairo.
54. *Ibid.*
55. *Ibid.* Parliamentary Questions, 29 May 1922, Mr. Cecil Harmsworth, Under-Secretary of Foreign Affairs responding to question from Lieutenant-Colonel James.
56. *Ibid.*
57. Marlowe: *Anglo-Egyptian Relations*, p.240.
58. Letter from Townsend, senior staff at Anglo-Egyptian Bank in Cairo, to Mr. Raoul Hector Foa, chairman of Anglo-Egyptian Bank, London, 21 May 1920.
59. FO141/494/14268. General Manager's Office, Cairo Station, to the Adviser, Ministry of Communications, 20 February 1922.
60. *Ibid.* From Under Secretary of State, Ministry of Communication, to General Manager of Egyptian State Railways, Cairo, 28 January 1922.
61. *Ibid.* General Manager's Office, Cairo Station to Ministry of Communications, recording the number of Egyptian and English personnel in the company, 15 September 1922.
62. *Ibid.* General Manager's Office, Cairo Station to the Adviser, Ministry of Communications, 20 February 1922.
63. *Ibid.* Financial Adviser's letter, 4 May 1922.
64. *Ibid.* Minutes of residency, 16 July 1922.
65. *Ibid.* Letter from Abdel Khalik Pasha Sarwat, President of Council of

Ministers (Prime Minister) to High Commissioner, 13 November 1922.
66. *Ibid.* Letter from Lord Allenby to Mrs. Brown, 4 June 1922, and also in letter from Lieutenant-Colonel Cuthbert James (MP) to Cecil Harmsworth, Under-Secretary of Foreign Office.
67. *Ibid.* Minutes in Residency, 13 March 1922.
68. *Ibid.* High Commissioner to Foreign Secretary, Marquess Curzon of Kedleston, 14 August 1922.
69. *Ibid.* Minutes of Residency, 13 March 1922.
70. *Ibid.* High Commissioner to Curzon, 14 August 1922.
71. *Ibid.* Foreign Office to High Commissioner Allenby, 25 November 1922.
72. *Ibid.* High Commissioner to Sarwat Pasha, 24 October 1922.
73. FO141/748/8882. George Swan, Secretary of Egypt General Mission to British Consul in Cairo, 17 March 1919.
74. Telegram, 17 October 1919, in archives of letters from Anglo-Egyptian Bank staff, Barclays Archives. (Emphasis mine.)
75. Letter from the Alexandria branch of the Anglo-Egyptian Bank to W. R. Carruthers, Manager in London, 26 May 1921, Barclays Archives.
76. FO141/434/10684. Letter from Buchanan in Foreign Office to High Commissioner, 25 November 1919.
77. FO141/748/8882. Top Secret Foreign Office telegram to High Commissioner, 16 December 1919.
78. FO141/494/14268. Foreign Office to High Commissioner, 16 August 1922.
79. FO141/748/8882. Letter from probably Residency to Mr. Alban, Consul-General, Alexandria, 12 December 1919.
80. *Ibid.* Letter from James Morgan, Acting Consul, British Consulate, Cairo to Residency, 1919.
81. *Ibid.* Letter from British Consul General in Alexandria to High Commissioner, 25 November 1919.
82. *Ibid.* Memo from Captain Heard, Acting Consul-General in Cairo to Mr. Furness, 28 May 1921.
83. *Ibid.* Memo from Office of Acting Adviser of Interior, 19 February 1922.
84. *Ibid.* Memo from Captain Heard to Furness, 28 May 1921.
85. *Ibid.* Memo from Residency, 23 June 1921.
86. FO141/664/2476. Congreve to Residency, 3 August 1921.
87. FO141/749/8882. First Secretary of Residency in Alexandria to Adviser, Ministry of Interior, recalling a conversation with Congreve, 23 June 1921.
88. *Ibid.* Letter from General Clayton, Adviser to Ministry of Interior, to Residency, 20 August 1921.
89. FO141/664/2479. Captain Huggett to High Commissioner Allenby, 18 September 1922.
90. *Ibid.* High Commissioner to Huggett, 24 September 1922.
91. 'Business in Egypt: after war trade prices,' *Egyptian Gazette*, 18 January 1919, p.4.

92. *Ibid.*
93. *National Bank of Egypt, 1898–1948* (Cairo: National Bank of Egypt Printing Press, 1948), p.51.
94. *Ibid.*, p.49.
95. FO141/503/16984. Restriction on English teachers, 1919.
96. *Ibid.* In 1913 a P&O ticket, Egypt to England, first-class, £14, and second class, £9; In 1922, first-class ticket, £46, and second class, £32.
97. *Ibid.* After six years, only 25 piastres per month increase, and after eight years, and increase of E£3.25 per month on a salary of just E£36 per month.
98. Letter from Anglo-Egyptian Bank staff to Mr. Raoul Hector Foa, Chairman of AEB in London, 4 February 1920, Barclays Archives.
99. *Ibid.* Towsend to Carruthers, Manager in London, 29 July 1920.
100. *Ibid.* Letter from C. W. Green, Manager of Anglo-Egyptian Bank, Alexandria, to Foa, Chairman of AEB in London, 7 October 1919.
101. FO141/581/9132. J. W. Eady in report, 19 April 1919.
102. *Ibid.*
103. Advertisement for 'Gabardine and Khaki for officers and Palm Beach suitings made by John Collacott and Son,' *Egyptian Gazette*, 30 August 1919, p.8.
104. *Ibid.*, 'The British boycott: slight effect in Cairo,' 9 January 1922, p.4.
105. FO141/581/9132. Mr. C. R. Beasley, agricultural expert, at Advisory Board of Non-Official British Community, 19 April 1919.
106. *Ibid.*
107. FO141/494/14268. General Manager's Office at Cairo Station to Ministry of Communications, Cairo, 15 September 1922.
108. *Ibid.*
109. 'Egyptian Delta Light Railways,' *Egyptian Gazette*, 17 September 1919, p.5.
110. *Ibid.*
111. *Ibid.*
112. *Ibid.*
113. Blunt to Carruthers, Bank Manager of Alexandria branch to Manager in London, 19 March 1919, letters from Anglo-Egyptian Bank staff, Barclays Archives, Manchester.
114. *Ibid.*, Blunt to H. A. Richardson, Chairman of Anglo-Egyptian Bank in London, 11 April 1919.
115. *Ibid.*, C. W. Green, new manager in Alexandria to Mr. Foa, chairman of Anglo-Egyptian Bank, 20 September 1919.
116. *Ibid.*, Green to Foa, 23 September 1919.
117. *Ibid.*
118. *Ibid.*, Green to Foa, 1 October 1919.
119. *Ibid.*
120. *Ibid.*, Telegram 17 October 1919.

121. *Ibid.*, Green to Directors, 21 November 1919.
122. FO141/581/9132. Minutes of meeting between Allenby and some members of the Non-Official British Community, 19 April 1919.
123. *Ibid.* Letter from High Commissioner Allenby to Lord Curzon, Foreign Secretary, 15 December 1921.
124. *Ibid.* Dr. Beddoe's report, 20 June 1919, pp.12–13.
125. *Ibid.* Kingsford, report of Non-Official British Community, 20 June 1919.
126. *Ibid.* Kingsford, report of the Council of Cairo Non-Official British Community, 22 November 1919.
127. *Ibid.*
128. FO141/799/14023. Letter from Kingsford to Allenby, 8 December 1921.
129. Letters from Anglo-Egyptian Staff, Walton to Carruthers, 25 May 1921.
130. *Ibid.* Walton to Foa, 28 April 1922.
131. Robert L. Tignor, *Modernisation and the British Colonial Rule in Egypt, 1882–1914* (Princeton: Princeton University Press, 1966), p.276.
132. Suzanne Brugger, *Australians in Egypt, 1914–1919* (Melbourne: Melbourne University Press, 1980), p.111.

Conclusion

1. J. W. A. Young, unpublished papers, ch. 16, p.15 (Middle East Centre Archives, St. Antony's College, University of Oxford).
2. Mabel Caillard, *A Lifetime in Egypt: 1876–1935* (London: Grant Richards, 1935), p.247.
3. *Ibid.*
4. FO141/451/4612. 1922 Church Annual Report, All Saint's Church, 31 December 1922. (Emphasis mine.)

BIBLIOGRAPHY

Unpublished Sources

1. Archives

All Saints' Church archives, Cairo.

St. Andrew's Church archives, Cairo.

Barclays Group archives, Wythenshawe, Manchester: Correspondence between staff in Egypt with managers in London of the Anglo-Egyptian Bank.

Church Missionary Society archives, University of Birmingham Special Collections: Incoming letters from missionaries in Egypt to mission leaders in London.

Church College archives, Cambridge University: Private papers and correspondence of Sir Cecil Spring Rice.

King's College archives, Cambridge University: Private papers and correspondence of Charles Robert Ashbee.

Special Collections, University of Exeter: Archives of the Barker family, 1850–1956, MS 238, Boxes 1 and 3.

Imperial War Museum, London: Diaries, letters or memoirs of:
Capt. R. B. Gillet, 2nd Battalion Hampshire Regiment (from transcript of BBC recording).
Lady Harkness.
Mrs. G. M. A. Horsford.
Second Lieutenant C. G. Meudell.
C. H. Rastell.
Lady Beatrice Rochdale.

BIBLIOGRAPHY 297

Manchester Central Library, Archives Department: Manchester Chamber of Commerce, minutes, Middle East and North Africa section (1916–1926), report after J. P. Foster's address, 12 November 1917.

National Army Museum, London: Private letters of Sergeant Harry Hopwood.

Public Record Office, The National Archives, London:
F0141: Foreign Office correspondences regarding Egypt.
F0633/87: Cromer's papers.
F0841: Cairo Consular Courts.
F0847: Alexandria Consular Courts.

St. Antony's College, Middle East Centre Archive, University of Oxford: Archives of the Barker family, 1856–1958, GB165–0493, Box 14.

Private papers of:
Harry Boyle.
Sir Milne Cheetham.
Sir Bertram Hornsby.
Sir Alex William Keown-Boyd.
Sir F. T. Rowlatt.
Sir Richard Vaux.
J. W. A. Young.

2. Theses

Al-Roumi, Mohammad, *Kuwait and Malta: British Imperial Policy, 1899–1939* (MA dissertation, University of Malta: 1980).
Bailey, John Paul, *The British Community in Argentina* (PhD thesis, University of Surrey, 1976).
Datta, Damayanti, *The Europeans of Caluctta, 1858–1883* (PhD thesis, Churchill College, University of Cambridge, 1995).
Glavanis, P. M., *Aspects of the Economic and Social History of the Greek Community in Alexandria during the 19th Century* (PhD thesis, Hull University, 1989).
Hanley, Will, *Foreignness and Localness in Alexandria, 1880–1914* (PhD dissertation, Princeton University, 2007).
Johnson, Valerie, *British Multinationals, Culture and Empire in the Early Twentieth Century* (PhD thesis, King's College, University of London, 2007).
Lissauer, F., *British Policy Towards Egypt, 1914–1922* (PhD thesis, London School of Economics, University of London, 1975)
Mak, Lanver, *The British Community in Occupied Egypt, 1882–1922* (PhD thesis, School of Oriental and African Studies, University of London, 2002).
Minkin, Shane, *In Life as in Death: The Port, Foreign Charities, Hospitals and*

Cemeteries in Alexandria, Egypt, 1865–1914 (PhD dissertation, New York University, 2009).

Roussos, Sotirios, *Greece and the Arab Middle East: The Greek Orthodox Communities in Egypt, Palestine and Syria, 1919–1940* (PhD thesis, School of Oriental and African Studies, University of London, 1995).

Sedra, Paul, *Textbook Maneuvers: Evangelicals and Educational Reform in Nineteenth-Century Egypt* (PhD Dissertation, New York University, 2006).

Published Sources

1. Government Publications

BRITISH GOVERNMENT
Command Papers relating to assault on British officers near Cairo, 23 July 1901.
Command Papers, 706, *Accounts and Papers, State Papers*, no. 76. Vol. CXXX, 1902 (Egypt, No. 3, 1902).

EGYPTIAN GOVERNMENT
Recensement Général de l'Egypte, 1882, Tome II, Ministry of Finance, Census Department (Le Caire: Boulaq, 1884), Arabic version.
Recensement Général de l'Egypte, 1882, Tome Deuxième, (Le Caire: Impremiere Nationale de Boulaq, 1884).
Recensement Général de l'Egypte, 1897, Tome Premier, (Le Caire: Imprimerie Nationale, 1898).
Census of Egypt, 1907 (Cairo: National Printing Department, 1909).
Census of Egypt, 1917, Vol. II, from Ministry of Finance, Statistical Department, (Cairo: Government Press, 1921).

2. Business Publications

Egyptian State Railways and Port of Alexandria, Report of the Board of Administration, 1900 (Cairo: Egyptian Railways Printing Office, 1901).
Egyptian State Railways and Telegraphs and Light Railways of Egypt, 1913 Report (Cairo: Printing Office of the Administration, 1914).
National Bank of Egypt, 1898–194, 50th Anniversary Report (Cairo: National Bank of Egypt Printing Press, 1948).

3. Maps

Residential Map of Gezira, the Survey of Egypt, 1907, in F. T. Rowlatt's Hanging File, Middle East Centre, St. Antony's College, University of Oxford.
Residential Map of Zamalek and 'Liste des abonnes de Zamalek, 1920,' Ministry of Finance, Survey of Egypt, Cairo in Serge Weber, 'Zamalek depuis la période anglaise, caractéristique socio-économique, fonctions d'un quartier du Caire', Format 4, 1618 (Cairo: CEDEJ, 1994).

Map of Cairo, no. 64480 (4): Edward Stanford, 12, 13, 14, Long Acre W.C., London: 16 June 1906.

General Map of Cairo, no. 64480(6), Survey of Egypt, 1920.

4. Newspapers and Periodicals

Egyptian Gazette, 2 January 1893–31 December 1938, Cairo.

Sphinx, 12 February 1916–31 March 1917, Cairo.

Church Missionary Society Intelligencer, London.

5. Books and Articles

Abdel Kader, Soha, *Egyptian Women in a Changing Society, 1899–1987* (Boulder, CO: Lynne Reinner Publishers, 1987).

Abu-Fadil, Magda, 'Gezira Club—still the 'in' place to be,' *The Middle East* (September 1990), p.43.

Abu-Lughod, Janet, *Cairo: 1001 Years of the City Victorious* (Princeton: Princeton University Press, 1971).

Adelson, Roger, *London and the Invention of the Middle East: Money, Power, and War, 1902–1922* (London: Yale University Press, 1995).

Aldcroft, Derek H. and Peter Fearon (eds), *British Economic Fluctuations* (London: St. Martin's Press, 1972).

Aldridge, James, *Cairo* (London: MacMillan, 1969).

Allen, Roger, *A Period of Time: A Study and Translation of Ḥadīth 'Īsā ibn Hishām by Muḥammad al-Muwayliḥī* (Reading: Ithaca, 1992).

'Al-Rafa'ī, Abd al-Rahman, *Al-tarāja'wa-1 -intakas min al-iḥtilāl ila thawra 1919* (Cairo: Dar al-Ḥalāl, 1990).

Anderson, Benedict, *Imagined Communities: Reflections on the Origin and Spread of Nationalism*, revised and extended ed. (London: Verso, 1991).

Anglesey, Marquess of, *A History of the British Cavalry, 1816–1919: Vol. V: Egypt, Palestine and Syria, 1914 to 1919* (London: Leo Cooper, 1994).

Arkell, V. T. J., *Britain Transformed: The Development of British Society since the Mid-Eighteenth Century* (London: Penguin Education, 1973).

Auchterlonie, Paul, 'A Turk of the West: Sir Edgar Vincent's career in Egypt and the Ottoman Empire', *British Journal of Middle Eastern Studies* 27/1 (2000), pp.49–67.

Bacharach, Jere L., *The Middle East Studies Handbook* (London, Cambridge University Press, 1984).

Baraka, Magda, *The Egyptian Upper Class between Revolutions: 1919–1952* (Reading: Ithaca, 1998).

Barth, Fredrik, 'Enduring and emerging issues in the analysis of ethnicity,' in Cora Govers and Hans Vermeulen (eds), *The Anthropology of Ethnicity Beyond 'Ethnic Groups and Boundaries'* (Amsterdam: Het Spinhuis, 1994), pp.11–32.

Barthes, Roland, *Mythologies*, trans. by Annette Lavers (London: Granada, 1973).

Bartlett, C. J., *The Global Conflict: The International Rivalry of the Great Powers, 1890–1990*, 2nd ed., (London: Longman, 1994).

Bashford, Alison, *Imperial Hygiene: A Critical History of Colonialism, Nationalism and Public Health* (New York: Palgrave MacMillan, 2004).

Beckett, Ian, 'The Nation in Arms,' in Ian Beckett and Keith Simpson (eds), *A Nation in Arms: A Social History of the British Army in the First World War* (Manchester: Manchester University Press, 1985), pp.1–35.

Benin, Joel, *The Dispersion of Egyptian Jewry: Culture, Politics, and the Formation of a Modern Diaspora* (Berkeley: University of California Press, 1998).

Benin, Joel and Zachary Lockman, *Workers on the Nile: Nationalism, Communism, Islam and the Egyptian Working Class, 1882–1954* (London: I.B.Tauris, 1988).

Berdine, Michael D. *The Accidental Tourist, Wilfrid Scawen Blunt and the British Invasion of Egypt in 1882* (Oxford: Routledge, 2005).

Bickers, Robert, *Britain in China: Community, Culture and Colonialism* (Manchester: Manchester University Press, 1999).

Blake, Matilda M., 'Are women protected?' *The Westminster Review*, CXXXVII (1892), pp.43–8.

Blunt, Wilfrid Scawen, *My Diaries: Being a Personal Narrative of Events, 1888–1914* (London: Martin Secker, 1932).

Botman, Selma, *Engendering Citizenship in Egypt* (New York: Columbia University Press, 1999).

Bowman, Humphrey, *Middle East Window* (London: Longmans Green, 1942).

Boyle, Clara, *A Servant of the Empire: A Memoir of Harry Boyle* (London: Methuen & Co., 1938).

Brendan, Piers, *Thomas Cook: 150 Years of Popular Tourism* (London: Serber & Warburg, 1992).

Briggs, Martin, *Through Egypt in Wartime* (London: Unwin, 1918).

Brookes, Barbara, *Abortion in England, 1900–1967* (London: Croom Helm, 1988).

Brooks, Chris, *Signs for the Times: Symbolic Realism in the Mid-Victorian World* (London: George Allen & Unwin, 1984).

Brown, Aldred, 'All Saints' Church,' in Arnold Wright (ed), *20th Century Impressions of Egypt: Its History, People, Commerce, Industries and Resources* (London: Lloyd's Greater Britain Publishing Co., Ltd., 1909), p.202.

Brubaker, Rogers and Frederick Cooper, 'Beyond Identity,' *Theory and Society* 29 (2000), 1–47.

Brugger, Suzanne, *Australians and Egypt, 1914–1919* (Melbourne: Melbourne University Press, 1980).

Budge, E. A. Wallis, *Cook's Handbook for Egypt and the Sudan* (London: Thomas Cook and Son, 1906).

Buettner, Elizabeth, *Empire Families: Britons and Late Imperial India* (Oxford: Oxford University Press, 2004).
Burrell, Arthur, *Cathedral on the Nile: A History of the All Saints Cathedral, Cairo* (Oxford: Amate Press, 1984).
Butcher, Edith Louisa, *Egypt As We Knew It* (London: Mills & Boon, Ltd., 1911).
——, *Things Seen in Egypt* (London: Seeley and Co, Ltd, 1910).
Butcher, John G., *The British in Malaya, 1880–1941* (Oxford: Oxford University Press, 1979).
Caillard, Mabel, *A Lifetime in Egypt: 1876–1935* (London: Grant Richards, 1935).
Cain, P. J. 'Character and imperialism: the British financial administration of Egypt, 1878–1914' *Journal of Imperial and Commonwealth History* 34/2 (June 2006), pp.177–200.
Cain, P. J., and A. G. Hopkins, 'Gentlemanly capitalism and British expansion overseas II: new imperialism, 1850–1945,' *Economic History Review*, 2nd series, XL/I (1987), pp.1–26.
Cannadine, David, *Ornamentalism: How the British Saw their Empire* (Oxford: Oxford University Press, 2001).
Cecil, Lord Edward, *The Leisure of an Egyptian Official* (London: Hodder & Stoughton, 1921).
Clark, Anna, 'Domesticity and the problem of wifebeating in nineteenth-century Britain: working-class culture, law and politics,' in Shani D'Cruze (ed), *Everyday Violence in Britain, 1850–1950: Gender and Class* (London: Pearson, 2000), pp.27–40.
Clark, Peter, *Sociability and Urbanity: Clubs and Societies in the Eighteenth Century City* (Leicester: Victorian Studies Centre, University of Leicester, 1986).
Cohen, Anthony, 'Boundaries of consciousness, consciousness of boundaries: critical questions for Anthropology,' in Cora Govers and Hans Vermeulen (eds), *The Anthropology of Ethnicity Beyond 'Ethnic Groups and Boundaries'* (Amsterdam: Het Spinhuis, 1994), pp.59–79.
——, *The Symbolic Construction of Community* (London: Routledge, 1993).
Cole, Juan Ricardo, 'Feminism, class, and Islam in turn-of-the-century Egypt,' *International Journal of Middle East Studies*, 13 (1981), pp.387–407.
Coles, Pasha, *Recollections and Reflections* (London: The Saint Catherine Press, 1918).
Colley, Linda, 'Does Britishness still matter in the twenty-first century and how much and how well do the politicians care?' in Tony Wright and Andrew Gamble (eds), *Britishness: Perspectives on the British Question* (Chichester: Wiley-Blackwell, 2009), pp.21–31.
Collins, Jeffrey G., *The Egyptian Elite under Cromer, 1882–1907* (Berlin: Klaus Schwarz Verlag, 1984).
D. J. Coppock, 'The causes of business fluctuations,' in Derek H. Aldcroft and

Peter Fearon (eds), *British Economic Fluctuations* (London: St. Martin's Press, 1972), pp. 188–219.
Cornell, Stephen and Douglas Hartmann, *Ethnicity and Race: Making Identities in a Changing World* (London: Pine Forge Press, 1998).
Crabb, Jack A., Jr., *The Writing of History in Nineteenth-Century Egypt: A Study of National Transformation* (Cairo: AUC Press, 1984).
Cromer, Lord, *Modern Egypt*, Vol. II (London: Macmillan, 1908).
Crinson, Mark, *Empire Building: Orientalism and Victorian Architecture* (London: Routledge, 1996).
Cronin, Stephanie, 'Introduction' in Stephanie Cronin (ed), *Subalterns and Social Protest: History from Below in the Middle East and North Africa* (London and New York: Routledge), pp.1–22.
Cuno, Kenneth M. and Michael J. Reimer, 'The census registers of the nineteenth-century Egypt: a new source for social sistorians,' *British Journal of Middle Eastern Studies*, 24/2 (1997), pp.193–216.
Darwin, John, *Britain, Egypt and the Middle East: Imperial Policy in the Aftermath of War, 1918–1922* (London: MacMillan, 1981).
Day, Henry, *A Cavalry Chaplain* (London: Heath Cranton Ltd., 1922).
D'Cruze, Shani, *Crimes of Outrage: Sex, Violence and Victorian Working Women* (London: UCL Press, 1998).
——, *Everyday Violence in Britain, 1850–1950: Gender and Class* (London: Pearson, 2000).
De Saram, Brian, *Nile Harvest: The Anglican Church in Egypt and Sudan* (Bournemouth: Bourne Press, 1992).
Deeb, Marius, 'The socioeconomic role of the local foreign minorities in modern Egypt, 1805–1961,' *International Journal of Middle East Studies* 9 (1978), pp.11–22.
Dirks, Nicholas B., 'Introduction: colonialism and culture,' in Nicholas B. Dirks (ed), *Colonialism and Culture* (Ann Arbor: University of Michigan Press, 1992), pp.1–25.
Douglas, William A., *Letters and Memorials* (Edinburgh: Andrew Brown, 1920).
Dubow, Saul, 'Race, civilisation and culture: the elaboration of segregationist discourse in the inter-war years,' in Shula Marks and Stanley Trapido (eds), *The Politics of Race, Class and Nationalism in Twentieth Century South Africa* (London: Longman, 1987), pp.71–94.
Dumett, Raymond E., 'Exploring Cain/Hopkins paradigm: issues for debate; critique and topics of new research,' in Raymond E. Dumett (ed), *Gentlemanly Capitalism and British Imperialism: The New Debate on Empire* (London: Longman, 1999), pp.1–42.
Eickelman, Dale, *The Middle East: An Anthropological Approach*, 2nd ed. (Englewood Cliffs, New Jersey, Prentice-Hall, 1989).
Elgood, P. G., *Egypt and the Army* (London, Oxford University Press, 1924).
Emsley, Clive, *Crime and Society in England, 1750–1900*, 3rd ed. (London: Pearson Longman, 2005).

Ernst, Waltraud, 'Idioms of madness and colonial boundaries: the case of the European and 'native' mentally ill in early nineteenth-century British India,' *Comparative Study of Society and History* 39/1 (1997), pp.153–81.

Fahmy, Khaled, 'For Cavafy, with love and squalor: some critical notes on the history and historiography of modern Alexandria,' in Anthony Hirst and Michael Silk (eds), *Alexandria, Real and Imagined* (Aldershot: Ashgate Publishing, 2004), p.272.

Frietag, Ulrike and Nora Lati, 'Cities compared: cosmopolitanism in the Mediterranean and adjacent regions,' project description, (version 2, 2007), http://halshs.archives-ouvertes.fr/docs/00/14/93/27/PDF/Freitag-Lafi-Cosmopolitanism.pdf

Gairdner, Canon Temple, 'The Nile valley in war-time: a word to the homebase,' *Church Missionary Society Gleaner*, XLVI/543 (May 1919), pp.70–2.

Ghosh, S. C., *The Social Condition of the British Community in Bengal, 1757–1800*, (Leiden: E. J. Brill, 1970).

Glazer, Nathan, and Daniel Patrick Moynihan, 'Introduction', in Nathan Glazer and Daniel Patrick Moynihan (eds), *Ethnicity: Theory and Experience* (Cambridge, MA: Harvard University Press, 1975), pp.1–26.

Goldberg, Ellis, 'Peasants in revolt—Egypt 1919,' *International Journal of Middle East Studies* 24 (1992), pp.261–80.

Gorman, Anthony, 'Foreign workers in Egypt 1882–1914: subaltern or labour elite?' in Stephanie Cronin (ed), *Subalterns and Social Protest: History from Below in the Middle East and North Africa* (London: Routledge, 2007), pp.237–59.

Govers, Cora and Hans Vermeulen, 'From political mobilisation to the politics of consciousness,' in Cora Govers and Hans Vermeulen (eds), *The Politics of Ethnic Consciousness* (London: MacMillan Press, 1997), pp.1–30.

——, 'Introduction' in Cora Govers and Hans Vermeulen (eds), *The Anthropology of Ethnicity Beyond 'Ethnic Groups and Boundaries'* (Amsterdam: Het Spinhuis, 1994), pp.1–9.

Habakkuk, H. J., 'Fluctuations in house-building in Britain and the United States in the nineteenth century,' in Derek H. Aldcroft and Peter Fearon (eds), *British Economic Fluctuations* (London: St. Martin's Press, 1972), pp.236–67.

Harrison, Thomas Skelton, *The Homely Diary of a Diplomat in the East, 1897–1899* (New York: Houghton Mifflin Co., 1917).

Harvey, Margaret, *The English in Rome: 1362–1420: Portrait of an Expatriate Community* (Cambridge: Cambridge University Press, 1999).

Hatem, Mervat, 'Through each other's eyes: the impact on the colonial encounter of the images of Egyptian, Levantine-Egyptian, and European women, 1862–1920,' in Nupur Chaudhuri and Margaret Strobel (eds), *Western Women and Imperialism: Complicity and Resistance* (Bloomington: Indiana University Press, 1992), pp.35–58.

Hitchcock, Tim, 'A New history from below,' *History Workshop Journal* 57 (2004), 294–8. http://muse.jhu.edu/journals/history_workshop_journal/v057/57.1hitchcock.html

Hitchcock, Tim, Peter King and Pamela Sharpe, 'Introduction: chronicling poverty – the voices and strategies of the English poor, 1640–1840,' in *Chronicling Poverty—The Voices and Strategies of the English Poor, 1640–1840* (London: MacMillan, 1997), pp.1–18.

Hitchcock, Tim and Robert Shoemaker, *Tales from the Hanging Court* (London: Hodder Education, 2007).

Hobsbawm, E. J. 'History from below—some reflections,' in Frederick Kranz (ed), *History From Below: Studies in Popular Protest and Ideology* (Oxford, 1988), 13–27.

Hopwood, Derek, *Egypt: Politics and Society 1945–1984*. 2nd ed. (London: Allen & Unwin, 1987).

——, *Tales of Empire: The British in the Middle East, 1880–1952* (London: I.B.Tauris, 1989).

Hourani, Albert H., *Minorites in the Arab World* (London: Oxford University Press, 1947).

Hoyle, Mark S. W., *The Mixed Courts of Egypt* (London: Graham & Trotman, 1991).

Hunt, E. H., *British Labour History, 1815–1914* (London: Weidenfield & Nicolson, 1981).

Hunter, Archie, *Power and Passion in Egypt: A Life of Sir Eldon Gorst, 1861–1911* (London: I.B.Tauris, 2007).

Hunter, F. Robert 'Tourism and empire: the Thomas Cook and Son enterprise on the Nile, 1868–1914,' *Middle Eastern Studies* 40/5 (2004), pp.28–54.

Ilbert, Robert, *Alexandrie, 1830–1930: Histoire d'une Communauté Citadine*, Vols. I and II (Le Caire: Institut Francais d'Archéolgie Orientale, 1996).

Jeffrey, Keith, *The British Army and the Crisis of Empire, 1918–1922* (Manchester: Manchester University Press, 1984).

Johnson, Valerie, 'British identity was forged by Imperial overseas encounters,' http://www.voxeu.org/index.php?q=node/1186 (June 2008).

Karsh, Efraim, and Inari Karsh, *Empires of the Sand: The Struggle for Mastery in the Middle East, 1789–1923* (Cambridge, MA: Harvard University Press, 1999).

Keegan, John, 'Foreword', in Ian Beckett and Keith Simpson (eds), *A Nation in Arms: A Social History of the British Army in the First World War* (Manchester: Manchester University Press, 1985), pp.viii–x.

Kent, Christopher, 'Victorian social history: post-Thompson, post-Foucault, postmodern,' in *Victorian Studies* 40/1, (Autumn 1996), pp.97–133.

Keown-Boyd, Henry, *Soldiers of the Nile: A Biographical History of the British Officers of the Egyptian Army* (Hertsfordshire: Thornbury Publications, 1996).

Kertzer, David, *Ritual, Politics and Power* (New Haven: Yale University Press, 1988).
Khouloussy, Hanan, *For Better, For Worse: The Marriage Crisis that Made Modern Egypt* (Stanford: Stanford University Press, 2010).
Kitroeff, Alexander, *The Greeks in Egypt, 1919–1937: Ethnicity and Class* (London: Ithaca, 1989).
Klein, F. A., 'Letters from Egypt, 22 January 1885,' *CMS Intelligencer* X (September 1885), pp.673–6.
Krämer, Gudrun, *The Jews of Modern Egypt, 1914–1952* (London: I.B.Tauris, 1989).
Landes, David, *Bankers and Pashas: International Finance and Economic Imperialism in Egypt* (New York: Harper, 1958).
Liddle, Peter, 'The Dardanelles Gallipoli campaign: concept and execution,' in Peter Liddle (ed), *Home Fires and Foreign Fields: British Social and Military Experience in the First World War* (London: Brassey's Defence Publishers, 1985), pp.101–4.
Lopez, Shaun, 'Football as national allegory: Al–Ahram and the Olympics in 1920s Egypt,' *History Compass*, 7/1 (2009), pp.282–305.
Mabro, Robert, 'Alexandria 1860–1960: the cosmopolitan identity,' in Anthony Hirst and Michael Silk (eds), *Alexandria, Real or Imagined* (Aldershot: Ashgate Publishing, 2004), pp.247–62.
MacMunn, George, and Cyril Falls, *Military Operations: Egypt and Palestine* (London: His Majesty's Stationery Office, 1928).
MacPherson, W. G., *Medical Services General History, Vol. III* (London: His Majesty's Stationery Office, 1924).
Makdisi, Ussama, *Artillery of Heaven: American Missionaries and the Failed Conversion of the Middle East* (London: Cornell University Press, 2008).
Mansfield, Peter, *The British in Egypt* (London: Wiedenfeld & Nicolson, 1971).
Marlowe, John, *Anglo-Egyptan Relations, 1800–1956,* 2nd ed. (London: Frank Cass & Co, Ltd., 1965).
Marshall, J. E., *The Egyptian Enigma, 1890–1928* (London: John Murray, 1928).
Marsot, Afaf Lutfi al-Sayyid, *Egypt and Cromer: A Study in Anglo-Egyptian Relations* (New York: Praeger, 1969).
——, *A Short History of Modern Egypt* (London: Cambridge University Press, 1985).
McCord, Norman, *British History 1815–1916* (Oxford: Oxford University Press, 1991).
McIntyre, John D. Jr., *The Boycott of the Milner Mission: A Study in Egyptian Nationalism* (New York: Peter Lang, 1985).
McPherson, Bimbashi, and Barry Carman, *A Life in Egypt* (London: BBC, 1983).
Mellini, Peter, *Sir Eldon Gorst: The Overshadowed Proconsul* (Stanford: Hoover Institute Press, 1971).
Miller, David, 'Reflections on British national identity,' *New Community* 21/2 (April 1995), pp.153–66.

Milner, Sir Alfred, *England in Egypt* (London: Edward Arnold, 1904).
——, *England in Egypt*, 13th ed. (London: Edward Arnold, 1920).
Mitch, David F., *The Rise of Popular Literacy in Victorian England: The Influence of Private Choice and Public Policy* (Philadelphia: University of Pennsylvania Press, 1992).
Mitchell, B. R., *British Historical Statistics* (Cambridge: Cambridge University Press, 1988).
Mitchell, Timothy, *Colonising Egypt* (New York: Cambridge University Press, 1988).
Monroe, Elizabeth, *Britain's Moment in the Middle East, 1914–1971* (London: Chatto & Windus, 1981).
Moulder, P. E., 'The lives of working women – by one of them,' *Good Words* XXXIX (1898), pp.636–9.
Nelson, Nina, *Shepheard's Hotel* (London: Barrie & Rockcliff, 1960).
Oldenburg, Veena Talwar, *The Making of Colonial Lucknow* (Delhi: Oxford University Press, 1989).
Onley, James, *The Arabian Frontier of the British Raj: Merchants, Rulers, and the British in the Nineteenth-Century Gulf* (Oxford: Oxford University Press, 2007).
Oppenheim, J-M. R., 'Le Sporting Club: symbole et enjeu social,' *La Revue de L'Occident Musulman et de la Mediterreanée (ROMM)*, 46, (1987), pp.168–75.
Osterhammel, Jürgen, *Colonialism: A Theoretical Overview* (Princeton: Markus Wiener Publishers, 1997).
Ouditt, Sharon, *Fighting Forces, Writing Women* (London: Routledge, 1994).
Owen, Roger, *Cotton and the Egyptian Economy, 1820–1914* (Oxford: Oxford University Press, 1969).
——, *Lord Cromer: Victorian Imperialist, Edwardian Proconsul* (Oxford: Oxford University Press, 2004).
——, *The Middle East in the World Economy, 1800–1914* (London: Methuen, 1981).
Papastergiadis, Nikos, 'Tracing hybridity in theory,' in Pnina Werbner and Modood Tariq (eds), *Debating Cultural Hybridity: Multi-Cultural Identities and the Politics of Anti-Racism* (London: Zed Books, 1997), pp.257–81.
Patterson, Orlando, 'The nature, causes, and implications of ethnic identification,' in Charles Fried (ed), *Minorities, Community and Identity* (New York: Springer-Verlag, 1983), pp.25–50.
Penfield, Frederick C., *Present-Day Egypt* (New York: The Century Co., 1903).
Philipp, Thomas, 'Demographic patterns of Syrian immigration to Egypt in the nineteenth century: an interpretation,' *Asian and African Studies* 16 (1982), pp.171–95.
——, *The Syrians in Egypt, 1725–1975* (Stuttgart: Steiner-Verlag-Wiesbaden-GmbH, 1985).

Porter, Brian, 'Britain and the Middle East in the Great War,' in Peter Liddle (ed), *Home Fires and Foreign Fields: British Social and Military Experience in the First World War* (London: Brassey's Defence Publishers, 1985), pp.159–74.

Powell, Eve Troutt, *A Different Shade of Colonialism: Egypt, Great Britain, and the Mastery of Sudan* (London: University of California Press, 2003).

Raafat, Samir, 'The Anglo-American Hospital approaches its centennial,' *Egyptian Mail*, 13 January 1996 and *Cairo Times*, 28 May 1998, (from Raafat's website: www.egy.com).

——, *Cairo: The Glory Years: Who Built What, When, Why and for Whom?* (Alexandria: Harpocrates Publishing, 2003).

——, 'Gezira Sporting Club milestones,' *Egyptian Mail*, 10–17 February 1996 (from Samir Raafat's website: www.egy.com).

——, *Maadi: 1904–1962: Society and History in a Cairo Suburb* (Cairo: Palm Press, 1994).

Reimer, Michael J., *Colonial Bridgehead: Government and Society in Alexandria, 1807–1882* (Cairo: AUC Press, 1997).

——, 'Urban government and administration in Egypt, 1805–1914,' *Die Welt Des Islams*, 39/3 (1999), pp.289–318.

Renford, Raymond K., *The Non-Official British in India to 1920* (Delhi: Oxford University Press, 1987).

Rich, Paul J., *Chains of Empire* (London: Regency Press, 1991).

Richmond, J. C. B., *Egypt 1798–1952: Her Advance Towards a Modern Identity* (London: Methuen & Co., 1977).

Robb, George, *White-Collar Crime in Modern England: Financial Fraud and Business Morality 1845–1929* (Cambridge: Cambridge University Press, 1992).

Robinson, Ronald, and John Gallagher, 'The imperialism of free trade,' *Economic History Review*, 2nd series, VI/ I (1953), pp.1–15.

Rodd, Sir James Rennell, *Social and Diplomatic Memoirs, 1894–1901* (London: Edward Arnold & Co., 1923).

Rodenbeck, Max, *Cairo: The City Victorious* (Cairo: American University in Cairo Press, 1999).

Rodwell, Edward, *The Mombasa Club* (Mombasa: Mombasa Club, 1988).

Ross, Robert and Gerard J. Telkamp (eds), *Colonial Cities: Essays on Urbanism in a Colonial Context* (Lancaster: Martinus Nijhoff Publishers, 1985).

Rubenstein, W. O., *Britain's Century: A Political and Social History, 1815–1905* (London: Arnold, 1998).

Russell, Sir Thomas, *Egyptian Service, 1902–1946* (London: John Murray, 1949).

Sattin, Anthony, *Lifting the Veil: British Society in Egypt, 1768–1956* (London: Dent, 1988).

Seawright, Sarah, *The British in the Middle East* (London: East and West Publications, 1979).

Sedra, Paul D., 'John Leider and his mission in Egypt: the evangelical ethos at work among nineteenth-century Copts,' *The Journal of Religious History* 28/3 (October 2004), pp.219–39.

——, *From Mission to Modernity: Evangelicals, Reformers and Education in Nineteenth Century Egypt* (London: I.B.Tauris, 2011).

Shalabi, Helmi Ahmed, A*l-Ḥukm al-Maḥallī wa-1 -majālis al-baladiyya fi Miṣr mundhu nash'atihā ḥatta 'āmm 1882* (Cairo: GEBO, 1987).

Sharkey, Heather, *American Evangelicals in Egypt: Missionary Encounters in an Age of Empire* (Oxford: Princeton University Press, 2008).

——, 'Muslim apostasy: Christian conversion, and religious freedom in Egypt: a study of American missionaries, Western imperialism, and human rights agendas,' in Rosalind Hackett (ed). *Proselytization Revisited: Rights Talk, Free Markets and Culture Wars* (London: Equinox, 2008), pp.140–66.

Shils, Edward, 'Primordial, personal, sacred, and civil ties,' *British Journal of Sociology* 8 (1957), pp.130–45.

Simkins, Peter, 'Soldiers and civilians: billeting in Britain and France,' in Ian Beckett and Keith Simpson (eds), *A Nation in Arms: A Social Study of the British Army in the First World War* (Manchester: Manchester University Press, 1985), pp.165–91.

Sinclair, Georgina, 'Book review for Barry Godfrey and Graeme Dunstall (eds), *Crime and Empire 1840–1940; Criminal Justice in Local and Global Context*, (Cullompton: Willan Publishing, 2005) in *Crime, History and Societies* 11/2 (2007), pp.155–7.

Sindall, Rob, 'Middle-class crime in nineteenth-century England,' *Criminal Justice History: An International Annual* IV (1983), pp.23–40.

Sinha, Mrinalini, 'Britishness, clubbability, and the colonial public sphere: the genealogy of an Imperial institution in colonial India,' *Journal of British Studies*, 40 (2001), pp 489–521.

Sladen, Douglas, *Egypt and the English* (London: Hurst & Blackett, Ltd., 1908).

——, *Oriental Cairo: The City of the 'Arabian Nights'* (London: Hurst & Blackett, Ltd., 1911).

Starkey, Paul, and Janet Starkey (eds), *Travellers in Egypt* (London: I.B.Tauris, 1998).

Starr, Deborah, *Remembering Cosmopolitan Egypt* (New York: Routledge, 2009).

Steevens, G. W., *Egypt in 1898* (New York: Dodd, Mead and Company, 1899).

Stockwell, A. J., 'The white man's burden and brown humanity: colonialism and ethnicity in British Malaya,' *The Southeast Asian Journal of Social Sciences* 10/1 (1982), pp.44–68.

Stoler, Ann Laura, *Carnal Knowledge and Imperial Power: Race and the Intimate in Colonial Rule* (Berkeley: University of California Press, 2002).

——, 'Rethinking colonial categories: European communities and the boundaries of rule,' *Comparative Study of Society and History* 31 (1989), pp.134–61.

Storrs, Sir Ronald, *Orientations* (London: Nicholson & Watson, 1937).

Strobel, Margaret, *European Women and the Second British Empire* (Bloomington: Indiana University Press, 1991).
Thompson, E. P., 'History from below,' *The Times Literary Supplement* (7 April 1966), pp.276–80.
Tignor, Robert L, 'The economic activities of foreigners in Egypt, 1920–1950: from Millet to Haute bourgeoisie,' *Comparative Studies in Society and History* 22/3 (1980), pp.416–49.
———, *Modernisation and British Colonial Rule in Egypt, 1882–1914* (Princeton: Princeton University Press, 1966).
Toffelson, Harold, *Policing Islam: The British Occupation of Egypt and the Anglo-Egyptian Struggle over Control of the Police, 1882–1914* (London: Greenwood Press, 1999).
Tranter, N. L., *Population and Society, 1750–1940: Contrasts in Population Growth* (London: Longman, 1985).
Vander Werff, Lyle, *Christian Mission to Muslims—The Record: Anglican and Reformed Approaches in India and the Near East* (Pasadena: William Carey Library, 1977).
Vatikiotis, P. J., *The Modern History of Egypt* (London: Weidenfield and Nicolson, 1969).
Verdery, Katherine, 'Ethnicity, nationalism and state-making: ethnic groups and boundaries past and future,' in Cora Govers and Hans Vermeulen (eds), *The Anthropology of Ethnicity Beyond 'Ethnic Groups and Boundaries'* (Amsterdam: Het Spinhuis, 1994), pp.33–58.
Ward, Paul, 'The end of Britishness? A historical perspective,' *British Politics Review: Journal of the British Politics Society* 4/3 (summer, 2009), p.3.
Watson, Charles R., *In the Valley of the Nile: A Survey of the Missionary Movement in Egypt* (London: Fleming H. Revell Co., 1908).
Weber, Max, *Economy and Society: An Outline of Interpretative Sociology*, ed. by Guenther Roth and Claus Dittrich (Berkeley: University of California Press, 1968).
Webster, Anthony, *The Debate on the Rise of the British Empire* (Manchester: Manchester University Press, 2006).
Welch, William M., Jr., *No Country for a Gentleman: British Rule in Egypt, 1883–1907* (London: Greenwood Press, 1988).
Whitehead, Clive, 'British colonial education policy: a synonym for cultural imperialism?' in J. A. Mangan (ed), *Benefits Bestowed: Education and British Imperialism* (Manchester: Manchester University Press, 1988), pp.211–30.
Willcocks, William, *Sixty Years in the East* (London: Blackwood & Sons, 1935).
Winter, Jay, 'Army and society: the demographic context,' in Ian Beckett and Keith Simpson (eds), *A Nation in Arms: A Social History of the British Army in the First World War* (Manchester: Manchester University Press, 1985), pp.193–209.
Wood, H. F., *Egypt Under the British* (London: Chapman-Hall, 1896).

Wright, Arnold (ed), *Twentieth Century Impressions of Egypt: Its History, People, Commerce, Industries and Resources* (London: Lloyd's Greater Britain Publishing Co., Ltd., 1909).

Zubaida, Sami, 'Middle Eastern experiences of cosmopolitanism,' in Steven Vertovec and Robin Cohen (eds), *Conceiving Cosmopolitanism: Theory, Context and Practice* (Oxford: Oxford University Press, 2002), pp.32–41.

INDEX

Abbassiyya 36, 100–1, 179, 188
Abdine 34, 36
Abdin Square 224
Alcohol and alcoholism 155, 175,
  194, 199, 242
Alderson, George Alexander 106, 132
Allenby, High Commissioner First
  Viscount Sir Edmund 172,
  218–19, 226, 236,
Alexandria 5, 8–9, 24, 26, 31–32,
  38–39, 41, 46, 56, 58–59, 66,
  86, 92–94, 105, 114, 125, 128,
  131–32, 143, 146, 154, 157–58,
  163, 166, 169–70, 182, 187,
  189–91, 205–8, 227, 229,
  234–35
  British Benevolent Fund 221
  City Police 165, 182, 186
  Sporting Club 94
  Swimming Club 158
Alimony 153, 155
Allies 150, 187, 209
All Saints' Church 3, 34, 36, 76,
  91, 107–8, 110, 115, 134–35,
  140–41, 242
American and Americans 97, 102–3,
  110, 113, 133, 147, 149, 159,
  171, 175, 216
Anglo-American Hospital 90, 102–4,
  111, 149, 152, 168, 193, 242

Anglo-Egyptian Bank 3, 91, 131–32,
  158, 165, 182, 185, 211, 227,
  231, 234, 237–38, 243–44
Arabic 12, 24, 55, 56, 58, 59, 62, 78,
  81, 87, 119, 134
Armenian and Armenians 23–24, 63,
  109, 135, 171
Ashbee, Charles Robert 149–52, 186
Assiut 58–59, 223–24
Australia and Australians 20, 49,
  64–65, 79, 135, 147, 187, 191,
  194–45, 197, 199
  Australian Imperial Force 65
  Australian and New Zealand Army
    Corps (ANZAC) 206
  Soldiers 64–65, 187, 191–92, 206,
    211–12
  Troops' misbehaviour 194–95
Austrian and Austrians 27–28, 170–71
Austro-Hungarian 26, 28, 65, 177,
  187, 207
  Business and businessmen 207–10,
    213, 243–44
  Hospital 103–4, 188

Barclays Group archives 3
Barker, Sir Henry Edward and family
  9, 62, 132, 190
Bengal, British community and
  Britons of 89, 115

Boulaq 36, 48, 91, 139–40, 165, 188, 233
Boundaries 18, 50–54
　Ambiguous 64, 68
　Between Britons and Egyptians 57, 60, 62, 81, 175
Boyle, Harry 57
British
　Agency 58, 78, 96, 114, 152
　Architects 93
　Army of Occupation 11, 18, 20, 22, 34, 117, 121, 135, 157, 160, 179–80
　Balls, ballrooms and dances 41, 99, 135, 175, 179, 192–93
　Bankers, Bank officials and employees 9, 125, 128, 131, 135, 143, 158, 175, 182, 185, 193, 203, 218, 228, 231–32, 235, 242–43
　Businessmen and merchants 5, 8–9, 18, 23, 41, 94, 125, 132–33, 135, 143, 175, 207–8, 229–30, 232, 237, 240, 242
　Chamber of Commerce 3, 70, 133, 181, 194, 202–4, 208–10, 236, 244
　Civil service 2–3, 11, 24, 26, 41, 92, 122, 125, 128, 131, 136, 143, 184–85, 215, 231, 241–42
　Community at odds with British authorities 199–204, 220–227, 237–38
　Constable 165, 171, 174
　Consul General 10–11, 19, 34, 36, 65, 91, 96, 102, 119, 135, 141, 169, 175, 178, 180, 185
　Consulate 34, 71, 77–78, 138, 140, 178, 184, 203, 229
　Consular courts 2, 87, 146–47, 161, 169, 222–23
　Consular court records 2, 131, 146, 162, 167
　Criminals 80–81, 146, 162, 175

British (cont.)
　Domestic servants and maids 17, 123, 140, 143, 157–58, 168–69, 242
　Engineers 158, 165, 175, 229, 233–34, 242–43
　Flag 86
　Foreign Office 10, 69–70, 88, 104, 113, 150, 226, 228, 237–38
　From the British Isles 4, 18, 31–34, 37–38, 41, 44, 46, 48, 118–19, 122–25, 128, 130, 138, 147
　Government 5, 18, 38, 75, 96, 112–13, 116, 154, 177, 181–85, 202–4, 210, 215–19, 238–39
　Government Exchequer Bonds 202–4
　High society 192
　Identity 5, 48–49, 53–54, 72, 82, 95, 113, 241
　Imperial command 65, 220, 222
　Imprisonment 152–57, 163–171
　Journalist 159–60
　Lawyers 38, 88, 118–19, 131–32, 135, 139, 143, 152, 159, 170, 175, 186, 242–43
　Lower-class 46, 74, 117–18, 121, 135–39, 142–44, 162, 242
　　Rank and file 121, 179, 199
　　Working-class 4, 7, 8, 27, 44, 46, 97, 117–18, 136, 138–43, 158, 199, 242
　Military 10–11, 22, 27–28, 36, 41, 44, 55–56, 94, 100–8, 121–33, 155, 163, 167, 171, 177–84, 199, 201, 212, 216, 220–21, 229–30, 243
　　Barracks 36, 100–1, 111, 139, 164–65, 179, 180, 183
　　Demobilisation 171, 214, 220–25, 238, 243
　　Chaplains 76, 107, 134–35, 160, 182, 186, 198, 244

British (cont.)
  Nationality 20, 48, 68, 70–71, 76, 80–82, 184, 241
  Nationality and Status of Aliens Act 69, 71
  Non-Official British Community 222, 235–39, 243
  Nurses 3, 55, 104, 118, 153, 179, 187–190, 194, 196, 212, 243
  Occupational differences in Alexandria and Cairo 125
  Office clerk 1, 97, 118, 136–38, 143, 162, 165–66, 242
  Officers 8, 37, 54–56, 65, 94, 99, 108, 115, 117, 121, 135, 142–43, 167, 179, 188–93, 220–23, 228, 230
  Officials or civil servants 3, 8, 13, 18, 24, 38, 41, 55–58, 81, 92–97, 101, 113–14, 117–123, 125, 130, 133–36, 139, 143, 150–51, 181–83, 211–15, 228–31, 236–37, 240–42
  Poorer families or poor 6, 36, 66, 77, 107, 139–141, 181, 193, 204
  Prisoners and separation from Egyptian prisoners 80–81, 157
  Protectorate 13, 69, 80, 89, 109, 112, 177, 186, 208–9, 219, 240
  Railway workers 36, 48, 97, 107, 139–40, 143, 242
  Red Cross 188–89, 193–94
  Refugees Fund 193
  Religious affiliations 41
  Residency 34, 91, 121, 125, 150, 240
  Residential quarters 38, 90, 92, 241, 244
  Rifle clubs 182, 229–30
  Salaries 97, 118, 120–121, 131, 134, 137–39, 143, 206, 211, 215, 221, 231–33
  Sick 36, 158, 187–91, 198, 201

British (cont.)
  Soldiers 22, 98, 108, 122, 142, 175, 180, 183, 189, 212, 220, 223–25, 228
  Soldiers' Café 197–98
  Sports and sporting culture 86, 92, 95–99, 179, 195–99
  Tailors 123, 136–38, 143, 242
  Teachers 55–56, 59, 94–95, 118–19, 123, 131, 135, 143, 150–51, 175, 186, 229–31, 238, 242–43
  Travellers 4, 9, 86
  Union in Egypt 236
  Upper class 3, 38, 117–21, 131–35, 142–43, 145, 149, 242
  Upper middle-class 8, 106, 118, 130–39, 143, 175, 241
  Women 39, 46, 64, 75–82, 128, 141, 187–93, 197, 241
Britishness 49, 53–54, 64
Brunyate, William 89
Butcher, Dean Charles Henry 76, 107, 134
Butcher, Edith Louisa 76
Bywater, Eliza 59, 134

Cairo 4–9, 22, 24, 27–41, 46, 56–62, 76–80, 86, 90–96, 99–115, 119–122, 125–28, 131–143, 146–99, 205–11, 216–18, 224–230, 234, 241, 244
  Amateur Repertory Players 196
  British community 32, 34, 36
  Churches and Cathedrals 3, 22, 34–41, 44, 75–76, 86, 91–92, 107–116, 134–45, 169, 175, 179, 191, 196, 220, 240–44
  Department stores 24
  Electric Railways 38
  Purification Committee 171
  Soldiers' Recreation Club 197–98
  Camel Transport Corps 212

Capitulations 11, 20, 27, 49, 64, 82,
    88, 146, 174, 176, 186, 207–8,
    214, 219, 222–25, 238, 241–43
    Imminent abolition of 68–72
Cecil, Lord Edward 96, 120, 132
Census and census records 3, 5,
    8, 15–16, 20, 22, 26, 31–34,
    36, 38, 41, 44–48, 67,
    119–22, 125–130, 143, 147,
    178, 183–84, 241–42
Chambers, Oswald 197
Cholera 57, 148
Christian 12, 41, 134, 196, 237
    Background 39, 41
    Faith, Gospel and Christianity 11,
        59, 61–62, 76, 80, 109, 111, 199
    Wife or women 73–80
    Worship 108
Christmas Day 114–15
Church Missionary Society 41, 59,
    105, 134, 182, 186
    Archives 2
Conscription 55, 183–85
Consulate, American 86
Convalescent Outings Society 198
Cook, John Mason 9, 133
Cook, Thomas 9, 34, 133, 165–66, 244
Coptic Church 75
Copts 61, 81
    Sympathising with Muslims
        against British occupation 62
    Converting to Protestantism 11
Cosmopolitanism 12
Cotton trade 9–12, 24, 28, 58,
    132–33, 212, 214–15
    Boom in Egypt 26–27
Crime and criminals
    Abortion 156–57, 242
    Assault 1, 148, 152–54, 158–59,
        167, 175, 242
    Bigamy 148, 170, 242
    Domestic violence 153–155, 158,
        175
    Ellis, Michael 1, 167

Crime (cont.)
    Embezzlement 148, 162, 165, 175,
        242–44
    Extortion 148, 162, 168, 175
    Fraud 1, 8, 148, 161–66, 175,
        242–44
    Hayes, John 164–165
    Helfield, Charles 1, 162–64
    History of, 5, 7, 145, 243
    Libel 148, 160–61, 175, 242
    Prostitution 141, 147–48, 170–76,
        194
    Rape 1, 148, 168–69, 175, 242,
        244
    Suicide 147, 157–58, 175, 242
    Theft 8, 148, 162, 167, 175, 242
Cromer, Lord 18–19, 54, 58, 60–64,
    67, 79, 100, 102, 106, 110,
    113–14, 119, 134, 158

Davies Bryan 164
Deaconesses' Hospital 156, 158
Dean's Building School 36, 37, 105,
    107, 111
Denshawai incident 176
De Villa-Clary, Conte Mario 66–68
Disturbances, demonstrations,
    protests 143, 218–19, 223,
    230–39, 243

Eastern Telegraph Company 34, 229,
    230
Eastern Telegraph Rifle Club 230
Economic recession, setbacks,
    downturns 214, 222, 230, 238
Egypt General Mission 227
Egyptian
    Gazette 3, 142, 160, 182, 195, 224
    Delta Light Railways 37, 132, 154,
        169, 234, 244
    Expeditionary Force 154, 229
    Labour Corps 154, 212

Egyptian (cont.)
  Nationalists, nationalist movement 13, 58, 69, 75, 150–51, 176–77, 180, 185, 214–17, 228, 230–39, 244
  State Railways 10, 131, 154, 166, 224–26, 233–34
Egyptians
  Europeanised 60–61, 64
  Rural 15
  Wealthy 63, 95, 141
Empain, Baron Edouard 38
Empire Day 114–15, 194
English Club of Alexandria 56
English language 70, 86–87, 146, 241
Englishman 63, 69, 81, 96, 146, 222, 227
Ethnic identity
  Ambiguous boundaries and hybrid identities 52, 54, 64, 72
  Clear or fixed boundaries 50, 52, 54, 61, 64, 72, 80–81
European or Europeans
  Commerce 28
  Community or communities 22, 99, 102
  Quarter 34, 59, 90–91, 193, 217
  White-skinned 49, 64–65
Ezbekiyya 34, 91, 93, 111, 140, 172, 196–98

Fabry, Edward 143
Football 58, 87, 95, 98–99, 105, 199
France 10, 87, 177, 217
French
  Education 61, 64, 105
  Enterprise and business 9–10, 24, 195
  Hospital, 103, 111
  In Egypt 10, 26–28, 48, 56, 60
  Language 55, 62, 87, 88, 131, 136
  Legal system 88, 89

French (cont.)
  Military 187
  Prostitutes 170–71
Foster, J. P. 88, 152
Fourteen Points 217

Gallipoli 110, 187–93, 206
German and Germans
  Business 102–3, 136, 207–10, 213, 243–44
  Hospital 102–3, 111, 149, 163
  In Egypt 26–28
  Prostitutes 171
Germany 78, 102, 177, 180, 187, 207, 210
Gezira Island 34, 38, 90–92, 97, 103, 111, 149
Gezira Palace Hotel 90, 99, 188
Gezira Sporting Club 56, 58, 90, 94–97, 121, 165, 175, 192, 201
Greek and Greeks
  Artisans, merchants and workers 26, 136, 205
  Church and Hospital 103, 110–11
  Community in Egypt 7, 20–23, 28, 69, 184
  Education 105–6
  Marriage with British 170
  Midwife 156–57
  Prostitutes 170
Gorst, Sir Eldon 19, 58, 96–97, 185

Helwan, and as place of healing, 34, 37–38, 91, 169, 189
Heliopolis 34, 37–38, 48, 91, 97, 99, 188
History from below 7, 117, 242–43
Hospitals 55, 59, 86, 93, 103, 133, 154–63, 171, 174, 187–96, 199–202, 226, 242–44

India 4, 7, 9, 11, 18, 20, 39, 54, 86, 116, 121, 178
Indian and Indians
  British subjects 16, 19–20, 39, 122, 184
  Designs of housing 54, 99
  Military hospital 194
  Soldiers 65, 179, 188, 191, 194, 205, 220, 223–24
Intermarriage 72–75, 79, 241
  Foreign Marriages Act 75, 80
Islam and Islamic 39, 77, 93, 176, 212
Italian and Italians 22 –23, 26, 28, 56, 69, 87, 93, 102–3, 111, 136, 164, 170–171, 228

Jews and Jewish 23–24, 37, 41, 53, 136, 171
  British subjects 39
Jockey Club 97

Khedive 9, 10, 11, 27, 111, 119, 136, 178
  Abbas II Hilmi 62, 177
  Ismail 27, 90, 177
Kitchener, Lord 102, 104, 109–10, 180, 205
Kitchener Memorial Hospital 102, 104

Levantine 24, 56, 63–84, 81, 105, 107, 115, 205
Loder, John de Vere 58–59

Maadi 34, 36–38, 48, 91
Maadi Soldiers' Club 197–98
Malaya 7, 86, 97, 115–16
  Malaysia 73
Malta 4, 18 –19, 66, 68, 164, 170, 217

Maltese 66–68, 81, 105, 119, 122, 135, 171, 241
  Benevolence and Benevolent Society 66–68
  British subjects 16, 19, 20, 38–39, 49, 64–66, 146, 184
Manchester 3, 39, 133, 166
Marriage 16, 71–80, 154–155, 164, 170
Maxwell, Sir John 182–83, 200, 205
McMahon, Sir Henry 103–4, 111–12, 200, 208
Mena House Hotel 99
Military Football League 199
Military Service Act 183
Milner Mission 219, 228, 238,
Misconduct 5, 8, 120, 145–51, 161, 175–76, 198, 242
Missionary and missionaries 3, 8, 11– 12, 18, 36, 41, 57, 59, 123, 134–35, 143, 168–69, 175, 182, 186, 227–229, 242–43
  Bywater, Eliza 59, 134
  Gairdner, Temple 59, 134, 196, 210
  Hollins, J. G. B. 59
  The Orient and the Occident 59, 134
  Thornton, Douglas 59, 134
Mixed Courts 87–89, 116, 186, 222, 241
Mombasa and Mombasa Club 86, 93–94, 116
Muhammad Ali 26, 216
Muslim and Muslims 11, 41, 59–61, 64, 73–81, 155, 214, 219, 237
Mustafa Kamel 58

Naggiar, Victor 70–71, 133
National Bank of Egypt 131–132, 167, 182, 196, 210
Negligence 145–149, 152, 155, 175

New English School 105–107, 111
New Zealand and New Zealanders 110, 137, 147, 187, 191, 194, 199, 205–6

Offences Against the Person Act 156
Old Khedivial Club 56
Orientalism 6
Ottoman 11, 116, 119, 146, 164, 187, 212
   Bank 166
   Empire, territory or territories 9, 23, 68, 87, 112, 177–78, 207, 214
   Millet system 68
   Subjects 23
Overland route 9–10

Paris, of the Middle East 90
Paris Peace Conference 216–19
Palestine 39, 110, 128, 178, 188, 193, 212, 218
Patriotic League of Britons Overseas 194
Pharaoh's Foot 182–183
Population
   British in Egypt 18, 31–32, 34, 48, 54, 103, 118, 179, 193
   Europeans in Egypt 24–28, 31
   Growth of British in Egypt 18–23
Port Said 5, 31, 146–148, 165, 205, 218, 228
Professional misconduct
   British doctor 148
   British lawyers 151–152
   British teacher 149–151
Protestants and Protestantism 11–12, 31, 39–41

Qasr el-Nil Barracks 36, 111, 164, 179
Queen Victoria 67, 102, 105, 114

Railway Institute Club 97, 137
Requisition 28, 188–89, 199–202, 211–12, 216, 243
Revolutionary period 3, 12, 178, 214, 219, 223, 230, 235, 239, 241, 243–44
Rowlatt, Sir F.T. 38, 196
Russia 177, 187
Russian and Russians 26–28, 87, 170–71, 187

Scottish 4, 53, 108, 132, 147, 159
   Soldiers 108, 206
Septicaemia 156–57
Shepheard's Hotel 9, 34, 91, 115, 135, 189, 193, 196
Silk imports 24
Smouha, Joseph 39, 166
Social Darwinism 72–73
Soldiers' Club 121, 196–98
Soldiers' Entertainment Committee 196
St. Andrew's Church 3, 34, 41, 91, 140
St. Mark's Church 93, 196
Suez 5, 9, 31, 93, 178, 227–230
Suez Canal 9–10, 13, 24, 28, 177–78, 205, 219, 238
Suez Canal Company 34
Supreme Consular Court 146, 160–61
Sultaniyya Training College 150–51
Syrians 23–26, 63, 106

Treaty of Union in 1707 53
Turf Club 34, 55–58, 95–97, 210

'Urabi Revolt 10, 15

'Veiled Protectorate' 10
Venereal Disease 154, 158, 171, 174
Victoria College 63–67, 105–107,
　　111, 199–201, 212, 242–43
Voluntary Aid Detachments 189

Wafd Party 216–217
Weber, Max 50
Wilson, President Woodrow 217
Wingate, Sir Reginald 97, 107, 179,
　　186, 217
World War, First 5, 9 ,12, 20, 22,
　　24, 27, 55, 57, 64–65, 101,
　　108, 110, 112, 128, 131, 138,
　　150, 174, 177–178, 199, 210,
　　212–14, 219, 222, 241–44

Young Men's Christian Association
　　94, 197–199
　　Soldiers' Club 196

Zaghlul, Saad 216–218
Zamalek 34, 36, 38, 48, 91, 94, 111